BESTSELLING BOOK SERIES

# Wills and Es[...] Canadians For[...]

by Margaret Kerr and JoAnn Kurtz

## Margaret and JoAnn's Top Ten Reasons to Create an Estate Plan and Make a Will

1. **Your family won't starve in the cold.** Without an estate plan you may not leave enough money to your family to make sure they'll always be warm and well fed.
2. **Less of your estate will pay a permanent visit to the income tax department.** Without an estate plan you won't be able to take advantage of tax-saving strategies.
3. **Your family won't have to weep before a judge to get the right to manage your estate.** If you don't make a will naming an executor, someone close to you will have to start a court proceeding to be appointed the administrator of your estate. Until the court makes a decision, no one will be able to touch your property.
4. **Your estate won't lose money after your death.** Without a will you won't be able to give an executor flexibility to sell or keep certain property and to make bold investment decisions.
5. **Your estate will be able to pay off your credit cards and still have something left for your family to go on a shopping spree.** Without an estate plan, your estate may not have the money it will take to pay off your creditors *and* hand over a good sum to your family.
6. **Your family will be able to keep the heirloom brass spittoon lovingly handed down from generation to generation instead of getting cash with no sentimental value.** Without a will, your administrator may have to sell your property and hand out cash.
7. **The business you built up from scratch can be more easily passed on to the person of your choice — or at least not sold at a loss.** Without an estate plan, you can't be sure where the business will end up and how much it will be worth when it gets there.
8. **Your children won't be left to play in the traffic.** Without a will, your wishes about who will look after your children may never be known.
9. **Your provincial government won't be playing piggy bank with your children's money.** Without a will that sets up a trust for young children until they come of age, the provincial government will hold any property you leave the kids — until they reach the age of majority.
10. **Your provincial government won't be playing piggy bank with *all* your money.** Without a will, your property will be given away to your lawful husband or wife and blood relatives according to rules set by provincial law. If you don't have a lawful spouse or any blood relatives — even though you have a long-time companion, a lover, friends, or a favourite charity — your property will all go to the provincial government.

...For Dummies®: Bestselling Book Series for Beginners

# Wills and Estates For Canadians For Dummies®

## Let Margaret and JoAnn Help You Decide If You Need Life Insurance

***You need life insurance if:***

- Someone you support will still need your income when you're no longer alive to earn it.
- You're likely to die leaving a large debt and you want it paid without eating into the capital of your estate.
- You want to create a fund to pay funeral costs, taxes, and probate fees.
- You want to leave money you wouldn't otherwise have to a family member, friend, or charity.

***You don't need life insurance if:***

- You don't have anyone who depends on you for support.
- You have no large debts or expenses.
- You have plenty of cash or property in your estate to pay funeral expenses, taxes, and probate fees.
- You don't need or want extra money to leave to family, friends, or charities.

## Margaret and JoAnn's Tips for Reducing Taxes for Your Estate

- Leave capital property that has gone up a lot in value to your spouse.
- Name your spouse as beneficiary of your RRSPs and RRIFs.
- Leave your children or grandchildren cash or property that has not gone up a lot in value.
- Use the principal residence exemption to leave your vacation property to your children without triggering a capital gain.
- Give away capital property while you're still alive if you have a capital loss to offset any capital gain
- Donate money to charity in your will.
- Make sure your will gives your executor power to use your unused RRSP contributions to make a contribution to your spouse's RRSP.
- Give your executor enough information to make use of any unused capital losses when you die.

## Information Your Family and Executor Will Need When You Die

- Whether you want to donate your organs.
- What kind of funeral you want.
- Where to find your will.
- Where you keep your important documents.
- The location of your safety deposit box and where to find the key.
- Particulars of any insurance policies on your life.
- Information about your bank accounts, investments, pensions, and other property.
- Details of your debts.
- The name and address of your lawyer, financial adviser, and insurance agent.

WILEY
wiley.com



Cheat Sheet $2.95 value. Item 3-16-4.

For more information about John Wiley & Sons Canada, Ltd call 1-800-567-4797.



***...For Dummies®: Bestselling Book Series for Beginners***

# Wills and Estates For Canadians FOR DUMMIES® Planning Kit®

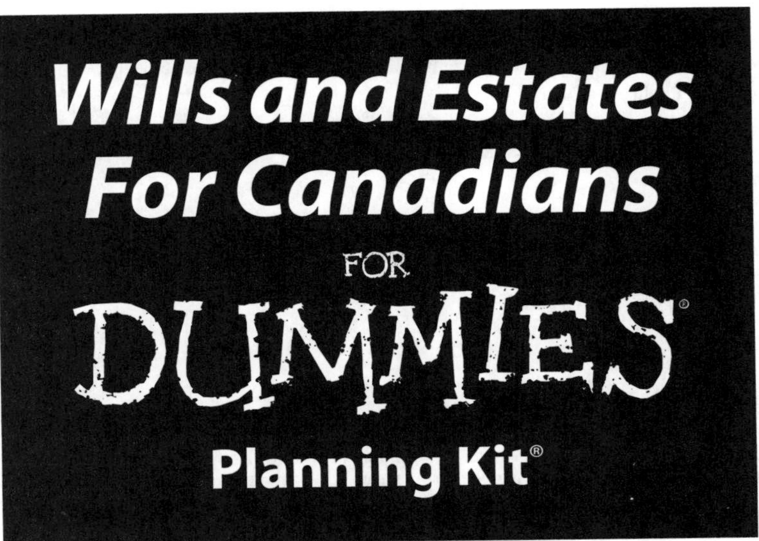


**by Margaret Kerr**
**and JoAnn Kurtz**

John Wiley & Sons Canada, Ltd

◆ Toronto, ON ◆

**Wills and Estates For Canadians For Dummies® Planning Kit**

Published by
**John Wiley & Sons Canada, Ltd**
22 Worcester Road
Etobicoke, ON M9W 1L1
www.wiley.ca



Canadian Cataloguing in Publication Data

Kerr, Margaret Helen, 1954–

Wills and estates for Canadians for dummies planning kit

Includes CD-ROM.
Includes index.
ISBN: 1-894413-17-2

1. Estate planning — Canada — Popular works. 2. Wills — Canada — Popular works. I. Kurtz, JoAnn, 1951– . II. Title: Wills and estates for Canadians for dummies planning kit.

KE5974.K47 2000 346.7105'2 C00-931654-X
KF750.K47 2000

Printed in Canada

1 2 3 4 5 TRI 04 03 02 01 00

Distributed in Canada by John Wiley & Sons Canada, Ltd.

For general information on John Wiley & Sons Canada, Ltd, including all books published by Wiley Publishing, Inc., please call our warehouse, Tel: 1-800-567-4797. For reseller information, including discounts and premium sales, please call our sales department, Tel: 416-646-7992. For press review copies, author interviews, or other publicity information, please contact our marketing department, Tel: 416-646-4584; Fax: 416-236-4448.

# About the Authors

**Margaret Kerr** and **JoAnn Kurtz** first met when they were junior lawyers in a law firm. Because their offices were side by side, they were frequently to be found carrying on entertaining and often risqué conversations, especially whenever the senior partner walked by. When Margaret and JoAnn left the firm to pursue other opportunities (as they say), it looked like the perfect co-authorship was ended before it even started.

During their years apart, JoAnn ran a general law practice and started a family, while Margaret practised in the areas of legal research and civil litigation and honed her equestrian skills. They met again by chance when they were both teaching in the Bar Admission Course, each having discovered a taste for inflicting information about law on innocent minds. JoAnn suggested that Margaret join her in teaching law at a community college and the two were briefly reunited under one roof.

Now co-authorship could not be held off by fate any longer. One day JoAnn's husband said to JoAnn and Margaret, "You two could write a book about buying a home." "Of course we could," they said, tossing their heads, and they immediately did so. *The Complete Guide to Buying, Owning and Selling a Home in Canada* (1997) became a Canadian bestseller, and the second edition is coming out at the very same time as this book.

Margaret and JoAnn made two strange discoveries after writing one book together — first, that they had fun writing as a team; and second, that writing books is addictive. The world just didn't seem quite right without an editor demanding a complete manuscript exactly when JoAnn was experiencing a major family crisis or Margaret was away on business. So they started churning out books: *Canadian Tort Law in a Nutshell* (1997) (with Larry Olivo), *Make It Legal: What Every Canadian Entrepreneur Needs to Know About the Law* (1998), *Residential Real Estate Transactions* (1998 — JoAnn briefly deserted Margaret to write this book with Joan Emmans), *Legal Research Step by Step* (1998 — Margaret retaliated by writing a book all by herself), and *Facing a Death in the Family* (1999). Since all this activity plus their day jobs clearly wasn't enough to keep them busy, Margaret and JoAnn also started writing a weekly column ("Homeowner's Handbook") in 1997 for the Toronto Real Estate News, created their own Web site (`www.kerr-and-kurtz.com`), and joined a speakers' bureau (Speaker Solutions — at `www.speakersolutions.com`). They are currently pursuing plans to write books on small business, family law, and cars and driving.

The Canadian media couldn't help noticing the deluge of books; and JoAnn and Margaret have happily done numerous radio, TV, and newspaper interviews as well as author appearances.

Margaret and JoAnn can't decide if they need their heads examined for obsessively writing books — but you can be fairly sure that if they do have their heads examined, they'll write a book about it.

# Dedication

This book is affectionately dedicated to Mary Jane Woods.

# Authors' Acknowledgements

We didn't achieve brilliant success with this book all by ourselves. We had help and we're very grateful for it.

We'd like to thank our editor, Joan Whitman (she's the first editor we've ever actually wanted to thank — congratulations, Joan!); our patient and hard-working copyeditor, Lisa Berland; our production editor, Rebecca Conolly (who made sure our book went through production in a timely and orderly way, despite our last-minute changes); our proofreader, Kelli Howey; and production manager, Donna Brown.

Then thanks to the following people and organizations who provided us with information: Mary Jane Woods, Bernice Henry, Royal Trust, the Canadian Bar Association — Ontario, and the Law Society of Upper Canada. Thanks also to Scotiabank and Dye and Durham, for providing material for the CD. And thank heaven for the Internet Movie Database.

A big thank you to the people who reviewed chapters of the book for us — Suzette Blom, Joan Emmans, and Michael Engelberg.

Finally we want to thank our families, who, due to constant insertion of each co-author into the other co-author's family life, no longer know which one of us goes with which family — but fortunately don't seem too worried about it.

## Publisher's Acknowledgements

We're proud of this book; please send us your comments at canadapt@wiley.com.

Some of the people who helped bring this book to market include the following:

***Acquisitions and Editorial***

**Editorial Director:** Joan Whitman

**Associate Editor:** Melanie Rutledge

**Assistant Editor:** Kim Herter

**Substantive/Copy Editor:** Lisa Berland

**Editorial Assistant:** Stella Partheniou

***Production***

**Director of Production:** Donna Brown

**Production Editor:** Rebecca Conolly

**Layout and Graphics:** Kim Monteforte, Heidy Lawrance Associates

**Proofreader:** Kelli Howey

**Indexer:** Belle Wong

***Special Help***

Michael Kelly

---

***John Wiley & Sons Canada, Ltd***

Bill Zerter, Chief Operating Officer

Robert Harris, Publisher, Professional and Trade Division

***Publishing and Editorial for Consumer Dummies***

Diane Graves Steele, Vice President and Publisher, Consumer Dummies

Joyce Pepple, Acquisitions Director, Consumer Dummies

Kristin A. Cocks, Product Development Director, Consumer Dummies

Michael Spring, Vice President and Publisher, Travel

Brice Gosnell, Publishing Director, Travel

Suzanne Jannetta, Editorial Director, Travel

***Publishing for Technology Dummies***

Andy Cummings, Acquisitions Director

***Composition Services***

Gerry Fahey, Executive Director of Production Services

Debbie Stailey, Director of Composition Services

# Contents at a Glance

**Introduction** ........ 1

**Part I: Estate Planning Basics** ........ 7

Chapter 1: What Is Estate Planning Anyway? ........ 9
Chapter 2: What Are You Worth on the Hoof? Financial Planning Basics ........ 21
Chapter 3: Head 'Em Up & Move 'Em Out: Planning Your Financial Future ........ 35
Chapter 4: Income Tax 101(a)(i): Some Tax Basics ........ 49
Chapter 5: The Taxman Cometh: Taxes and Your Estate ........ 61

**Part II: Estate Planning Tools** ........ 83

Chapter 6: Wish You and Your Income Were Here — Do You Need Life Insurance? ........ 85
Chapter 7: Money to Die For: The Mysteries of Life Insurance Revealed ........ 97
Chapter 8: Free to a Good Home: Giving Away Your Things before You Die ........ 113
Chapter 9: Pass the Buck: Using Trusts in Estate Planning ........ 125

**Part III: Creating an Estate Plan** ........ 145

Chapter 10: A Crew for Your Ship of Estate: Beneficiaries and Executor ........ 147
Chapter 11: Who's Minding the Kids? Planning Your Children's Future ........ 161
Chapter 12: Giving Them the Business: What to Do with the Family Firm ........ 177
Chapter 13: You Gave at the Office, But . . . — Charitable Donations ........ 193
Chapter 14: Goodbye to All That: Plan Your Funeral and Organ Donation ........ 211

**Part IV: Putting Your Plan into Action** ........ 229

Chapter 15: If There's No Will There's No Way: Why You Need a Will ........ 231
Chapter 16: The Will: An Alien Document Form ........ 245
Chapter 17: The Best Laid Plans: What Can Go Wrong with Your Will? ........ 265
Chapter 18: Affairs to Remember: Who'll Manage Your Money For You? ........ 283
Chapter 19: While You're Up, Get Me a Ventilator: Who'll Care For You? ........ 299

**Part V: Do You Need Professional Help?** ........ 315

Chapter 20: The Best Defence: Your Lawyer as Your Estate Planning Coach ........ 317
Chapter 21: Who's on First? The Rest of Your Estate Planning Team ........ 335

Part VI: You're Not Done Yet .......................................349
Chapter 22: Tidy Up before You Go-Go — Putting Your Affairs in Order ................351
Chapter 23: It's Even Better the Second Time Around: Updating Your Estate Plan ................365

Part VII: The Part of Tens .......................................383
Chapter 24: Ten Questions to Ask before You Hire a Lawyer ................385
Chapter 25: Ten Tips for Using Your Computer for Estate Planning ................389

Appendixes.......................................393
Appendix A: Prepare to Meet Your Lawyer ................393
Appendix B: Instructions for Your Executor ................403
Appendix C: Inventory for Your Executor ................409
Appendix D: About the CD ................413

Index .......................................425

Book Registration Information .......................Back of Book

# Cartoons at a Glance

*By Rich Tennant*

"You have to put some instructions in your will, Mr. Snead. You can't be sure that haunting your executor will work."

*page 229*

"Okay, you can call him Ben. But only we'll know it's short for Beneficiary."

*page 145*

"I know I should tidy up, but I'm convinced that as long as I'm this disorganized I can't die."

*page 349*

"According to this financial calculator, we won't have an estate to leave until 2018."

*page 383*

The 5th Wave By Rich Tennant

"No, I don't have a P.F.P. or S.F.C. from the I.C.B., but I do have an R.F.P. from the C.A.F.P."

*page 315*

"You'll find it interesting working with Mr. Barnum. He's quite creative in his use of estate planning tools."

*page 83*

The 5th Wave By Rich Tennant

"Actually, Mr. Custer, the estate planning process isn't this painful for everyone."

*page 7*


***Fax:*** 978-546-7747

***E-mail:*** richtennant@the5thwave.com

***World Wide Web:*** www.the5thwave.com

# Table of Contents

**Introduction ........ 1**

Why You Need This Book ........ 1
How to Read This Book ........ 2
What's in This Book ........ 3
Part I: Estate Planning Basics ........ 3
Part II: Estate Planning Tools ........ 3
Part III: Creating an Estate Plan ........ 3
Part IV: Putting Your Plan into Action ........ 4
Part V: Do You Need Professional Help? ........ 4
Part VI: You're Not Done Yet ........ 4
Part VII: The Part of Tens ........ 5
Icons ........ 5

**Part I: Estate Planning Basics ........ 7**

**Chapter 1: What Is Estate Planning Anyway? ........ 9**

What Exactly Is Your Estate? ........ 9
What Is Estate Planning? ........ 11
What you need to know to get started ........ 11
This is not a one-time thing ........ 12
Why Do You Need to Do Estate Planning? ........ 12
What Tools Are Used in Estate Planning? ........ 14
When Should You Make an Estate Plan? ........ 15
What about Your Needs? ........ 16
What If You Become Physically or Mentally Incapable? ........ 17
Should You Get Professional Help? ........ 18
You've Likely Heard Enough for the Moment ........ 19

**Chapter 2: What Are You Worth on the Hoof? Financial Planning Basics ........ 21**

Start with a Round-Up of What You've Got ........ 21
Figuring out what you own ........ 22
Figuring out what you owe ........ 25
Figuring out your net worth ........ 26
Take a Hard Look at Your Income and Expenses ........ 27
Figuring out what you earn monthly ........ 27
Figuring out what you spend monthly ........ 28
Take a Rest ........ 33

Chapter 3: Head 'Em Up & Move 'Em Out: Planning Your Financial Future ....35

What Do You Want and When Do You Want It? ....35
The long and the short of your goals ....36
Your goals in case of emergency ....36
The make and model of your goals ....36
You can't do everything ....37
Income Minus Outgo Equals Savings ....37
Increasing your income ....37
Cutting your expenses ....39
You've Saved Some Money — Now What? ....42
Pay off your credit cards ....42
Set aside your savings ....42
Develop an investment strategy ....43
Hope for the Best, Be Prepared for the Worst ....44
Life insurance ....45
Disability insurance ....45
Overhead expense insurance ....46
Out-of-country medical insurance ....47
Liability insurance ....47
Critical illness insurance ....48
Long-term-care insurance ....48

Chapter 4: Income Tax 101.1(a)(i): Some Tax Basics ....49

Taxes on an Estate ....49
Tax for Toddlers ....50
Income and capital gains ....50
Capital gains ....51
Capital losses ....54
Taxable income ....56
Back to Taxes on an Estate ....58
What should your tax planning goals be? ....58
What should your tax planning strategies be? ....59

Chapter 5: The Taxman Cometh: Taxes and Your Estate ....61

The Story So Far ....61
Should You Leave Everything to Your Spouse? ....62
Capital property ....62
RRSPs and RRIFs ....64
Should You Put Your Money into Your Principal Residence? ....67
What is a principal residence? ....67
But can you make use of the principal residence exemption? ....67
But be careful! ....68
Should You Give Things Away Now? ....69
Will you actually reduce capital gains tax for your estate? ....70
Will you actually reduce your income taxes now? ....71
Will you be sorry? ....71

Should You Freeze Your Estate? ....71
Types of estate freezes ....72
Don't try this at home, kids! ....75
Should You Donate Something to Charity? ....75
Some Tax Planning Takes Place after You Die ....76
RRSPs ....76
Capital losses and spousal rollovers ....76
Putting It All Together ....78
When the Taxman Finally Arriveth . . . With the Bill ....78
Estimating the tax ....79
Where will the money come from? ....80
Make sure the wrong person doesn't get stuck with the bill ....81
A Word about Foreign Taxes ....81
Probate Fees ....82

*Part II: Estate Planning Tools* ....83

**Chapter 6: Wish You and Your Income Were Here — Do You Need Life Insurance?** ....85
What Is Life Insurance? ....85
Do You Need Life Insurance? ....86
How Much Life Insurance Do You Need? ....87
If you need insurance to replace your income ....87
If you need insurance to pay a debt or expense ....91
If you need insurance to leave money ....91
Who Should Get the Insurance Money When You Die? ....91
What if you name an individual as your beneficiary? ....92
What if you name your estate as your beneficiary? ....92
What if you create an insurance trust? ....93
Any Other Chance Your Family Will Get Some Money When You Die? ....94
Pension plan and death benefits ....94
Windfalls ....94

**Chapter 7: Money to Die For: The Mysteries of Life Insurance Revealed** ....97
What Kind of Life Insurance Should You Get? ....97
Term insurance ....97
Permanent insurance ....98
What are the advantages and disadvantages of term insurance? ....99
What are the advantages and disadvantages of permanent insurance? ....99
Variations on a theme ....100
Where Do You Get Life Insurance? ....102
Individual insurance ....102
Group insurance ....105

How Do You Get Life Insurance? ....105
Getting individual insurance ....106
Getting group insurance ....107
How Much Will Insurance Cost? ....108
The amount of insurance ....108
Term insurance or permanent insurance ....108
Insurance rating factors ....108
Comparison shop ....110
Individual insurance or group insurance ....111
What Does a Standard Life Insurance Policy Say? ....111
Individual insurance ....111
Group insurance ....112

**Chapter 8: Free to a Good Home: Giving Away Your Things before You Die ....113**

Why Give Your Property Away While You're Alive? ....114
What Is a Gift? ....114
How Do You Make a Gift? ....115
Can You Give Away Your Property without Meaning To? ....116
A gift made against your will is not a gift ....116
A promise to give a gift is not a gift ....117
But a promise to give a gift in return for something is a different matter ....117
Will You Live to Regret This Gift? ....118
Can you afford the gift? ....118
Will you have to pay tax on your gift? ....119
Is There a Safer Way Than Giving a Gift? ....120
A loan ....121
A rental ....121
An investment ....121
A sale ....122
RESPs ....122
Co-ownership ....122
A trust ....123

**Chapter 9: Pass the Buck: Using Trusts in Estate Planning ....125**

What Is a Trust? ....125
More about the players ....126
More about the property ....126
Why Set up a Trust? ....127
Kinds of Trusts ....128
Testamentary Trusts ....129
Spousal trust ....129
Trust for a minor ....130
Spendthrift trusts ....131
Special needs trust ....132
Pet trusts ....133
Trust for a charity ....133

Living Trusts ....................133
Creating an estate freeze ....................134
Keeping a gift confidential ....................135
Looking after someone with special needs ....................135
Giving to charity ....................135
Avoiding probate fees ....................136
A Trustee You Can Trust ....................136
What does a trustee do? ....................136
What are the legal responsibilities of a trustee? ....................137
What are the powers of a trustee? ....................138
Choosing a trustee ....................138
Paying a trustee ....................139
Trusts and Taxes ....................140
On the creation of the trust ....................140
During the operation of the trust ....................141
When your trust comes of age at 21 ....................142
On the termination of the trust ....................143
The Care and Feeding of a Trust ....................143
Set-up fees ....................143
Ongoing fees ....................143
Winding-up fees ....................144

*Part III: Creating an Estate Plan* .................... 145

**Chapter 10: A Crew for Your Ship of Estate: Beneficiaries and Executor** .................... **147**

Your Beneficiaries ....................147
The people you want to provide for ....................148
The people you have to provide for ....................151
The people you decided not to provide for ....................154
Your Executor ....................155
What does an executor do? ....................156
What are the legal responsibilities of an executor? ....................157
Choosing your executor ....................158
What to do with an executor who's a landlubber ....................159
All Hands on Deck ....................159
Beneficiaries ....................160
Executors ....................160

**Chapter 11: Who's Minding the Kids? Planning Your Children's Future** .................... **161**

Once upon a Time . . . ....................162
The Story Takes a Grimm Turn ....................162
If one parent dies but the other is still alive and has custody ....163
If one parent dies and that parent had sole custody ....................163
If both parents are dead ....................166

Wicked Witch or Fairy Godparent? ....167
Testamentary guardian, a.k.a. fairy godparent ....168
Preventing the fairy godparent from dissolving when splashed with water ....170
The Duties of a Fairy Godparent ....171
Guardian of the person and guardian of the property ....171
Instructions for the guardian(s) ....171
The Little Bag of Gold ....172
Where will the money come from? ....172
How will the money be managed? ....173
Who will manage the money? ....174
The Hut at the Edge of the Forest ....175
Happily Ever After ....175

**Chapter 12: Giving Them the Business: What to Do with the Family Firm ....177**

Take Stock of Your Situation ....177
You may already be sold short ....178
You may have options ....179
Market Timing ....183
If you hold for the family ....184
If you decide to sell ....185
Place Your Orders ....185
If your business is a sole proprietorship ....185
If your business is a partnership ....186
If your business is a corporation ....187
Don't Forget to Hedge ....189
Someone who can step in ....189
Insurance for your business ....190
At the close ....191

**Chapter 13: You Gave at the Office, But . . . — Charitable Donations ....193**

Thinking about Giving to Charity ....194
Why give to charity? ....194
How much should you give? ....194
What are the tax advantages to leaving money to charity? ....195
Choosing the Right Charity ....196
A charity that does the right kind of good ....197
A charity that's not good enough to be true ....197
A charity that's on good terms with Canada Revenue ....198
A charity that looks a gift horse in the mouth ....199
A charity that can't take a hint ....199
A charity that will put your name up in lights ....200
Making Sure Your Donation Gets Where You Want It to Go ....200
Get the charity's name right ....201
Guard against the charity's untimely end ....201

Planned Giving ....201
Ways to Give to Charity ....202
Gifts of cash made by will ....202
Gifts of specific property made by will ....203
Gifts of life insurance ....204
Gifts of RRSP or RRIF proceeds ....206
Charitable gift annuities ....207
Charitable remainder trusts ....209
Memorial donations ....209

**Chapter 14: Goodbye to All That: Plan Your Funeral and Organ Donation ....211**

The Last Word ....211
The High Cost of Death ....212
It's Your Funeral ....213
At the home sweet funeral home ....213
Shop 'til you drop ....214
Slip into something comfortable ....215
The funeral services contract ....216
At Your Disposal: Earth, Air, Fire, or Water? ....218
Earth ....218
The cemetery ....219
Interment rights ....219
Interment, or the yawning grave ....220
The monument ....220
Extras ....220
Water ....222
Fire ....223
How much will you get burned for? ....224
Ashes to dust ....224
Air ....224
The Gift That Keeps on Giving: Organ and Body Donation ....225
Consenting to body part donation ....225
This won't hurt a bit ....226
No one thinks you're sexy anymore but someone may still want your body ....227

***Part IV: Putting Your Plan into Action ....229***

**Chapter 15: If There's No Will There's No Way: Why You Need a Will ....231**

Where Will Your Property Go without Your Directions in a Will? ....232
If you are married ....232
If you are married with children ....233
If you are not married but you have children ....233
If you are not married and you have no children ....234
If you don't want this to happen to you . . . ....234

Who Will Administer Your Estate? ....235
How will an administrator be found? ....236
The application for letters of administration ....236
What Difficulties Will Arise in the Administration of Your Estate? ....237
A stranglehold on the administrator ....237
Increased taxes ....239
Government meddling ....241
Mystery beneficiaries ....242
What Happens to Your Estate If You Have a Will? ....242

**Chapter 16: The Will: An Alien Document Form ....245**

Get Ready, Get Set, Get Lost ....245
. . . To Discover Strange New Words . . . ....246
In Low Orbit around a Will ....250
Identification ....250
Revocation of other wills ....250
Naming the executor ....250
Leaving property to the executor in trust ....251
Payment of debts ....252
Distributing the remaining property to the beneficiaries ....252
Executor's powers ....256
Signing a Will ....260
The testator must be legally capable of making a will ....261
Legal formalities for signing and witnessing a will ....261
After the Will Is Signed ....263
Do-It-Yourself Wills ....264
Holograph wills ....264

**Chapter 17: The Best Laid Plans: What Can Go Wrong with Your Will? ....265**

It's Unsinkable ....266
Of Course It Will Hold! ....266
What can happen if you choose the wrong executor? ....267
What can happen if you don't take debts and taxes into account? ....268
What can happen if you neglect your spouse or dependants? ....269
What can happen if you don't set up a trust for beneficiaries who are minors? ....270
What can happen if you don't name someone to look after your children? ....271
What can happen if you don't make a plan to pass on your business? ....271
Trust Me, I Know What I'm Doing ....272
Residue ....272
Unclear wording ....273
Unconsidered "what-ifs?" ....274
Insufficient power to the executor ....276
Now I really do know what I'm doing ....277

What Happens If You Touch These Two Wires Together? ....................277
Signed and witnessed ....................278
Mental competence and free will ....................279
Don't Worry, It's Not Loaded ....................280
There's a Great View If You Just Lean Over Here ....................281
I Wish I Hadn't Done That . . . ....................282

**Chapter 18: Affairs to Remember: Who'll Manage Your Money For You? . . . . . . . . . .283**

What Will Happen If Your Physical or Mental Health Fails? ....................284
Looking after income ....................284
Looking after business ....................285
You'd be surprised how often you need your mind ....................286
Looking for help! ....................287
The Solution to Your Management Problems ....................287
Powers of Attorney Come in Different Models ....................288
Enduring or continuing power of attorney ....................288
General or specific power of attorney ....................288
What's in a Power of Attorney? ....................290
What's Involved in Preparing a Power of Attorney? ....................291
The attorney ....................291
The powers ....................292
The process ....................293
Once the Power of Attorney Has Been Prepared ....................294
What Happens When Your Attorney Takes Over? ....................295
The duties of an attorney ....................295
What Happens If There Is No Power of Attorney? ....................296
Seat-of-the-pants arrangements ....................297
Formal arrangements ....................297
Government arrangements ....................298

**Chapter 19: While You're Up, Get Me a Ventilator: Who'll Care for You? . . . . . . . . . .299**

What Happens If You're Sick and Can't Speak for Yourself? ....................300
Why Is Your Consent Needed for Treatment? ....................301
Are There Special Rules about Giving Consent to Treatment? ....................302
What Kind of Treatment Are We Talking About? ....................303
Treatment that prolongs life ....................303
Treatment that eases death ....................304
What kind of treatment do you want? ....................305
How Can You Make Your Wishes Known? ....................305
What does a living will say? ....................306
How do you make a living will? ....................308
After you've made a living will ....................309
What Happens When Your Living Will Comes into Effect? ....................310
Arrangements If You Haven't Made a Living Will ....................311
Guardian of the person ....................312

## Part V: Do You Need Professional Help? ......................315

### Chapter 20: The Best Defence: Your Lawyer as Your Estate Planning Coach ........................................317

Why Do You Need a Lawyer? ....................318
- What about those guys who are sort of minor league lawyers? ....318
- Stick to the majors ....................320

When Do You Need a Lawyer? ....................320
- When you're planning your estate and your will ....................320
- When you start to put your plan into action ....................322
- When it comes time to put pen to paper ....................322
- After you're gone ....................323

What Lawyer Do You Want? ....................323
- A lawyer who knows something about wills and estates ....................324
- A lawyer you like . . . or at least don't loathe ....................325

Where Is the Lawyer You Long For? ....................326
- Recommendation ....................326
- Investigation ....................326
- Interview ....................327
- Decision ....................327

How Much Do Lawyers Charge? ....................328
- Yeah, okay, so how do they charge? ....................328
- Billing at an hourly rate ....................328
- Charging a flat rate ....................329
- Charging a contingency fee ....................330

What Should You Expect of Your Lawyer? ....................330

What Do You Do If Your Lawyer Annoys You . . . Or Worse? ....................331

How Do You Get the Most from Your Lawyer? ....................332

### Chapter 21: Who's on First? The Rest of Your Estate Planning Team . . .335

The Coach, You've Met ....................335

Now Say Hello to the Boys on the Bench ....................336

A Professional Accountant ....................336
- Types of professional accountants ....................337
- How do accountants charge for their services? ....................338
- How do you find an accountant? ....................338

A Financial Planner ....................339
- Are there any qualifications out there? ....................339
- How are financial planners paid for their services? ....................340
- How do you find a financial planner? ....................342
- What do you do if your financial planner drops the ball? ....................343

Banks, Trust Companies, and Credit Unions ....................343

Life Insurance Agents or Brokers ....................344
- How are agents and brokers paid for their services? ....................344
- How do you find an insurance agent or broker? ....................345

Forget about Stealing All the Way to Home Base ....................346

We're Back to the Coach Again ....................346

Part VI: You're Not Done Yet .......................................349

Chapter 22: Tidy Up Before You Go-Go — Putting Your Affairs in Order .......................................351

How Can You Prevent Your Death from Causing Confusion in Your Family? .......352
Before you kick the bucket .......352
After you kick the bucket .......352
What Documents and Instructions Will Your Family Need? .......353
If you don't just drop dead but become incapacitated before you die .......353
When you die .......354
What Documents Will Your Executor Need? .......354
The duties of an executor .......354
Where Are Your Documents Now? .......363

Chapter 23: It's Even Better the Second Time Around: Updating Your Estate Plan .......................................365

What's Involved in Reviewing Your Estate Plan? .......365
Why Do You Need to Review and Revise Your Estate Plan? .......366
When Should You Revise Your Estate Plan? .......367
Changes in Your Personal Life .......368
If you get married .......368
If your spouse dies .......369
If your marriage breaks down .......369
If you have children .......371
If you develop serious health problems .......371
If a family member develops special needs .......372
Changes in your residence .......372
Changes in your executor's life .......374
Changes in Your Financial and Economic Life .......374
Changes in the nature and value of your property .......374
Changes in your business .......375
Changes in the Law .......376
Tax law .......376
Family law .......377
Succession law .......377
Other areas of law .......377
How Do You Change Your Will? .......378
Making a codicil .......378
Revoking and replacing your will .......379
A codicil or a new will? .......379
Don't Forget Your Pensions and Insurance Policies .......379
Life insurance policies .......380
Pension plans .......380
RRSPs and RRIFs .......381

And Don't Forget Your Power of Attorney and Living Will Either .........381
Power of attorney .........381
Living will .........382

**Part VII: The Part of Tens .........383**

**Chapter 24: Ten Questions to Ask before You Hire a Lawyer .......385**
Ask the Lawyer .........386
Then Ask Yourself .........388

**Chapter 25: Ten Tips for Using Your Computer for Estate Planning . . .389**
Get Financial Planning Help .........389
Find Income Tax Info .........390
Look for Insurance Help .........390
Locate Legal Information .........390
Get Government Information .........390
Find Help with Funeral Planning .........391
Look into Organ Donation .........391
Investigate Charities .........391
Research Your Living Will .........391
Get Organized .........392

**Appendix A: Prepare to Meet Your Lawyer .........393**

**Appendix B: Instructions for Your Executor .........403**

**Appendix C: Inventory for Your Executor .........409**

**Appendix D: About the CD .........413**
System Requirements .........413
Installing the Programs from Microsoft Windows .........415
Installing the Programs from a Macintosh .........416
What You'll Find .........417
Windows programs .........417
Macintosh programs .........419
A note about shareware .........421
Forms and other documents .........421
Financial calculators .........423
If You've Got Problems (of the CD Kind) .........423

**Index .........425**

# Introduction

NEWS FLASH: The end of the world is coming! Well, not the end of the entire world, just the end of *your* world. It's probably not coming today, and it's probably not coming tomorrow or even next week. But the nasty truth is that we're all going to die some day.

We usually can't tell very far ahead what day our world will end. But we can plan ahead against that day — and there are good reasons for doing that. There are *no* good reasons for pretending that we're going to live forever and that death is what happens to other people but not to us.

Planning ahead involves creating an estate plan and making a will, power of attorney, and living will. An estate plan is a strategy for increasing the amount of cash and property you own in your lifetime, and for giving it to others after your death (sometimes even before your death). A will is a legal document that comes into effect when you die and sets out the plan you've made to give your property to others. A power of attorney is another legal document. It gives a person you choose the ability to handle your financial affairs when you're still alive but you can't handle them yourself. A living will, also a legal document, gives a person you choose the ability to make decisions about your personal care when you're still alive but you can't make them yourself.

Estate planning and wills were not invented for controlling people who want to keep their hands on their property after they're dead. (Well, they weren't invented *just* for never-say-die controllers. . . .) They were invented for people who want to make sure that, after their death, life goes on fairly smoothly — financially if not emotionally — for their family and friends.

## Why You Need This Book

When we go, we can't take much with us. In fact we can't take anything with us — not the stock portfolio we built up so carefully, not the brass spittoon that's been in the family for generations, not even a stick of gum. Our possessions stay behind.

They may as well stay with people we choose rather than go to people the provincial government chooses or be spent on government taxes and fees that could (at least in part) be avoided. And if there are people you really want to have your money and other property, why not leave them as much as possible?

This book will tell you how to plan for the end of life by creating an estate plan, making a will, and making a power of attorney and living will. If you don't make any plans, there may not be enough money available to look after you and your family before your death and to support your family comfortably after your death. If you don't make any plans, on your death more of your property will be eaten up in taxes and government fees and less of it will go to your family and friends. If you don't make any plans, your property will go to certain of your relatives named in a list created by your provincial government — you won't get to choose which relatives and how much, and not a penny will go to your friends or to your favourite charity. If you don't make any plans and you're short on relatives, all of your property will go to your provincial government.

This book was written for people who aren't lawyers or accountants or insurance brokers or financial planners but who want to know how to plan their estate and make their will. (Lawyers, accountants, insurance brokers, and financial planners are welcome to read this book too.) We don't assume that you have any background knowledge about law or income tax or insurance policies or funeral planning or anything else. We start at the beginning of each subject and build up information about it. We avoid using technical language when it's not necessary, and we explain technical terms in plain English if you need to know them.

# How to Read This Book

Our editor pounded it into our heads that we shouldn't assume that people would read this book in any particular order, and many chapters can be read on their own. However, there are a few pairs of chapters that are really two-parters — and you'll understand part two a lot better if you've read part one first. We let you know which chapters those are. Apart from that you can dip into a chapter here and a chapter there if you like. On the whole, though, you'll probably get more out of this book if you start at the beginning, proceed to the middle, and continue on to the end (although not all in one sitting).

You can, of course, leave out chapters that you think are unimportant to you. If you don't have children, you could skip the chapter on making arrangements for your children to be looked after following your death. If you don't own a business, you could skip the chapter on passing on your business. But then you'll miss some of the stories we tell in sidebars, and you wouldn't want to do that.

# What's in This Book

This book is divided into seven parts, each covering a major area of estate planning. The chapters within each part cover specific topics in detail.

## Part I: Estate Planning Basics

In this part you'll find the basic information you need to understand the estate planning process. In Chapter 1 we explain what your estate is, and what estate planning is and why you need to do it. In the following two chapters we offer a bit of advice about how to measure and manage your estate while you're still alive — in Chapter 2 we set out the basics of financial planning and in Chapter 3 we share tips gleaned from experts about increasing the value of your estate. In Chapters 4 and 5, probably the scariest parts of this book, we tell you about the Canadian tax system and the impact of the federal Income Tax Act on estate planning. But don't worry, we also tell you how to work with the income tax rules to keep taxes on your estate as low as possible. Then, as a bonus, we explain what probate fees are and offer some strategies for keeping them down too.

## Part II: Estate Planning Tools

In Part II we introduce you to the tools commonly used to plan an estate. Chapter 6 helps you figure out whether you need life insurance and, if you do, how much. Chapter 7 delves into the difference between term life insurance and permanent life insurance and gives you the information you need to decide which kind is right for you. In Chapter 8 we talk about giving away your property before you die, and explain why there are no such things as simple gifts. In Chapter 9 we talk your ear off about testamentary trusts and living trusts. In case you just can't wait — trusts are a way to give property away while still keeping some control over it.

## Part III: Creating an Estate Plan

In Part III we start to take you through the estate planning process. Chapter 10 organizes you to choose the people you'll give your estate to (your beneficiaries) and the person who will manage your estate until it has been completely given away (your executor). In Chapter 11 we let you know what will happen to your young children if you die before them and how to make the best advance arrangements for their care. In Chapter 12 we explain what you have to do in order to pass your business on to family members or other people of your choosing. Chapter 13 helps you decide whether to give a gift to charity and when to do it (while you're alive or in your will). Chapter 14, destined to become a cult classic, gives you the lowdown on planning your funeral and donating your organs.

## Part IV: Putting Your Plan into Action

In Part IV we get down to the nitty-gritty of estate planning — creating the documents required to carry out the plan you've worked so hard on. In Chapter 15 we set out all the unpleasant things that will happen if you don't make a will and in Chapter 16 we actually show you a will, in all its glory. It may take you a while to recover from that chapter. And Chapter 17 won't give you much help in recovering, because it tells you all the things that can go wrong if your will isn't done right. In Chapter 18 we talk to you in our perky way about making arrangements to manage your finances in the event that you become disabled before you die; and in Chapter 19 we cover arrangements to manage your physical care if you become unable to make decisions.

## Part V: Do You Need Professional Help?

In this part we take a little pity on you and tell you how to get help with all the things we've told you you'd better do if you know what's good for you. Chapter 20 sets out the role of a lawyer in estate planning and gives step-by-step instructions on how to find a lawyer. Chapter 21 does the same for other people who can assist you — accountants, financial planners, insurance agents and brokers, and so on.

## Part VI: You're Not Done Yet

Just when you think it must surely be all over by now, along comes Chapter 22. In that chapter we encourage you to put your affairs in order so you won't drive your executor to an early grave or make your estate impossible to manage. It's at this point that you'll probably want to throw the book through a plate glass window. But if you resist that impulse in Chapter 22, you'll almost certainly give in to it in Chapter 23, where we cheerily tell you that the only way to avoid going through the whole estate process again . . . maybe many times . . . is to die as soon as you've made your first estate plan and signed your first will.

## Part VII: The Part of Tens

In Chapter 24 we build on our advice in Chapter 20 and suggest 10 questions for you to ask a lawyer before you hire him or her. In Chapter 25 we offer 10 tips for using your computer in the estate planning process.

# Icons

We use a number of icons in this book to guide you to information that's particularly important or useful . . . or in one case, that's particularly easy to ignore.

This icon draws your attention to important information that you've probably already forgotten if we told you about it before or that we want you to remember in the future.

This one reminds you that there are some things you mustn't do without getting professional help from a lawyer.

And this one lets you know it's probably safe to jump to the next paragraph, especially if your eyes are already glazing over from reading the paragraph that came before. But seriously, if you're really interested in understanding the topic you should read these detailed definitions and explanations.

This icon alerts you that we're saying something that could save you time, trouble, or money. When we hit a bull's-eye, it could save you all three.

This ominous icon suggests not very subtly that you're heading for trouble and very possibly complete disaster if you don't follow our advice to the letter.

Finally, this icon identifies material that — you guessed it — you will find on the CD-ROM as well.

# Part I
# Estate Planning Basics

"Actually, Mr. Custer, the estate planning process isn't this painful for everyone."

## In this part . . .

This part introduces you gently to estate planning. We hardly ask you to think about your approaching end at all! Instead we tell you exactly what estate planning is, help you figure out the present size of your estate and give you some suggestions about increasing it, and explain how Canadian tax laws affect your estate plan.

# Chapter 1

# What Is Estate Planning Anyway?

### *In This Chapter*

- Discovering what estate planning is and why you need to do it
- Understanding what your estate is
- Knowing when you should make an estate plan
- Learning about estate planning tools
- Planning in case of physical or mental incapacity before you die
- Getting professional help with estate planning

Here's the good news about estate planning, right up front: *You* have an estate! You don't have to be a sports star, a computer maven, or to have inherited old family money to have an estate or to need to do estate planning.

Now for the bad news about estate planning: It forces you to think about death — and not just in an abstract philosophical kind of way. It forces you to think about your own death. It also forces you to think about leaving family and friends behind, when they still need you to be there.

You're probably not going to enjoy the estate planning process very much, but we explain why you should do it even though it's not a lot of fun. And after you've done it you'll feel a kind of virtuous glow because you've taken important steps to make things easier for the people you care about when you die.

In this chapter we're going to ease you gently into estate planning. We'll briefly discuss the main things you need to know, and then in the following chapters we go into more detail.

## What Exactly Is Your Estate?

We keep talking about this estate of yours — we seem to be quite convinced that you have one, don't we? Before you start wondering why the butler and chauffeur didn't show up for work this morning, we'd better give you a little more detail about what your estate is.

Your estate is made up of everything you own. That makes sense so far, right? But in legal terms, your debts — everything you *owe* — are also part of your estate, since what you own must be used to pay off your debts when you die. (We show you how to take stock of your estate in Chapter 2.)

Everything you own includes:

- A home, cottage, or other real estate
- A boat, a car, or other motor vehicles
- Any money you have in cash, bank accounts, or certificates of deposit
- Any investments you hold, such as shares, bonds, or mutual funds
- Your valuable personal belongings, such as computers, stereo systems, TV and VCR, jewellery, artwork, antiques, silver and fine china, or collectibles such as a complete set of Elvis Plays Las Vegas memorial plates
- Your other belongings that may have value only as part of your household, such as furniture, kitchen utensils, linens, and clothing
- Any business you run as a sole proprietor or partner

The things you own are referred to in law and accounting as your *assets.* We'll try not to refer to them as "assets," but we may forget every now and then because we're lawyers and it's hard for us not to throw around words like "assets" and "estate."

Everything you owe includes:

- A mortgage on your home or other real estate
- Personal loans that have not been paid off
- Business loans made to you personally (if you're a sole proprietor or partner, you and your business are one and the same)
- Unpaid credit card balances
- Other unpaid bills
- Unpaid income taxes

Then there are some other things that, while not technically part of your estate, need to be taken into account when you think about who has to be looked after by you and how much they'll need to keep going:

- **Life insurance:** If you have a life insurance policy, when you die either your estate or an individual (or individuals) you name as beneficiary, whichever option you have chosen, will receive the insurance proceeds. (We tell you more about insurance in Chapters 6 and 7.)

- **Pension plans:** If you are a member of an employee pension plan, your spouse or a person you name as beneficiary may be entitled to receive a pension after your death or to receive a one-time payment.
- **Government benefits:** Your spouse and/or children may be entitled to receive either a pension or a one-time payment from the Canada Pension Plan, Old Age Security, Veterans' Affairs, or Workers' Compensation after your death.

Besides being what you own and owe, your estate is also a legal being that comes into existence on your death — sort of like a ghostly lingering reminder of you. It has some of the same legal rights that you had when you were alive, such as the right to enter into contracts and to sue and be sued. It also has some of the duties you had, the principal one being the duty to pay income tax. At various places in this book we'll be talking about your estate's activities, so don't let it throw you for a loop.

# What Is Estate Planning?

Estate planning is essentially two things: planning to build up cash and other property in your estate, and planning what you want to happen to that property after you die.

We know this sounds pretty materialistic and self-centred, as though the point of your whole life is to accumulate money right up to the very end and then to control that money from beyond the grave. In fact, estate planning is not a selfish activity — it's not really about *you* at all, it's about the people who are important to you and whom you want to look after . . . not just for your lifetime but for their lifetime.

## What you need to know to get started

Estate planning is not rocket science, but it isn't a one-step process either. It involves identifying your estate to begin with, figuring out how to increase it if possible, and then deciding who you want to have it.

In order to start planning your estate you need to have a clear idea about the following matters:

- What do you own and what do you owe?
- What ways can you find of owning more and owing less so that you have more to leave behind?

- Whom do you want to (or have to) provide for after you're gone, and how much do they need?
- What are the best ways of providing for them?

It looks like you're going to have to take a hard, cold look at your financial situation *and* your family relationships and obligations. Yikes! Don't try to do both on the same day! Maybe not even in the same week. But you can't put it off too long — you do have to do it in the same lifetime.

### This is not a one-time thing

Estate planning is not a one-time exercise, either. Well, okay, it is if you kick the bucket immediately after making your plan and putting it into effect. But we wish you a very long and prosperous life full of exciting incidents like love, marriage, babies, divorce, business start-ups, and lottery jackpots. And whenever an exciting incident occurs in your life you need to review your estate plan and make any changes that seem necessary.

When you're young and single, you may want your money to go to a brother or sister if something happens to you, or to friends or a charity. But once you settle into a serious relationship or marry, you'll probably want your partner to get most of what you own. (You picture your bereaved partner lounging on your favourite sofa, playing your classic Sinatra . . . or Ricky Martin . . . CDs and thinking tearfully of you.) If you have a young family, you'll want to make sure that they will have enough money to live comfortably without your income, and that there will be someone to look after the kids (and money to do it with) if both parents meet an untimely end.

If you're divorced, you may want to make sure that all your money goes to your children and that your ex never gets a red cent of it. And if you remarry and start a second family, you need to balance your responsibilities to your first family with your commitments to your new one. If you have grown children, you probably want an estate plan that treats each of them fairly, while taking into account their different abilities, needs, and interests. When you get older, you may have to put the needs of a frail spouse above those of your children. Or you may be sick of all of your relatives and determined to give everything to a home for stray cats.

## Why Do You Need to Do Estate Planning?

Notice that we're not asking, Do You Need to Do Estate Planning or Not? You do need to do it, so don't argue. And here are the main reasons why you need to plan your estate. You want to make sure that when you die:

- You have done everything in your power to see that your family has enough money to manage without you — it takes planning to set aside and invest money for your family (see Chapters 2 and 3) and to make sure that you have enough insurance (see Chapters 6 and 7).
- Your property goes to the people *you* want to have it — if you die without a valid will, the provincial government decides who gets your property based on rules set by provincial law, and it may well not go to the people you have in mind (see Chapter 15).
- A person *you* choose will look after your estate — without a valid will, there will be no executor named by you who will have the automatic right to look after your estate; instead, someone (usually a family member) will have to apply to the court to be appointed to look after it (see Chapter 15).
- You have a say in who will look after your children — if both you and the children's other parent die, a will is the best way to let your surviving family and the courts know whom you would like to care for the children (see Chapter 11).
- Your debts can be paid with the least damage to your estate — if you make no plan for payment of your debts, there may not be enough cash available to pay them (see Chapter 17). If you leave no will, the person appointed to look after your estate will have to sell some of your property to get the necessary cash, without any guidance from you about what to sell and what to keep in order to give to a particular family member or friend.
- The capital gains taxes your estate has to pay will be as low as possible — when you die your estate is taxed as if you had sold everything you owned just before you died, and without proper tax planning the bill can be high (see Chapters 4 and 5).
- The probate fees your estate has to pay will be as low as possible — in almost all provinces probate fees are calculated according to how much your estate is worth; with advance planning you can reduce the value of your estate for probate purposes, and so reduce these fees (see Chapter 5).
- The future of any business you own has been looked after — you need to plan ahead, whether you want your business to carry on (who should look after it?) or whether you want it to be sold (how to get the most money for it?). (See Chapter 12.)

Here's a final, even more morbid, reason to plan your estate. As part of the process you can let your family know what you'd like done with your body. (Oddly enough, your body is not part of your estate, unlike the other things that belonged to you when you were alive . . . it belongs to your executor or, if you have no executor, your closest relative.) You can make your wishes known about organ donation (yes or no) and funeral arrangements (plain oak casket or the King Tut special, burial or cremation, flowers or donations to a favourite charity), so that your family members don't have to go through the stress of making choices they think you'd approve of, or maybe even end up fighting.

# What Tools Are Used in Estate Planning?

Uh oh, things are starting to sound technical here. So we're going to need "tools" to do this estate planning business, are we? Like what? A level to make sure that all family members are treated equally? A shovel to beat off Canada Revenue?

Actually, we had something a little less physical in mind . . . although it's probably not a bad idea to keep that shovel handy. Once you know what your estate consists of and what you want to give to whom, you can choose some estate planning tools to help you do what you want.

The most commonly used estate planning tools are:

- **A will:** A will is a written, signed, and witnessed document that states how you want your property to be given away after you die, and appoints an *executor* to look after your property and debts after your death. We strongly advise that you have a lawyer prepare your will. (We tell you more about wills in Chapters 15 and 16.)
- **Gifts given during your lifetime:** A gift is a transfer of all of your rights over a piece of property. (Once you make a gift, you no longer have the right to hold on to the thing given or to sell it or to take it back from the person you gave it to or to leave it to another person in your will.) Giving a valuable gift usually has tax consequences for the giver. "Tax consequences" is a fancy way of saying "tax payments." We tell you more about gifts in Chapter 8.

- **Trusts:** A trust is another way to give property away during your lifetime. But instead of giving the property directly to the person you want to have the use of it (the *beneficiary*), you give the property to another person you choose (a *trustee*) to hold and look after it for the use of the beneficiary. Why, you may be asking, would anyone want to do a weird thing like this? The main reason is to prevent the beneficiary from having total control of the property (for example, if the beneficiary is a child, or mentally disabled, or hopeless about business matters; or if you want one person to have use of the property in the short term but want a different person to become the owner of the property at a later date). There can be income tax benefits to setting up a trust. If you decide to set a trust up, you'll need a professional — an estates and trusts lawyer or a tax lawyer, to advise you and to do the paperwork. (For more on trusts, see Chapter 9.)

- **Joint ownership of property during your lifetime:** Joint ownership while you're alive allows you to control who gets the jointly owned property when you die. You can own property jointly with another person (or with other people) in all provinces other than Quebec. All sorts of property (real estate, bank accounts, mutual funds or other investments) can be owned in this way. When you die, your share in the property will automatically pass to the surviving owner. It's not necessary to mention the property in your will in order to pass it on to the surviving joint owner. In fact you can't deal with joint property by will even if you want to.
- **Life insurance:** Life insurance is a kind of bet that you make with an insurance company. You're betting that you'll die and the life insurance company is betting that you won't. If the life insurance company loses, it has to pay up on the bet — that's the proceeds of the policy. A life insurance policy will help you ensure that your family has enough money after you die to replace the income you will no longer be around to earn, or to help them pay off taxes or other debts without using up your estate. The downside (apart from the fact that in order to win the bet you have to die)? Many insurance policies end when the insured reaches retirement age — in other words, just when your chance of winning starts to improve.

# When Should You Make an Estate Plan?

Most people put off estate planning because they don't want to face the certainty of dying. Some people are even afraid that doing some estate planning makes them more likely to die. As experts in this area, we are in a position to give you some scientific facts about estate planning and death. Statistics do indeed show that 100% of people who have planned their estate die. However, statistics also show that 100% of people who *haven't* planned their estate die. We can assure you that there is no cause-and-effect relationship between estate planning and death. There is however a cause-and-effect relationship between a lack of estate planning and wasted time, trouble, and aggravation for the people you care about.

So, since estate planning isn't going to kill you, when's the best time to do it? You should make an estate plan as soon as you have any significant property (and you care who's going to get it) or as soon as there is anyone who is financially dependent on you, whichever happens sooner. You are legally able to make a will when you're quite young — as soon as you are 18 years old (even younger in some limited circumstances, as we explain in Chapter 16). Don't assume that estate planning is something to do when you're "old," because you don't have to be old to die, you just have to be alive. Anyway, if we waited until we were "old" none of us would ever do any estate planning: No matter how old we get, we don't think of ourselves as old. Old is what other people get.

Going through the estate planning process once is not the end of the matter. Estate planning is a continuing process because you will have to change your estate plan as changes occur:

- **In your personal life.** You should review your estate plan if you marry. Have a look again when you have children and as they grow up, leave home, and start to earn their own living. Think about changing your will if your spouse or partner dies or if you divorce or even if you separate and meet someone new.
- **In your business life.** If you start a business either alone or with others, you should review your estate plan to make sure it deals with your business's debts and with whether your business will fold or carry on under new management when you die.
- **In your executor's life.** You may need to change your will if the person you have named as your executor is no longer willing or able to take on those duties, or if you decide that you need someone with more sophisticated business or investment skills. (Hey, we're not saying a thing against Cousin Joe. He's a good guy . . . but does he know a stock option from a distributor cap?)
- **In the value of your property.** If the value of the property you own goes way up or down in value, you may want to make changes to your estate plan to deal with the change in the taxes your estate will have to pay and with the debts your estate may have. You may also want to re-think how you've divided up your property in your will if you're trying to treat everyone equally.

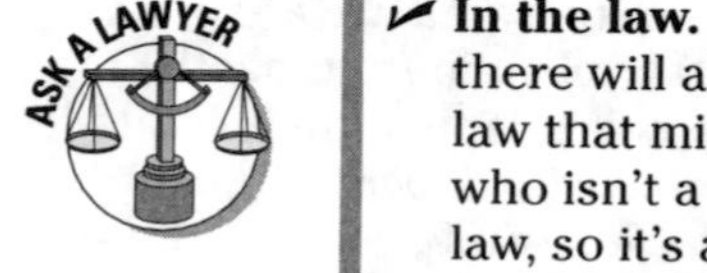

- **In the law.** Between the time you plan your estate and the date you die there will almost certainly be changes to tax law, family law, and estate law that might require changes to your estate plan. It's hard for someone who isn't a lawyer watching eagle-eyed for changes to keep tabs on the law, so it's a good idea to have a lawyer review your estate plan every now and then.

## What about Your Needs?

You're not dead yet. When you put together your estate plan don't get so carried away with looking after everybody when you're dead that you forget to look after yourself while you're still alive.

What if you build up your investments but never have any money for new clothes, a night out, or a vacation? Suppose you were to give your cottage to your children on the understanding that you had the use of it for a few weeks every year? How happy would you be if they couldn't afford or couldn't be bothered to maintain it properly and it turned into a dump, or they squabbled with you about when it was your turn and when it was theirs? What if you made your unmarried significant other a joint owner with you of the house *you* bought . . . only to find one day that significant other had run off with your best friend — and now wanted to sell the house to finance a honeymoon in Rio de Janeiro?

You must make sure that your plans leave you with enough money and property (and enough control over your money and property) to last you until you die.

# What If You Become Physically or Mentally Incapable?

Now isn't that a cheery thought. But while you're confronting your own mortality, you have to also think about the possible decline before your ultimate fall.

A complete estate plan includes a plan for any time during your life that you can't manage your own financial affairs — not only if you get Alzheimer's disease but if a car accident leaves you in a coma, or if you have an operation that puts you out of commission for even just a short time, or, on a happier note, if you're spending two or three months in Florida during the winter and you want someone to be able to look after things while you're away.

The tool used for managing financial matters is a *power of attorney*. A power of attorney is a written, signed, and witnessed document that gives the person of your choice (called an *attorney* in most provinces) authority to handle your legal and financial affairs.

You also have to think about what you want done if your health declines to the point that you are no longer able to make decisions about your own health care. When that happens, someone else has to make decisions on your behalf — but who do you want that someone to be? And what decisions do you want that person to make? If you go into cardiac arrest or stop breathing, do you want to be brought back to life and kept alive no matter what shape you're in? Or would you prefer to let nature take its course? If you're dependent on machinery such as a ventilator to keep you alive, are there some circumstances in which you'd like someone you trust to give the order to pull the plug?

The tool used to deal with health matters is a *living will*. A living will is a written document that sets out your wishes about your health care, and that appoints a person (family member or friend or anyone you wish) to make health care decisions if you become unable to make those decisions for yourself. If you don't have a living will, provincial law tells doctors and hospitals which of your nearest and dearest they should turn to for instructions. First on the list is a spouse, then adult children, and so on. If you run out of close relatives, the doctors and hospitals may have to ask a government official what to do with you. Now *there's* a thought to frighten you out of six months' life.

## Should You Get Professional Help?

In a word, yes! We want to make this very clear. Estate planning and will preparation are dangerous territory for the do-it-yourselfer. The law in these areas is very complicated.

If you make a mistake in preparing or signing your own will and power of attorney, they may not do what you want them to do, or, even worse, they may be totally invalid. And let's not even think about what will happen if you make a mistake in planning to reduce the taxes on your estate.

But naturally you're worried about the cost of professional help. Will you have anything left in your estate after you pay for it? Obviously cost will be related to the amount of work you want done. If you have a large estate and need to make complex arrangements to reduce taxes, sure it will be expensive. On the other hand, a will is a real bargain as far as legal services go. Most lawyers look on wills as "loss leaders." They hope the executor will ask them to do the legal work for the estate after you die, so they don't charge very much to do the will.

Lawyers are not the only professionals who can help you in planning your estate. Although a lawyer (or, in Quebec and British Columbia, a notary) with experience in will preparation should always be used to draft the actual legal documents and can usually give you much of the estate planning advice that you need, other professionals can also help in the financial, investment, and tax-saving part of the planning process. They include

- Accountants
- Financial planners

You may also be able to get advice from people or institutions you may deal with while building or planning your estate, such as

- Insurance agents or brokers
- Trust companies or banks
- Stockbrokers and mutual fund agents or brokers

Even with professional help, the more you know the better. That's where this book will come in handy. We'll take you through the process of estate planning, financial planning, and preparing a will and other documents so that you can get the most out of your professional advisers.

# You've Likely Heard Enough for the Moment

You're probably beginning to see that there's more to estate planning than just taking out a life insurance policy, naming a beneficiary for your RRSP, or preparing a will. Estate planning can serve different purposes, and those purposes can change from time to time. You have to plan carefully to make sure that you are meeting your goals, and that you don't meet one of your goals at the expense of others. In other words, you've got some work to do.

We expect you've contemplated your own demise sufficiently for one sitting. And in Chapter 2 we ask you to contemplate your personal finances. If we were you, we'd take a walk in the sunshine or scarf down some chocolate before proceeding to that exercise.

# Chapter 2

# What Are You Worth on the Hoof? Financial Planning Basics

### *In This Chapter*

- Understanding why you need a financial plan
- Taking stock of what you own and owe
- Taking stock of what you earn and spend

Financial planning is about setting goals, and keeping an eye on your progress toward those goals. When you head off on a financial journey, it helps to know where you're starting from so you know how far you have to go. And once you're on the trail, knowing where you started from lets you measure how far you've come.

Don't get the wrong idea about this chapter and the next one. They're not intended to be a complete discussion of financial planning. We can only just begin to touch on this subject: It would take a whole book (at least!) to cover the topic thoroughly. (A good start is *Personal Finance For Canadians For Dummies* by Eric Tyson and Tony Martin.) Besides, we are not financial planners. In fact, one of us is not even particularly well planned financially, which caused the other to laugh hysterically quite often while we were writing this chapter.

## Start with a Round-Up of What You've Got

In order to take stock of what you've got, you'll need to get an accurate idea of what you own and what you owe. Once you've got those numbers, you can calculate your present net worth.

We know that this seems like an awful lot of work. But there are good reasons for going through this process. Since your main object in creating a financial plan is to increase your net worth, you need to do a baseline calculation. (Then you need to re-calculate your net worth every year, to see how much it has grown.) In addition, your net worth calculation will be useful when you sit down to create your estate plan, because you'll know exactly what your estate consists of.

## Figuring out what you own

Make a list of everything you own and its value. You can be high-tech or low-tech — use your computer and a personal finance program or a plain piece of paper and a pencil. You may find Table 2-1 on page 24 helpful.

Start the list with the things that are easiest to value:

- **Bank accounts:** Check your bankbook or most recent bank statement to find out what your current balance is.
- **Guaranteed investment certificates:** Look at the certificate to see how much you originally invested and call your bank or trust company to find out how much interest has accumulated since that time.
- **Government savings bonds:** Look at the face amount and maturity date on the bond and call your bank or trust company to find out how much interest has accumulated since the bond was issued. (For Canada Savings Bonds you can check the CSB calculator on the Internet at www.csb.gc.ca.)
- **Stocks, corporate bonds, and mutual funds:** If you have a broker, you get an account statement monthly or (if you don't do a lot of buying and selling) at the end of any month in which there's been activity in your account. Ask for a statement if you haven't received one recently. If you don't have a broker you can find out the value of publicly traded shares and bonds by checking the stock quotation pages in the business section of your newspaper or a stock quotation Web site on the Internet.
- **RRSPs:** Call your bank, trust company or other plan administrator for the current balance if you don't get regular account statements.
- **Life insurance policies:** Call your insurance company or agent to see if you have the right to cash in any of your policies before you die (and if so, for how much right now).
- **Employment pension plans:** Ask your employer to give you a statement of the present value of your pension (it's not necessarily the same as the total of your contributions and your employer's contributions plus interest).

- **Money owed to you by others:** If you are in business as a sole proprietor or as a partner in a firm, include the amounts of any bills you have sent to your clients or customers and that haven't yet been paid (and then hope you'll get paid).

Then look at the things you own that you could sell if you needed to. Their value is the amount that a stranger who actually wants them would be willing to pay for them (this is called *fair market value*).

- **Your home, cottage, or other real estate:** Look at ads in the newspapers to see the asking price of properties similar to yours (the sale price may be higher or lower than that); or for a fee you can have a real estate agent or appraiser value your property.
- **Cars, boats, or other vehicles:** Check newspaper ads to see what a vehicle of your make, model, and year is selling for privately, or call a dealer. A dealer would likely offer you a lower price than a private buyer.
- **Artwork and antiques:** Visit art galleries or antique shows to find out how much similar items are selling for. You can consult a dealer about the value of your property, but a dealer will probably charge to give you a careful valuation.
- **Jewellery:** Browse around pawn shops or jewellery stores that sell estate jewellery to learn the resale value of your pieces, or ask a jeweller for an opinion (you might have to pay for anything more than a casual answer).
- **Furniture and household contents:** Go to second-hand shops to find out what your sofa, dining room table, and bedroom suite are worth on the open market.
- **Your business, if you own one:** Conservatively speaking, your business is worth at least as much as its parts (equipment, inventory, accounts payable, property owned or leased, etc.) could be sold for. Estimate the fair market value of those parts. Your business may be worth more than the value of what it owns, if it has a fabulous reputation or a great location or an incredible client base. You would need to pay a business valuator to put a price on your business if it could be sold as a whole rather than sold off piece by piece. If your business is essentially you personally providing a service (say dressmaking or accounting), it may not be worth much to anyone but you.

You'll quickly discover that you paid a lot more for your belongings than you can hope to sell them for.

**Table 2-1 What You Own**

| *Item* | *Value* |
|---|---|
| Bank accounts | $______ |
| | ______ |
| | ______ |
| Guaranteed investment certificates | $______ |
| | ______ |
| | ______ |
| Canada Savings Bonds | $______ |
| | ______ |
| | ______ |
| Shares | $______ |
| | ______ |
| | ______ |
| RRSPs | $______ |
| | ______ |
| | ______ |
| Life insurance policies that can be cashed in | $______ |
| | ______ |
| | ______ |
| Employer pensions | $______ |
| | ______ |
| Money owed to you | $______ |
| Your home | $______ |
| Other real estate | $______ |
| | ______ |
| Cars and other vehicles | $______ |
| | ______ |
| Boats | $______ |

| *Item* | *Value* |
|---|---|
| Artwork | $__________ |
| | __________ |
| | __________ |
| Antiques | $__________ |
| | __________ |
| | __________ |
| Other collections | $__________ |
| | __________ |
| Jewellery | $__________ |
| | __________ |
| Furniture | $__________ |
| Appliances | $__________ |
| Other household contents | $__________ |
| Your business | $__________ |
| **Total** | $__________ |

## Figuring out what you owe

This may be something you'd rather not think about. How much do you owe and whom do you owe it to? The only good news here is that you won't have a lot of trouble finding out how much you owe, because your creditors have an unpleasant habit of reminding you about it on a regular basis. There's a table on the next page to help make this job a bit easier.

Make a list of everyone you owe money to and the current balance that you owe in each case:

- **Mortgages:** Call your mortgage lender to find out your outstanding principal balance.
- **Car loans:** Call the lender (bank or financing company) to find out the outstanding balance.
- **Other personal loans:** Again call the lender to find out your outstanding balance.

- **Student loan:** You may receive regular statements; if not, call the bank.
- **Credit card balances:** Check your most recent monthly statements.
- **Outstanding income tax installments or arrears:** Check your reminders from Canada Revenue.
- **Real estate taxes:** Look at your municipal tax bill for the total amount of your annual taxes (it will also show any outstanding unpaid amount) and deduct any payments you've made, or phone your municipal tax department to check.

Table 2-2 may be useful in this very unappealing job.

**Table 2-2 What You Owe**

| *Item* | *Value* |
|---|---|
| Mortgages | $________ |
| | ________ |
| Car loans | $________ |
| | ________ |
| Other personal loans | $________ |
| | ________ |
| Student loans | $________ |
| Credit cards | $________ |
| | ________ |
| | ________ |
| Income tax installments or arrears | $________ |
| Real estate taxes | $________ |
| **Total** | $________ |

## Figuring out your net worth

Your net worth is what you would be worth financially after paying off all of your debts. (We'd like to assure you that your many good qualities make you worth a lot in ways other than financial. Just thought we'd tell you that now before you do the arithmetic and start screeching that you're a failure.) To calculate your net worth, subtract the total of your debts from the total value of what you own. (You can use Table 2-3.)

| Table 2-3 | | Your Net Worth |
|---|---|---|
| What you own (total from Table 2-1) | | $________ |
| | – | |
| What you owe (total from Table 2-2) | | $________ |
| | = | |
| Your net worth | | $________ |

# Take a Hard Look at Your Income and Expenses

Financial planning also involves confronting how much you earn and how much you spend. You have to invest if you want to increase your net worth. You can't invest unless you have money to do it with. To have money, you first have to make it and then not spend it all.

Start by calculating, on a monthly basis,

- What you earn, and
- What you spend

## Figuring out what you earn monthly

This is the easy part.

If you are an employee and are paid a salary, just look at your pay stub for the amount you are paid before deductions (this is called your *gross pay*). Note how frequently you are paid, and then convert the amount to a monthly figure:

- If you are paid every week, multiply your weekly salary by 4.33. (You don't just multiply by 4 because there are more than 4 weeks in a month. If each month had only 4 weeks, the year would have only 48 weeks, not 52.)
- If you are paid every two weeks, divide your biweekly salary in half, and then multiply by 4.33.
- If you are paid twice each month, multiply your salary by two.
- If you are paid monthly, the arithmetic has already been done for you. But if you're feeling left out of this exercise, you can multiply your salary by one.

Your income also includes any benefits that you receive from your employer on a regular basis, such as car, living, or travel allowances. These benefits will be shown on your pay stub. Remember to convert them to monthly amounts too.

If you are self-employed, or if you are an employee who can't accurately predict your regular income (for example, if you work on commission or depend on tips), you have to estimate your present income based on how much you have earned in the past. Look at your income tax returns for the last several years and see how your income has changed from year to year. If your income has gone up a certain percentage each year, then it's reasonable to assume that your income for this year will be that much more than your income was last year. When you arrive at your best estimate of what your income will be for this year, divide that figure by 12 to get your monthly income.

If you receive income from a pension of some kind, you are probably paid on the same schedule as an employee (monthly, every two weeks, etc.). Use the figures above to calculate your monthly income.

If your income includes investment income, royalty payments, or rental income that is paid other than monthly, check your income tax returns from past years to estimate your likely income for this year (estimate low rather than high), and then divide by 12.

## Figuring out what you spend monthly

This is the hard part.

To begin with, it's a lot of work to sort through all the bits and pieces of paper of your life to track down what you spend. But there's also a sense of impending doom that when you total everything up you'll be faced with damning evidence that you do spend more than you earn. And perhaps worst of all is the nagging feeling of guilt that you have nothing to show for what you've spent, because so much of it has been spent on things you didn't really need . . . and have already tired of or thrown out. Well, all we can say is that you have to face this beast if you're to have any hope of controlling it.

If you're simply living from paycheque to paycheque, you're never going to get ahead, and an unexpected illness or expense can put you into serious debt. And if you're regularly spending more than you earn, sooner or later you'll end up bankrupt.

But let's get started. If it turns out to be as bad as you fear, you can cheer yourself up by buying something expensive and totally unnecessary!

### Identifying your expenses

You have to track down what you spend money on, and how much. Your expenses include

- **Deductions from income:** Income tax, Canada Pension Plan (or Quebec Pension Plan) premiums, Employment Insurance premiums, pension plan or automatic RRSP payments, provincial health tax surcharge in some provinces, union dues, and anything else that's deducted from your paycheque.
- **Housing expenses:** Rent or mortgage payments, utilities, property taxes, and home insurance.
- **Other household expenses:** Groceries and household supplies, cleaning help, lawn care, and snow removal.
- **Transportation:** The cost of running your car (gas, maintenance, parking, insurance) or getting around by public transit.
- **Monthly loan payments:** Payments for loans other than a mortgage.
- **Clothing:** Clothing for yourself and your family.
- **Health expenses:** Uninsured medical services, prescription drugs, medical supplies, and dental costs.
- **Life and health insurance premiums.**
- **Personal grooming expenses:** Haircuts, facials, and massage (to help you forget that you're living beyond your means), dry cleaning.
- **Entertainment expenses:** Eating out, movies, sports equipment and fees, club fees, and vacations.
- **Children's expenses:** Daycare, toys, bribes and guilt offerings, lessons, and activity fees.
- **Support payments:** For children or spouse, if you're separated or divorced.
- **Pets' expenses:** Food, vet care, boarding or daycare fees.
- **Charitable donations.**

Don't just guess at your expenses. Go through all your monthly bills to see what your regular payments are, and then look through your cheque book and credit card bills for the last year to see what else you've been spending your money on. If you seem to go through lots of cash you can't account for, try using a debit or credit card as much as possible for two or three months — your statement will show where the money went — and also make a note of anything you pay for in cash.

### Adding up your expenses

Once you know what you spend, you have to convert the numbers into monthly figures. Take your weekly expenses (like groceries) and multiply them by 4.33 (the number of weeks in a month). Take yearly expenses (like insurance premiums or membership dues) and divide them by 12. Take occasional expenses (like clothing or car repairs) and add them up for the year and then divide by 12.

Table 2-4 should help you identify what your expenses are. Total up your monthly expenses and compare what you spend to what you earn on a monthly basis.

If you're spending more than you earn, you're going to have to cut back. So we've included room in the table for you to put in the reduced amounts if you decide you have to make cuts in your budget.

**Table 2-4 Your Monthly Expenses**

| *Expense* | *Monthly Amount* | *Reduced Monthly Amount* |
|---|---|---|
| Deductions from income | | |
| Income tax | $________ | $________ |
| Canada Pension Plan | ________ | ________ |
| Employment Insurance | ________ | ________ |
| Employer pension | ________ | ________ |
| Union or other dues | ________ | ________ |
| Group insurance | ________ | ________ |
| Savings plans | ________ | ________ |
| Other deductions | ________ | ________ |
| Housing | | |
| Mortgage or rent | ________ | ________ |
| Property taxes | ________ | ________ |
| Condominium fees | ________ | ________ |
| Home insurance | ________ | ________ |
| Maintenance and repairs | ________ | ________ |

| *Expense* | *Monthly Amount* | *Reduced Monthly Amount* |
|---|---|---|
| Gardening and snow removal | $________ | $________ |
| Water | ________ | ________ |
| Electricity | ________ | ________ |
| Gas or oil | ________ | ________ |
| Telephone | ________ | ________ |
| Cable TV | ________ | ________ |
| Internet connection | ________ | ________ |
| Household expenses | | |
| Groceries | ________ | ________ |
| Household supplies | ________ | ________ |
| Cleaning help | ________ | ________ |
| Loan payments | | |
| Bank loans | ________ | ________ |
| Credit card payments (on previous balances) | ________ | ________ |
| Other | ________ | ________ |
| Support payments | ________ | ________ |
| Transportation expenses | ________ | ________ |
| Lease payments | ________ | ________ |
| Car insurance | ________ | ________ |
| Car loans | ________ | ________ |
| Maintenance and repairs | ________ | ________ |
| Gasoline | ________ | ________ |
| Parking | ________ | ________ |
| Public transit | ________ | ________ |

*(continued)*

**Table 2-4 *(continued)***

| ***Expense*** | ***Monthly Amount*** | ***Reduced Monthly Amount*** |
|---|---|---|
| Clothing | | |
| Self | $____________ | $____________ |
| Spouse | ____________ | ____________ |
| Children | ____________ | ____________ |
| Health expenses | | |
| Uninsured medical services | ____________ | ____________ |
| Dentist/orthodontist | ____________ | ____________ |
| Drugs | ____________ | ____________ |
| Insurance | | |
| Life | ____________ | ____________ |
| Disability | ____________ | ____________ |
| Health | ____________ | ____________ |
| Other | ____________ | ____________ |
| Grooming | | |
| Haircuts | ____________ | ____________ |
| Dry cleaning | ____________ | ____________ |
| Other | ____________ | ____________ |
| Entertainment | | |
| Meals out | ____________ | ____________ |
| Movies, plays, concerts, sporting events | ____________ | ____________ |
| Vacation | ____________ | ____________ |
| Club fees | ____________ | ____________ |
| Sports equipment | ____________ | ____________ |
| Gifts | ____________ | ____________ |

| *Expense* | *Monthly Amount* | *Reduced Monthly Amount* |
|---|---|---|
| Newspapers, magazines, and books | $________ | $________ |
| Other | ________ | ________ |
| Children's expenses | | |
| School fees | ________ | ________ |
| Day care | ________ | ________ |
| Babysitting | ________ | ________ |
| Lessons and activities | ________ | ________ |
| Summer camp | ________ | ________ |
| Other | ________ | ________ |
| Pet expenses | ________ | ________ |
| Savings | ________ | ________ |
| Charitable Donations | ________ | ________ |
| **Total** | $________ | $________ |

# Take a Rest

There's nothing more exhausting than running after your money to see where it went! It moves a lot faster than you do, and it can slip between cracks that you can't even see. In the next chapter we'll give you some help to round it up and get it trotting in the right direction.

# Chapter 3

# Head 'Em Up & Move 'Em Out: Planning Your Financial Future

### *In This Chapter*

- Setting financial goals
- Increasing your income or reducing your expenses
- Paying off your credit cards
- Finding ways to set aside the money you've saved
- Developing an investment strategy
- Planning for emergencies

If you're going through all the effort of planning your estate, why not make it as big as possible? In this chapter we're going to talk to you about taking what you have now and making it grow — not only for your family and others you care about when you die, but also for yourself while you're still alive.

## *What Do You Want and When Do You Want It?*

Once you've been through Chapter 2 and know where you are financially (and you may have a low opinion of the neighbourhood), you can start thinking about where you would like to be — tomorrow, next month, next year, in 20 years. That means setting short-term, medium-term, and long-term goals. Unless you're really lucky, you won't be able to meet them all without adjusting some of them downwards.

## The long and the short of your goals

Your short-term goals are about surviving in the here and now — having enough money to pay for a place to live, food, clothing, and transportation. Short-term goals also involve things you want rather than need, like sports activities, a night out at the movies or a concert, and dinner in a restaurant every now and then.

Your medium-term goals are about the kinds of things you want in the not-too-distant future, like new furniture, a vacation, a new car, a house, a cottage, or start-up funds for a business.

Your long-term goals include things like an education fund for your children or grandchildren, a retirement fund for yourself, and a decent-sized estate to leave to your family when you die.

## Your goals in case of emergency

In addition, you should have emergency planning goals. They include life insurance to provide for your family if you die, disability insurance to look after yourself and your family if you are sick or injured, and enough money set aside to cover between three and six months' worth of basic expenses in case you lose your job. We go over emergency planning goals in more detail in a section called "Hope for the Best, Be Prepared for the Worst."

## The make and model of your goals

All of these goals involve a range of possibilities, from the cut-rate model to the super-luxury one. If your goal is dining out occasionally, your choice runs the gamut from a hamburger drive-in to the trendiest, most expensive spot in town. The home you have in mind to buy might be anything from a semi-detached in the suburbs to a monster house with a Jacuzzi in every closet. Your retirement goals might revolve around an apartment in the city or a house on the beach in Hawaii. Your emergency goals could focus on a first-aid kit and some cough syrup or the equivalent of a full year's income stashed away.

You need to have a fairly clear idea of what your goals are and what they will cost, and the date when you want to achieve them. Then you can start making realistic plans to reach them.

## You can't do everything

Mid-term, long-term, and emergency planning goals all have something in common — you have to save money to pay for them. And as we said before, unless you're really lucky, you don't have enough money to get all of the things you want now *and* to save. You're going to have to choose. Do you want to live for today? Or do you want to plan for tomorrow?

If you decide to pay attention to your future, you will have to come up with some money to save today. You want to save enough of your income (aim for 10 to 20 percent of your net or take-home pay) to accomplish your medium-term, long-term, and emergency planning goals.

# Income Minus Outgo Equals Savings

Unless you want to go more and more into debt, what you spend plus what you save must equal no more than what you earn. There's no way around this equation. If you want to have more to save, you either have to increase your income or cut your expenses.

## Increasing your income

We'd all love to increase our income . . . especially if it doesn't involve doing any extra work. But to return to Planet Earth — is there a realistic way to increase your income?

### Can you get a raise?

Do you think your present employer will give you a raise? The fact that you need more money will not be reason enough for your employer to increase your salary. You have to convince your employer that it's in the company's interest to pay you more, because you're valuable to the company or because another employer would like to hire you away. Before you ask for a raise put together some evidence (of your value to this employer or another) to support your request.

### Can you work more?

If you can't arrange to be paid more for the work you already do, you may be able to do more work, either by working overtime at your own job or by taking on a second job. This requires energy and stamina, not to mention an understanding spouse and children and a dog that's outgrown chewing the furniture.

Working overtime is the simplest way to earn more money — if the work is available and if your employer pays for overtime. You don't have to find a second job or waste time travelling from one job to another. You'll also get paid the same as or more than for your regular work.

If working overtime is not an option, you may consider moonlighting at a second job or at your own business. Your ability to do either will depend on the demands of your current job.

Your current job may make moonlighting a breeze, because your work schedule gives you several days off at a stretch. For example, a firefighter we know runs a small furniture upholstering business. He assures us that every firefighter has a business on the side. But if you work fixed business hours, let alone any extended hours, you may not have the time that a second job or a business requires.

If you are considering a second job, ask yourself whether you can commit to the work schedule that it will likely demand. If you are thinking of starting your own business, remember that even though you'll have some flexibility you still must be available when your clients or customers need you. And be warned that starting up your own business, even a part-time one, can take lots of time but carries no guarantee of financial success.

Before you go to work for someone else or for yourself, make sure that doing so won't get you fired from your day job. If you signed a contract when you were hired, read it to make sure that it doesn't say that you will not do any outside work. If you were given a booklet of company policies at the time you were hired, make sure that one of those policies does not prevent you from taking on outside work. If your contract or employee handbook says you must have your employer's permission before doing any outside work, be sure to get it. Even if you have no written contract or policy book, you cannot compete with your full-time employer or make use of or reveal your employer's trade secrets or information about your employer's customers or clients.

### Can you find a new job?

If working at two jobs doesn't appeal to you, maybe it's time for a new job that pays more. You can explore the job market by speaking to placement agencies, reviewing newspaper ads and job-related Internet Web sites, and talking to your network of contacts at other companies.

Check out any potential employer's pension and benefits plan, because if you have a pension and benefits with your present employer, the benefits you give up may offset the increase in salary.

### Can you send your family out to work?

Another way to increase your family's income is to put your family members to work. If your spouse isn't already working, maybe it's time to become a two-income family. (If you have young children, make sure that the cost of child care will not amount to more than the extra income your spouse can earn.) Older children could be encouraged to get an after-school job and to assume responsibility for some of their personal expenses. (Reality check: You could end up doing the kid's job . . . and delivering papers, although time-consuming, does not pay particularly well.)

### Can you rent out space in your home?

You might also consider taking in a boarder if you have an extra bedroom or a basement apartment. You may know, through friends and co-workers, of someone who would like to rent a room. If you live reasonably close to a college or university, you may be able to rent to a student. (Call the college or university housing office.) English language schools often attract foreign students who need somewhere to live for the length of their course. (Look in the Yellow Pages under "Schools — Language.") Some public school boards take in foreign visa students and help them arrange home-stays with families in the area. (Telephone your local school board to see if your family qualifies as a home-stay family.)

If you're thinking about renting out space, you should probably check with your municipality to see if it's allowed by the by-laws. (Or you can keep your mouth shut and hope that your neighbours don't turn you in.) If you rent, check with your landlord to see if the lease allows it. If you've got a basement apartment, you should check with the local fire department to make sure it's safe.

## Cutting your expenses

If you can't increase your income enough or at all, you'll have to examine your expenses to see where you can make cuts. Start by looking for savings that won't seriously affect your lifestyle. You'll feel better about cutting expenses if the cuts don't sting too much.

- Make sure you're not paying more income tax than you have to. Each year make the maximum contribution to your Registered Retirement Savings Plan and make sure that you have taken all available deductions and claimed all possible tax credits (consider having a professional review your tax return at least one year as a cross-check).
- Renegotiate your mortgage. If you can reduce your interest rate, you will reduce your monthly mortgage payments. If you renew your mortgage early, you may be able to "blend and extend" your mortgage by extending your mortgage at an interest rate somewhere between your existing rate and the current rate.

If your mortgage does not contain a prepayment privilege, you may have to pay a penalty to renegotiate your mortgage that more than offsets your savings.

- Make sure you are not paying more in property taxes than you have to. Find out what taxes other homeowners in your area are paying on houses similar to your own. For information, try the municipal assessment office, your local ratepayers' association, or a friendly discussion with your neighbours. If your taxes are out of whack, you can ask to have them reassessed downward. A word of caution though: If you ask for your property taxes to be reassessed, they can be increased rather than decreased.
- Don't overpay for your home and car insurance. Contact other insurance companies to see if they will offer you a lower premium for a similar policy. Speak to your own insurance company to make sure you are not paying for coverage you don't really need and that you are getting all available discounts. Consider increasing your deductible (the amount you have to pay towards repair or replacement when you make a claim on your insurance). While you'll have to pay for a greater share of the loss if you ever have to make a claim, your premium may go down considerably.
- Reduce your utility costs. To save on electricity bills, turn off lights when you leave the room, use lower-watt light bulbs, use your clothes dryer less. To save on your fuel bills, switch to natural gas from oil or electricity, put a timer on your thermostat so the heat turns down automatically when you're asleep or the house is empty during the day, and don't heat or air-condition rooms you don't use (shut them off). To reduce your water bill, get rid of your lawn and plant shrubs and perennials instead or install brick walkways and a patio, run only full loads in the washer and dishwasher, and put a water-filled jug or other plastic container in your toilet tank to reduce the amount of water you use when you flush. To reduce long distance telephone bills, look for a long distance carrier that can offer you a better rate on the calls you regularly make, and try to make more of your calls in off-peak hours.
- Pay less for groceries and household supplies — buy no-name products instead of name brands, buy in bulk, or join one of the wholesale superstores.
- Reduce your monthly credit card payments (but we don't mean you should just stop paying). If you are carrying an unpaid balance from previous months, shop around for a credit card that offers a lower monthly rate and transfer your outstanding balance to the new card, or take out a personal loan at a lower interest rate and use the loan to pay off your credit cards.

Neither a lower interest rate card nor a personal loan will do you any good at all if you're just going to run up the balance again.

- Don't pay for benefits you don't need. You and your spouse may have similar benefits packages at work; if you are required to make a contribution to the cost of those benefits and you don't gain an advantage from the extra coverage, speak to your employee benefits representative to see if you can opt out.
- Stop buying meals at work — bring your own breakfast and lunch instead. It's amazing how easy it is to spend $50 or much more a week on restaurant and take-out meals.
- Use your car less — gas and parking can cost a small fortune, so walk short distances, bike longer distances, and take public transit when it's not too inconvenient.
- Pay less for the clothes you want (even if you can't stand shopping at discount stores). Many stores have in-season sales offering savings of 25% or more. Since many stores start selling summer clothes at the beginning of February and winter clothes in August, the actual season has hardly begun when the sales start.
- Don't have clothes dry-cleaned simply for convenience if you can wash them yourself.
- Get haircuts and manicures for less — community colleges and private schools that train hairdressers and estheticians often have clinics where services are provided by students (under professional supervision) at very low prices. Getting a haircut from a student can be a bit nerve-wracking, however.
- Cut your entertainment expenses (and still have a good time) — most movie theatres have lower prices on certain days of the week, and some restaurants have lower prices on certain days or in the early evening. If you enjoy going to concerts or the theatre, you can often get rush tickets at a substantial discount on the day of the performance. If you hate waiting until the last minute, you may be able to save money by buying a subscription series.
- Get out of the habit of buying expensive gifts for everyone. If you have a big extended family or a huge network of children's friends to give birthday gifts to, make up your mind which small subgroup is going to get something nice . . . and resign yourself to looking cheap to everyone else.
- Save on vacations — book off time for a vacation and then choose your destination from sell-offs that are available in the week or two before you leave. For greater variety and savings, try to travel at off-peak times if you can.

In addition to these fairly painless ways to save money, you can get others from books on living simply or from simple-living newsletters and tip sites on the Internet. Try the suggestions for three months and then calculate your expenses again. You may be surprised by how much you've been able to save.

Or then again, you may find it's a case of no pain, no gain, and the cuts you've made still don't allow you to save (or worse, haven't pulled you out of the hole). Then you may have to give up things that are important to you, like new clothes, cleaning help, help with lawn care or snow removal, your favourite sport or activity, expensive entertainment like concerts and sports events, vacations, your car, or even your house or apartment if you really can't afford to live there. On the bright side, if your circumstances are that desperate, estate planning will seem like a pleasant diversion to you.

# You've Saved Some Money — Now What?

You've reduced your expenses and you now finally spend less than you earn. What should you do with this extra money?

## Pay off your credit cards

Your absolute first priority should be to get rid of your credit card debt if you have any because you're paying a very high rate of interest on the money you owe.

Calculate how much it will cost you each month to pay off your balance in one year. If you can't possibly afford those payments, see what it will cost you to do it in two years or even in three. Then make a promise to yourself to make those payments every month until the balance is down to zero.

Until you've paid off the balance, don't use your credit cards to buy anything else; use cash or a debit card. And once your credit card debts are paid in full, don't run an outstanding balance again! Never put more purchases on your credit cards than you can pay for in full when you get the bill.

## Set aside your savings

After dealing with your credit card balances, you can start squirrelling away the money you've saved. Here are some strategies to keep your savings out of your untrustworthy hands and get them working for you.

- Open a savings account. When you go to the bank to cash your paycheque or to deposit it into your chequing account, take 10 to 20 percent (or whatever you can afford) off the top and deposit it into a savings account. If your pay is automatically deposited into your chequing account, transfer the amount to your savings account as soon as you're paid. See if you can arrange for your bank to make the transfer for you automatically.

- Enroll in your employer's payroll deduction savings plan if there is one. Many employers offer programs for the purchase of Canada Savings Bonds or for RRSP contributions.
- Use an automatic contribution plan. Instead of or in addition to a payroll savings plan, you can arrange with your RRSP provider, mutual fund plan, or other investment fund to make a fixed contribution that is taken from your bank account once a month.

## Develop an investment strategy

Once you have money to invest, you need a strategy for investing it wisely. Look at books that deal specifically with financial planning or investing (such as *Investing For Canadians For Dummies,* by Eric Tyson and Tony Martin), or get professional advice. Here is a *very* simplified version of the things that the books and experts often say:

- Your investments should match your goals. For example, if you're saving for something in the short term or if you've set aside money for emergency purposes, invest the money in such a way that you can get at it quickly without paying a penalty.
- Your investments should act your age. If you're younger you can afford to take more risks than if you're older, because you have more time to recover from any costly mistakes.
- Take advantage of RRSP tax savings. Since one of your investment goals is to save for your retirement, use RRSPs as much as possible. Every dollar you put into your RRSP is deductible from your current income, and all income earned by your RRSP investments is tax-free until you withdraw the funds.
- It's usually better to own than to loan. You can invest money by either lending it to others to invest for their own profit or by owning things that you hope will go up in value. You're a lender when you put money in the bank or when you buy government or corporate bonds. The bank, corporation, or government gets the use of your money and in return agrees to pay back your money with interest. You're an owner when you buy things like real estate or shares in a corporation. The things you own may earn you income, such as rent or dividends, but they may also go up in value, so that you can sell them for a profit. Owning gives you two ways to make money — income and profit. On the downside, owning is riskier than lending, because the thing you buy can go down in value instead of up.
- You have to balance risk against return. The general rule is that the safer the investment the lower the return. You have to decide whether you are willing to run the risk of losing your investment altogether in order to

get a chance at a high rate of return. Your decision will depend on your temperament, your age, and your goal in investing. You should be less willing to take risks if you are older or need the money in the near future, because you won't have time to recoup your losses if the investment goes bad.

- Balance your investments. You should have a mixture of different types of investments: bonds, shares or real property, and cash. Some of your investments can be high risk as long as the majority of them are not.
- Don't follow financial advice blindly. Many people who call themselves financial advisers earn commissions when they sell financial products to you. Make sure their advice is in *your* interest, not just theirs.

# Hope for the Best, Be Prepared for the Worst

When we talked about setting goals in financial planning at the beginning of the chapter, we told you to think about the things you want. For your financial plan to be really useful, it also has to take into account things you *don't* want, such as job loss, serious illness, and death. If one of these unwanted things happens and you are not prepared, the results can be financially disastrous.

One recommendation we made in the section "What Do You Want and When Do You Want It?" was to set up an emergency fund to cover three to six months' worth of expenses in case you lose your job. This fund will also be available if you're faced with an unexpected major expenditure.

The other recommendation we made was to take out insurance. Life insurance and disability insurance are essential if you have a family to care for (and disability insurance is desirable even if you have just you to care for), and out-of-country medical insurance is essential if you leave Canada even for a day-trip to the States. Critical illness insurance and long-term-care insurance are things you might want to think about. And liability insurance is a must if you own or rent a place to live.

Insurance is a confusing field, and insurance companies don't seem to be in a big hurry to make everything crystal clear. That's why we're going to explain a bit about the insurance we've said you need.

## Life insurance

Life insurance will pay a pre-agreed amount of money (the face amount of the policy) to a person you name as beneficiary or to your estate when you die.

Don't think you're getting away with anything just because this section is so short. We tell you more than you ever wanted to know about life insurance in Chapters 6 and 7.

## Disability insurance

Disability insurance pays you a pre-agreed amount of money each month if you are unable to work because of illness or injury. It is designed to replace the income you will not earn if you cannot work.

### Do you need disability insurance?

If you are eligible for disability benefits from the federal or provincial government, you may think buying disability insurance is a waste of money. However there's a catch with most government plans. Provincial worker's compensation will cover you only if you are injured on the job. Employment Insurance will pay you benefits if you lose your job because you're disabled, but they usually end after several months . . . and your inability to work may continue much longer. You must be very seriously disabled to be entitled to Canada Pension Plan benefits, and the payments are quite low. So government benefits don't take the place of disability insurance.

If you're independently wealthy, or if you have a spouse who earns enough to pay all the bills and you're just working for personal fulfillment, then you probably don't need disability insurance. But the bottom line is, if you or your family need your paycheque to meet expenses, you need disability insurance.

### Where do you get disability insurance?

Most large employers and some smaller employers offer group disability insurance. If your employer does not offer group disability, you may be able to get it through a trade union, a professional organization, or an alumni association. If you can't get group disability insurance you can usually buy an individual disability insurance policy from an insurance company.

Group insurance policies are generally much less expensive than individual policies, and if you have group insurance through an employer, the employer may pay part of the premium.

Group policy applications do not usually require you to fill out a medical questionnaire or have a physical examination, unlike individual policy applications. If you have a pre-existing physical or mental condition, you may not be able to get individual coverage, or it may be very expensive or may not cover you for the pre-existing condition.

### How much disability insurance do you need?

You need a large enough payment each month to replace the income you will not receive if you can't work.

If you personally pay the premiums for your disability insurance, the benefits you receive will be tax-free, and so you will need disability insurance that pays your *net* salary amount (what you receive each month after taxes are deducted). If your employer pays the premiums, the benefits you receive will be taxable, and so you will need insurance that pays your *gross* salary amount (what you receive before taxes are deducted).

### When are you entitled to receive benefits?

You have to be disabled to receive monthly payments from your insurance company. At the simplest level, "disabled" means unable to work due to illness or injury. The definition of disability, however, is different from policy to policy. Some policies will pay benefits if you are unable to work in your own occupation, even though you are physically or mentally able to work at some other type of job. These policies are called *own occupation* or *regular occupation* policies. Other policies will pay benefits only if your disability prevents you from working at *any* occupation for which you are suited based on your education, training, and experience. Yet other policies will pay benefits based on your inability to work in your own occupation for a year or two, and then will continue to pay only if you are so disabled that you can't work in any suitable occupation.

With all policies there is a waiting period between the time you become disabled and the time the benefits become payable. The minimum waiting period in most policies is 30 days. If you have group disability insurance you have no say in what the waiting period is, but if you have private disability insurance you can choose a longer waiting period. The shorter the waiting period, the more the insurance will cost.

## Overhead expense insurance

If you have a business that cannot operate if you are disabled, you should also consider having an overhead expense policy to pay the fixed expenses of your business (such as rent and salaries) that will continue even though the business is not making any money.

## Out-of-country medical insurance

If you leave Canada for even a short period of time, you should have out-of-country medical insurance. If you need medical treatment while outside Canada your provincial health insurance plan will usually pay only a small part of the cost — the same amount it would pay a doctor or hospital in your province (and in Canadian dollars at that!). That payment would cover just a fraction of the cost of treatment in the United States. In addition to covering your actual medical expenses, out-of-country coverage often reimburses you for the lost portion of your trip and for the cost of bringing you home.

You may already have some out-of-country coverage if you have extended health care benefits through your employer. You may also have some coverage through one of your credit cards. (Read their coverage provisions carefully before you decide to rely on them. Many policies still leave you with thousands of dollars to pay.) Otherwise, you can buy coverage for one particular trip, for a number of trips over a maximum number of days, or for an extended stay outside the country. Policies are available from travel agents, banks, some credit card companies, and organizations like the Canadian Automobile Association. Or you can get year-round coverage from an insurance company, so you never have to think about buying insurance before you head for the border. The cost of out-of-country medical insurance rises with your age.

## Liability insurance

Liability insurance covers you if you are sued because you accidentally harm someone else. If someone makes a claim against you, your insurance company must defend any lawsuit against you and pay the amount of any settlement or judgment.

If you have a homeowner's or tenant's insurance policy, you have liability insurance that protects you if you accidentally injure someone (either at your home or elsewhere) who is not a member of your household. If you have an automobile insurance policy, or drive an insured vehicle with the owner's permission, you have liability insurance that protects you if you accidentally cause injury while driving.

If you have a business, and if it's possible for you or an employee accidentally to cause physical or financial harm to a customer or client, then your business should be covered by business liability insurance.

## Critical illness insurance

Critical illness insurance gives you a one-time payment if you suffer (and survive) a major illness such as heart attack, stroke, kidney failure, life-threatening cancer, paralysis, or major surgery such as a coronary bypass or major organ transplant. Not all policies cover all possible illnesses, so you may decide to insure against the diseases you dread most or that run in your family. The payment is tax-free and, unlike disability insurance, is not tied to your ability to work.

The cost of this kind of policy depends on your age and health, and the amount of the benefit to be paid.

## Long-term-care insurance

Provincial health insurance does not pay the full cost of care you receive outside a hospital or doctor's office. If you become disabled and need help to continue to live in your own home, home care is available — but in most provinces there are (low) limits on the amount of home care that you can receive for free. After that you and your family will have to pay, and it could easily cost you hundreds of dollars a month. If you go into an extended care facility, the cost of medical, nursing, and most personal care is covered by provincial health insurance — but you normally have to make a co-payment (depending on the province, from a few hundred to a few thousand dollars each month) toward the cost of room and board.

Long-term-care insurance pays a fixed amount per day for care if you suffer from a disabling condition or chronic illness and need to have in-home caregiver assistance or to live in a long-term-care facility. Once you require care, there is often a waiting period before insurance payments will begin.

When you take out a policy, you choose the period of coverage. Its length is reflected in the cost of the premium, as is your age (the older and the more likely you are to need long-term care soon, the higher the premium). A person with Alzheimer's might need several years' coverage, while a person who suffered a stroke or heart attack might only need a few months' coverage (. . . or none at all). As with critical illness insurance, you may want to review your family's medical history before choosing the coverage.

# Chapter 4

# Income Tax 101.1(a)(i): Some Tax Basics

### In This Chapter

- Defining income and capital gains
- Learning how income and capital gains are taxed
- Understanding some of the special rules that apply between spouses
- Discovering how your estate will be taxed
- Deciding what your tax goals for estate planning should be

There are no "death taxes" or "inheritance taxes" in Canada (Yay!), but that doesn't mean that there are no taxes payable following a death (Boo!). Taxes at death can be quite substantial, but with proper estate planning you can keep them to the minimum possible. Alas, before you can do any planning, you need to understand basic tax. That's what this chapter is about.

One more thing before we get started. You're probably used to talking about "Revenue Canada" when you mutter rude things about the tax authorities under your breath. Recently Revenue Canada changed its name to "Canada Customs and Revenue Agency." (Did they think we wouldn't recognize them under a new name when they came calling?) That name is a real mouthful, so people have taken to nicknaming it "Canada Revenue." That's what we're going to call it too. When you see Canada Revenue in this chapter instead of Revenue Canada, it's not because your eyes have gone crossed from reading about taxes.

## Taxes on an Estate

When you die, you may be gone . . . but you're not forgotten by the tax authorities. Under income tax law, your estate is born as a brand-new taxpayer that comes into existence on the date of your death.

Your estate (via your executor) has to file estate tax returns annually, starting from the year in which death occurred until the year in which the last property of the estate is given out to the beneficiaries. Filing has two purposes: to report income of the estate (so it can be taxed in the estate), and to give Canada Revenue information about distributions of income from the estate to beneficiaries (so the income can be taxed in the hands of the beneficiaries).

Estates are taxed in much the same ways as individuals. So you have to know something about how individuals are taxed before we can tell you how estates are taxed.

# Tax for Toddlers

There's probably no one in Canada who really understands income tax — and if you doubt it all you have to do is try reading the Income Tax Act. But if you do that, you'll need years of expensive psychotherapy and counselling to overcome the resulting traumatic stress disorder . . . and that would eat into the estate you're building . . . so let's forget that and move right along into the world of Tax Made (sort of) Easy.

In this section we're going to tell you briefly about

- Income and capital gains
- Calculation of taxable capital gains
- Calculation of taxable income
- Special rules for spouses

## Income and capital gains

In Canada, individuals pay federal and provincial income tax on their *income* and on their *capital gains*. Examples of income are:

- Salary or wages
- Commissions
- Tips
- Rental payments received
- Interest payments received
- Dividends on shares
- Profits from an unincorporated business

Capital gains are profits from the disposition (such as a sale or a gift) of *capital property,* which is property with a long-term value, such as

- Shares in a corporation
- Real estate (but not your *principal residence*, which is what your home usually is — see Chapter 5 for more on your principal residence)
- Valuable art, jewellery, collectibles, or antiques

Income and capital gains are taxed differently. Income tax is calculated on the full amount of an individual's income. Capital gains tax is calculated on one-half (changed recently from two-thirds) of a capital gain.

## Capital gains

We're going to start with capital gains because, as we tell you in Chapter 5, tax on capital gains, rather than tax on income, is usually the big thing people have to worry about when they're doing estate planning.

A taxpayer can make a capital gain by disposing of capital property for more than it cost, or have a capital loss by disposing of capital property for less than it cost. (We'll tell you later what you do with a capital loss.)

### Calculation of taxable capital gains

It's easiest to explain how to calculate a capital gain by starting with a sale of capital property. And in everyday life most capital gains arise from a sale. The amount of a capital gain on a sale is calculated by looking at two things:

- The cost of the capital property, which is the purchase price plus other costs of acquiring the property (such as legal fees, commissions, licensing fees, the cost of borrowing money to buy the property, and the cost of improving the property). The cost of capital property, once all of these things are taken into account, is called the *adjusted cost base*.
- The amount received on the sale of the capital property, which is the selling price minus the cost of selling the property. The cost of selling includes such things as repairs, advertising, legal fees, and commissions. This sale amount, once everything is taken into account, is called the *adjusted sale price*.

A capital gain (or capital loss) is the difference between the adjusted sale price and the adjusted cost base. If the adjusted sale price is higher than the adjusted cost base, you have a capital gain. If it's lower, you have a capital loss.

Only a portion of any capital gain is taxable. That portion is added to your income and is taxed as part of your income at standard income tax rates. The portion has changed from time to time. Before 1972, capital gains weren't taxable at all. Then for many years, one-half of a capital gain was taxable. Recently, three-quarters of a capital gain has been taxable. But in the year 2000, the portion has fallen twice — first to two-thirds and then again to one-half. (And we don't even want to guess what may happen by the time you're reading this book!) For capital gains made on or after October 18, 2000, one-half of any capital gain is your *taxable capital gain*, and is added to your income. If you made a capital gain before October 18, 2000, you should check with Canada Revenue to see what portion of the gain is taxable.

(The calculation of the capital gain or loss is a bit more complicated if you used the property for business purposes and claimed *capital cost allowance* — that's depreciation, or a gradual loss in value — against the property. In that case you'll need to talk to Canada Revenue or get advice from an accountant.)

Maybe this would be a good time to give an illustration of how a capital gain is calculated. Have a look at "Emma has a capital gain."

## Emma has a capital gain

Emma started hitting the garage sales after she heard that a man in Moncton had bought a grimy old painting for $5 that turned out to be a Rembrandt worth $2.5 million. At one sale she bought a box of costume jewellery for $50. Among the rings was a white stone in a really ugly setting. She took the ring to a jeweller, who told her that it was a one-carat diamond with a small chip in it. The jeweller thought the diamond would be worth about $2,000 without the chip. She paid the jeweller $250 to recut the stone to remove the chip. Three years later, Emma's neighbour, John, got engaged to Emma's sister, Isabella. (The match was set up by Emma.) John told Emma he was going to buy Isabella a nice ring. Emma mentioned that she had a good-sized diamond and asked John if he'd like to buy it. He agreed, on the condition that Emma have the stone properly appraised. So Emma went back to the jeweller and paid $75 to have the stone appraised. The appraisal certificate stated that the stone was worth $2,200. John paid the full $2,200.

Assuming that Emma reports a capital gain on her income tax form for the year, this is how she would figure it out:

**1. *Adjusted cost base calculation***

| | | |
|---|---|---|
| | Purchase price of the ring | $50 |
| + | Improvements to the ring | 250 |
| = | Adjusted cost base | $300 |

**2. *Adjusted sale price calculation***

| | | |
|---|---|---|
| | Sale price | $2,200 |
| – | Cost of appraisal | $75 |
| = | Adjusted sale price | $2,125 |

**3. *Capital gain calculation***

| | | |
|---|---|---|
| | Adjusted sale price | $2,125 |
| – | Adjusted cost base | $300 |
| = | Capital gain | $1,825 |

**4. *Taxable capital gain calculation***

| | | |
|---|---|---|
| | Capital gain | $1,825 |
| × | 50% | |
| = | Taxable capital gain | $912.50 |

So Emma, as a law-abiding taxpayer, would put $912.50 on her income tax form as a taxable capital gain and would pay tax on that amount as part of her income.

### If it walks like a capital gain and it quacks like a capital gain . . .

In Emma's case, we assumed that she got the capital gain by selling something she had bought. But you can also end up with a capital gain on capital property

- That you didn't buy — that was given to you as a gift, or that you inherited, or that you received as part of an employment package (such as shares or stock options).
- That you didn't sell — that you gave away to someone as a gift, or that you moved from an investment account into your RRSP.
- That you own at the time you die — Canadian tax law makes the peculiar assumption that immediately before you die you dispose of all of your capital property (this is called a *deemed disposition*).

When you become the owner of property in a way other than buying it, tax law says that you acquired the property for its *fair market value* (the going price in the open market) on the day the property came into your possession.

When you give away capital property, tax law says that you are disposing of the property at fair market value. Even though you're not actually getting a cent for your property, you're triggering a capital gain (or loss) that has to be reported in your income tax return for the year. And when that happens, you — or your estate, if you're dead — have to come up with cash to pay the tax on the capital gain.

If you trigger a capital gain on property that you didn't buy in the first place or sell in the second place, how the heck are you supposed to figure out what the capital gain is? Well, you have to find out what the fair market value of the property was when you got it and when you disposed of it. This is easy with publicly traded stocks, for example, because a broker can tell you what a stock was worth on any given day. But suppose that you inherited a cottage from your parents and then gave it to one of your children. With property like real estate, art, or jewellery, you'd have to get an expert's appraisal of the value at the time of acquisition and/or disposal.

And now for a strange tax fact: If you've owned property for many years (shares in a corporation, or a family cottage, for example), for capital gains purposes you're responsible for the increase in value of the property only since December 31, 1971. That's because capital gains were not taxable in Canada before that date. As a result, owners of capital property don't have to go back any further than that when they're figuring out the adjusted cost base of their property.

### Capital gains tax and spouses

A taxpayer ordinarily has to pay capital gains tax whether the property is sold or given away, or "deemed" (by Canada Revenue) to have been disposed of, if the capital property has gone up in value. However there is an exception when a taxpayer transfers property to his or her spouse. No capital gain is triggered.

Spouses, for tax purposes, are two people who live together in a *conjugal* (marriage-like) relationship and have done so continuously for at least 12 months. They don't have to be married to each other. The two people can be of the same sex.

When a taxpayer transfers property to a spouse, the spouse automatically steps into the shoes of the taxpayer and gets the original adjusted cost base of the capital property along with the property. It is as if the spouse acquired the property at the same time and for the same price as the taxpayer did. This is called a *spousal rollover*. (Isn't this a great name? Unfortunately that's as far as the income tax people went and there is no spousal heel or spousal stay or spousal sit-up-and-beg in tax law.)

There is an automatic rollover — of the property, you understand, not of the spouse — any time a taxpayer transfers property to a spouse during the marriage (or marriage-like relationship). When the spouse ultimately sells the property, he or she includes one-half of any capital gain, calculated using the *original* adjusted cost base, in his or her income. (Canada Revenue can *attribute* the capital gain back to the spouse who originally owned the property; in other words, make that spouse pay the capital gains tax.) A taxpayer who doesn't think this whole idea of rollovers sounds like a heck of a lot of fun can choose not to have one.

We know you enjoyed singing along with the last capital gains tax illustration, so we've composed another illustration that you'll like just as much. Turn to "David and Lisa roll over." It shows how a spousal rollover works.

## Capital losses

Hey! Did we catch you thinking how much fun it would be to take out the garbage just about now or clean the cabinet under the bathroom sink? You can't leave yet. We haven't tormented you nearly enough — we're just getting warmed up. Next we're going to tell you, as promised, about capital losses. To remind you, a taxpayer has a capital loss by disposing of capital property for less than it cost.

Question: You have to pay tax on one-half of a capital gain — but what do you do with a capital loss?

Answer: If you have a capital loss in the same year that you have a capital gain, you can deduct the capital loss from the capital gain before calculating your taxable capital gain. If your capital loss is more than your capital gain, you have taxable capital gains of zero in that year. However, you can use a capital loss to reduce only a capital gain in that year: you can't use a capital loss to reduce income in that year. What you *can* do is carry any extra capital

## David and Lisa roll over

David bought shares in a corporation and paid $100,000 for them. He also paid a commission of $2,000. Seven years later, he transferred the shares to his spouse, Lisa. At that time they were worth $135,000, but David didn't ask Lisa to pay him anything (he said she could show her gratitude by not giving him a kiss). Two years later, Lisa sold the shares for $142,000 and paid a commission of $2,500. There was an automatic spousal rollover because David did not choose *not* to have the rollover. So — who pays tax, how much, and when?

1. David pays no tax at all when he transfers the shares to Lisa. The automatic spousal rollover that happened when David transferred to Lisa meant that no capital gain was triggered for David.
2. When Lisa sells the shares, David is not the owner of the shares. He won't have any tax liability as long as Canada Revenue doesn't decide to attribute the capital gain back to him (which it could do under certain circumstances that would take too long to explain here) and make him pay the taxes. Instead, Lisa pays tax when she sells the shares because she's the owner of the shares.

But how much does she pay? How does she calculate the capital gain? First of all, Lisa's cost of acquiring the shares, that is, her adjusted cost base, is not zero, even though she paid nothing for the shares. And it's not $135,000, even though that was the value of the shares when she acquired them. Because of the spousal rollover, Lisa's adjusted cost base is exactly the same as David's. That's the cost of the shares plus the cost of acquiring the shares (the commission), or $102,000.

Once you figure that out, the rest is easy. All you have to do is calculate Lisa's adjusted sale price.

$142,000 – $2,500 = $139,500

Then subtract the adjusted cost base from the adjusted sale price to get the capital gain.

$139,500 – $102,000 = $37,500

Then you take one-half of the capital gain and plunk it onto the income tax return as the taxable capital gain.

$37,500 × 50% = $18,750

Is this plain in your brain?

loss back to any of the preceding three years to reduce taxable capital gains you had earlier. You have to file a new return to get back tax you paid in the preceding year or years. If you still have any unused capital losses, you can carry them forward indefinitely.

### When's a capital loss not a dead loss?

Now here's an amazing thing. Canadian tax law actually gives you a reason to die (other than the ordinary ones of sheer annoyance or apoplexy) if you have capital losses larger than your capital gains. In your very last income tax return, which is filed after you're dead, capital losses can be used to reduce income!

There are special rules that apply to capital losses in your last or *terminal* return. That's the return filed by your executor for the tax year in which you die. In the terminal return, capital losses must first be used to reduce capital gains, but if there are any losses left over they can be used

- First, to reduce your other income in the taxation year in which you die,
- Then to reduce your other income in the taxation year before the year you die.

This gives you a whole new perspective on your inexorably approaching death, doesn't it?

## Taxable income

We've concentrated on calculation of capital gains so far because it's the most important stuff to know about if you're estate planning. However, the rules about calculation of taxable income have a bearing on RRSPs (Registered Retirement Savings Plans) and RRIFs (Registered Retirement Investment Funds) if they're a part of your estate, so we're going to talk a bit about income now.

### Calculation of taxable income

In the annual tax return, a taxpayer is required to list his or her income from all sources, including employment income or income from an unincorporated business, pension income, amounts withdrawn from an RRSP or RRIF, benefits from various sources, investment income, and rental income. These different types of income are added together to arrive at the taxpayer's *total income*.

Taxpayers are allowed certain *deductions* from their total income to arrive at their *taxable income*, the income on which federal and provincial income tax is calculated. Allowable deductions include:

- RRSP contributions
- Annual union or professional dues
- Attendant care expenses that allowed the taxpayer to earn income
- Certain child care expenses

### Tax brackets

Individual taxpayers don't pay tax on their taxable income at one single rate. Instead, they can pay tax at up to four different rates. As income increases, the percentage rate at which it is taxed also increases in steps or by brackets.

It's hard to generalize about the combined rate of federal and provincial tax, because provincial tax rates vary from province to province, and both federal and provincial rates change from time to time. In fact, federal tax rates were recently reduced (the new rates take effect in the 2001 taxation year), and some provincial tax rates are changing too (and not always down). Roughly speaking, as of 2001,

- If your taxable income is up to approximately $30,000, you'll pay tax at a rate of about 24% (however, the basic personal exemption tax credit reduces the tax payable on approximately $7,000 of this amount to $0).
- If your taxable income is between approximately $30,000 and approximately $60,000, you'll pay tax at a rate of about 24% on taxable income up to $30,000 and at a rate of about 35% on taxable income between $30,000 and $60,000.
- If your taxable income is between approximately $60,000 and $100,000, you'll pay tax at a rate of about 24% on taxable income up to $30,000, at a rate of about 35% on taxable income between $30,000 and $60,000 and at a rate of about 40% on taxable income between $60,000 and $100,000.
- If your taxable income is over approximately $100,000, you'll pay tax at a rate of about 24% on taxable income up to $30,000, at a rate of about 35% on taxable income between $30,000 and $60,000, at a rate of about 40% on taxable income between $60,000 and $100,000 and at a rate of about 50% on taxable income over $100,000.

Keep in mind that these are very rough estimates. So don't trust us, check the combined federal/provincial rate in your province.

"Maurice's brackets" gives an example of how tax brackets work.

## Maurice's brackets

Maurice is a stockbroker and cricket player with a taxable income of $115,000. From Canada Revenue's point of view, his income is made up of several blocks of money — $30,000 + $30,000 + $40,000 + $15,000 (= $115,000 in total). On the first block of $30,000, he pays tax in his province at 24% ($5,520 when the basic personal exemption tax credit is figured in); on the second block of $30,000 he pays tax at 35% ($10,500); on the $40,000 block he pays tax at 40% ($16,000); and on the $15,000 block he pays tax at 50% ($7,500). So because of the tax bracket system, the amount of tax he pays on the last $15,000 of his taxable income is more than he pays on the first $30,000.

# Back to Taxes on an Estate

As we tell you at the beginning of this chapter, estates are taxed in much the same ways as individuals. Income and one-half of any capital gain are taxed at the personal income tax rates discussed in the section above on tax brackets. One big difference is that an estate cannot claim any personal tax credits, other than the charitable donation tax credit, and so always has a higher taxable income — and therefore pays more tax — than a living person with the same total income. However, income earned by the estate (say from investments or renting out property) that is paid out or due to be paid out to a beneficiary named in the will is not considered income of the estate but rather income of the beneficiary.

Here's an example. Your mother, Matilda, left you corporate shares in a shady used car business started by her father. Your mother's will directed that the shares are to be held in trust for you until you are 25 years old (you're 21 now), and the executor is to pay you the dividends earned by the shares. The dividends are income earned by the estate. But because the dividends are to be paid to you, your mother's estate is not taxed on the income; you are.

There is no capital gain or loss for an estate when property is transferred from the estate to a beneficiary under the will or under the provincial law (the law of *intestate succession)* that comes into play when a person dies without leaving a valid will. That's because the estate is deemed by Canada Revenue to have acquired the property of the person who died at its fair market value, on the day he or she died. (You may have been wondering who exactly was buying all your property when you were so busy immediately before your death selling it. Now you know.) At the same time, and somewhat confusingly, tax law also assumes that the person who died disposed of his or her property on death directly to the beneficiaries.

## What should your tax planning goals be?

Let's face it. If you had your way, you wouldn't pay any taxes at all, ever. Unfortunately, the government frowns on this approach to tax paying. They call it tax *evasion* and send you to jail if they catch you doing it. Tax *avoidance,* on the other hand, is perfectly legal. It's not a crime to plan your affairs in such a way that you pay the least amount of tax legally possible. However, just because tax avoidance is legal doesn't mean that the government likes it. So almost as fast as taxpayers and their advisers come up with ways to avoid paying taxes, the government changes the legislation to close the loopholes that let them do it. It's an exciting cat and mouse game that makes tax planning quite the industry in Canada.

Now that we've told you that you can't do what you really want to do, which is pay no taxes, what should your goals be if you're going to do strictly legal tax planning? The usual goals in tax planning for estate purposes are to

- Pay as little tax as you legally can.
- Delay paying tax for as long as you legally can.
- Make sure that the taxes are the responsibility of the person you choose.

Sometimes achieving one goal means you can't achieve another. For example, sometimes in order to pay less tax, you have to pay it sooner rather than later. Also, while these are the usual tax planning goals, they are not your only goals. You shouldn't plan your estate just to avoid taxes. You must never lose sight of your other estate planning goals, which are (in case they've slipped what's left of your mind after dipping into this chapter) to make sure that:

- Your property goes to the people you want to have it.
- Your debts and taxes can be paid without selling property you would like your family to keep.
- Your family has enough money to manage after you die.
- You have enough money and property to last until you die.

Everyone's goals will be a little different. The only thing everyone has in common is a need to know about tax law.

## What should your tax planning strategies be?

Chapter 5 is entirely about taxes and estate planning, but we're going to give you a little preview here of what you'll find there.

There is no one-size-fits-all approach to tax planning for estate purposes. Your situation is unique, so we can't tell you how to plan your estate to avoid all tax possible. What we can and will do is tell you what kinds of strategies there are and what may happen if you decide to use a particular strategy.

There are several strategies to avoid or delay paying taxes that knowledgeable people take into account:

- **Leave everything to your spouse.** Our income tax laws are drafted in such a way that there are very few taxes payable when you give money and property to your spouse. The big tax bill comes when you pass on your money and property to your children or grandchildren. As a result, leaving everything to your spouse is an effective way to delay paying tax.

- **Put your money into your principal residence.** Because a principal residence is usually exempt from capital gains tax, you can leave it to your children or grandchildren without having to pay tax. So putting your money into your principal residence is an effective way to avoid paying tax.
- **Leave money to charity.** Your estate will get an income tax deduction for any money you leave to charity in your will. So leaving money to charity is an effective way to reduce the amount of tax your estate will pay when you die.
- **Give things away now.** On your final tax return, capital gains tax has to be paid as if you had sold everything you owned just before you died. The more you give away when you are alive, the less you will own when you die, and the less tax your estate will have to pay. You may, however, end up having to pay tax now.
- **Freeze your estate.** An estate freeze may be an effective way to delay paying some tax. There are a variety of ways to change the ownership of property so that your children or grandchildren, and not you or your estate, will be responsible for the capital gains tax on future increases in value of the property.

We tell you lots more about each of these strategies in Chapter 5. See you there . . . last one in's a rotten egg!

# Chapter 5

# The Taxman Cometh: Taxes and Your Estate

### *In This Chapter*

- Discovering the tax strategies for estate planning
- Knowing what tax-avoidance strategies are available only after your death
- Pre-planning to pay your estate's tax bill
- Dealing with foreign taxes
- Minimizing probate fees

Unless you already know a lot about basic income tax, you have to read Chapter 4 before you read this chapter. So have you read Chapter 4? Are you still conscious? Good. If we don't have to stop to revive you we can roll merrily along. Now that you know more than you ever wanted to know about income tax, it's time to apply your general knowledge more specifically to estate planning. What can you do in planning your estate to keep the tax department from being your biggest and happiest beneficiary?

By the way, this chapter is a bit long and involved. Better pack a lunch and a pillow.

## The Story So Far

You escaped from Chapter 4 with your life and at least a little of your sanity. . . . In case you're afraid to venture back into that chapter, we'll quickly recap the tax planning strategies we said we'd investigate in this chapter. They are:

- Leaving everything to your spouse
- Putting your money into your principal residence

- Giving some of your property away now
- Freezing your estate
- Leaving money to charity

# Should You Leave Everything to Your Spouse?

In order to make use of this strategy, you first have to have a spouse. (We define "spouse" in Chapter 4.) But we don't encourage you to put tax avoidance above your own personal happiness — don't acquire a spouse just so you can minimize estate taxes. If you do, you might be found floating face-down in the bathtub some day, while your spouse is seen elsewhere drinking champagne and waving around your life insurance policy.

If you already have a spouse, you may want to leave everything to him or her anyway, no matter what the tax consequences are. On the other hand, you may be thinking about leaving some or all of your estate to your children, grandchildren, or others. So let's look into the pros and cons of leaving property to your spouse.

## Capital property

Your capital property is subject to capital gains tax. Capital property, as we explain in Chapter 4, is property with long-term value, and you are deemed by Canada Revenue to have sold all of your capital property for its fair market value just before you die (this is called a *deemed disposition*). If what you owned went up in value after you got it, your estate will have a capital gain, one-half of which is taxable.

This rule about your capital property does not apply to any property that you leave to your spouse in your will. The gift of the property in your will is not treated as a disposition of the property at its current value. Instead, there is an automatic spousal rollover, and the gift is treated as a disposition of the property at its original cost to you. (If you've already forgotten what spousal rollovers are, you can refresh your memory in Chapter 4.) When you dispose of your property for the same price at which you bought it, there is no capital gain. So because of the spousal rollover, your estate will not have to pay any capital gains tax on the transfer.

But when your spouse decides to sell the property, or when your spouse dies, he or she is taxed on the increase in the value of the property from the time *you* got the property, not from the time *he or she* got the property.

## Jules and Jim decide whether or not to roll over

Jim bought for $10,000 shares that would be worth $110,000 when he died. He could leave the shares to his spouse or his son.

**Case #1:** Jim leaves the shares in his will to his wife, Jules. When he dies, there is an automatic spousal rollover of the shares, and there's no capital gain and no tax payable by Jim's estate. If Jules sells the shares five years later for $170,000, her capital gain will be calculated on the sale price of $170,000 minus Jim's purchase price of $10,000, for a capital gain of $160,000, 50% of which (or $80,000) is taxable. Jules has to pay the tax, but she has the money to do so with what she received on the sale of the shares. If Jules doesn't sell the shares and still owns them when she dies, her estate will have to pay capital gains tax based on the value of the shares when she dies.

**Case #2:** Jim leaves the shares in his will to his son, Jim, Jr. (Actually Jim, Jr., was named not after his father but after his parents' good friend, Jim.) There is a deemed disposition by Jim just before his death of the shares for $110,000 and a capital gain of $100,000, 50% of which (or $50,000) is taxable. Jim's estate has to pay the tax on that capital gain, leaving less money in his estate for his son or other beneficiaries. If Jim, Jr., sells the shares five years later for $170,000, his capital gain will be calculated on the sale price of $170,000 less the value of the shares when he got them from his father's estate, which was $110,000. That will result in a capital gain of $60,000, 50% of which (or $30,000) is taxable. Jim, Jr., will have to pay the tax on that capital gain.

In both cases the government collects tax on capital gains of $107,200, but when Jim leaves the shares to his spouse, no tax is payable until Jules sells the shares, and then it is all paid by Jules, not by Jim's estate. When Jim leaves the shares to his son, a good chunk of the tax is payable immediately by Jim's estate.

We show you in Chapter 4 how a spousal rollover of capital property works when both spouses are alive. Above (in "Jules and Jim decide whether or not to roll over") is an illustration of how the rollover works following the death of spouse number one. We don't want you to get bored (you're already tired and aggravated), so in "Jules and Jim" we also show you what happens to the same piece of property if it's left to a child instead of the spouse.

It's clear that if you leave all of your property to your spouse, your estate will not have to pay any capital gains tax at all. But what if you don't want to leave everything to your spouse? What if you want to leave something to your children? Is there any way that the spousal rollover can help you?

In fact, there is. You can still take advantage of the spousal rollover by leaving property that is subject to capital gains tax to your spouse while leaving property that is not subject to capital gains tax to your children or others. The story (next page) of "Bob and Carol and . . . Alice" gives an example.

The spousal rollover applies when you leave your property directly to your spouse. It will also apply if you leave your property *in trust* for your spouse in your will if the will is drafted so that

## Bob and Carol and . . . Alice

Carol has shares worth $100,000 that she bought for $20,000, and she also has $100,000 in cash. She wants to divide her estate equally between her husband Bob and her daughter Alice.

**Case #1:** If Carol leaves the shares to her daughter and the cash to her husband, there will be a deemed disposition of the shares on her death for $100,000 and a capital gain of $80,000, 50% of which (or $40,000) is taxable. Carol's estate will have to use some of the $100,000 in cash to pay the tax on that capital gain, leaving less money for Bob. In effect, Alice will get the shares, while Bob will get the tax bill.

**Case #2:** If Carol leaves the shares to her husband and the cash to her daughter, there will be an automatic spousal rollover of the shares, and there will be no capital gain and no tax payable by the estate. Alice will get $100,000 in cash and Bob will get shares worth $100,000.

- Your spouse has the right to receive all of the income earned by the trust for the rest of his or her life, and
- No one but your spouse has the right to receive any of the income or the property of the trust as long as your spouse is alive.

We tell you more about trusts in Chapter 6. Bet you can hardly wait.

# RRSPs and RRIFs

A Registered Retirement Savings Plan (RRSP) contribution is fully deductible from the taxpayer's income. You don't pay any income tax on money that you earn that you put into an RRSP. So if you have income in a particular year of $40,000 and you make an RRSP contribution of $3,000 in that year, your income is reduced like magic to $37,000 for that year. Whenever you withdraw money from your RRSP, it's taxed as income in the year of withdrawal.

So if you have income in a particular year of $40,000 and you withdraw $3,000 from your RRSP that year, your income is increased to $43,000 for that year. When you reach age 69 (actually, you get to the end of the year), you have to withdraw everything from your RRSP, but you can roll it over into a Registered Retirement Investment Fund (RRIF) so that you don't have to pay tax on the income that has accumulated in the RRSP over the years. You then have to make annual withdrawals from your RRIF and pay tax on those withdrawals as income.

## Death of a taxpayer

A taxpayer who dies is deemed by Canada Revenue to have cashed in all RRSPs (and also RRIFs) before dying, and the full amount of the RRSPs or RRIFs must be added to income in the terminal return.

Now here's the first twist. For estate planning purposes, an RRSP or RRIF is not treated simply as cash in the estate if it's given as a gift in your will or it's directed to someone you've named as beneficiary of your RRSP or RRIF. When tax has to be paid on the RRSP or RRIF amounts that are added to income, the tax doesn't come straight out of the RRSP or RRIF. The tax comes first out of ordinary cash in your estate. So what can happen when you give someone your RRSP or RRIF is that the person gets the full amount of money in the RRSP or RRIF, but anyone who was supposed to get cash from your estate gets less because it's being used to pay the tax on the RRSP or RRIF.

Now for the second twist. If you make your spouse the beneficiary of your RRSP or RRIF and the proceeds are paid into your spouse's RRSP or RRIF, the money in the RRSP or RRIF is not added to your estate's income and no tax will be payable by your estate or by your spouse. (And your spouse will still have the right to make his or her usual RRSP or RRIF contribution.) If you name your estate as beneficiary of your RRSP or RRIF and your spouse is the beneficiary of your estate, the money in your RRSP or RRIF will be taxed in the hands of your spouse and no tax will be payable by your estate, as long as your spouse and your executor file a *refund of premium* form with Canada Revenue. Your spouse will have the right to avoid paying tax on the proceeds by depositing the RRSP or RRIF proceeds into his or her RRSP or RRIF. (Again, your spouse will still have the right to make his or her usual RRSP or RRIF contribution.)

Likewise, if you name a child or grandchild who is financially dependent on you as a beneficiary of your RRSP or RRIF, or you leave the RRSP or RRIF to him or her in your will, your estate will not have to pay any tax as long as the beneficiary and your executor file a refund of premiums form. The full amount of the RRSP or RRIF will be taxed as income in the hands of your child or grandchild. (The way in which the amount will be taxed depends on whether your child or grandchild is under the age of 18 and/or suffers a physical or mental disability.)

As we keep seeing, life . . . or death . . . is simple if you want to leave everything to your spouse. Your estate will not have to pay any tax. But supposing you don't want to leave everything to your spouse? You may have good and valid reasons. It's none of our business. Anyway, supposing you'd like to leave something to your children or even a friend? You can use your knowledge about how RRSPs and RRIFs are taxed to make sure that both your spouse and someone else of your choice will get the most out of your estate while Canada Revenue gets the least. See "Mike's RRSP" on the next page.

### What's the best way to pass on your RRSP or RRIF?

If you want your spouse to get the money from your RRSP or RRIF, it is usually better to make him or her the beneficiary of the plan rather than having the plan go through your will because

- Your spouse will be able to get the money more quickly if he or she is named as the beneficiary.

## Mike's RRSP

Mike has an RRSP worth $100,000 and $100,000 in cash. He would like to divide his estate equally between his wife, Pat, and his adult son, who could use the money to bolster his Internet business that sells golf and tennis balls.

If Mike leaves his RRSP to his son and the cash to Pat, in his terminal return he will be taxed as if he had extra income of $100,000 in the year of his death. Assuming that Mike's estate is taxed in the top bracket (we explain tax brackets in Chapter 4), this income will be taxed at 50%, and Mike's estate will have to pay $50,000 in tax out of the cash set aside for Pat. Mike's son will get the whole RRSP, and his wife will get only $50,000 in cash.

If, on the other hand, Mike leaves the RRSP to his wife and the cash to his son, neither his wife nor his estate will have to pay any tax on the RRSP. Pat will get the full $100,000 RRSP, and Mike's son will get $100,000 in cash.

- Your estate's probate fees will be lower (we discuss probate fees later in this chapter).
- The money will not be used to pay the debts of your estate.

If you want someone other than your spouse to get the money from your RRSP or RRIF, it's usually not a good idea to name that person as beneficiary of the plan. It's usually not even a good idea to leave the RRSP or RRIF directly to that person in your will. It's probably better to name your estate as beneficiary of your RRSP or RRIF and simply divide your estate among the people you choose. The story of "Bill and Ted's estate adventure" shows why.

## Bill and Ted's estate adventure

Let's say you have $100,000 in cash and $100,000 in an RRSP, and you would like to divide your estate equally between your sons, Bill and Ted.

If you name Bill as beneficiary of your RRSP and you leave Ted the cash in your will, here's what happens. Your estate will be taxed as if you had additional income of $100,000 (the amount in your RRSP) in the final year of your life. Assuming the RRSP income is taxed at 50%, your estate will have to pay $50,000 in tax out of the cash you had set aside for Ted. Bill will get the whole RRSP, and Ted will get only $50,000.

If, instead, you name your estate as beneficiary of your RRSP and your will says that your estate is to be divided equally between your sons, here's what happens. Your estate will be taxed the same way as before. But now your estate will be able to pay the $50,000 tax bill out of the $200,000 in cash it has, leaving $150,000 to be divided equally between Bill and Ted. Each of them will get $75,000. Excellent!

# Should You Put Your Money into Your Principal Residence?

Just to recap, so that this concept is etched permanently into your brain no matter how much you'd like to forget it, when you dispose of capital property at a profit you trigger a capital gain, and capital gains tax becomes payable. (You'll find an explanation of capital gains taxes in Chapter 4.) A home, cottage, or vacation property is a form of capital property. As with all other kinds of capital property, when you die you will be deemed to have sold the property the day before you die. If the property went up in value after you got it, there will be a capital gain.

Now with most capital property, one-half of that capital gain would be taxable. But if this home or cottage or vacation property is your *principal residence,* your estate won't have to pay any capital gains tax.

## What is a principal residence?

Here we go again, insisting that you listen to some incredibly boring definition before we'll let you in on a tax secret. A principal residence can be any residential property that you inhabit or your spouse or your child ordinarily inhabits during the year. It does not have to be your main residence. Your cottage or vacation home can qualify as a principal residence as long as you occupy or your spouse or at least one of your children occupies the property for some time during the year.

There is a catch here. The catch is that, since 1982, a family is allowed only one principal residence each year. If you own only a house or only a cottage, the one property you own will be your principal residence. But what if you own both a house and a cottage? In that case, when you sell or give away the property — or die, more to the point — you (or your executor) must choose one of them to be your principal residence and to qualify for the capital gains exemption.

## But can you make use of the principal residence exemption?

Because of the principal residence exemption, you can leave your principal residence to anyone you choose without worrying about your estate (or anyone else) having to pay capital gains tax on it. Whoopee!

If your only objective in planning your estate is to keep your taxes to a minimum, and if you've carefully followed and understood everything we've said to you so far about taxes and your estate, you're thinking right now that you'll leave your principal residence to your children and leave your spouse some other property that's subject to capital gains tax. Great plan . . . let's start the engines and see if it will fly.

### If you have only one residence

If you have only one property that qualifies for the principal residence exemption, and that property is your family home, you probably want to leave the property to your spouse, not to your kids. If you do that, there's already an automatic spousal rollover that keeps your estate from having to pay capital gains tax, so the principal residence exemption doesn't add anything extra here.

And if you and your spouse own your family home as joint tenants (as most couples do), you can't leave your home to your kids even if you want to. That's because when you die, your share of the home will automatically pass to your spouse, no matter what your will says. Your share of the home will not become part of your estate.

All in all, you won't be able to make much use of the principal residence exemption if you own only one residential property.

### If you have two residences

The principal residence exemption can be very useful, however, if you own more than one residential property. If you own a home and a cottage, for example, you can take advantage of the principal residence exemption to leave your home to your spouse and your cottage to your children. Your estate will not have to pay any capital gains tax on your home because of the spousal rollover. Your estate will not have to pay any capital gains tax on the cottage if your executor names your cottage as your principal residence.

## But be careful!

Simplicity is a relative concept as far as taxes are concerned . . . but things are fairly simple if you never use your principal residence exemption from capital gains tax until you die. However, things will work out very differently if you have used your principal residence exemption in the past. That's because you can only have one principal residence in any given year. Look at "Thelma and Louise go to the cottage" to see the effect of this rule.

### Thelma and Louise go to the cottage

Let's say you bought a home in 1985 for $200,000 and sold it in 1995 for $400,000. You used the principal residence exemption at the time and paid no capital gains tax on the sale of the house. You now have $400,000 in guaranteed investment certificates instead of a house. You also own a cottage, which you bought in 1985 for $50,000 and which is now worth $400,000 because some Hollywood actors moved into the area in 1996. You want to divide your estate equally between your daughters, Thelma and Louise. Louise has always loved the cottage so you leave it to her, and you leave the cash to Thelma.

You may think that, because of the principal residence exemption, no tax will be payable on the increase in value of the cottage, but you would be wrong. And why is that? Because you used your principal residence exemption when you sold your home, and you are only allowed to have one principal residence in any year. By using the principal residence exemption for the house sale, you in effect said that the house was your principal residence from 1985 to 1995. Your executor can't now say that your cottage was your principal residence for 1985 to the present, because you've already said that your home was your principal residence from 1985 to 1995. Your cottage can be your principal residence only from the date in 1995 when the house was sold. That means that there will be a taxable capital gain on the increase in value of your cottage from 1985 to 1995. If your cottage was worth $100,000 in 1995, the capital gain will be $300,000, 50% of which (or $150,000) will be taxable. If the capital gain is taxed at 50%, your estate will have to pay $75,000 in capital gains tax out of the cash you had set aside for Thelma. The result? Louise will get a cottage worth $400,000, and Thelma will get only $325,000 in cash instead of the $400,000 you thought you were leaving her. Better leave her your car as well.

# Should You Give Things Away Now?

There are many reasons why you may want to give things away to others before you die:

- You may take pleasure in watching them enjoy your gifts while you're still alive. Conversely, you may take sadistic pleasure in watching some of your friends and relations seethe because you gave gifts to others and nothing to them.
- You may own property that is too expensive or too much trouble for you to keep up any more.
- You may hope to keep your family from fighting over how to divide your estate after you die.
- You may hope to save taxes either for yourself now or your estate later.

If you're dead set on giving your property away while you're still alive, there are a couple of ways to do it. You can make an absolute gift of the property by giving away full or part ownership of it, or you can create a trust and transfer the property to the trust. We'll tell you more about gifts and trusts in Chapters 8 and 9.

At the moment, however, we're going to look at the tax reasons for giving your things away while you're still alive. The two major possible tax advantages to giving things away are

- To reduce the capital gains tax your estate will have to pay when you die. Your estate pays capital gains tax as if you sold everything you owned on the day before you die. So, the less you own at the time you die, the less tax your estate will have to pay.
- To reduce your income tax now. If you give away property that is earning income, the income earned by the property in the future will be paid to the new owner and should be taxed in the hands of the new owner.

Notice that we told you that these things are *possible* advantages. We want to look at each of them a little more closely, because neither of them is a sure thing.

## Will you actually reduce capital gains tax for your estate?

There is a capital gains tax advantage for the estate only if you give away capital property that has increased in value. There is no capital gains tax advantage to giving away cash or cash-like investments such as GICs or treasury bills, because they do not go up in value, and so your estate will not have to pay any capital gains tax on the deemed disposition of these items when you die.

While it's true that if you give away capital property that has increased in value your estate will not have to pay any capital gains tax later, *you* may have to pay capital gains tax now! (And if the gift is to your spouse and your spouse sells the property at a profit before you die, Canada Revenue has the power to attribute the capital gain back to you; in other words, tax you as if the capital gain is yours.)

It doesn't usually make sense to pay taxes now if you can put them off until later. However, you may be willing to pay some capital gains tax now if you believe that the property will increase in value a lot more before you die. It may also make sense to give away property now if you have a capital loss that you can use to offset the gain, so that no tax will be payable.

### Will you actually reduce your income taxes now?

Even though the new owner of the property will receive the income from the property, *you* may still have to pay the tax on it. Depending on whom you give the property to, Canada Revenue may attribute the income back to you and tax you as if the income continues to be yours. (Canada Revenue will tax the income in the hands of the person who will pay tax at the higher rate.) Here's what Canada Revenue can do:

- If you give income-producing property to your spouse or to a trust for your spouse, Canada Revenue has the power to tax you on any interest or dividend income or any capital gains from that property in the future.
- If you give income-producing property to a child or grandchild under the age of 18, Canada Revenue has the power to tax you on any interest or dividend income from the property in the future (but your child or grandchild will be responsible for any future capital gains). You cannot be taxed on the income earned by property that you transfer to your adult child or grandchild.

### Will you be sorry?

Are you quite sure you want to give away your property? If the tax consequences of giving away your property don't put you off generosity, there's still a little more to think about. Whatever your reasons for considering giving your money or property away while you're still alive, you should ponder the matter before you give up control over property that's important to you. And you must also keep enough money and property for yourself that you don't go from being financially independent to being dependent on others.

## Should You Freeze Your Estate?

You may have heard people use the term *estate freeze* and wondered what they were talking about. The term "estate freeze" can be used to describe any of several estate planning techniques that are used to reduce the capital gains tax that you would otherwise have to pay when you leave capital property to your children or grandchildren when you die. They are used for capital property that is expected to increase a lot in value in the future.

Estate freezes are all designed to transfer your property out of your hands so that you cap the amount of capital gains tax you'll ever pay. (You may have to pay capital gains tax on the current value of the property.) If the property goes up in value in the future, whoever gets the property from you — usually someone in the next generation or even the one after that — will have to pay capital gains tax on that future increase.

## Types of estate freezes

There are really complicated estate freezes and less complicated estate freezes. There are no simple estate freezes.

### A gift

A gift of your property to a child or grandchild is a relatively simple form of estate freeze. (In the previous section we told you about the advantages and disadvantages of giving your property away.) When you give your property to your child or grandchild you pay capital gains tax exactly as if you sold the property at its current fair market value. Your child or grandchild has to pay the tax on any capital gains that accumulate in the future.

Don't forget that *you* may get stuck paying annual taxes on income from the property as long as your child or grandchild is under 18!

"Harold's estate freeze" (next page) shows an estate freeze using a gift.

### A sale

Another way of creating an estate freeze is to sell your property to your child or grandchild at its current fair market value. You pay the capital gain based on the sale price of the property, and your child or grandchild will have to pay any future capital gains when the property is sold or otherwise disposed of. You can set up the transaction so that your child does not pay you right away but instead gives you a *promissory note,* which is a document in which your child promises to pay the sale price when you demand it. The advantage of using a promissory note is that that you don't have to pay tax on the entire sale price at once — Canada Revenue lets you spread out the capital gain over up to five years.

Look two pages over at "Frankie sells Johnny a painting."

If you don't in fact want any money from your child or grandchild, you don't ever have to demand payment during your lifetime. (You'll still have to pay the capital gains tax either in a lump or spread out over five years.) Your child or grandchild will have to pay your estate the amount of the promissory note when you die (and can buy life insurance on your life to get the money to do so) unless you forgive the promissory note in your will.

## Harold's estate freeze

Harold owned shares that cost him $10,000 and that went up in value to $50,000. He had a hunch that the shares would go up dramatically in the future and so he gave them to his daughter, Maude. Harold's hunch about the shares was right. When Harold died (too bad he didn't have a hunch about that chandelier as well), the shares were worth $100,000. Maude held onto the shares until this year, when she sold them for $150,000.

Here's how Harold and Maude were taxed:

- When Harold gave his shares to Maude, he was taxed as if he had sold them for their then current value of $50,000, for a capital gain of $40,000, 50% of which (or $20,000) was taxable. Because Harold had an income that year of $100,000, the capital gain was taxed at the highest rate, 50% in Harold's province. He had to pay tax of $10,000, but it was an amount Harold could easily afford.
- When Harold died, no capital gains tax on the shares was payable by his estate because the shares already belonged to Maude.
- When Maude sold the shares this year, she had a capital gain of $100,000 (the sale price less the value of the shares when Harold gave them to her), 50% of which (or $50,000) is taxable. Maude, like her father, was a high earner, so her capital gain was also taxed at the rate of 50%. She had to pay tax of $25,000, and had the money to do so out of the proceeds of sale of the shares.

If Harold had not had the foresight to put this relatively simple estate freeze in place, this is what would have happened:

- When Harold died, he would have been deemed by the tax department to have disposed of the shares at their then current value of $100,000, resulting in a capital gain of $90,000, 50% of which (or $45,000) would have been taxable. At the tax rate of 50%, Harold's estate would have had to pay $22,500 in tax. If there was not enough cash in Harold's estate to pay the tax, Harold's executor would have had to sell some of Harold's other property to come up with the money.
- Under tax law, Maude would have been deemed to receive the shares from her father's estate for $100,000. When Maude sold the shares, she would have had a capital gain of only $50,000 (the sale price less the value of the shares when Harold died), 50% of which (or $25,000) would have been taxable. At Maude's tax rate of 50%, she would have had to pay tax of $12,500.

In either case, the total amount of tax would be the same — $35,000. So an estate freeze didn't save the family tax dollars at all. But in the first case the timing of the taxes caused less inconvenience to the parties. Notice, however, that it caused less inconvenience only because Harold had the cash to pay the capital gains tax while he was alive, and because his estate was cash-strapped.

### *A trust*

In another form of estate freeze, you can set up a trust that you manage for your children or grandchildren and give property to the trust. (You can find out about trusts in Chapter 9.) This will allow you to keep some control over the property. You have to pay capital gains tax as if you sold the property at its fair market value when you handed it over to the trust. You won't have to

### Frankie sells Johnny a painting

Frankie owned a Group of Seven painting that she received under her mother's will in 1975. Its value then was $40,000. She sold it to her son, Johnny, for $100,000, its fair market value at the time, and received in exchange Johnny's promissory note.

In that year and in each of the following four years, Frankie asked Johnny to pay $20,000 of the full amount. Frankie's capital gain in total was $60,000, of which 50% ($30,000) was taxable. Instead of adding $30,000 to her taxable income in the first year, Frankie added $6,000 in each of five years. Since her ordinary income was $90,000, the added amount did not take her income into the top tax bracket (see Chapter 4), so Frankie did not have to pay tax at the top rate of 50% on any of the taxable capital gain. If she had been required to pay the entire tax in the year she sold the painting, she would have had to pay tax at 50% on a substantial part of the capital gain.

pay the tax on future capital gains; it will have to be paid by either the trust or the beneficiaries of the trust, depending on the circumstances.

- If the trust sells the property and continues to hold the proceeds of sale in trust, the trust will pay the tax.
- If the trust sells the property and pays the proceeds of sale to the beneficiary, the trustee decides whether the trust or the beneficiary will pay the tax.
- No tax is payable when the trust ends and the trustee transfers the property to the beneficiary, but the beneficiary takes over the property at the trust's adjusted cost base. (We explain adjusted cost bases in Chapter 4.) When the beneficiary disposes of the property, he or she is taxed on the capital gain from the time the property was transferred by you to the trust.

### A corporation

In all three of the above types of estate freeze, you will have to pay tax now as the cost of handing over responsibility for future capital gains tax to your children or grandchildren. There is one type of estate freeze in which you don't have to pay any capital gains tax until you die — an estate freeze involving a corporation. This kind of estate freeze is very complicated and is usually used to pass on a business or real estate investments.

You create a corporation and transfer ownership of property to the corporation in return for shares in the corporation. You give your children shares in the corporation as well. The corporation is organized using different classes of shares, so that you take shares that give you voting rights and control over the corporation and you give your children shares that go up in value as the property goes up in value. If the estate freeze is set up properly, there is a rollover (similar to a spousal rollover) when you transfer your property to the corporation, and the transfer doesn't trigger any capital gains tax at the time.

When you die, your estate pays capital gains tax on the value of your shares in the corporation — which will be the same as the value of the property when you transferred it to the corporation. If your children ever sell their shares, they will pay capital gains tax based on the increase in the value of the property from the time it was transferred into the corporation. (If the corporation, which is separate from the humans who control it, sells the property, it will pay capital gains tax based on the increase in value of the property from the time it was transferred to the corporation. The proceeds from the sale, less the cost of paying the tax, could then be paid out to the shareholder children in the form of dividends.)

### Don't try this at home, kids!

Estate freezes involving trusts or corporations are not do-it-yourself projects. If you are thinking about an estate freeze, you need professional tax and legal advice. And if you have to stop to think about whether you can afford to pay for fancy advice, trust us, you don't need to think about an estate freeze — you don't have enough money to make an estate freeze worthwhile!

## Should You Donate Something to Charity?

If you leave money or property to a registered charity, your estate will be able to claim a tax credit in your terminal tax return against the income tax it would otherwise have to pay. Your estate will be allowed to claim a tax credit of 17% of the first $200 in donations and 29% of donations from $200 up to the full amount of your taxable income reported in your final tax return. The amount of tax that your estate would otherwise pay is reduced by the amount of this tax credit.

If the charitable donations in your will are more than your net income in your final tax return, your executor has the right to refile your tax return for the year before you died and use the remainder of the donation to get a tax credit to reduce that year's taxes after the fact. (Your estate will get a refund.)

It is important to know how to make charitable donations in the right way in order to get the maximum tax benefits possible. We tell you more about giving money to charities in Chapter 13.

# Some Tax Planning Takes Place after You Die

There are some tax-saving strategies that can be put into effect only after you die. That probably means your involvement with these strategies will be minimal. . . .

## RRSPs

If you have not used up your RRSP contribution allowance for the year in which you die, your executor can contribute the unused portion to your spouse's RRSP after you die, and can use the contribution as a deduction in calculating taxable income on your final tax return.

## Capital losses and spousal rollovers

If you have any unused capital losses when you die, it may make sense for your executor to elect *not* to take a spousal rollover on some of the assets you leave to your spouse. (It's automatic unless the executor chooses not to have it.)

There are two things to remember here. First, a capital loss occurs when property goes down in value between the time you get it and the time you dispose of it, and capital losses can be deducted from capital gains before capital gains tax is calculated. Second, a spousal rollover does not eliminate capital gains taxes, it just postpones them until your spouse sells or gives away the property, or until your spouse dies. And then, your spouse (or your spouse's estate) will have to pay capital gains tax based on the increase in value from the time when *you* first got the property, not when your spouse got the property.

Now that we've re-stuffed your brain with the knowledge about tax law that leaked out since you began this chapter, let's get back to the point we were trying to make. If you have unused capital losses, your executor can apply them to reduce capital gains on the transfer of property to your spouse at market value. If your executor does not use these capital losses in your final tax return (or by refiling for previous years), they are lost. By using your capital loss to offset capital gains at the time of your death, the executor makes two things happen. One, your estate will have no capital gain now, and two, your spouse's capital gain in the future will be lower because it will be calculated using the value of the property when your spouse gets the property, not when you got the property.

Example, anyone? Well, since you asked, have a look at "Victoria's executor takes advantage."

Your executor needs to know about your unused capital losses before he or she can make the decision to opt out of the spousal rollover. Make sure that you tell your executor where to find your past income tax records and other documents that contain this information. We'll nag you about organizing all of your records for your executor in Chapter 22.

## Victoria's executor takes advantage

Victoria loved to invest in the stock market. She had some good years and some bad years. The year before Victoria died was a bad year. She bought shares for $50,000 at the beginning of the year, but they went down and down in value. In December, she sold the shares for $10,000. She ended the year with a capital loss of $40,000. Undaunted, Victoria used her remaining $10,000 to buy shares in another company early the next year. Several months later, the shares shot up to $50,000 virtually overnight. The shock of joy was too great, and Victoria left her entire estate to her husband Victor, including her extensive men's wear collection. One year later, when the shares had gone up to $100,000, Victor decided to sell the shares, feeling that tracking their meteoric rise reminded him too painfully of his wife.

Let's look at two scenarios, one in which the automatic rollover takes place, and one in which it doesn't:

- **Victoria's executor allowed the automatic spousal rollover to take place.** The new shares were transferred to Victor at Victoria's original cost base of $10,000, so her estate did not have a capital gain and did not have to pay capital gains tax. But when Victor sold the shares one year later, his capital gain was $90,000 — the difference between the sale price of $100,000 and Victoria's purchase price of $10,000 — 50% of which (or $45,000) was taxable. The capital gains took Victor into the top tax bracket and was taxed at 50%, so Victor had to pay $22,500 in tax. Victor was not able to take advantage of Victoria's capital loss from the year before she died to offset his capital gain.

- **Victoria's executor opted out of the spousal rollover.** The new shares were transferred to Victor from Victoria's estate at their then current market value of $50,000, resulting in a capital gain to the estate of $40,000. However, Victoria's executor was able to apply her capital loss of $40,000 from the year before to offset this capital gain completely. As a result her estate did not have to pay any tax on the transfer. When Victor sold the shares one year later, his capital gain was only $50,000 — the difference between the sale price of $100,000 and the value of the shares when he got them from Victoria's estate. The taxable capital gain was $25,000. It was taxed at a rate of 50% so Victor had to pay $12,500 in tax — but that was just over half of what he would have paid if there had been a spousal rollover.

# Putting It All Together

This is where we're going to summarize all the tax tips we've given you in this chapter. (If you'd known we were going to do this, you could have avoided the agony of slogging through the whole chapter.) So here are the tips:

- Leave to your spouse the property that will attract the most tax:
  - Capital property that has gone up a lot in value.
  - RRSPs and RRIFs (and, to reduce probate fees and to avoid the claims of creditors, name your spouse as beneficiary in the RRSP contract rather than in your will).
- Leave children and grandchildren assets that attract little or no tax:
  - Cash.
  - Property that has not gone up a lot in value.
  - A second residence — use the principal residence exemption to leave your vacation property to your children, without triggering a capital gain.
- Give away capital property while you're still alive if you think it will go up a great deal in value by the time you die *and* you will either not have a large capital gain now, or you have a capital loss to offset any capital gain.
- Donate money to charity in your will.
- Make sure that your will gives your executor the power to use your unused RRSP contributions to make a contribution to your spouse's RRSP.
- If you have any unused capital losses, keep information about them where your executor can find it, so that your executor can decide whether to opt out of the spousal rollover for some of your property.

# When the Taxman Finally Arriveth . . . With the Bill

We've told you a number of ways that you may be able to reduce the tax that your estate will have to pay on the property you own when you die. But unless you leave everything to your spouse, your estate will have to pay something. To be prepared for that unhappy time, you should:

- Estimate how much tax your estate will have to pay in your terminal return.
- Decide where the money will come from to pay it.
- Plan so that the wrong person doesn't get stuck with the bill.

## Estimating the tax

You can't know what property you will own when you die or what it will be worth. All you can do is estimate your taxes (over and above your usual tax bill) based on your present situation. To keep your estate plan current, you'll need to do this from time to time. Start by going to Table 2-1 in Chapter 2 and making a list of everything you own.

Make a list of everything that you are *not* leaving to your spouse. Don't worry about property that will not be subject to capital gains, such as cash, GICs, treasury bills, or your principal residence. Estimate your capital gain for each remaining piece of property by doing the calculation shown in Table 5-1.

**Table 5-1 Estimate Your Capital Gains**

| | | | |
|---|---|---|---|
| | Current fair market value of property | $________ | |
| – | Estimated costs to sell, if any | $________ | |
| = | Adjusted sale price | $________ | (A) |
| | Purchase price of property (or fair market value of property when you acquired it, if you didn't buy it) | $________ | |
| + | Costs of buying (if any) | $________ | |
| = | Adjusted cost base | $________ | (B) |
| | A – B = Capital gain | $________ | |
| × | 50% (or × 0.50) = Taxable capital gain | $________ | (C) |

When you have done this calculation for everything you own, add the taxable capital gains figures together for your total taxable capital gains and call it amount (D).

Now you know how much your taxable capital gains will be, but you're not finished yet. You haven't taken into account the tax you will have to pay on any RRSPs or RRIFs that you do not leave to your spouse. Remember that the full value of your RRSPs and RRIFs will be taxed as income received by your estate. So add together the balances in all of your RRSPs and RRIFs and add that total to your taxable capital gains total. That combined total is the amount on which your estate will be taxed as a result of the gifts you are making in your will.

Use Table 5-2 to do the rest of the calculation.

**Table 5-2 Add Deemed Income from Gifts of RRSPs and RRIFs**

| | | |
|---|---|---|
| Total taxable capital gains | $_________ | (D) |
| + RRSPs and RRIFs not left to spouse | $_________ | |
| = Amount in your estate that is subject to tax | $_________ | (E) |

Finally, estimate the tax rate that will be applied to the capital gains and RRSPs and RRIFs. Let's do this the lazy way. After you dispose of all your capital property the day before you die, and after all of your RRSPs or RRIFs are rolled in, there's a very good chance you'll have made it into the top tax bracket. So assume a tax rate of 50% . . . if that's not true in your case, you'll be too embarrassed to tell anyone anyway. Use Table 5-3 to calculate your taxes.

**Table 5-3 Calculate the Actual Amount of Tax Payable in Your Terminal Return**

| | | |
|---|---|---|
| Amount in your estate (over and above your final year's income) that is subject to tax | $_________ | (E) |
| × 50% = Tax payable | $_________ | |

## Where will the money come from?

Once you have an idea of how much tax your estate will have to pay, think about where the money will come from to pay it. Canada Revenue doesn't like to wait to be paid — although your executor may be able to work out a deal with them if there is difficulty in paying the tax owing right away. Here are the usual possibilities for paying the tax bill:

- Your estate may be rolling in cash and there will be enough of it to pay the tax.
- If your estate does not have enough cash to pay the tax, it may have valuable property that can be sold and turned into cash. If you would like your executor to sell (or not to sell) specific property, you should leave instructions in your will to that effect.
- If there is not enough cash in the estate or you don't want non-cash property in your estate sold, you'll have to buy enough (additional) life insurance to cover the expected tax bill.

- If your estate owes tax money and simply does not have enough cash or property to cover the bill, Canada Revenue can go after the executor personally if he or she transferred cash or property out of the estate to the beneficiaries before the taxes were paid. But if the executor didn't do that and there still isn't enough money to pay the taxes due in the terminal return, the tax authorities have to go whistle. They can't get it out of your executor or surviving family or friends.

### Make sure the wrong person doesn't get stuck with the bill

Throughout this chapter we have shown you examples of situations in which one beneficiary receives a piece of property while another beneficiary gets stuck paying the taxes. That's because of a rule of estates law that the taxes and other debts of your estate are to be paid using the *residue* of your estate (anything you have not left as a specific gift to a specific individual) first, then out of cash gifts to specific individuals, then out of non-cash gifts (they'd have to be sold for cash, of course). Keep that in mind when you plan your gifts under your will. You can plan around this in several ways:

- Make sure that you have enough cash, through insurance or otherwise, to pay all of your taxes so that gifts of cash to named individuals are not affected.
- Divide your estate among your beneficiaries in shares instead of leaving them specific property. That way they'll share equally in losses to tax or debt payments.
- State in your will that the person who gets a particular piece of property is responsible for any taxes on that property. Then you won't run into the problem of one person getting the property and another person footing the tax bill.

## A Word about Foreign Taxes

If you live or own property in another country, your estate may be subject to foreign income tax or inheritance taxes. You should get advice from a lawyer and/or accountant in that country. Ask your Canadian accountant or lawyer for a recommendation.

# Probate Fees

Probate fees are fees charged by the provincial *surrogate court* (the court that handles wills and estate matters) for its work in checking out a will to see that it's valid and formally appointing the executor. In theory they are administrative fees, but in fact they are more like a tax because, in most provinces, they are based on the value of the property in the estate rather than on the amount of work that the court does. Probate fees can amount to thousands of dollars.

Property that is not part of the estate (jointly owned property, life insurance proceeds, pension plans, and RRSPs payable directly to a beneficiary) does not have to be included in calculating the value of the estate for probate fee purposes. Any of the tax strategies mentioned in this chapter that reduce your taxes by reducing the overall value of your estate will also reduce your probate fees.

Not all wills have to be probated, because some kinds of property can be transferred to a beneficiary without a probated will. Your will will have to be probated if your estate has even one piece of property that can be transferred only with a probated will. (After you die, your executor should consult a lawyer about whether or not your will has to be probated.) Once your will is probated, the probate fees are calculated on the value of all of the property in your estate.

Theoretically, it's possible to have two wills (one for the property that needs probate and the other for the property that doesn't). Your executor could then probate only the one will, and pay probate fees based only on the property dealt with in that will. Don't even *think* about trying this without the help of a lawyer! If either will is drafted incorrectly, one will may cancel out the other.

# Part II

# Estate Planning Tools

"You'll find it interesting working with Mr. Barnum. He's quite creative in his use of estate planning tools."

## In this part . . .

This part lets you make the acquaintance of some tools that are commonly used in estate planning. We help you decide whether or not you need life insurance and (if you do) how much and what kind. We also explain the use of gifts given during your lifetime as part of your estate plan, and the use of trusts created during your lifetime or after your death. (A trust allows you to give your property away — like a gift — but keep some control over it — unlike a gift.)

## Chapter 6

# Wish You and Your Income Were Here — Do You Need Life Insurance?

### *In This Chapter*

- Getting acquainted with life insurance
- Deciding whether you need life insurance
- Figuring out what pension and death benefits your survivors might be eligible for
- Calculating how much life insurance you need
- Guessing whether your family will get a windfall if you die uninsured

In Chapter 3 we talk about how to build up an estate so that you'll be able to take care of your family (or friends, or a favourite charity) after you're gone. Building an estate isn't the only way to carry out that goal — you may be able to accomplish the same thing without going through all the hard work of earning and saving. You may be able simply to arrange to have a sum of money paid to your estate or an individual on your death. Does this sound like the answer to your prayers? Does it still sound like the answer to your prayers when we tell you we're talking about life insurance?

We're not going to badger you to buy insurance in this chapter. We're just going to help you decide whether you need it or not. Some people do, some people don't.

## *What Is Life Insurance?*

A life insurance policy is a legal agreement between the owner of the policy and an insurance company. The owner of the policy agrees to pay *premiums* to the insurance company in return for the insurance company's promise to pay a specified sum of money (the *face amount* of the policy) to a named person (the *beneficiary* of the policy) when the person whose life is insured (the *life insured*) dies. The face amount of the policy is not subject to income tax when it's paid out.

The owner of the policy is not necessarily the person whose life is insured. Someone else, for example the beneficiary, can own the policy and pay the premiums. But not just anyone can insure another person's life. The owner of a policy of insurance must have an *insurable interest* in the life of the insured person. An insurable interest means a close relationship, whether a family or business relationship, which creates a reason for the owner of the policy to want the life insured to stay alive. (Well, that's the theory, anyway. We're sure you have your own thoughts about people in close relationships you'd just as soon see dead.) Insurance companies get nervous about people who insure the lives of others who have no good reason to keep those others alive, and who stand to make a lot of money if they die.

A life insurance policy is legal contract, but it's also a bet. When you take out a life insurance policy, you're betting that the life insured is going to die while the policy is in force. Naturally, you're hoping that the insured is *not* going to die, or at least not any time soon. The insurance company, on the other hand, is betting that the life insured won't die — or at least not until so much has been paid in premiums that the insurance company won't lose money by paying the face amount of the policy.

# Do You Need Life Insurance?

Not everyone needs life insurance. To help you decide whether or not you do, we'll tell you the usual ways people use life insurance, and you can see if any of them apply to you. Life insurance is used

- To replace the income you won't be alive to earn for the people you support. Without your income, or insurance to replace it, your family may have to change their lifestyle drastically, if they can get by at all.
- To pay off a large debt, such as a mortgage on your home or a large personal or business loan, or pay for a major expense like a university education for your children. Without your income or insurance, your family may not be able to pay the debt or expense and so may have to eat into the capital of your estate.
- To pay off expenses related to your death, such as funeral costs, lawyer's fees, taxes, and probate fees. These debts and expenses don't exist until you die and, without insurance, are normally paid out of your estate.
- To leave money you wouldn't otherwise have to a family member, friend, or charity. You may want to create more money when you die, so that you have more to give away.

You don't need life insurance if you

- Don't have anyone who depends on you for support.
- Have no large debts or expenses.
- Have plenty of cash or property in your estate to pay funeral expenses, lawyers' fees, and taxes.
- Don't need or want extra money to leave to family, friends, or charities.

And even if you do support other people or have debts or major expenses, you still may not need insurance if there will be enough money in your estate without insurance.

# How Much Life Insurance Do You Need?

The amount of insurance you need depends on the reason or reasons you need the insurance and how much other money will be available to meet those needs when you die.

Once you know how much insurance you need, you have to calculate how much you can afford, and you can then decide how much you actually want to buy.

## If you need insurance to replace your income

You want your family to be able to live as well after you die as they do now. How much insurance do you need for them to be able to do that? In order to answer that question, you have to work out a few things first:

- What your family's expenses will be.
- What other income your family will have.
- Whether there will be a shortfall between your family's income and expenses.
- What lump sum of money will be required to make up any shortfall.

### What will your family's expenses be?

The monthly expense calculation in Chapter 2 will give you a pretty good idea of your family's expenses, at least if you die in the very near future. You have to make adjustments, though, to take into account the fact that you won't be around. When you're gone, your personal expenses will go too, but there may be new expenses to take their place because your family may have to pay someone to do some of the things that you do for free, like child care or household maintenance and repairs.

You also have to look into the future, and make adjustments for how your family's expenses may change over time. Are your family's expenses likely to go up or down? If your children are young, the expenses will grow with them. If your children are older and ready to leave home, your spouse will no longer have to support them and may even be able to move to a smaller, less expensive home.

### What other income will your family have?

How much income will your family have when you die and your salary goes west with you? Your panicky answer of "Nothing! They'll be destitute and living on the streets!" probably is not correct. Sit down, put a cold compress on your forehead, and think rationally about whether your family will have any of these things:

- **Your spouse's income.** If your spouse works or has investment income, that income will probably continue to be available to pay the family's expenses.
- **Pension plan payments.** If you have a pension plan through work or any union, professional, or fraternal organization, or if you are a veteran who is eligible for Department of Veterans' Affairs benefits, your spouse and/or dependent children (those under the age of 18, or between 18 and 25 and in full-time attendance at school) may be entitled to receive a monthly pension and/or a lump sum payment. Speak to the administrator of your pension plan or contact the DVA to see how much your family members will be entitled to receive and for how long.
- **Canada Pension Plan death benefits.** Your estate may be entitled to receive a lump-sum death benefit, your spouse may be entitled to receive a monthly survivor's benefit, and your dependent children may be entitled to receive a monthly orphan's benefit. Contact Health Canada to find out how much your spouse and/or children will likely receive.
- **Old Age Security benefits.** If you are or your spouse is receiving Old Age Security payments, your spouse may be eligible for increased benefits after you die. Even if neither of you is receiving anything at the time of your death, benefits may be available for your spouse if he or she is between 60 and 65. You can get information about these benefits from Health Canada, Income Security Program.
- **Other death benefits.** If you belong to any organization, social club, or lodge, it may provide death benefits to your estate or surviving family. Contact the organization to find out.

- **Income earned by your estate.** If there is cash, or investments or rent-producing property, in your estate, there will be income in your estate. How much income, of course, depends on the size of your estate and interest rates, going rental rates, and so on.

For pensions or death benefits, a "spouse" might or might not have to be legally married to you or be of the opposite sex, depending on the wording of the legislation, pension plan, or other agreement.

### What will the shortfall be?

Add up all of your family's likely expenses. Then add up all of your family's likely income. Subtract the expenses from the income. If your family's expenses are more than your family's projected income without your salary, you need enough insurance to make up the shortfall.

### What lump sum of money will be needed to make up the shortfall?

To cover a shortfall, you need a sum of money that will produce enough income to make up for the shortfall as long as it lasts. That's easy for us to say, you're thinking, but how on earth do you calculate something like that without a crystal ball? We admit that it's difficult to do — you do need to be able to see into the future, or at least to be able to make a good guess about:

- How long your family will need the extra money. You have to estimate how long your children will be dependent and how long your spouse is likely to live (if he or she is not self-supporting) and will need an income.
- What future interest rates are likely to be — because that determines how much income will be earned from the lump sum.
- What the rate of inflation is likely to be — because that affects how your family's expenses will increase.
- What your spouse's (and other supporting family members') income tax rate is likely to be — because that determines how much will be available after taxes to pay expenses.

There are professionals, called *actuaries,* who develop tables to help life insurance companies, accountants, and other financial advisers do these calculations. Working with assumptions about the things we've talked about above (interest rates, inflation, life expectancy of a spouse), an actuary can name the sum of money that your family will need. It's an amount that will produce a little less income than is needed to cover expenses each year, so that every year it will be necessary to spend a bit of the lump sum. If all of the actuary's assumptions turn out to be right, at the end of the time for which the income was needed, all the income *and* the lump sum will be gone.

You're not an actuary (well, most people who are reading this aren't actuaries). How do *you* figure out how much insurance you need? There are several possibilities:

- Ask an insurance agent, broker, or insurance company representative. You should be aware, however, that most insurance professionals are paid a commission based on the amount of insurance they sell, so there may be a motive to overstate the amount of insurance you need. Make sure you get an explanation of how the amount was arrived at.
- Visit insurance company Web sites. Some of them include interactive pages that will calculate how much insurance you need based on the amount of income you want to replace. Unfortunately, these Web sites don't tell you the assumptions (such as interest rate or inflation) they are relying on in doing their calculations.
- Look at *Personal Finance For Canadians For Dummies*, by Eric Tyson and Tony Martin. You'll find a table in Chapter 18 of that book that helps you estimate the amount of insurance you need.
- Ask your accountant, if you have one. You may have to pay for your accountant's time, but the answer you get should be accurate, reliable, and unbiased.

We can also suggest a much simpler approach. Just look at the amount you've calculated to be your family's expected shortfall and figure out what lump sum, if invested at today's interest rates, would produce the right amount of income to cover the shortfall. It's not as precise as the answer an actuary would come up with, and in fact it may lead you to buy more life insurance than a strict actuarial calculation would. That's because you're not aiming for an amount that will be used up over time. Instead, when the income is no longer needed the lump sum will still be there. You can use this calculation to check the recommendation an insurance agent makes about how much insurance you need.

### Another option

You may be able to find an insurance company that offers a policy that pays a specified amount of money to the beneficiary each month instead of one lump sum. You may even be able to get a policy in which the payment is indexed to the cost of living so that it goes up with inflation. This type of insurance is called a *reversionary annuity* or *contingent annuity* policy. With a policy like this, you don't have to go through the contortions of figuring out what lump sum will produce the income needed — you just have to guess what income will be needed and for how long.

### If you need insurance to pay a debt or expense

If you need insurance to pay off a large debt such as a mortgage on your home or to pay for a major expense like a university education for your children, you need insurance in the same amount as the debt or expense. So this calculation is a pretty simple one.

### If you need insurance to leave money

This is another simple calculation. How much money do you want to leave to your family, friends, or charity? That's the amount of insurance you need to buy.

## Who Should Get the Insurance Money When You Die?

When you die, the insurance company will pay the proceeds of the policy to the person named as beneficiary in the policy. That means you have to choose a beneficiary as well as deciding how much coverage you need. Your choice of beneficiary will be related to the reason you're buying the policy, but the choice may not be obvious. For example, just because you take out an insurance policy so that you can leave some money to a charity doesn't necessarily mean that you should name the charity as the beneficiary. You have to choose the beneficiary carefully so that you can meet your overall estate planning objectives. You need to discuss this matter with the professional (lawyer, accountant, financial planner) who's helping you to plan your estate.

There are three ways of naming a beneficiary. You can

- Name an individual (or two or more individuals) as your beneficiary.
- Name your estate as your beneficiary.
- Create an *insurance trust* and direct the insurance company to pay the proceeds to a trustee who will hold them on behalf of a beneficiary.

## What if you name an individual as your beneficiary?

If you name an individual as your beneficiary, the proceeds of your policy will be paid directly to that person when you die. None of the money can be used to pay off the debts of your estate, because it's not part of your estate. No probate fees are payable on the money either, again because it's not part of your estate (see Chapter 5 for more on probate fees). On your death, your beneficiary can apply directly to the insurance company for payment of the proceeds and does not have to wait for your executor to make a payment out of the estate.

It's possible to name a beneficiary *irrevocably.* If you do so, you won't be able to change the beneficiary or deal with the policy in any way without the consent of the beneficiary.

There are a few disadvantages to naming an individual as your beneficiary:

- If you decide to change your beneficiary, you have to notify your insurance company in writing. The insurance company will pay out the proceeds only to the beneficiary named officially in its records.
- If you decide to change your will, you may have to think about changing your beneficiaries under your insurance policy too, to make sure that your choice of beneficiary still meets your estate planning objectives.
- If your beneficiary is a child, the insurance company can't just pay the money to the child. It will have to be paid into court and a government official will look after the money until the child comes of age.

If you want to name an individual as your beneficiary, you should name an alternate beneficiary in the policy as well. If you don't and your beneficiary dies before you do, the insurance proceeds will be paid to your estate.

## What if you name your estate as your beneficiary?

If you name your estate as your beneficiary, when you die the insurance company will pay the proceeds of your policy to your executor and the insurance proceeds will be part of your estate. The money will be divided among your family and/or friends in the way you have instructed in your will. If you don't have a will, the money will be divided among your family according to the law of your province (see Chapter 15).

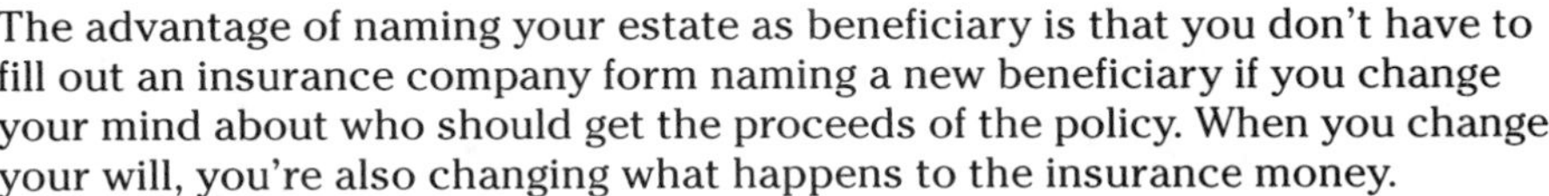

The advantage of naming your estate as beneficiary is that you don't have to fill out an insurance company form naming a new beneficiary if you change your mind about who should get the proceeds of the policy. When you change your will, you're also changing what happens to the insurance money.

There are two disadvantages to naming your estate as beneficiary:

- The insurance proceeds can be used to pay your debts. Your executor must pay your debts before dividing your estate among your heirs. So if you name your estate as your beneficiary, some of the money may go to your creditors and not your family.
- The insurance proceeds are subject to probate fees. Probate fees are court fees that in most provinces are calculated on the value of an estate. If the insurance proceeds are paid to your estate, they will be included when the probate fees on your estate are calculated, and so the fees will be higher. Probate fees are paid out of the estate.

## What if you create an insurance trust?

You can create a trust to hold insurance proceeds on behalf of your beneficiaries, and tell your insurance company to pay the proceeds to the person you name as trustee. When you create the trust, you have to give instructions to the trustee about what you want him or her to do with the proceeds.

For example, you might create an insurance trust if you have young children and you don't want the government to manage the money for them if you die before they reach the age of majority. You might direct your trustee to keep the money invested for your children and to use the income the money earns to pay your children's expenses until they come of age.

You can also use an insurance trust to divide up your life insurance proceeds the same way you are dividing up your estate in your will. You can even have your executor act as trustee. If you are careful in the way the trust is worded, the insurance proceeds will not be considered to be part of your estate, and will therefore not be subject to probate fees or claims by your creditors.

You can create a trust in your will or by using a separate document called a *trust agreement.* The will or trust document has to be prepared by a lawyer. We tell you a lot more about trusts in Chapter 9.

# Any Other Chance Your Family Will Get Some Money When You Die?

If you decide not to gamble with the insurance companies and you don't take out a life insurance policy, is there the slightest hope that your family will receive some kind of payment on your death? The answer could be yes, and we're not talking about miracles. Depending on various circumstances (including the exact way in which you meet your end), there might be a little money for your family, and there might even be a lot of money — in fact, as much money as if you had bought an insurance policy.

## Pension plan and death benefits

We'll do the boring money first. As we discussed earlier in the section "How Much Life Insurance Do You Need," on your death your family may be eligible for benefits from the government, an employer, or an organization of which you were a member. To recap, your family may be eligible for one or more of:

- Pension plan payments from an employer, union, or professional or fraternal organization, or from the Department of Veterans' Affairs
- Canada Pension Plan death benefits
- Old Age Security benefits
- Death benefits from an organization, social club, or lodge

## Windfalls

Now we'll do the exciting, unexpected money.

There are lots of different ways to die. If you're, um, lucky, you might die as the result of someone's careless act (called *negligence* in law). Most businesses, governments, and even individuals are insured against injuring or killing someone through their own negligence in certain circumstances. Your surviving family will have the right to sue any organization or person whose carelessness caused your death.

Among the businesses that get sued for negligently causing death are transportation companies (airlines, railroads, bus companies, cruise lines) and any business that puts a vehicle on the road, manufacturers (of pharmaceuticals, industrial chemicals, industrial equipment, household appliances, or anything that turns out to be dangerous), and hospitals. These are just a few examples. You should know that your family probably won't be able to sue your own employer but will be able to make a claim to the provincial workers' compensation board.

Governments (federal, provincial, or municipal) can be sued for various negligent acts of their employees, which might include, for example, running over bystanders in high-speed police chases, fatally injuring people during arrests, and failing to make sure that the drinking water is safe with the result that illness or death occurs.

Individuals are most often sued for negligent driving that causes death, but can be sued for any kind of negligent behaviour such as drunken boating or medical malpractice (doctors only).

Far less likely, you might die as the result not of someone's careless act but of their intentional act — you might be shot in a robbery, for instance. If someone deliberately kills you, your family can sue that person for *wrongful death*. Your family would also be able to make a claim to the provincial criminal injuries compensation board . . . which is a good thing, because killers can't get insurance that will compensate their victims and most killers don't have big bank accounts. However, neither do criminal injury compensation boards.

If you are killed by a negligent or intentional act, your family will have the right to sue the perpetrator of the act for *damages*, which is money compensation for the loss they've suffered. They will be able to ask for, and may be awarded by a court or receive through a settlement with the perpetrator's insurance company, money to compensate for many different things, including

- Your funeral expenses
- The loss of your care and companionship
- Their emotional suffering caused by your death
- And most important financially, the loss of your earnings over the period of time they were needed to support family members

A court award or a settlement could end up providing your family with as much money as a life insurance policy. By the way, even if you've got life insurance, your family can still sue.

To end this chapter on a cheerful note, in the very remote event that you're killed in an airplane crash during an international flight, your family would probably immediately be offered the equivalent of US $135,000 by the airline without having to sue the airline. (Why is a long dull story which begins with something called the Warsaw Convention.) But your family could still sue the airline if they felt you were worth more.

# Chapter 7

# Money to Die For: The Mysteries of Life Insurance Revealed

### In This Chapter

- Deciding on the kind of life insurance you want
- Choosing your beneficiary
- Finding out how much life insurance costs
- Figuring out where and how to get life insurance
- Learning what a standard life insurance policy says

Any kind of insurance can overheat your brain when you try to understand the ins and outs, especially when they're presented to you in Insurance Company Speak. That's why we're going to do our best in this chapter to demystify life insurance for you. In Chapter 6, we discuss whether you need to buy life insurance. If you do, in this chapter we arm you to go out and talk fearlessly to insurance agents.

## What Kind of Life Insurance Should You Get?

You wouldn't think it from the large number of names that insurance companies bandy about for their policies, but there are only two basic types of insurance. They are *term insurance* and *permanent insurance*.

### Term insurance

Term insurance provides life insurance coverage for a fixed period, or *term*. If the insured person dies during that term, the insurance company will pay a specified sum of money (the *face amount* of the policy) to the beneficiary. If the insured person dies after the term ends, the insurance company doesn't have to pay anything at all.

A term insurance policy can have a term of one year, five years, ten years, fifteen years, twenty years, or even longer. At the start of the term, the insurance company will set an annual premium rate based on your age and health, the amount of coverage, and the length of the term. The younger and healthier you are, the less likely you are to die and the lower your premiums will be. The longer the term is, the higher the premium will be, because even if you are young and healthy when you buy the insurance, you will become older, less healthy, and more likely to die before the insurance expires.

At the end of the term one of three things may happen:

- The insurance policy may simply expire — in which case you will have to buy new insurance, the cost of which will depend on your age and health at that time. If you have become very unhealthy, you may not be able to get insurance at all.
- The insurance policy may be renewable. You may be able to renew the policy for a previously agreed premium, if the policy guaranteed this right. Most term policies cannot be renewed past the age of 70. But if you're a term insurance junkie, don't despair! It is possible to get term insurance up to age 100 and even beyond under a *Term to 100* policy. In some versions of these policies, if the insured reaches the age of 100 coverage continues even though premiums no longer have to be paid. In other versions, if the insured lives to be 100, coverage ends but the insurance company will pay out some or the entire face amount of the policy.
- You may be able to convert the policy into permanent insurance before you reach the age at which the policy can no longer be renewed.

## Permanent insurance

Permanent insurance has quite a few aliases, such as whole life, universal life, and guaranteed life, but all permanent insurance policies have two important features. First, the insurance policy will remain in effect until you die, no matter how ancient you are by then, provided you pay your premiums. Second, the policy combines insurance with a savings feature. Some of your premium dollars pay the life insurance costs, but some are invested so that your policy has a *cash surrender value* that goes up as time goes by. If you decide to cancel the policy, the insurance company will pay you the cash surrender value of your policy.

## What are the advantages and disadvantages of term insurance?

The main advantage of term life insurance is its lower cost. While no insurance policy is cheap, term insurance can cost from one-quarter to one-tenth the price of the same amount of permanent insurance. That means that you can get a lot more insurance coverage for your premium dollar than you can with permanent insurance. This is especially important to people with young families, who have high insurance needs at a time of their life when their expenses are high.

The main disadvantage of term life insurance is that the only way to get any money from your insurance company is to die. (This is a bit extreme, don't you think?) If you stop paying the premiums, or you reach the maximum age under the policy, the policy simply ends and you don't receive a cent — even though you may have paid hundreds or thousands of dollars in premiums over the years.

## What are the advantages and disadvantages of permanent insurance?

Permanent insurance is promoted by insurance companies as having numerous advantages. However, many of these advantages aren't that advantageous on closer examination. Let's look at some of the claims made for permanent insurance.

- *Advertised advantage:* Your insurance coverage will not end when you reach a certain age — it will continue in place until you die.

  *Reality:* As you get older, your need for life insurance usually goes down. When you reach the age at which your term insurance coverage ends, you will probably need a lot less insurance than before. You might not need any at all. But if you still want insurance, you can get it by converting some of your term policy coverage into a permanent policy, or by buying a new, smaller permanent life insurance policy. Although the premiums for a new policy when you are older will be quite expensive, the combined cost of the premiums for your original term policy and for the new permanent policy will probably be a lot lower than the permanent policy premiums you would pay over the length of the larger permanent policy.

- *Advertised advantage:* You have an investment as well as insurance, and a tax-deferred investment at that — the cash value grows over time, and you don't have to pay income tax on what your policy earns unless you take the earnings out before you die.

*Reality:* Insurance is not a very good investment. Other investments earn a lot more money than a permanent insurance policy. And while it's true that the earnings on a permanent policy are tax deferred, investing in an RRSP is a much better way to get a tax deferral. With an RRSP, the money you invest is deductible from income, you will almost certainly earn more on your investment, and the income earned is not taxable until you cash in the RRSP.

- *Advertised advantage:* Permanent insurance is a form of forced savings — if you're good at paying your bills but not good about saving money, at least part of your insurance bill is going toward savings.

  *Reality:* You can participate in other forms of forced savings, such as payroll savings plans.

- *Advertised advantage:* You can borrow against the cash value of your policy at a reasonable rate of interest.

  *Reality:* Think about it — you're borrowing your own money!

- *Advertised advantage:* The premiums don't go up as you get older — they remain constant throughout the life of the policy.

  *Reality:* Instead of having a policy with premiums that get very high when you get older, you have premiums that start high and stay high.

- *Advertised advantage:* You may not have to pay premiums at all after a certain number of years. If the cash surrender value of your policy gets high enough, instead of paying more each year, your premiums may be paid out of the interest earned on the cash surrender value.

  *Reality:* If interest rates go down and your policy doesn't earn enough to cover the premiums, premiums will be deducted from the cash surrender value of the policy and the cash surrender value will go down.

The main disadvantage of permanent insurance is its cost. Coverage under a permanent insurance policy is much more expensive than the same amount of coverage under a term insurance policy — as we told you above, it can be as much as ten times more expensive. And it is questionable whether the advantages are worth the extra cost.

All in all, we think you'll find that as insurance, permanent insurance is too expensive, and that as an investment, it's not a great investment.

## Variations on a theme

Now we're going to touch on a few variations on term life insurance.

### Joint policies

Normally if you wanted life insurance on two different people, you'd have two separate policies and the insurance company would pay up when each person died. A joint insurance policy insures two lives, but the insurance company only pays the face amount of the policy once, when one of the joint insured people dies — depending on the policy, the payment will be made when the first person dies or when the second person dies. Generally speaking, the premiums on a joint policy are cheaper than the premiums on two separate policies. (And you're thinking: They darn well better be, since the insurance company only pays once!)

Under a *first-to-die policy*, the insurance company pays the face amount of the policy when the first of the two insured people die. You might consider taking out a first-to-die policy if you and another person, usually a partner or a spouse, are in a situation in which either of you would need money if the other one died. For example, if you and your spouse have a debt, such as a mortgage, that you need both of your incomes to pay, you might want enough insurance to pay off the debt if either one of you dies. You might also use this type of policy if you own a business with someone else and have an agreement that if one of you dies, the other will buy that partner's share of the business from the partner's estate. A first-to-die policy on each other's lives would give you the money to buy out your partner's share.

Under a *second-to-die policy*, the insurance company pays the face amount of the policy when the second of the two insured people die. You might consider taking out a second-to-die policy if your family will need money only after you and your spouse both die. This type of policy is most commonly used to cover capital gains taxes (see Chapter 4). Generally, capital gains taxes do not have to be paid when the first spouse dies if that spouse leaves property to the other spouse, but have to be paid only when the second spouse dies and the property is then left to the children or others.

### Mortgage insurance

If you and your spouse have a mortgage on your home, your mortgage lender has probably offered you the opportunity to buy *mortgage insurance* to pay off the mortgage if one spouse dies. Mortgage insurance is simply a first-to-die term insurance policy. Before you take out the policy, shop around and see if you can get the same amount of term insurance somewhere else for less money.

### Accidental death insurance

*Accidental death insurance* is term insurance that provides coverage only if you die in an accident. If you die of natural causes, for example of a heart attack after narrowly avoiding being killed in an accident, your beneficiary will get nada. You can buy accidental death insurance on its own, or you can buy a *double indemnity* rider to your life insurance policy — an addition to your policy under which your beneficiaries will be paid double the face amount of the policy if you are killed accidentally. However, accidental death insurance is more often found as part of a travel insurance package that includes other things like out-of-country medical, trip cancellation, and lost baggage insurance — it's term insurance for a very short term (the length of your trip).

Also available is *flight insurance* (in travel insurance packages and from machines at the airport). Your beneficiary only collects if you're killed in a plane crash. Flight insurance is alluringly inexpensive because air crashes, although extremely scary to contemplate and highly publicized when they occur, are very rare.

The bottom line about insurance that picks and chooses the way you're going to die is this: You either need life insurance or you don't. If you need it, you should buy ordinary term insurance and have coverage all the time for all possible ways of kicking the bucket. If you don't need insurance, then don't buy it, no matter how cheap it is or how nervous you are about having an accident.

# Where Do You Get Life Insurance?

Where you go looking for a life insurance policy depends on whether you have in mind *individual insurance* or *group insurance*. Individual insurance is a contract between the owner of the policy and an insurance company, and any individual can apply for coverage from any insurance company. Group insurance is a contract between a group (such as a company, a trade union, a professional organization) and a particular insurance company. Only members of the group (the employees, the union members, the professionals) are eligible to apply for coverage from the insurance company.

Permanent insurance is available only through individual policies, while term insurance is available through either individual or group policies.

## Individual insurance

When you buy individual insurance you have several decisions to make. You have to decide which insurance company you want to deal with. Then you have to decide whether to buy your insurance directly from the insurance company or through an agent or broker. And if you decide to work with an agent or broker you have to decide which agent or broker to use.

### Which insurance company should you deal with?

A major factor in your choice of insurance company will be which company offers you the most reasonable rate for the insurance you want. You should get quotes from several insurers before you buy a policy. We tell you more about how to comparison shop under the heading "How Much Does Insurance Cost?" later in this chapter.

Another factor you should take into account is the financial health of the insurance company. The insurance industry is very highly regulated, and the provincial government examines an insurance company's financial health when it decides whether or not the company should be (or should continue to be) licensed to carry on business. If you're concerned about the financial condition of a particular insurance company, you can get information from an insurance broker, from the Canadian Life and Health Insurance Association, and from reports issued by rating agencies such as Moody's Investors Service, Inc., and Standard and Poor's Corp.

You're going to be with your chosen insurance company for a long time . . . you hope. You don't want to monitor the company's financial health hourly as you would an Internet stock. So you'll be relieved to learn that, although life insurance policies are not insured by the federal government the way bank or trust company deposits are, all life insurance companies that conduct business in Canada contribute to a fund that compensates policy holders if their insurance company fails. If your insurance company doesn't last as long as you do, the fund will pay a maximum of $200,000 for each life insured at any one company. If you need more than $200,000 of life insurance, you won't be fully protected if you have all of your insurance with one company. Your alternative is to have several policies of no more than $200,000 with different companies, but this will probably cost more than having one policy for the full amount you need.

A final factor in your choice of insurance company is the way in which you want to buy your insurance — from an agent or a broker, or directly from a company.

### Agent, broker, or buy direct?

Most life insurance is sold through agents and brokers who earn commissions based on the amount and kind of insurance they sell. But more and more insurance companies are selling their policies directly to the public.

Agents and brokers work for themselves or for insurance agencies or brokerages, not for the insurance company. They are regulated and licensed by provincial governments. We use the term insurance *agent* to mean a person who deals with only one insurance company and sells only that company's policies. We use the term insurance *broker* to mean a person who deals with and sells the policies of several companies. A broker can get quotes for you from several companies, while an agent can get you insurance only from one. So if you choose to work with an agent, make sure that you have checked out the insurance company as well as the agent.

You can buy directly from an insurance company, for example through the company's Web site or over the phone. You can also buy insurance from one of the banks or trust companies that have set up insurance departments. Their staff is usually made up of salaried employees rather than commission-earning salespeople — however it's their job to sell insurance for their employer. You may pay less for the policy because you'll be dealing with staff who are employed by the insurance company rather than with independent salespeople, but do some comparison shopping to make sure.

If you decide to buy insurance through an agent or broker, he or she can give you advice about

- How much insurance you need
- The kind of policy to buy
- Completing the formal application process

If you buy directly from an insurance company you may be on your own here.

When you're dealing with insurance agents and brokers, you should keep in mind that they are paid a commission by the insurance company for each policy they sell. Generally speaking, the more expensive the policy, the higher the commission, and commissions for permanent policies are a lot higher than the commissions for term policies. It makes it rather tempting for an agent or broker to try to sell you more insurance than you need. Also, the more insurance a broker sells for a particular company, the higher the rate of the broker's commission, so even an independent broker may be inclined to push one insurance company's products over another's.

These facts of insurance life make it very important for you to be careful in choosing an agent or broker to deal with. So how do you find a trustworthy one? Ask for recommendations from your family and friends, from your lawyer or accountant, or from the agent or broker you deal with for your car or home insurance (if you've been satisfied with his or her work). Once you have a recommendation, speak to the agent or broker and:

- Find out about his or her experience and qualifications. Some agents and brokers hold various professional designations, such as Chartered Life Underwriter (CLU), Chartered Financial Planner (CFP) and Chartered Financial Consultant (CHFC). These designations mean that the agent or broker has taken courses and examinations in insurance and financial planning topics.

- Ask for references from other clients if you'd like to know more about an agent or broker's past performance.
- Get a sense of whether the agent or broker is someone you can trust and feel comfortable working with.

After you've chosen a person, don't just blindly follow the advice you are given. Ask lots of questions, such as how the agent or broker arrived at the recommended amount of insurance, why the broker is recommending one insurance company over another, and how much commission is payable on any particular policy.

### Group insurance

In order to get group life insurance, you have to belong to a group . . . and the group has to offer group insurance. (Have you noticed that this book is full of brilliant insights?)

The most common source of group insurance is an employer. If your employer offers group coverage you would have been told about it when you were hired or when it was first introduced as a benefit. To be eligible for employer group insurance you generally have to be a full-time employee, although some employers also offer coverage to part-time employees. Usually you must be employed for one to three months before you are eligible for coverage. You must apply for coverage within a short time after becoming eligible (as a rule, one month) or you may not be able to apply at all, or you may have to provide evidence that you are healthy.

Alternatively, you may be eligible for group life insurance through membership in a union or professional or other association (such as a university alumni association). If you are a member of such a group, call the organization to find out whether or not it offers group life and, if so, whether you are eligible for coverage and what the cost is.

## How Do You Get Life Insurance?

The process of applying for life insurance varies according to whether you are getting individual insurance or group insurance.

## Getting individual insurance

If you apply for individual insurance, you will have to fill out a form that asks your age and sex, and detailed questions about

- Your current health
- Your medical history
- Your family's medical history as it relates to any hereditary medical conditions
- Your past and present use of alcohol, tobacco, and drugs
- Your past and present participation in dangerous activities, such as flying (as a pilot or crew member), motor vehicle racing, parachuting, hang gliding, and scuba diving, and your intention to participate in those activities in the future
- Whether you have any other insurance policies, and whether you have ever applied for and been denied insurance coverage

You will also have to sign a consent form authorizing all of your doctors to disclose information about your medical history to the insurance company. Depending on your age, your medical history, and the amount of insurance you are applying for, you may have to undergo a medical examination by a doctor or nurse chosen by the insurance company.

It is very important to be absolutely honest in filling out the application form and in answering any questions asked during your medical examination. If you make a mistake, leave out information, or tell a lie, your insurance company may have the right to terminate the policy for up to two years after the policy comes into effect. After two years, the insurance company still has the right to terminate your policy for wrong information, but only if you were trying to defraud the insurance company.

### If your application is approved

If the insurance company approves your application, the insurance policy does not take effect unless

- A copy of the policy has been delivered to you, your agent, or your beneficiary
- The first premium has been paid
- There has been no change in your health or lifestyle that would affect the insurance company's decision to insure you between the time your application was completed and the time the policy was delivered

### If your application is not approved

If your application isn't approved and you're working with an agent or a broker, ask him or her to ask the insurance company for an explanation. If you applied for insurance directly from the insurer, ask the insurance company yourself.

If your application was turned down because of a medical condition, you want to know whether the insurance company relied only on information in your questionnaire and medical examination and your doctors' records, or whether it relied on information obtained from the Medical Information Bureau.

The Medical Information Bureau (MIB) is an organization of life insurance companies that operates a medical information exchange on behalf of its members. Whenever you apply for insurance, you consent to the insurance company giving the medical information they get from you to the MIB and to the MIB giving whatever medical information they have about you to the insurance company. The MIB may have a medical file on you, just like a credit rating bureau may have a credit file on you. If the insurance company relied on information from the MIB in deciding to reject your application, you have the right to ask the MIB to give you any information it has about you. If you find a mistake, you can contact the MIB in Toronto to seek a correction.

If there has been no mistake or misunderstanding, don't give up hope. Just because one insurance company has turned down your application doesn't mean that every insurance company will do the same thing. Ask a broker to look for another company that may consider granting coverage to someone with your particular medical problem.

## Getting group insurance

How you go about applying for group insurance depends on the nature of the group.

In order to get group life insurance from your employer, you have to make a written application to your employer once you become eligible under the plan (usually one to three months after starting your employment). Most employer group life insurance policies do not require the individual members of the group to provide evidence of good health, and so the application form is very short. If you apply as soon you become eligible, your insurance will take effect as soon as your employer receives your written application. If you wait more than about a month to put in your application, you will probably have to fill out an insurance company form and perhaps even have a medical exam to satisfy the insurance company about your health and lifestyle.

If you are taking out group life insurance with a non-employer group, the insurance company may require proof of good health and lifestyle. In that case, the application form will be more detailed, and the approval process longer.

# How Much Will Insurance Cost?

Insurance premiums differ in price considerably — and not just from insurance company to insurance company, but from person to person. How much your insurance will cost will depend on

- The amount of coverage you want
- Whether you buy term insurance or permanent insurance
- Insurance industry rating factors
- Whether you comparison shop for the best price for similar policies
- Whether you buy individual insurance or group insurance

## The amount of insurance

Insurance premiums are quoted per thousand dollars of coverage, so the more insurance you buy, the higher your premium will be. (We discuss how much insurance you need to buy in Chapter 6.)

## Term insurance or permanent insurance

As we mentioned, the cost of permanent insurance coverage can be up to ten times the cost of the same amount of term insurance coverage.

## Insurance rating factors

At the beginning of this chapter, we said that when you buy a life insurance policy you're placing a bet with the insurance company about when you're going to die. Betting with an insurance company is like gambling at a casino, and the insurance company is the casino. A casino that wants to stay in business makes sure that the odds favour the house so that it doesn't have to pay out more winnings than it has budgeted for.

To check that the odds remain in their favour, insurance companies collect information about the general population. While it is impossible to predict when any one person will die, it is possible to predict quite accurately, based on death statistics, the number of people out of a large group who will die during a given period of time. If an insurance company insures a large number of people who as a group resemble the general population, using statistical *mortality tables* it can predict how many will die each year. Then it can budget for the number of claims it will probably have to pay and set premiums accordingly — with people who are statistically more likely to die in the year being charged higher premiums than those who are statistically less likely to die.

Insurance companies also collect information about each applicant to make sure that the applicant doesn't have a greater-than-statistically-average risk of dying. (Insurers believe that people who are more likely to die are also more likely to want insurance, so they are immediately suspicious of anyone who wants to buy what they're trying to sell.) This screening process is called *underwriting.* An underwriter decides whether a particular applicant runs an average risk of dying, a lower than average risk of dying, or a higher than average risk of dying. A person with an average risk of dying will be charged a *standard* premium. A person with a lower than average risk of dying will be charged a *preferred* premium. A person with a higher than average risk of dying will either be charged a higher premium or will be refused coverage altogether, depending on how high the risk is.

All of this means that an insurance company sets your premium according to the following rating factors:

- **Your age and sex:** Rates are different for sex as well as age because for men and women of the same age the likelihood of dying at any given age is different.
- **Your health:** People who already have certain kinds of health problems (just to name a few examples, cancer, heart disease, or emphysema; or less advanced problems such as high blood pressure or diabetes) are more likely than the average person to die sooner rather than later.
- **Whether or not you smoke:** Insurance company executives were among the first to take seriously the warnings on cigarette packages that smokers are more likely than non-smokers to get sick and die.
- **Whether or not you engage in dangerous activities:** Some activities, such as flying small airplanes, car racing, parachuting, and scuba diving, are associated with a higher fatal accident rate than, say, walking the dog or going to a hockey game.

Just to give you an idea of how your rating factors affect insurance premiums, Table 7-1 shows the standard annual insurance premiums for $100,000 of ten-year term insurance, depending on age and sex. The price ranges reflect the fact that not all companies charge exactly the same amount for a premium.

Table 7-2 gives you an idea of how much money you would save on the same amount of insurance if you qualified for preferred premiums because you were in ideal health and did not engage in any dangerous activities.

**Table 7-1 Standard Annual Insurance Premiums for $100,000 of Term Life Insurance, by Age and Sex**

| *Age* | *Female* | *Male* |
|---|---|---|
| 30 | $ 110–187 | $ 131–204 |
| 40 | 145–212 | 137–240 |
| 50 | 219–341 | 304–462 |
| 60 | 454–730 | 618–1,035 |
| 70 | 1,129–2,439 | 1,645–4,013 |

**Table 7-2 Preferred Annual Insurance Premiums for $100,000 of Term Life Insurance, by Age and Sex**

| *Age* | *Female* | *Male* |
|---|---|---|
| 30 | $ 110–140 | $ 123–159 |
| 40 | 134–165 | 137–186 |
| 50 | 188–249 | 226–327 |
| 60 | 320–527 | 448–733 |
| 70 | 885–1,395 | 1,390–2,243 |

As you can see by comparing standard and preferred premiums, good health and a safe lifestyle become more important the older you get.

## Comparison shop

The cost of the same amount and type of insurance coverage can vary widely from insurance company to insurance company, as the two tables above show. And paying more may not get you any more in terms of reliability or service. To make sure that you don't pay more than you have to, compare the prices of several insurance companies.

You can compare insurance prices by

- Speaking to an insurance broker. An insurance broker who deals with a number of companies can find out what each would charge you for the same insurance. You can ask the broker whether there is any reason to justify a higher premium from a particular company.

- Speaking to insurance agents for several companies. Ask each one to tell you what their particular company would charge you for the insurance coverage you are interested in. (But who in their right mind would want more than one insurance salesperson at a time after them?)
- Using the Internet. There are Web sites that will give you comparative quotes. A good site is Compulife's Term4sale, located at www.term4sale.com.

## Individual insurance or group insurance

Almost everything we've told you so far about the cost of insurance applies only to individual insurance policies. It does not apply to group life insurance policies.

If you are eligible for group life insurance, your age, sex, health, and lifestyle do not affect your premiums. Everyone in the group is charged the same premium per dollar of insurance, so the only thing that will affect the cost is the amount of insurance you buy.

Group life insurance policies are convenient because, as a rule, you simply enroll through your company or other group and do not have to complete any health and lifestyle questionnaires or go through any form of medical examination. However, the premiums may not be cheaper than those for an individual life insurance policy, especially if you're in good health.

# What Does a Standard Life Insurance Policy Say?

Have you ever felt a burning desire to read a life insurance policy? We thought not. We didn't feel a burning desire either, but we read one anyway — and now we're going to tell you what's in there just in case you never get around to looking for yourself. What's in a policy depends (once again) on whether the policy is an individual policy or a group policy.

## Individual insurance

There are certain things that every individual insurance policy contains:

- The name of the insurance company
- The name of the insured person
- The name of the beneficiary

- The amount of money to be paid on the death of the life insured (or a method for calculating the amount)
- The amount of the premium (or a method for calculating the premium)
- Any grace period for paying a premium — if you don't pay your premium your policy will *lapse* (end). By statute, there's a grace period of at least 28 days after the due date for the payment. During that period you're still covered and you can still make your payment to keep the policy in force
- When the policy takes effect
- When the policy ends

Most policies also contain a clause stating that no money will be paid under the policy if the insured commits suicide within two years after the policy takes effect.

Permanent life insurance policies also include clauses dealing with the cash value of the policy. Term insurance policies may have a clause allowing the insured to convert the policy to permanent insurance before the policy expires.

## Group insurance

In group insurance there is no contract between the insurance company and the individual group members whose lives are insured. The contract is between the insurance company and the group — employer company, labour union, or professional or other organization — known as the *contracting party*. Only the contracting party gets a copy of the insurance contract. However, the insurance company must provide a certificate or other document for the contracting party to deliver to each group member. This document sets out

- The name of the insurance company
- A contract number or other identification of the contract
- The amount of insurance on the group member (or a method to determine the amount)
- The circumstances in which the insurance will terminate

Instead of getting a copy of a life insurance policy, the individual members of the group may be given a brochure setting out the main details of the insurance policy.

# Chapter 8

# Free to a Good Home: Giving Away Your Things before You Die

### *In This Chapter*

- Looking into making a gift of your property while you're alive
- Figuring out the best way to make a gift
- Learning how to avoid gift-giving mistakes
- Discovering the best ways to give

Maybe you wandered into this chapter thinking that you'd like to give a grandchild something that belonged to your parents, to link the generations of your family. Or you've been toying with the idea of helping your children pay for their children's education. Or you may feel that your dear nephew's business would be successful if only he had a chunk of your cash to put into it. Aha! you say to yourself. A gift would be the very thing.

Then your eye started travelling. You saw that we've written paragraphs and paragraphs and probably pages and pages (good guess) about gifts . . . and you think we're loopy. You've been giving gifts since you could hold a pudgy little hand out to someone you loved. How complex can gift-giving be if you could do it before you could walk or talk?

Gifts aren't quite as innocent as they look . . . lawyers got there first! A gift is actually a legal transaction with a whole set of rules attached to it, and a whole bunch of potential problems trailing behind it.

# Why Give Your Property Away While You're Alive?

Giving things away while you're still alive is one way to make sure they actually get to the people you want to have them. After you're dead, you might have to rely on the kindness of strangers, or worse, of relatives. And there may be other reasons why you don't want to wait until you're dead:

- A family member or friend may need financial help now — why not do the generous thing? It will head off those calculating looks that accompany the greeting, "How are you?"
- You may be thinking of the pleasure it will give you to see your family or friends enjoying your gifts while you're still alive.
- Your property (especially a house or cottage) may be eating up too much of your money, time, and effort to keep up.
- You may entertain some strange hope that if you divide up your property now it will prevent your family from fighting over it after you're dead. (And you're right! They'll fight with you instead of with each other later.)
- After reading Chapter 5 on taxes and estate planning, you may believe that there will be tax advantages for you now in a gift or for your estate or a beneficiary when you die.

# What Is a Gift?

Legally speaking, giving a gift means unconditionally transferring ownership and control of your property to another person. Does that sound like what you want to do? Or do you really want the recipient to do what you tell him to do with your former property?

Once you've made a gift of a piece of your property, you have no rights over the property any more. If it's money, you can no longer keep it under your mattress or in your safety deposit box or in your bank account without the permission of the recipient. If it's a house or a cottage, you can no longer live there — or even visit — without the permission of the recipient. If it's a car, you can't drive it without the permission of the recipient. If it's a painting, you have no say in how it's framed, and if it's a vase, you can't tell the recipient to put it away for safekeeping or to display it in the living room.

The person to whom you give the gift, on the other hand, now has all the rights over the property that you used to have. The new owner can sell the gift, or spend it foolishly and contrary to your wishes, or deliberately destroy it, or carelessly lose it, or give it away, or trade it for something she likes better, or pawn it, or mortgage it, or paint it a funny colour. Legally speaking, it's none of your business what the new owner does with your gift.

Chances are, though, that emotionally and morally speaking, you haven't achieved a state of total detachment from the gift. What the new owner of your lovely gift does with it may drive you nuts . . . and there will be nothing you can do about it. Once you've made a gift, you can't get it back — unless the new owner decides to give it to *you* as a gift, or agrees to let you buy it back.

We're not trying to scare you. Well, yes, we *are* trying to scare you. The recipient of your gift may be happy to do exactly what you would like, and you'll be pleased and the world will generally be a better place. But many people have given gifts that were not used in the way the giver anticipated, and the results have not been pretty — extending as far, sometimes, as a family feud that never healed. Be sure, before you give a gift, that you are fully aware of what gift giving means.

# How Do You Make a Gift?

No, we're not going all Martha Stewartish on you. We're not talking crafts. We're not even talking gift-wrapping. We're talking about the elements that must be present if you want to make a valid gift. Only if you make a valid gift will the new owner be legally able to sell it, mortgage it, spend it foolishly, or do any of the other things that are likely to upset you.

In order for you to make a valid gift,

- You must be the owner of the property. You can't give away property that belongs to your spouse or your children or that you own with someone else (unless you get that other person's consent).
- You must intend to make a gift. You must mean to give away ownership and control of the property completely and permanently, not just partly or temporarily.
- You must hand over the property and/or transfer legal ownership (depending on the nature of the property). You must actually turn the property you are giving away over to the person you are giving it to. You have to hand the person the jewellery or cash, or have the furniture delivered to him or allow him to take it away. You have to move out of the house or cottage, unless you've been given permission to stay on or leave your belongings there. If the property is something that requires registration of ownership, such as a car, a house or cottage, or investments, you must sign and hand over the title documents as well.

- The person to whom you are making the gift must accept the gift — not usually a problem . . . although if the person says she doesn't want it you can't force her to take it. Leaving it on her doorstep after she's said no doesn't make it hers or require her to take it in out of the rain.

# Can You Give Away Your Property without Meaning To?

Now that we've warned you that a gift may not be exactly the ticket for you and your loved ones, you may be wondering if you can give a gift without really wanting or intending to. Sometimes you can. And you may or may not be able to get out of it.

## A gift made against your will is not a gift

Even if you meet all the legal requirements to make a valid gift, as we set out in the list above, there's one additional requirement before the recipient is the undisputed owner of your property. You must also be making the gift voluntarily.

- You must be mentally competent. You don't have the necessary intention to make a gift unless you are able to understand the legal and practical meaning and consequences of making the gift. You might be mentally incompetent for a time because of anesthesia or drugs or alcohol or a head injury. You might be mentally incompetent permanently because of Alzheimer's or a stroke or other brain damage.
- You must not be acting under *duress* (violence or threats of violence to force you to make the gift).
- You must not be acting under *undue influence* (pressure put on you to make a gift, if the pressure results from the nature of your relationship with the person who'd like you to make a gift). For example, if you're physically frail and you rely on an individual to look after you, that individual's expressed interest in getting a gift might be considered undue influence. In addition, you'll be fascinated to know that whenever you give a gift to your lawyer the law presumes that there has been undue influence.

If you give a gift at a time when you are either temporarily or permanently mentally incompetent, or if you give a gift because you were threatened or felt pressured to give it, you (if you're mentally competent) or your family (if you're not) can apply to a court to have your gift cancelled and returned.

### Ada's piano

Ada was very fond of her sixteen-year-old grand-niece, Flora, who visited Ada every weekend for tea and at the end of her visit always played the piano for Ada. One day, Ada said to Flora, "You play that piano so beautifully that I am going to give it to you for your next birthday." Flora continued to visit Ada and play her piano, but on Flora's next birthday Ada gave her a sweater. Flora was disappointed, not least because the sweater was something she wouldn't be caught dead in. But she was well brought up and said nothing to Ada about the piano. In fact if Flora had consulted a lawyer about the promised gift, she would have found that she had no legal right to make Ada give her the piano, despite Ada's clear promise.

## A promise to give a gift is not a gift

Suppose you're in your right mind, not under pressure, and not being threatened with a long walk off a short pier. Suppose that in a moment of affection you've promised to give someone something. Can you be forced to go through with your promise and make the gift?

If the moment of affection passes, or if you simply forget that you made the promise, no one can make you give the gift as long as you received nothing in return for your promise. Have a look at the story of "Ada's piano," above.

## But a promise to give a gift in return for something is a different matter

If you promise someone a gift, there's nothing she can legally do to make you give it to her. However if you promise someone a gift and he promises you something in return or promises to do something valuable for you in return, there's a change of scene. You're out of the world of gifts and into the world of contracts. And in the world of contract law, a promise in exchange for a promise creates a contract that a court will agree to enforce. So you can be forced to go through with making the gift you promised. (Only now it's not really a gift, its legal name is *consideration* — the thing you give in exchange for the thing you receive.)

Let's look at "Ada's piano, second movement" to see how the story might have turned out differently if something else had been said.

### Ada's piano, second movement

In this variation on the example above, Ada said to Flora, "You play that piano so beautifully that I'd like to give it to you for your next birthday."

Flora replied, "I'd like that very much. I'll come and play the piano for you every weekend between now and then, and once the piano is mine I'll invite you to my house."

"That's settled, then," said Ada.

Flora showed up and played every weekend. In legal terms she gave her consideration, and when her birthday rolled around it was Ada's turn to give her consideration — to give Flora the piano as promised. Instead she gave Flora a sweater. In these circumstances, Flora could have sued Ada for the piano. But Ada was lucky. Flora was too well brought up to think of suing.

Not everyone is as polite as Flora! You must be careful not to promise to give something to a person who is doing something in return, *especially* if the person is not already getting paid for doing it. Unless, of course, you actually want to give the person something and you're not just making conversation. So if the kid next door likes to walk your dog after school and isn't being paid to do so, think a minute before you say you'll buy the kid her own purebred dog next Christmas. If your cousin, out of the goodness of his heart, picks you up and takes you grocery shopping every week, don't just blurt out that if he keeps on taking you shopping you'd like to thank him by giving him your hockey puck that was autographed by Rocket Richard.

# Will You Live to Regret This Gift?

For now, let's assume that you truly and genuinely want to give someone a gift and you have no doubt in your mind that your gift will be used exactly as you would like. There are still a couple of other things to consider before generosity overwhelms you:

- Are you giving away so much that you won't have enough money or property to look after yourself until you die?
- Will you have to pay taxes as a result of making the gift?

## Can you afford the gift?

As we've said, once you make a gift of something, you no longer own it and you can't get it back. So before you give anything away, make sure that you're leaving yourself enough money and property to look after yourself until you die. Think not only about your current circumstances, but consider what your financial needs will be if you become ill and unable to look after yourself, or if your spouse needs special care. Will you still have enough?

You may be thinking about giving away something that earns income, such as cash that earns interest, shares that pay dividends, or real estate that brings in rental income. Stop to think how much income the property earns for you and what income you will be left with if you give the property away. Will you still have enough income now? In the future?

You may be thinking about giving something away that does not earn income, like jewellery or a painting, or something that costs you money to maintain, such as a cottage. Stop to think about how much money you might get for this property if you were to sell it. Do you need that money now? Might you need it in the future?

## Will you have to pay tax on your gift?

Taxes may turn out to be another cause for regret.

In Chapter 5, we tell you that there are two important possible tax advantages to giving things away while you're alive:

- You may reduce the capital gains tax your estate will have to pay when you die.
- You may reduce your income tax now.

But you may find that when you give a gift, the tax advantages won't work out quite the way you're hoping. Instead, Canada Revenue may come snuffling up and ask for a gift from you too.

### Reduced capital gains tax later

You might be planning to give away cash, stocks, valuable artwork, collectibles, or real estate like a house or cottage, and you're wondering whether giving these things now will relieve your estate of some of the tax burden.

There is no capital gains tax payable, ever, on cash, GICs, or treasury bills because cash, or any investment that is essentially cash, does not go up in value. Your estate won't pay capital gains tax on such things when you die. So there's no capital gains tax advantage to giving a gift of cash.

By disposing of property that does go up in value (investments, artwork, real estate), you may be reducing capital gains payable on your death. On the other hand, you may have to pay capital gains tax yourself now, if the property has increased in value since you got it. If the gift is to your spouse you won't pay any capital gains tax because of the spousal rollover (see Chapter 4). But if your spouse sells the property at a profit before you die, Canada Revenue has the power to *attribute* the capital gain back to you; in other words, make *you,* rather than your spouse, pay the capital gains tax.

If you have to pay capital gains tax, the amount will be calculated as if you had sold the property at fair market value, even though you are actually giving it away. It doesn't make much sense to pay tax now rather than later — especially since you have no profit from a sale to pay tax with — unless

- You believe that the property will increase a lot in value between now and the time of your death, and for whatever reason you don't want your estate to have to pay tax on the entire gain from the time you acquired the property to the time you die.
- You have a capital loss that you can use to offset the capital gain and reduce the tax payable.

### Reduced income tax now

You may want to give away property or an investment that is generating income for you because you don't need the income and you'd rather not pay the associated income tax. You probably want to give the income-producing property to someone who will pay tax in a lower tax bracket, thus rescuing part of the income from the claws of the government.

There could be some bad news here. Even though the new owner of the property will receive the income from the property, *you* may still have to pay the tax on it. Depending on whom you give the property to, Canada Revenue might think you were trying to *income-split* (share income within a family unit in order to reduce the tax payable on it) and might attribute the income back to you and tax you as if the income continues to be yours.

If you give income-producing property to your spouse or to a trust for your spouse, the tax authorities have the power to tax you on any interest, dividend, or capital gains income from that property in the future. If you give income-producing property to a child or grandchild under the age of 18, the tax department has the power to tax you on any interest or dividend income (but not capital gains) from the property in the future. Some good news — you cannot be taxed on the income earned by property that you transfer to your adult child or grandchild, or to a friend or passing stranger.

## Is There a Safer Way Than Giving a Gift?

You love your family and your friends . . . but if you don't trust them any further than you could throw a woolly mammoth, then maybe a gift is not the best way to show your love. Luckily, there are alternatives.

## A loan

If a family member or friend needs money to make a major purchase such as a house or a car, you could make a loan instead of a gift. Your loan can be accompanied by a *promissory note* (a promise to repay), with a repayment schedule drawn up to reflect the borrower's financial circumstances. You can charge interest if you like (less than a bank would charge, if you're feeling kind), or make the loan interest-free (if you're feeling extra kind). If you receive interest, you're supposed to report it in your income tax return.

If your friend or relative knows that the money is supposed to go back to you some day, she'll probably be more careful about what she does with it . . . even if there's a chance that you'll someday forgive the loan.

If the loan is to buy a house or cottage and you'd like more reassurance that the money will come back to you, you can have a mortgage registered against the property for the amount of the loan. That will give you the right to take and sell it if the loan is not paid. If you want to do the business properly, you should have the property appraised to make sure that its value is at least equal to the value of your loan plus any other mortgages on the property. That way, if the property ever has to be sold you should be able to get your money back.

If the loan is for a car, you can register a *security interest* against the car. Like a mortgage, a security interest gives you the right to take and sell the car if the loan isn't paid.

If you're thinking along the lines of either a mortgage or a security interest, you need to chat with a lawyer.

## A rental

Instead of giving a house or cottage to someone who needs or wants it, you could hang on to the property as owner but rent it out to your family member or friend. If you aren't particularly concerned about income, you can even let him or her live there rent-free. If you do receive rental payments, you're supposed to report them as income in your tax return.

## An investment

If you're lending money to help out with a business venture, you can use a promissory note to encourage repayment, or you can even ask for security in the form of a mortgage on the borrower's home in the amount of the loan. In addition or instead, if the business is incorporated you can take back shares in the corporation which could pay you dividends as the corporation became more successful and/or give you some measure of control over the corporation's affairs. These are matters you should speak to a lawyer about.

## A sale

Instead of making a loan of your property, you could sell the property to your relative or friend for its full value on the open market or for as little as you like. You'd have to pay capital gains tax if the property has gone up in value since you got it. If you sell your property to a close relative, you would have to calculate the capital gain as if you sold the property for its current fair market value even if you're actually selling it to your relative for less. (Note, though, that if what you're selling is your principal residence there is no capital gains tax payable. See Chapter 4.)

The purchaser wouldn't necessarily have to pay you right away but could instead give you a promissory note, promising to pay at a later time or in installments. (If you were paid in installments you would be able to spread out any capital gain — and therefore any capital gains tax payable — over a period of up to five years.) You might want to register a mortgage against real property that you sell but don't get paid for in full immediately.

Someone who purchases your property, even for less than its value, is probably more likely to take care of it than someone who gets the property for free as a gift.

## RESPs

If you want to pay something towards a child's education and you're afraid that money you put in the kid's savings account might end up invested in computer games or snowboarding vacations, try a Registered Education Savings Plan (RESP). An RESP is a federal government strategy to let you save for a child's post-secondary education. You can start a plan for a child as soon as it's born and contribute up to $4,000 per year until the child reaches age 17. The maximum amount that can be contributed to a plan is $42,000. The income earned in the plan by your contributions is tax-free for you — it's taxed in the hands of the child once the child registers in a post-secondary program and starts to withdraw the money. However, unlike an RRSP, your contributions to the plan are not tax deductible.

The federal government has decided to dote on your young relatives too, and it has promised to add a grant of up $400 per year to each child's plan.

## Co-ownership

Another way to make a gift directly to a friend or family member without giving up total control is to give away a share in the property rather than giving away the entire property. If you own a cottage alone, you could transfer ownership of the cottage from yourself to yourself and the family member. If you have an investment account or money in a bank account, you could transfer ownership of the account from yourself to yourself and the friend.

If you decide to give away a share of your property, in all provinces other than Quebec you and the other person can own the property as either *joint tenants* or as *tenants-in-common.* (In Quebec there is no joint tenancy.) If you decide to own the property as joint tenants, when you die your share in the property will automatically pass to the surviving owner, no matter what your will says. The property does not become part of your estate. So if you change your ownership to joint tenancy you kill two birds with one stone — you give away a half-interest in your property now and arrange to give the other half interest when you die. If you own the property as tenants-in-common, your share of the property is part of your estate when you die and passes under your will.

If you give away only a share of your property, you are still an owner. You still get to use the property and to have a say in what happens to it. The amount of control you have depends on the kind of property involved.

If you become an owner together with someone else of a home or cottage or other real estate, both owners have an equal right to use the entire property, and neither owner can keep the other out of any part of the property. Either co-owner can sell her share of the property without the other owner's permission (this may not be true if the co-owner is your spouse and the property is your family home) — although to tell you the truth it will be almost impossible to find someone who will want to buy just a share of the property. Either owner can start court proceedings to force the sale of the entire property. (It is possible to change these arrangements by entering into a co-ownership agreement.) You'll need to see a lawyer about transferring real estate into joint ownership.

If you become a joint owner of a bank account or investment account (much like a joint owner of real estate), ordinarily either owner has access to the entire balance in the account. As a result you may find that you've given the whole account away even though you only intended to give half. You can arrange with the bank or investment company that both account holders must agree (usually by signing the withdrawal form) before any money can be withdrawn by either of them.

## A trust

You can put property such as investments or real estate into a *living trust*, and the trust holds the property for the beneficiaries you name. Then you name the trustees who look after the property (you can name yourself) and give them instructions about how to handle the property. Living trusts are a great invention for big-time control freaks, but they're expensive to set up (lawyers again) so the property has to be worth a lot . . . and so do you.

There's another little problem with trusts. If you put income-producing property into the trust and then name your spouse or minor children or grandchildren as the beneficiaries of the trust, the tax authorities can attribute the income back to you and make you pay the tax on it as if it were your own income.

If a trust sounds like the very thing for you, your whole soul will vibrate with excitement to hear that the entire Chapter 9 is devoted to trusts.

# Chapter 9

# Pass the Buck: Using Trusts in Estate Planning

### In This Chapter

- Getting acquainted with trusts
- Figuring out whether a trust is right for you and your family
- Creating a trust
- Choosing a trustee
- Paying the taxes associated with a trust
- Paying the ongoing expenses of a trust

The trust is one of the estate planning tools we threaten you with in Chapter 1. It hangs out back in the estate planning shed along with gifts, wills, powers of attorney, life insurance, and the odd cobweb.

Trusts are not for everyone. Not everyone needs one, and not everyone can afford one. After you've read this chapter, you'll have some idea of whether you fall into either of these two categories.

Now let's take the trust down off the shed wall and see what it can do.

## What Is a Trust?

A trust is a vehicle for giving property away but still keeping some control over it. Instead of giving the property directly to the person you want to have the use of it (the *beneficiary*), you (the *settlor*) give the property to a *trustee*, who carries out your instructions about how to manage the property for the use of the beneficiary. (Pay attention to the words in italics 'cause we're actually gonna use them in this chapter.) You can set up a trust during your lifetime or arrange for one to be set up after your death.

The whole idea of trusts is a bit weird because once the trust is set up, the property is owned in two different ways by two different kinds of people. The trustee is the *legal owner* of the property, and the beneficiary is the *beneficial owner* of the property. But the beneficiary can't get his hands on the property except for the bits that the trustee doles out. And the trustee can't do anything with the property except what she has been told to do by the settlor's instructions.

To add to the weirdness, even though you create a trust by giving property to the trustee and not to "the trust," the trust itself has an existence separate from the trustee and the beneficiary. The trust has to file tax returns and pay the trustee, and is responsible for paying for any professional services the trust requires (such as legal, accounting, and investing services) and for paying to maintain property in the trust (painting a cottage, for example).

But only lawyers think about the mysterious and mystical nature of a trust . . . and then as infrequently as possible — and preferably when they're getting paid to think about it. *You* don't have to think about it at all if you don't want to.

## More about the players

You can have more than one beneficiary for your trust, and the beneficiaries can either be named individuals (for example, Margaret Kerr and JoAnn Kurtz — feel free to make us the beneficiaries of your trust, since no one else has yet) or members of a *class* (for example, "my children" or "my grandchildren"). You can even have second-choice beneficiaries, who can step in if your first-choice beneficiaries die before the trust comes to an end.

You can also have more than one trustee for your trust. Trustees can be humans or they can be trust companies (more about this below under the heading "Choosing a Trustee"), or you can have both together.

And you, the settlor, can be a trustee if you're alive when the trust is created. Then you've really got things wrapped up — you can give yourself instructions about what to do with the property *and* you can carry them out. But no matter how hard a time you're having letting go of worldly things, you cannot be a trustee after you're dead.

## More about the property

Any kind of property can be put into a trust, including a house or cottage or art or musical instruments or racehorses. Settlors usually put into trust property that will produce income in the form of interest, dividends, rent, or royalties, such as:

- Cash from a bank account, from the sale of property, or from the proceeds of an insurance policy
- Shares in a corporation or mutual funds
- Commercial real estate
- Rights to a book, a song, a play, or a movie

## Why Set up a Trust?

If you want to give your property to someone, why not just give it and be done with it? If you read Chapter 8 about giving a gift, you don't need us to answer that question. You'll know some of the things that can go wrong with a gift. Setting up a trust is one answer to the problems that may arise from giving a gift straight out. In addition, only a trust will allow you to keep a specific sum of money or identified property together for a long period of time after your death and to be sure that it is used as you wish.

Trusts are most commonly set up for two particular reasons. The first reason is that the settlor wants to keep the beneficiary or those acting for the beneficiary from having total control over the property either for a period of time or permanently. Read about Estella's expectations for Pip.

### Estella has expectations for Pip

Estella was a wealthy woman who took an interest in her deceased husband's young cousin, Philip (usually known as Pip), who often dropped by to play cards with her. Pip's parents were both dead and Pip's guardians were his sister (who was abusive) and her husband (who was fond of a drink). Estella believed firmly in the value of a good education. She wanted to help Pip, but she was afraid that she might not live until Pip grew up. She also knew that if she gave the money directly to Pip an official of the provincial government would have to manage it until Pip turned 18 (see the "Trust for a Minor" section later in this chapter) and she had little faith in government officials. She had even less faith in Pip's sister and her husband, so she couldn't give the money to them to spend on Pip.

Estella decided to put a sum of money in trust for Pip, and she instructed the trustee to keep the money invested for Pip's benefit (to pay for schooling, voice coaching, rowing lessons, and suitable clothing) until he was 21 years old. Estella also instructed that when Pip turned 21, any money remaining in the trust was to be paid directly to him so that he could take a trip to the former penal colonies of Australia.

### Charlie's trust

Dr. Bruner has two sons, Raymond and Charlie. Raymond makes a good living selling vintage cars, but Charlie is autistic and needs constant professional care and supervision. Doc Bruner wants to make sure that Charlie will be properly looked after whether he (the Doc) is alive or not. So he puts $3 million into a trust and instructs the trustee to use the income, and capital as necessary, to pay for Charlie to live at a very expensive and well-run institution. Since there is no reason to tie up the money after Charlie's death, Doc Bruner instructs the trustee to pay out all money in the trust to Raymond when Charlie dies. If Raymond dies before Charlie, Doc Bruner instructs that the money is to be paid out to his favourite charity, the Wapner Law Foundation.

If the beneficiary is mentally disabled, or simply can't be trusted to handle the money, the settlor may want to keep the beneficiary from ever having control over the property. In that case, the trustee may be instructed to keep the money invested for the benefit of the beneficiary until his or her death, at which time the money and any accumulated income is to be paid to a different beneficiary. Have a look at "Charlie's trust," above.

The second reason for setting up a trust is that the settlor wants one beneficiary to have the use of the property in the short term, but wants another beneficiary to become owner of the property at a later date. Read "Luke's trust for Jackie," on the next page.

# Kinds of Trusts

There are two main types of trusts — *living trusts* and *testamentary trusts*. Testamentary trusts are much more common than living trusts.

A testamentary trust is created in the settlor's will and comes into effect when the settlor dies. The will names the beneficiaries of the trust and the trustee(s) and sets out instructions. The property in a testamentary trust comes from the settlor's estate.

A living trust (also called an *inter vivos* trust — Latin for "between the living") is set up while the settlor is still alive. It comes into effect as soon as the settlor signs a document called a *trust agreement* (which names the beneficiaries and trustee(s) and contains the instructions) and transfers property to the trustee. A living trust can be set up to continue after the settlor's death.

Either kind of trust has to be set up by a lawyer in order to avoid practical, legal, and tax problems.

### Luke's trust for Jackie

Nobody can figure out what Luke does for a living, but he sure does own a lot of blue-chip corporate shares. He wants to make sure that his wife, Jackie (who has recently been diagnosed with cancer), has a comfortable income until she dies if something happens to him, but he also wants to leave some property to his girlfriend, Isabel, in case she needs to buy more cameras. So in his will he has set up a trust for the shares, giving instructions to the trustee to pay any interest and dividends generated by the shares to Jackie during her lifetime, and to hand the shares over to Isabel on Jackie's death.

Both a testamentary and a living trust can be *discretionary*. This means that the trustee is given the power to decide how much income to pay the beneficiary in any year, and may even be given the power to pay out some of the capital of the trust if the income alone isn't enough for the beneficiary's needs. Or a trust can be *non-discretionary*. That means that the trustee can pay out only the specific amounts stated in the document that sets up the trust.

# Testamentary Trusts

Most wills contain some form of testamentary trust. Testamentary trusts come in different flavours. They include:

- A spousal trust — to provide for a spouse until his or her death
- A trust for a minor — to provide for a beneficiary under the age of 18
- A spendthrift trust — to provide for a beneficiary who has trouble handling money responsibly
- A special needs trust — to provide for a beneficiary who is physically or mentally unable to look after his or her own financial affairs
- A pet trust — to provide for a pet until its death
- A trust for a charity — to provide for a family member until his or her death, and then to give the property to a charity

## Spousal trust

When you set up a spousal trust, you instruct the trustee to invest the trust property and pay some or all of the income earned to your spouse until he or she dies. Then the trustee is instructed to give the trust property to someone else, typically your children or grandchildren, or a charity.

You might want to set up a spousal trust (as in "Harry and Sally") if

- Your spouse is unable to look after his or her own financial affairs properly because of illness, disability, or simple lack of knowledge and experience.
- You think that your spouse will remarry, and you want to make sure that the property in your estate will ultimately go to your children and/or grandchildren rather than to your spouse's next spouse.
- You have children from a previous relationship and you want to look after your spouse after you die but you also want to make sure that your estate will ultimately go to your own children and/or grandchildren rather than your spouse's.
- You want to reduce the tax your spouse will pay on the income earned by your estate. (Your spouse and the trust will each file separate income tax returns and each may pay income tax at a lower tax rate than if all of the income were reported on one tax return. See the section "Trusts and Taxes" later in this chapter.)

## Trust for a minor

You should include a trust in your will if you want to leave any of your property to someone who may still be under the age of majority when you die. If you leave property directly to a minor, by law it must be managed by the provincial government until the minor comes of age at 18 or 19, depending on the province.

### Harry and Sally

Harry's first wife died after they had been married for forty years. Two years later, Harry met (and married) Sally, whose husband had died five years before. They have been married for five years now and have been very happy together. Unfortunately, neither Sally nor her children are particularly fond of Harry's children, Marie and Jess. Sally has assured Harry that if he dies first, she will leave anything she gets from Harry to his children. But Harry is worried that after he's gone, Sally's children will persuade her to change her mind and leave everything to them instead. Harry decides to set up a spousal trust in his will and instruct his trustee to pay the annual income from the trust to Sally, with the property of the trust to be divided between Marie and Jess when Sally dies.

In a trust for a minor, you instruct the trustee to invest the trust property and to pay all or part of the income earned by the trust property to the beneficiary until he or she reaches the age of majority (or even older). When the beneficiary reaches the age you specify, the trustee gives the trust property directly to the beneficiary.

The trustee's instructions about the payment of income to the beneficiary can vary. For example, you may instruct the trustee to

- Pay the beneficiary all of the income earned by the trust every year.
- Pay only as much of the income earned by the trust as the trustee believes is appropriate, and to reinvest what's left over.
- Pay out some of the capital if the trustee believes that the beneficiary should be paid more than the trust earns in income in any year.
- Use the income of the trust to pay only certain types of expenses, such as school fees.

The trustee's instructions about turning over the trust property to the beneficiary can also vary. You may instruct the trustee to turn over all of the trust property to the beneficiary as soon as he reaches the age of majority or to wait until the beneficiary is older (and presumably wiser . . . of course he may be wiser about the wrong things). Or the trustee may be instructed to turn over the trust property in stages, for example half when the beneficiary turns 21 and half when she turns 25.

The trustee's instructions must be properly worded or the beneficiary may be able to get a court to order the trustee to turn over all of the property to her as soon as she reaches the age of majority, even though the will says to wait until the beneficiary is older.

## Spendthrift trusts

You might want to set up a spendthrift trust if you want to help support an adult child who has a history of failed business ventures or investments; has problems with gambling, alcohol, or drugs; or who simply has a money-squandering personality.

In a spendthrift trust, you instruct the trustee to invest the trust property and pay some or all of the income earned by the trust property to the beneficiary until the beneficiary dies. At that point the trustee is instructed to give the trust property to someone else, such as the beneficiary's children or a charity. Read about "The Finsbury trust," on the next page.

### The Finsbury trust

Morris Finsbury has two sons, Joseph and Masterman. Masterman is a wealthy and successful businessman. Joseph, on the other hand, has never found a place for himself in the business world. He is more interested in making statistical studies of obscure facts that rarely, if ever, have a commercial pay-off. He and his family manage to survive on the salary of his amazingly patient wife.

Masterman has told Morris that he has enough money and he should not leave any of his estate to him. Morris is concerned that if he leaves his estate outright to Joseph, he will waste it on fact-finding missions. Morris therefore decides to leave his estate in trust for Joseph. He instructs his trustee to keep his estate invested and to pay as much of the income as the trustee thinks is reasonable to Joseph to provide for himself and his family in any year, and to reinvest any income left over. When Joseph dies, the property of the trust is to be paid to his two children, Michael and Julia.

## Special needs trust

In a special needs trust, you instruct the trustee to invest the trust property and use some or all of the income it earns to look after the needs of the beneficiary until the beneficiary dies. When that happens, the trustee is instructed to give the trust property to someone else, such as another family member or a charity.

A special needs trust, like any trust, can be discretionary or non-discretionary — in other words, the settlor (that's you) can state how much is to be paid in any year to the beneficiary or can let the trustee use his own judgment about how much to pay out. But this matter must be given very careful thought if the beneficiary is receiving government assistance or services as a result of his disability. Eligibility for government assistance is usually tied to financial need, and the beneficiary's right to receive income from the special needs trust may put his right to assistance in jeopardy. In some provinces it may be possible for the beneficiary to stay eligible for assistance as long as the trust is discretionary.

If you are thinking about setting up a special needs trust in your will, you should consult with a lawyer who has experience working with people who are disabled and their families.

### Pet trusts

Pet trusts are for pets, but they're really for nervous pet owners. A pet is not an individual like a spouse or a minor child. A pet is property. So you can't leave money directly to a pet for food and vet bills — even if you're sure you could trust your cat to buy tuna instead of cat toys and to make annual appointments for shots.

People who have a pet and have family and friends who are pet people simply give the pet in their will to someone who will look after it, and then they also give a cash gift earmarked for the pet's future expenses. People who aren't sure that their nearest and dearest will look after the pet properly create a pet trust.

In a pet trust, the pet-owner legally gives the pet to a trustee (normally the executor) in his or her will and names a beneficiary who will have custody of the pet. Enough property is also given to the trustee to look after the pet's needs for the rest of its life, and to pay the beneficiary something for taking care of the pet. The trustee is instructed to pay money out to the beneficiary as long as the beneficiary is caring for the pet.

### Trust for a charity

A trust for a charity is any trust in which a charity is named to receive the trust property after the first beneficiary (the beneficiary who was getting the income) dies. We'll tell you more about trusts for charities in Chapter 13.

## Living Trusts

There are a number of ways that people, usually rich people, use living trusts, but only a few of them are directly related to estate planning. The non-estate-planning uses for living trusts include income splitting with family members, funding child support payments on marriage breakdown, and putting public office holders' investments in a blind trust. You don't need to know about that stuff, you only need to know about the estate planning uses of living trusts. These are:

- Creating an estate freeze
- Keeping a gift confidential
- Looking after someone with special needs
- Giving to charity
- Reducing probate fees

It will probably turn out that you don't really need to know about the estate planning uses of living trusts, either, but we're having so much fun here — why stop now?

## Creating an estate freeze

We tell you about estate freezes in Chapter 5. What do you mean, you read it but you've forgotten? Oh all right, we'll go over it again. Estate freezes are used to reduce the capital gains tax payable by the present owner on capital property expected to increase in value. The present owner may have to pay capital gains tax when she transfers the property to someone else, but whoever receives the property (usually a spouse, child, or grandchild) will have to pay the capital gains tax on any future increase in value.

Although you can do an estate freeze by giving the property directly to your children or grandchildren (or to whomever else you may want to have it), if you don't want their sticky fingers all over the property you can put it into trust for them instead.

If you use a trust for an estate freeze, there's a slight variation on the capital gains tax story (see Chapter 4 for the scoop on capital gains tax). When you set up the trust, you will have to pay capital gains tax as if you had sold the property at its fair market value when you handed it over to the trust. That part doesn't change. But afterwards, it could be the beneficiaries who have to pay any future capital gains tax, or it could be the trust itself.

- If the trustee sells the property and keeps the sale money in the trust, the trust will pay the tax.
- If the trustee sells the property and pays the sale money to the beneficiary, the trustee decides whether the trust or the beneficiary will pay the tax.
- When the trust ends and the trustee transfers the property in the trust to the beneficiary, no tax is payable by either the beneficiary or the trust. If the beneficiary afterward sells the property or disposes of it in some other way, the beneficiary is subject to capital gains tax.

If you give income-producing property directly to your spouse, the tax authorities have the power to tax *you* on any interest, dividend, or capital gain from that property in the future. (You can read more about this in Chapter 5.) If you give income-producing property to a child or grandchild under the age of 18, the tax authorities have the power to tax you on any interest or dividend (but *not* capital gain) from that property in the future. These things are also true if you put the income-producing property into a trust. (You have to be much sneakier than you think to get around Canada Revenue. They spend 365 days a year plotting ways to foil sneaky plans.)

## Keeping a gift confidential

Your will becomes a public document when you die. Anyone can ask to see the copy kept at the provincial surrogate court office. Consider *that* when you're obsessively dividing up your teacup or fishing lure collection among your nieces and nephews.

Now maybe you don't have a teacup collection but you do have a mistress. Or a special friend who wears his shirt unbuttoned to the navel to show off his six-pack. Or a child that you never got around to mentioning to your spouse. You'd like to give something to your mistress, friend, or child when you die, but you don't want your family to have a cow when your will is read and you don't want to become a myth in your former neighbourhood as a two-faced swine.

The answer for you is a living trust. If you set up a living trust, the property you put into the trust will never become part of your estate, and nobody except your trustee and the beneficiary needs to know anything about the arrangement. Of course, this is expensive and you may actually prefer to horrify your grieving relatives with your secret life.

## Looking after someone with special needs

A living special needs trust serves exactly the same purpose as a testamentary special needs trust. You may want to set the trust up while you are still alive, to continue after you die. That way you won't be wondering whether the matter will be properly taken care of when you're no longer around to oversee it.

## Giving to charity

It is possible to set up a trust in which you get the income from the trust property for as long as you (and your spouse) are alive and the charity gets the trust property after you (or after you and your spouse) die. This kind of trust is called a *charitable remainder trust.*

Why would you do this? It looks even weirder than the usual run of trusts. Well, you probably *wouldn't* do this.

It's true that you will get a tax credit for the donation when you set up the trust, but the credit is not likely to equal the full value of the property you give. The credit is discounted to take into account the fact that the actual change in ownership will not take place until some time in the future. But of course it's also true that when you put the property into the trust you are deemed to have disposed of it for income tax purposes. If the property has gone up in value since you acquired it, you will have to pay tax on the capital gain. The tax payable on the capital gain may well be greater than the tax credit for the donation.

So why are we even mentioning this dang-fool notion? Some people in Canada try to promote it because it works okay in the United States, where tax laws are different.

### Avoiding probate fees

If you set up a living trust, the property you give to the trust is no longer part of your estate, so it won't be taken into account in calculating your estate's probate fees. (We tell you more about probate fees in Chapter 5.)

But if the property has gone up in value since you acquired it, the saving in probate fees later will probably not be as large as the tax you will have to pay now on the capital gain. So this is kind of a stupid idea — unless you know that the value of the property is really going to take off sky-high between the time you set up the trust and the time you die. This is another scheme that worked better somewhere else. Probate fees aren't very high in Canada, but death duties in some other countries can be crippling.

## A Trustee You Can Trust

When you create a trust, you give ownership of your property to a trustee. This isn't as much of a gamble as you might think. The trustee has the settlor via the trust agreement or will and the provincial government via statute law looking over his, her, or its shoulder. Not to mention the beneficiaries watching like hawks.

### What does a trustee do?

It is the trustee's job to

- Manage the trust property, which might include buying and selling property and making investments.
- Pay out the income of the trust to the beneficiaries and transfer ownership of the property in the trust in accordance with the settlor's instructions.

- Account to the beneficiaries — that is, inform the beneficiaries in writing what property was received from the settlor, what income was earned by the trust property, what profits were made on the sale of trust property, and what money was paid out or what property was given to the beneficiaries. The trustee usually provides accounts when asking to be paid her fee.
- File income tax returns on behalf of the trust every year until the trust is wound up and to pay the tax out of the money in the trust.

## What are the legal responsibilities of a trustee?

A trustee has to

- Follow the settlor's instructions set out in the trust agreement or will.
- Obey provincial laws about trusts.
- Act with the highest level of trust, loyalty, and honesty (sorry if that disqualifies three-quarters of your relatives and half of your friends).
- Handle the property of the estate in the way a reasonably prudent business person would handle his or her own affairs (this probably disqualifies the rest of your friends and relations).
- Act in the best interest of the beneficiaries — and not play favourites if there are some beneficiaries who are entitled to the income from the trust and different ones who are entitled to receive the trust property after the income beneficiaries die.
- Carry out duties personally and not ask someone else to perform them, although a trustee is allowed to get professional advice and assistance.
- Not deal with the property for his or her own personal benefit (for example, not sell herself property that's in the trust unless the trust agreement or will specifically allows that).

A beneficiary can apply to the court to have a trustee removed if the trustee is not carrying out these responsibilities properly, or can sue a dishonest or incompetent trustee for losses the beneficiary has suffered.

Now you know why most people would rather be a settlor, dead or alive, than a trustee. To be a settlor, you just need to have property and someone you want to be nice to. To be a trustee, you need to have the character of a successful capitalist *and* a saint.

## What are the powers of a trustee?

Trustees get their basic powers to act from a provincial statute (called the *Trustees Act* in all provinces other than Quebec, where trust matters are dealt with in the *Civil Code*) and can be given extra powers in the will or trust agreement.

The powers given by the provincial statutes are very limited and conservative. For example, under the statutes, money can be invested only in incredibly boring and uncool things like government securities of Canada or a Canadian province; deposits or guaranteed investment certificates in a Canadian bank, trust company, or credit union; and first mortgages on land in Canada, as long as the mortgage is not for more than 75 percent of the value of the land. The purpose of restrictions like these is to keep the trust property as safe as possible.

If the settlor wants the trustee to rock a little, he can give the trustee broader investment powers in the trust agreement or will. The settlor can also give the trustee the power to decide how and when income from the trust is to be paid, and how and when the property of the trust is to be given to the beneficiaries. Then the trust is a discretionary trust. For settlors who have very controlling personalities ( . . . maybe you should see a therapist about that . . .) there is also the non-discretionary trust. The trust document sets out exactly how much income is to be paid and when, and what property is to be handed over and when, and the trustee has no power to stray from those instructions.

## Choosing a trustee

If you thought it was hard to find a mate, try looking for a trustee. The perfect trustee

- Is honest.
- Has the skill and knowledge to handle the trust investments.
- Has completely trustworthy judgment if you're allowing him or her discretion about the amount and timing of payment.
- Won't favour one beneficiary over another if there is more than one beneficiary.
- Has the time necessary to devote to trustee duties, and will be alive long enough to complete the duties.
- Is willing to take on the job.

A trustee does not have to be good-looking or rich, but what the heck. Might as well add those to the list too.

When you realize that you don't know anyone who meets all of the qualifications to be a perfect trustee (and you don't want to go with whoever is alive and willing in your circle of family and friends), you turn to a professional trustee. It's like looking for the right lover, only professional trustees and professional lovers hang out in different parts of town.

A professional trustee — that is, a *trust company* — may be the answer if

- You have no family member or friend who resides in your province or has enough time to devote to the duties of a trustee.
- The trust property is so valuable or complicated to manage that you need real expertise.
- The trust will last for a long time, for example because the beneficiaries are young children.
- The relationship between the beneficiaries (or between the beneficiaries and the potential human trustee) is so screwed up that it may be difficult for a family member or friend who becomes a trustee not to have a favourite.

You can name more than one person to act as a trustee. You might want to have a trust company as one trustee, and a friend or family member as another. (It might be a good idea to draft your will in such a way that your human trustees can hire a different trust company if they don't like the rates or service of the first one chosen.)

If you name more than one trustee, they have to act unanimously unless the trust agreement or will says they don't. (The trustees are allowed to bicker and whine without special permission.) If your trustees cannot get along, any of them can apply to the court to have one or more of the trustees removed. Setting up a trust is like creating your own soap opera!

If you name a human (as opposed to a trust company) as your trustee, be sure to name someone else as an alternate trustee in case your original trustee becomes unwilling or unable to carry out his or her duties before the trust ends. If you name only one trustee and that trustee dies, the executor of your trustee's will becomes trustee of your trust. And you have no idea where your trustee's executor might have been or what diseases he might have picked up along the way.

## Paying a trustee

Trustees are entitled to be paid, and the amount they get paid is set by the provincial statute governing trustees. Depending on the province, a trustee is usually entitled to an annual management fee that's a percentage (up to 6 percent) of the value of the trust property, and to additional fees calculated as a percentage (usually between 5 and 6 percent) of the income the trust earns. A trustee is also usually allowed to charge an additional fee for preparing the trust's annual income tax return. The actual amount of the trustee's fees will depend on how complicated the trust is and how much work is involved.

What happens in practice is that the trustee makes up a bill showing what she's entitled to be paid and why, and shows it to the beneficiaries. If they don't like what they see they can argue with the trustee, and if that doesn't work they can ask a court to look the bill over and decide if the amount is fair.

Family members or friends who act as trustees often waive their fees. Professional trustees, on the other hand, have a minimum annual fee, typically about $2,500. A trust company charges fees for its services over and above the compensation a trustee is entitled to claim under provincial trust legislation.

# Trusts and Taxes

Have you noticed that we manage to drag taxes into almost every single chapter, just to torture you? As if trusts weren't torture enough even without tax implications! Well, grit your teeth and let's get this over with. Taxes can raise their ugly heads at three points during the existence of a trust:

- On the creation of the trust (when the settlor transfers property into the trust)
- During the operation of the trust
- On the termination of the trust (when the trustee transfers the property in the trust to the beneficiaries)

## On the creation of the trust

You've probably already guessed by now . . . when you decide to create a trust, the thought has hardly entered your mind before you've got Canada Revenue breathing down your neck.

### Tax on the settlor

If the trust is a testamentary trust (in your will, remember?), the transfer into the trust takes place on your death. As we tell you in Chapter 4, Canadian tax law says that when you die you "dispose" of all of your property immediately before death and get its fair market value at the time. If the property has gone up in value since you acquired it, there's a taxable capital gain. The estate pays the tax on any capital gain (only because Canada Revenue hasn't yet found a way to follow taxpayers into the afterlife — but they're working on that).

If the trust is a living trust, tax law says that you dispose of the property to the trust for a price equal to its fair market value at the time. If the property has gone up in value since you acquired it, there's a taxable capital gain. You pay the tax. It's a drag, but look at it this way. It's a small price to pay for still being alive.

And now, ladies and gentlemen, back by popular demand — the spousal rollover! (Wild applause. See Chapter 4 if you've never heard of it.) Whether you're setting up either a testamentary trust or a living trust, you can avoid the dread spectre of capital gains tax if the trust is for the benefit of your spouse, *and* your spouse is entitled to receive all of the income of the trust, *and* no one other than your spouse is entitled to receive or use income or capital of the trust as long as your spouse is alive. If you create the trust this way, neither you (if you're alive when the trust comes into existence) nor your estate (if you're dead) will have to pay capital gains tax. That's because the trust steps into the shoes of the settlor and gets the property at the settlor's original adjusted cost base — so there's no capital gain to pay tax on.

## During the operation of the trust

Canada Revenue is only getting started when it dings the settlor or the estate for capital gains tax on creation of the trust. Next it settles down to slurp up some income tax . . . from everyone in sight.

### Tax on the settlor

If you create a living trust and give income-producing property to your spouse, Canada Revenue has the power to attribute to you both the income and capital gains the property earns in the future. The tax authorities can make you, the settlor, pay tax on the trust's income or capital gains.

If you create a living trust for children or grandchildren under the age of 18, Canada Revenue has the power to attribute income but not capital gains to you. So the settlor, you, can be made to pay tax on the trust's income.

Being taxed on attributed income is probably not enough to make you wish you were dead, but if you *do* happen to be dead there is no attribution of income or capital gains. The attribution rule doesn't apply to a testamentary trust — if income tax is payable, it will have to be squeezed out of the trust or the beneficiaries.

### Tax on the trust

A trust is a taxpayer, and it has to file an income tax return annually, declaring its income and capital gains. It can deduct certain expenses, including interest paid (if the estate borrowed money to invest in income-producing property such as shares, bonds, or rental property), investment management and accounting fees, and amounts paid to maintain trust property (for example, to re-roof a house held in the trust). However, unlike an individual (human) taxpayer, a trust cannot claim any personal tax credits except a credit for charitable deductions.

Testamentary trusts pay taxes at the same rate as individuals. (You can acquaint yourself with the tax-bracket system in Chapter 4.) But here we finally have some good news for you about taxes. A testamentary trust is a good way to split income for tax purposes. The beneficiary of the trust and the trust will each file separate income tax returns, and each may pay income tax at a lower tax rate than if all of the income were reported in one tax return. This translates into a lower tax bill than if the income earned on the estate property were taxed directly in the hands of the beneficiary (where it would be taxed along with his or her income from other sources).

Unlike a testamentary trust, a living trust is taxed on its entire taxable income at the highest marginal tax rate, which is about 50 percent, and so is not as useful for income-splitting purposes.

### Tax on the beneficiaries

Income earned by the trust property doesn't necessarily have to stick around in the trust to get taxed. If money received by the trust is paid out or payable to a beneficiary, the trustee can either declare that money as income in the trust's annual tax return or can issue a T3 slip to the beneficiary.

If the trustee chooses the first route, the trust pays any tax that's due. If the trustee chooses the second route, the beneficiary includes the money in his or her own return and pays any applicable tax. This sounds like a good reason for the beneficiaries to stay on the right side of the trustee. The trustee normally decides who should pay the tax based on which choice results in the lowest combined tax bill for the trust and the beneficiary.

## When your trust comes of age at 21

Under Canadian tax laws, trusts are deemed to dispose of all of their capital property at fair market value 21 years after the creation of the trust, and then every 21 years after that. The purpose of this rule is to prevent taxpayers from (oh, horrors!) using trusts to put off paying capital gains tax indefinitely.

### Tax on the trust

Happy birthday, dear trust, happy birthday to you! Or maybe we should say Trick or treat, shell out! Because if capital property in the trust has risen in value during the 21-year period since the trust was created, the trust has to pay tax on any capital gain.

## On the termination of the trust

When the trust ends and the trustee transfers the property to the capital beneficiary, no tax is payable by the settlor or the estate or the trustee or the beneficiaries. Everyone just walks out into the sunshine and goes tripping through the daisies.

Foolish reader! Don't you know there is no escape?

### Tax on the beneficiaries . . . later

On termination of the trust, the beneficiary takes over the property at the trust's adjusted cost base. That means that from Canada Revenue's point of view, the beneficiary acquired the property for whatever its cost when the trust acquired it, whether it came directly from the settlor or was bought by the trust afterwards. When the beneficiary disposes of the property that came from the trust, the beneficiary is taxed on any increase in value of the property from the time it came into the trust.

# The Care and Feeding of a Trust

We've finished talking about taxes . . . for now . . . and you should be eternally grateful for that. But we're going to continue to harp on the unpleasant subject of spending money. It will cost you to set up a trust, to maintain it, and to wind it up.

## Set-up fees

The main expenses in setting up a trust are legal fees, although for variety there may be some accounting fees too. You'll need advice on the tax implications of setting up your trust, and you'll have to have the trust documents drafted (a trust agreement for a living trust, and a will for a testamentary trust). You (if this is a living trust) or your estate (if this is a testamentary trust) may have to pay additional legal fees to transfer the trust property into the name of the trustee. As a rule of thumb, it's more expensive to set up a living trust than a testamentary trust.

## Ongoing fees

A trust has continuing expenses, which are paid out of the property in the trust. Not all of these expenses are applicable to every trust every year, of course, but here they are:

- Trustee's fees
- Lawyer's fees for legal advice
- Accountant's fees for accounting or financial advice and for accounting to the beneficiaries
- Broker's commissions on investments
- Safety deposit box rental

## Winding-up fees

A trustee is entitled to be paid a fee for transferring the property of the trust to the capital beneficiaries when the trust comes to an end. This fee is calculated as a percentage (usually between 1 and 2.5 percent) of the value of the trust property.

There may be lawyer's fees for transferring ownership of the trust property (such as a house, vehicle, or corporate shares, but not usually cash) to the beneficiaries.

There is no charge to you for winding up this chapter. If you enjoyed it as much as we did, feel free to read it again. No charge for a second reading either.

# Part III

# Creating an Estate Plan

"Okay, you can call him Ben. But only we'll know it's short for Beneficiary."

## In this part . . .

This part starts you off — at last! — on the process of planning your own estate. We help you choose people to give your property away to (your *beneficiaries*) and a person to manage your estate after your death until all the property has been given away (your *executor*). We tell you how to make arrangements to look after your young children after your death, how to pass on your business, and how to express your charitable feelings. We finish this part off by telling you how to plan your own funeral and (as if that's not enough) also your organ donation.

# Chapter 10

# A Crew for Your Ship of Estate: Beneficiaries and Executor

### *In This Chapter*

- Deciding whom you want to provide for after you're gone
- Deciding whom you are required to provide for after you're gone
- Figuring out the best way to do the providing
- Understanding what an executor does
- Choosing your executor

Captain on the bridge! That's you, the captain of your ship of estate.

In the preceding chapters we tell you about the reasons for estate planning, income tax concerns, and the main estate planning tools. If you've read them, your response was probably a hearty yo ho ho, and a bottle of rum. Now it's time to start using what you've learned . . . perhaps learned painfully (rum will do that to you) . . . and begin to create an estate plan.

The first step will be to assemble a crew for your estate — your *beneficiaries* (the people you will provide for in your estate plan) and your *executor* (the person who will manage your estate after you've sailed into the sunset).

## Your Beneficiaries

When you die, you have to give away everything you own. That means figuring out whom to give it to. This is the fun part of estate planning — you can reward those who've been good to you and punish those who haven't by giving a gift here, withholding a gift there. Some people make a hobby out of picking their beneficiaries and they revise their choices on an almost daily basis, according to who has pleased them or ticked them off most recently.

Not everyone can afford the fantasy of planning their estate just to get even with their family, friends, and acquaintances. Most people have obligations, and those obligations may extend past the end of life. Sometimes feelings and obligations match exactly — then Bingo! you choose a beneficiary without any trouble at all. But in other cases the feelings and obligations are completely at odds (feelings: good, obligation: none; or feelings: bad, obligation: heavy) and it becomes more difficult to make choices. In this section we're going to help you think about how to choose your beneficiaries, possibly including some people you wish were at the bottom of the sea.

In choosing your beneficiaries — and in deciding what to give them — you're going to have to consider

- Whom you really want to provide for *and* whom you merely have to provide for
- Your reason for providing for them
- The best way to do the providing

## The people you want to provide for

Unless you have the misfortune to come from a 100-percent dysfunctional family, it won't be difficult to settle on the people you actually *want* to give your money and belongings to. (And if you do hate everyone you know and would be keelhauled before you gave any of them a nickel, with luck you'll be able to leave everything to charity — preferably one that will really get up their noses.)

### Rounding up the usual suspects

Take a look around you to see the beneficiaries whom you'll want to provide for. They're the people you live with or spend your time with. As we mention in Chapter 1, who these people are may vary with your stage of life:

- When you're young and single, they're parents, brothers and sisters, friends, a charity, or a combination of these.
- When you marry or settle into a serious relationship, it will probably be your spouse or partner whom you want to get all or most of what you own.
- When you have young children, they'll likely be first in your mind.
- If you divorce, your children or other relatives will be at the top of the list and your former spouse may be right off it.
- Once your children are grown up and self-sufficient, grandchildren or a favourite charity may attract your attention.

### What's your reason for giving?

There are many different reasons to include certain family members or friends in your estate plan. The particular reason you have in each case will affect what you decide to give and how you go about giving it.

You may want to include someone in your estate plan in order to

- Provide ongoing support. Your spouse or children, or some other relative or friend, may need your financial assistance. It may take the bulk of your estate to do it.
- Help meet a particular goal. Finishing a university degree, starting a business, or buying a house requires cash. A gift of a specific amount of money will do the trick.
- Say thank you. An employee may have been very loyal, or a friend may have been especially kind when you were sick or in some kind of trouble. A gift of money or one of your personal possessions may be the answer.
- Pass on a family heirloom. You may have received furniture, photographs, or papers from your parents or grandparents that have been in the family for generations or that have special significance for your family. You'd like the heirloom to go to a relative who will value it and pass it on in turn.
- Leave a memento. A family member may have admired a piece of your jewellery or a friend may have shared your passion for collecting belly dancer figurines. A gift of a particular item would be appropriate.
- Show that he or she was in your thoughts. A gift of one of your personal possessions or a small sum of money will be appreciated.

### What's the right tool for making the gift?

The most obvious way to give to your survivors is to leave money or property in your will. But, as we say in Chapter 1, there are other ways of providing:

- Life insurance: You can name someone as beneficiary of a life insurance policy and your beneficiary will receive the insurance proceeds directly (see Chapters 6 and 7).
- RRSPs and RRIFs: You can name someone as beneficiary of your RRSP or RRIF and your beneficiary will receive the RRSP/RRIF proceeds directly (see Chapter 5).
- Pension plans: If you are a member of an employee pension plan, you may be able to name a beneficiary to receive a pension after your death or a one-time payment (see Chapter 6).
- Joint ownership of property: If you own property jointly with another person, when you die your share in the property will automatically pass to the surviving owner, without your having to mention the property in your will.

That's the how. Now what about the when? When do you want the person to get the money or property? Timing will also affect your choice of estate planning tool. You may want to provide for someone

- While you're alive: That means a gift (see Chapter 8) or a living trust (see Chapter 9).
- Immediately after your death: That means making a gift in your will (see Chapters 15 and 16) or naming the person as a beneficiary of your life insurance policy (see Chapter 6) or your RRSP or RRIF (see Chapter 5).
- After you die but not until someone else also dies: You may want your children to inherit your property, for example, but not until after the death of your spouse. That means setting up a trust in your will (see Chapter 9) to give your spouse the use of the property during his or her lifetime, and to hand the property over to your children when your spouse dies.
- After you die but not until the person reaches a certain age: You may not want your children to have total control over the inherited property until they are 25 years old, for example. That means setting up a trust in your will to keep your money invested for your children until they turn 25, and then to give them the property outright.

### Should you give to children directly or indirectly?

If you have children under the age of majority to deal with, there are some special concerns. You must decide whether to provide for them by making a gift to the children themselves or by making a gift to their parents (and benefitting the children by a trickle-down effect).

If you are married with young children, you certainly want to make sure that your children are supported after you die, but that doesn't necessarily mean that you have to give money to them directly by naming them as beneficiaries of your will and/or insurance policies. You can achieve your purpose by leaving your estate to your spouse, who will use it to support your children.

If you're dubious about what your spouse will do with the money, then you must name your children as beneficiaries to make sure that they are provided for. But if you want to leave money for your children, you must set up a trust in your will that will invest the money for the children, pay out income and capital as necessary, and turn the entire fund over to the children when they grow up. (See Chapter 11 for more about children and trusts.)

If you give a large sum of money directly to a minor child (under age 18 or 19, depending on the province), the provincial government will step in and put the money into a trust. The trust will be managed by a government official (called the *public trustee* in most provinces) and turned over to the child when he or she comes of age. Many people aren't all that keen on the way the provincial government manages their tax dollars and would be less than thrilled to have the government managing their personal money.

If you have grandchildren, nephews and nieces, or other children whose lot in life you'd like to improve, the question still arises — do you want them to benefit directly or indirectly? If you want the child to have a direct benefit, you can make a gift to be held in trust until the child comes of age. Have a look at the example of "Fletcher's *Mutiny*."

If you have education in mind, you can even set up a Registered Education Savings Plan to help out the child with university or college expenses (see Chapter 8). If you think it would be better to benefit the child indirectly, you can give a gift to the child's parents and make the entire family's finances healthier.

## The people you have to provide for

There are some people in your life whom you see more as ballast than crew. They're the people you have to provide for even though you may not want to — they have to be in your estate plan too.

You may think that you can do what you like with your property when you make your will, but you're wrong. For centuries, people making wills could do pretty much what they wanted — they had the *right of testamentary freedom.*

### Fletcher's *Mutiny*

William, an avid sailor, decided that his little nephew, Fletcher, should eventually inherit his beloved yacht, *Mutiny.* William intended to teach Fletcher to sail and navigate as he grew up so that he would be ready to take over *Mutiny* when he came of age. However, William saw a little flaw in this plan. He was about to set out on a solo voyage across the South Pacific in an open boat equipped with only a compass, a fishing line, and a few bottles of fresh water, and there was a slight possibility that he might never return from the trip. In the event that he went down with his ship, William's first thought was to leave money for sailing lessons to Fletcher's parents in his will together with the yacht, which Fletcher would take over when he was older. But Fletcher's parents were obsessed with their breadfruit investments and would almost certainly wind up spending some or all of the money and maybe even selling the yacht for investment capital.

The solution? William can set up a trust in his will. The trust could contain both the yacht and capital to pay for Fletcher's sailing lessons. When Fletcher comes of age, the trustee can transfer ownership of the yacht into Fletcher's name and give Fletcher any money left in the trust fund.

However, since the early years of the 20th century, certain limits have been placed on that freedom. Nowadays when you're making plans, you have to take into account the possibility that, once you've passed on, claims will be made against your estate by

- People who are dependent on you for support
- Your spouse
- People you've promised to provide for

### People who are dependent on you for support

Have you been giving money to certain family members or old pals for years and think it's high time they stood on their own two feet? So far you've never been able to work up the nerve to tell them you're turning off the tap, but you're looking forward to doing just that in your will. Well, we have some bad news for you — death is no certain escape from those relatives and friends who have attached themselves to you like barnacles.

Whatever province you live in, there is a law to make sure that your *dependants* — certain people you are required by law to support — will be looked after out of your estate.

The definition of a dependant varies from province to province. In some provinces only children or legally married spouses can be considered dependants. In other provinces unmarried spouses, parents, grandparents, or siblings can also qualify as dependants.

A person won't necessarily be considered a dependant just because he or she is related to you. The person must also be someone whom you were supporting (or under a legal obligation to support) at the time of your death. Likewise, a person won't be considered a dependant just because you were supporting him or her before you died. There must also be a recognized relationship between the two of you.

For example, your deadbeat friend who has been sleeping on your basement sofa and whose car loan you have been paying for the last six months would not qualify as a dependant. But your own child under the age of majority would qualify as a dependant whether or not you are providing support for him or her.

Provincial law allows a dependant to make a claim for support from your estate if you do not leave him or her enough money in your will. A judge would decide whether to provide for a dependant out of your estate by looking at things such as that person's other sources of income and ability to earn a living.

Dependants are given a fixed period of time, usually six months, in which to make a claim by starting a court action. Your executor cannot legally start giving your estate away to your chosen beneficiaries until the time limit for these claims has passed and no claim has been made.

Once someone has made a claim, your executor will not be allowed to give anything to your beneficiaries without first getting a court order, or else getting the consent in writing of everyone who has the right to make a claim against your estate as a dependant. If your executor does give any of your estate to your beneficiaries without consent or a court order, the executor could really land in the drink. He or she may personally have to pay the dependant if there's not enough money left in the estate.

If you have been supporting someone, or know or think that you have a legal obligation to support someone, tell your lawyer when you're making your will. Your lawyer can determine whether or not that person has the right to make a claim against your estate as a dependant. If the person does have a right, you should probably leave enough money in your will to support him or her. (Your lawyer will be able to help you figure out how much that is.)

There's not much to be gained by trying to leave a dependant out of your will. A dependant with any gumption will get the money out of your estate anyway — and your other beneficiaries won't get anything until the claim has been dealt with.

### Your spouse

In addition to being able to make a claim against you as a dependant, in some provinces your spouse may have rights to claim a minimum share of your estate. Some provinces have passed family law legislation that is designed to give a surviving spouse the same rights to a division of property that a spouse would have on a marriage breakdown. So if you're thinking that death would be a cheaper escape from your marriage than divorce, think again.

Like dependants, your spouse has a fixed period of time, usually six months, in which to make a claim by starting a court action. Your executor can't legally give any of your estate to your chosen beneficiaries until the time limit has passed without a claim, unless your spouse consents. If your spouse does make a claim, your executor will not be allowed to give anything to your beneficiaries until his or her claim is settled, unless your spouse consents. If your executor does give any of your estate to your beneficiaries without consent, the executor may personally have to pay some or all of any amount a court later awards to your spouse.

It looks like "'til death do us part" is a bit off the mark, doesn't it? Even if you're looking forward to death as a way of fleeing the clutches and financial demands of your spouse, if you live in a province that gives spouses a right to a share of an estate you have to leave your spouse the required amount.

When you talk to your lawyer about making your will, your lawyer will ask if you are married or separated. He or she will tell you whether or not your spouse has the right to make a claim for a share in your estate. If your spouse does have a right, you'll probably have to leave him or her enough money to satisfy it. (Again, your lawyer will be able to help you figure out how much that is.) As with your dependent relatives, there's little to be gained by trying to leave your spouse out of your will.

### People you've promised to provide for

Generally speaking, if you promise a person that you'll make a provision in your estate, he or she can't force your estate to carry through on your promise. That only goes for ordinary, run-of-the-mill promises, though. If your promise is contained in a contract, the person to whom you made the promise may be able to make a claim against your estate.

This kind of promise is most commonly found in separation agreements. A separation agreement may contain a promise by one of the spouses that

- His or her estate will continue to make support payments to a spouse and/or children. If you have made this kind of promise, you should make sure that you earmarked enough money in your estate for support payments. (Your lawyer will probably suggest that in your will you give your executor the right to try to negotiate a one-time payment to replace ongoing payments.)
- He or she will maintain a life insurance policy in a specific amount naming the spouse and/or children as beneficiaries, failing which the estate will be required to pay a fixed amount of money to the spouse and/or children. If you have made this kind of promise, you should make sure that you've got that life insurance in place!

If you have signed a separation agreement, show it to your lawyer when you go to talk about preparing your will.

## The people you decided not to provide for

Finally, there are people in your life who've walked the plank — these are the people you don't want to give anything to, don't legally have to give anything to, and don't intend to give anything to. In your estate plan you should pay attention to them as well.

What if you don't want to leave anything to someone who is a close relative? You've got your reasons. Perhaps you've already given a gift of money or property, or you believe that he or she doesn't need your money and property but other relatives do. Maybe you once made a substantial loan that was never repaid. Or maybe you just can't stand this person and the two of you have been quarrelling for years.

A close relative who feels entitled to be included in your will may be tempted to go to court to try to have your will set aside after your death. If your will does get set aside, then you have no valid will — and provincial rules about who shares in your estate if you die without a valid will (that is, if you die *intestate*) take effect (see Chapter 15). Depending on how close this relative is and what other relatives survive you, he or she might manage to get a chunk of your property. Learn from "Captain Adams' mistake."

It may be a wise idea to give an explanation in your will if you are leaving a close relative little or nothing. If you don't say anything at all about this person, the troublemaker could argue to the court that failing to remember him or her at all was evidence that your mind was in tatters when you made your will. If you mention the person and give a reason for cutting him or her out, it will make an attack from that quarter more difficult.

# Your Executor

You get to be captain on your ship of estate, but you need someone to carry out your orders when you're down in Davy Jones's locker. That's what your executor is for.

It will give you a jaunty, nautical air if you refer to your executor as your "XO" (no it doesn't mean love and kisses, it stands for Executive Officer). Or possibly it may send your family looking for your power of attorney and living will, convinced that you are no longer mentally capable of managing your own affairs.

## Captain Adams' mistake

Captain Adams, a widower, had two sons, Krill and Strannix. Because of their abusive behaviour towards him (maybe they would have turned out better if he hadn't given them such weird names), he had little to do with them after they grew up. He decided that he would make the beneficiaries of his estate his cook and his housekeeper, Casey and Jordan. He said nothing about his sons in his will, and after his death they challenged the will on the ground that he was not of sound mind when he made it. They pointed to the fact that he left nothing to his only relatives, and instead gave it all to two unrelated people who were living with him and had had an opportunity to influence his decision for their own benefit. The court agreed and set aside the will. In Captain Adams' province, if a person dies intestate and has children but no legally married spouse, the entire estate is divided equally among the children. So Krill and Strannix got all of their father's estate. To show there were no hard feelings, Casey offered them a cruise with dinner, and they graciously accepted.

## What does an executor do?

Before you can decide whom to name as your executor, you should know what it is your executor will have to do. Not everyone is cut out to be an executor, so you'll want to choose yours carefully.

Your executor (called a *liquidator* in Quebec and an *estate trustee with a will* in Ontario) must

- Make your funeral arrangements. An executor usually checks to see if you left any instructions and consults with the family about what you might have liked, but the executor has the legal responsibility to make your funeral arrangements and has the final say about them.
- Collect information about your estate. Your executor has to get a reasonable amount of information about the property you own and your debts (including the approximate value of both) in order to apply for letters probate, and locate and gather in your property.
- Protect the property of your estate. Your executor has to make sure that valuables (house, car, jewellery, artwork, and so on) are kept safe, and that the property of the estate is properly insured. If you leave behind a business or investments that need active attention, your executor has to look after them personally or else hire a skillful person to manage them.
- Apply, if necessary, for *letters probate* (known in Ontario as a *certificate of appointment of estate trustee with a will*). In order to administer your estate, your executor must be able to prove to the world that he or she has the legal authority to do so. The best proof is letters probate, a document from the provincial surrogate or probate court certifying that your will is valid. (Your executor may or may not have to apply for letters probate depending on the size and complexity of your estate. We tell you a bit more about this in Chapter 5.) In order to get letters probate, your executor will have to estimate the value of your estate and have the estate pay probate fees (in almost all provinces, probate fees are based on the total value of your estate).
- Gather in the property belonging to your estate. Your executor will have to track down everything that you owned and that now belongs to the estate, and, if necessary, transfer the registration of things that were in your name into the estate's name (real estate, vehicles, bank accounts, investments). Property that your executor must track down includes insurance proceeds, pension benefits, and survivors' benefits that are owed to your family.
- Make an inventory of the property in your estate and value the property. Your executor has to have a reasonably good idea of the value of your estate in order to get letters probate. But in order to complete your terminal tax return, your executor will have to know your exact income

in the year you died as well as the exact present value of your capital property *and* its value when you got it (for capital gains tax calculations). See Chapter 4 for more on capital gains taxes.

- Keep the money and investments in your estate properly invested. Your executor has to stash your cash in a safe place until he or she pays the estate's debts and taxes and distributes the remainder of the estate to the beneficiaries. An executor has to choose conservative, low-risk investments unless you give special instructions in your will (for example, that playing the futures market or day trading is okay). Your beneficiaries can sue your executor for making bad investments and reducing the value of the estate before it's given to them.
- Pay debts and taxes. Your executor must find out whom you owed money to (your creditors) and then pay them, and must also file your terminal income tax return and any outstanding past returns (and, as time passes, estate tax returns) and pay income taxes due. All payments come out of the estate, not the executor's pocket.
- Distribute your estate to the beneficiaries. Your executor has to hand over the property in your estate to your beneficiaries, following the instructions in your will. If your will creates a trust naming your executor the trustee, he or she will continue to hold onto the trust property and manage it on behalf of the beneficiaries of the trust, in accordance with the instructions in the will.
- Account to the beneficiaries. Your executor will have to give a statement to the beneficiaries that sets out what money and property were received and paid out on behalf of your estate.

## What are the legal responsibilities of an executor?

Your executor is a kind of trustee (we talk about trustees in Chapter 9) who must

- Follow the instructions set out in your will.
- Obey provincial laws about trusts.
- Act with the greatest trust, loyalty, and honesty.
- Deal with the property of the estate the same way a reasonably prudent businessperson would handle his or her own property.
- Act in the best interests of the beneficiaries and not favour some beneficiaries over others.

- Carry out duties personally and not pass them off to someone else (although it's okay for the executor to have professionals working for him or her, such as having a lawyer get letters probate or an accountant prepare tax returns or a broker give investment advice).
- Not try to make a personal profit from the estate or get a good deal for himself or herself on property from the estate.

## Choosing your executor

So far what you know about an executor is this: An executor has to perform fairly complex tasks like arranging your funeral and looking after and valuing real estate, investments, and personal possessions; has to manage the finances of your estate; has to deal with a lawyer or a court office to get letters probate; has to keep track of everything that comes into and goes out of your estate; and has to make sure your beneficiaries get what you want them to get. And an executor has to do all these things with honesty and loyalty, and do them as well as a reasonably careful businessperson would do them when dealing with his or her own property. (Read Chapter 17 to find out what can go wrong if you choose the wrong executor.)

Clearly, acting as an executor is not going to be as easy as falling out of a crow's nest. That means you don't want to choose someone who's going to have trouble fulfilling the role because his or her business or management skills are too limited to deal with the kind of property you're leaving. You also don't want to choose someone who won't want the job (a person named as executor doesn't have to accept) or who doesn't have time to do it. Likewise you'd prefer to avoid someone who's not likely to last as long as your estate — if you set up a trust for young children, for example, you don't want to name an executor who has one foot in the grave. Last but not least, you don't want an executor who's going to have trouble getting along with one or more of the beneficiaries, or who might find it hard to treat certain beneficiaries fairly.

Have a look at your potential crew members. Does anyone there fill the bill? There's no need to panic just because your family and friends are normal human beings instead of lawyers, accountants, bankers, or entrepreneurs. Most executors do not administer the estate all on their own. They hire a lawyer and perhaps an accountant to carry out many of these tasks. So if your estate is relatively simple, anyone who is honest and has good common sense and at least enough sophistication to work with a lawyer and/or accountant can be your executor.

If you think it will take more than one person to handle the challenge, you can name two or more individuals as co-executors. If your estate is complex, you can name a trust company such as Royal Trust or Canada Trust (their services may be expensive) as your executor, or as a co-executor with an individual. If you decide to go for co-executors, though, keep in mind that they have to act unanimously unless you say in your will that they don't. Then think about which would be worse — requiring your executors to agree about everything, or letting each one act alone?

Oh, and by the way, you should think about naming an alternate executor, especially if you've chosen to go with a single executor. If you don't name an alternate executor and the executor who's your only choice dies before you or refuses to act, someone will have to come forward and apply to the court to be made the administrator of your estate. If your executor dies after you and you haven't named an alternate executor, your executor's executor will become your executor.

### What to do with an executor who's a landlubber

Suppose you feel that you have to name some particular person as your executor in order to avoid hurting his or her feelings deeply, even though he or she isn't quite up to the job. Your spouse, for example, might be very offended at being rejected for the post.

You can take steps while you're alive or in your will to help the landlubber executor — throw a lifeline, as it were. For example, you can pair this executor with a more skilled and experienced executor by naming a more business-savvy friend or relative as co-executor. If your estate is complicated and has enough money to pay the extra fees involved, you can name a trust company, or a professional like your lawyer or accountant, as co-executor. Or you could start introducing your executor to your affairs gradually while you're alive and well (and hope you don't kick off before the executor gets the hang of them). You could also put together a team of professional advisers (lawyer, financial consultant, accountant, broker) and let your executor know they'll be available to help when the time comes.

## All Hands on Deck

Now you're ready to start signing on the crew. At this point, you can make a fairly realistic list of your beneficiaries and potential executors.

## Beneficiaries

Write down the names of the people you want to provide for, the people you legally have to provide for, and the people you can safely cut out of your will. Next to each name, note roughly how much that person needs from you or can extract from you under provincial law. If you're leaving a close relative out, briefly explain why.

Then, perhaps with your inventory from Chapter 2 in hand, suggest where the required amount for each person is going to come from: your property (be specific if you can, for example, "cottage," "mutual funds," or "RRSP"), an insurance policy, or pension benefits. You can also think about whether your gift should be given while you're alive or in your will.

Take this list with you when you meet your lawyer to talk about preparing your will. Your lawyer will help you fine tune your instructions to take into account the nasty tricks that debts and taxes can play on your choices.

## Executors

If you know a couple of people who would do a good job, great. You could name them as co-executors or as a first choice and an alternate. If you've got weak candidates, see how you could mix and match them to create a stronger team. If your estate is complicated and none of your friends or relatives is up to the job alone, consider pairing a family member who would really want the assignment with one of your professional advisers or with a trust company.

Once you've made a choice, speak to the person you've chosen and ask if he or she would agree to be your executor. If the person says, "I don't know anything about being an executor," hand over this chapter to read and then ask again. If the person of your choice says no, move on to someone else.

# Chapter 11

# Who's Minding the Kids? Planning Your Children's Future

### In This Chapter

- Knowing what will happen to your children after your death if you make no plans
- Choosing someone to look after your children if you die
- Finding out about the duties of a testamentary guardian
- Figuring out how to support your children financially after your death
- Finding out about the duties of a trustee if you set up a trust for your children
- Deciding where your children will live once you're gone

Once upon a time there was a poor but honest woodcutter who lived at the edge of a deep, dark forest. He and his wife and their two children were very happy. One day his wife died, but the woodcutter and his children, although they grieved, were still reasonably happy. To make them all happier, the woodcutter remarried, and now the children had a stepmother. Then the woodcutter died. The stepmother found the woodcutter's small bag of gold, which was all he had to leave to his children, and decided she would not share the gold. So she turned the children out of the house and they wandered weeping in the forest, hungry, cold, and afraid. After a time they came upon a delightful cottage made of gingerbread and candy. Because they were so hungry, they started breaking off bits of the cottage and eating them. The owner of the cottage, a wicked witch, came out to see who was snacking. When she saw it was two tender young children, she brought them inside and cooked them for her dinner. The end.

Fairy tales were scary when you were a kid, even when they had a happy ending. Now that you have kids yourself, some of the fairy tales are even scarier because you find it harder to believe in the happy ending. And the scariest of all fairy tales are the ones about orphaned children.

It won't help to hide under the covers or to ask for a night light to be left on. You might as well know what will happen to your children under the age of majority if you die before them — and what you can do to try to make sure they'll be safe and well cared for even though you're not there.

# Once upon a Time . . .

Before we get into what will happen to the kids when you die, we're going to tell you what the law says about who cares for the kids when their parents are still alive. This will delay the stuff about orphans, which you really don't want to hear about, and make it easier to understand when we get there.

In every province, both living parents are the *guardians* of their children. That means that they are both responsible for caring for the children and they both have the right to make decisions about how the children are raised — where they should live, what religion they should be raised in, where they should go to school, and what medical treatment they should have.

This two-parents, two-guardians arrangement is hunky-dory if both parents live together. Things get a little less hunky-dory and a little more complicated if the parents are separated or divorced. Then they will have to agree who will have *custody* of the children.

Custody and guardianship mean pretty much the same thing. The person who has custody of the children is the person with whom the children live and who cares for the children and makes the decisions that affect their lives. (This can be viewed as a responsibility or a privilege, depending on how your day has gone so far. By the way, what was that crashing noise coming from the kitchen?) The parents may agree that they will continue to share custody in some way — such as *joint custody*, which allows both parents to have a say in how the children are raised — or they may agree that only one of them will have custody.

If separated parents can't come to an agreement about custody, the courts will decide for them. Judges often prefer joint custody arrangements. If that's impossible because the parents won't cooperate, judges make their decisions by assuming that both parents have an equal right to care for their children but that custody should go to the one who can care for them best.

# The Story Takes a Grimm Turn

We can't put the scary part off any longer because this is a book about wills and estate planning, not about baby and child care. Now we're going to tell you what will happen to your kids following your death if you make no plans for their care. We'll start off with the least upsetting scenario, but matters will rapidly go downhill after that.

What happens to the children on the death of the first parent depends on the custody arrangements that existed beforehand.

## If one parent dies but the other is still alive and has custody

If the parents were sharing custody — either because they were living together as a family, or because, although separated or divorced, they had agreed to a joint custody arrangement, or because a court had ordered a joint custody arrangement — the surviving parent simply carries on as sole guardian of the children.

## If one parent dies and that parent had sole custody

If the parent who died had sole custody of the children, there are a number of things that could happen:

- Someone, perhaps the surviving parent, the new spouse of the parent who died, or a grandparent will come forward and offer to look after the children.
- More than one person — surviving parent, new spouse, grandparents, and maybe other relatives — will put in dibs on the kids and there will be a long, drawn-out, expensive fight over who gets to care for them. If the kids are this lovable, they may have a future in the entertainment business.
- No one will offer to take the children. The surviving parent may not want them and there may be no other close relatives or friends who feel a moral obligation towards them — or else everyone who *might* feel a moral obligation is already acquainted with the children. Having enjoyed the spectacle of them tearing around like banshees when they were not murdering each other over the TV, the toys, or the right to monopolize the bathroom, all potential caregivers run screaming in the opposite direction. Sadly, this may also be the case if a child has a disability and needs extra care.

### If only one person wants custody

There may be only one person interested in caring for the children. Or the entire family may have discussed the situation and agreed that a particular family member should care for the children.

The person who wants custody or guardianship of the children will have to apply to the court for a formal custody order. In a few provinces, a surviving parent who was not a guardian (because of an agreement or court order giving custody to the other parent alone) automatically becomes the guardian and does not legally need a court order. But even when there is no legal requirement to get a court order, a formal order may be necessary to allow the guardian to

- Receive any money for the children's care and upbringing that was left by the parent who died.
- Register the children in school.
- Consent to medical treatment on behalf of the children.

When an application for custody is made, the court has a duty to make sure that the person applying is capable of looking after the children and has a reasonable plan for their upbringing. This is true even if no one comes forward to oppose the application.

### If there's a custody battle

If the kids are popular and a fight erupts over who gets them, it will be up to the court to decide who gets custody. The judge hearing the application will base his or her decision on the best interests of the child. This means that the judge will want to hear about such things as:

- The family relationship between the children and each person claiming custody.
- The emotional ties between the children and each person claiming custody.
- The existing living arrangements between the children and any person claiming custody.
- The ability of each person claiming custody to look after the children.
- The plans of each person claiming custody for the care and upbringing of the children.
- The stability of the family life of each person claiming custody of the children.
- The children's point of view. In some provinces, they are even entitled to a lawyer to put their interests forward.

How these factors would play out in an actual custody battle would depend on the particular circumstances of the case. Read "Joanna vs. Shelby" (next page) for an example. Once you've read it, you may see some patterns.

A biological parent has a real advantage, even if he or she was not the greatest parent before the other parent's death. Unless the surviving biological parent is seriously unfit to look after a child, the courts will likely grant him or her custody. The only competition to watch out for is a relative or friend with whom

## Joanna vs. Shelby

Ted and Joanna were married and had an adorable little boy named Billy. Ted worked long hours at the office while Joanna stayed at home painting clouds on the ceilings and feeling unfulfilled. When Ted came home and announced that he'd received a wonderful promotion that would require him to work even longer hours at the office, Joanna packed up her paintbrushes and left. After a vicious custody fight in which Ted and Joanna each went to some trouble to prove that the other was a completely unfit parent, Ted got custody of Billy. Later, after the divorce decree came through, Ted married his secretary, Shelby. Several years passed, during which Ted and Shelby had two children of their own. Then Ted accidentally got run over in the driveway of Billy's school by a van driven by someone who didn't know about the one-way rule.

Joanna and Shelby both want custody of Billy. Competitors, on your marks, get set, go!

Joanna starts out ahead because she's Billy's biological mother. She starts out even further ahead because of her close relationship with Billy — he stays overnight at her place regularly, in a room with clouds painted on the ceiling.

But Shelby isn't far behind Joanna because Billy has lived with her for several years. The gap closes because she too has a close relationship with Billy, and it narrows even further because she and Ted had children. Giving custody of Billy to Joanna would mean separating him from his little half-brother and half-sister.

The competition heats up as we look at how well Joanna and Shelby are equipped to look after the kids. Shelby loses points for having poor income prospects as a secretary, while Joanna gains points for being a well-paid graphic artist. But Joanna will be docked points for her busy travel schedule.

Shelby can move up on the inside with her plans for where Billy will live. If she can afford to go on living in their current home, Billy won't have to change schools or lose his friends. She'll fall back if she's going to have to move from the neighbourhood to somewhere north of the treeline just to make ends meet.

Joanna lengthens her stride and gets ahead since she's currently in a stable relationship and Billy gets along well with her partner. But she falters because she's gone through several marriages or live-in relationships since leaving Ted.

Finally, Billy has a chance to influence the outcome of the competition. He's nearly a teenager now, and he may have a preference about where he'd like to live. He's old enough to vote with his feet, and it will be hard for his mother, his step-mother, or a court to force him to stay anywhere he doesn't want to stay. In the long run, Billy's preferences may settle the matter entirely.

the children lived before the death of the first parent. And the preferences of an older child are very important.

### If no one wants the kids

If there are no family members or friends who are willing and able to look after the children, the children will be considered *children in need of protection* under the province's child welfare legislation.

We don't do orphanages in Canada any more, so put out of your mind the sad picture of your children trudging up the steps of some grey and soulless institution. But don't worry, we've got other sad pictures to replace it. The children will be placed in the care of a child and family services agency, which will try to find them a foster home (they make an effort to keep families together in one foster home but it's not always possible). The children may be adopted, especially if they're quite young, perhaps by the foster parents or perhaps by someone else.

Child and family services agencies are fairly careful about picking foster parents, and they keep an eye on the children in foster care. The adoption process is quite lengthy and is geared toward investigating the adoptive parents to make sure they're fit. But there's no doubt about it, even a kind foster family or adoptive family isn't the same thing as *your* family.

Children who are not adopted are on their own as soon as they come of age (18 or 19 depending on the province). If they inherited property from the parent who died and that parent made no special trust provisions, the children will also receive the property as soon as they come of age. So your teenagers could be running around with no one to supervise them and their pockets full of cash . . . or with nothing in their pockets at all.

## If both parents are dead

To help you overcome the traumatic feelings you experienced when you read the title of this section, read the cheerful story called "Exit Mr. and Mrs. Smith" before we proceed.

### Exit Mr. and Mrs. Smith

Mr. and Mrs. Smith met a premature end, leaving behind five feisty children, ranging in age from fifteen down to five, and a dog. The children gave the child welfare authorities the slip and wandered around for some time, living off the land. Finally they wandered onto the country estate of Janice, a famous actress who was recuperating from a nervous breakdown. Upon finding them washing in her bird bath, she asked them into her home, fed them, and put them up for the night. After a couple of days' consideration, she told her child-hating fiancé/agent to get lost, married Jim, the handsome local minister, with her new husband adopted all five children and the dog, and retired from her high-paying and exciting career to become a housewife and mother.

Are you ready to go on now? However upsetting the things we have to tell you, they can't be harder to swallow than a story like that.

Now for the orphans. If the children have only one surviving parent who then dies, or if both parents die at the same time, the result will be the same. There is no person who has an automatic right to take over custody of the children.

We've already told you what may happen when we talked about the death of a parent who has sole custody of the children. But we'll go over it again just to grind the point in. If both of the children's parents are dead:

- One person may offer to look after the children. It will be up to the courts to decide whether that person is suitable — and if he or she is not, then the children will be turned over to the child and family services agency as a child in need of protection.
- Several people may offer to look after the children and then there will be a custody battle over them — but in this case no one has the advantage of being the children's parent, so the outcome of the fight may be harder to predict. With luck, at least one of the people who want custody will be someone the courts think is fit to have custody.
- No one may offer to look after the children. Then, once again, the children will be handed over to the child and family services agency.

# Wicked Witch or Fairy Godparent?

Maybe you have a stable marriage and your spouse is the world's best parent and you never travel together in the same car, bus, train, or airplane. You don't even go for walks together, and if one of you gets sick the other wears a surgical mask. Maybe you have a large and loving extended family, and if you and your spouse both die there will be no shortage of wonderful people to take over the care of your children. If this fairy tale is your life, you can keep on reading with a light heart.

But let's just suppose that your children's other parent has already left the scene, or that your supply of children-loving relatives and friends is scanty. Is there anything you can do to make sure that the kids will land with the fairy godparent of your choice — rather than with the wicked witch?

We have to tell you up front that there isn't anything you can do to guarantee absolutely that a person you choose to look after your children will end up looking after your children. But there are some things you can do that will improve the chances that your choice will be respected:

- You can name in your will the person you want to look after your children when you die.
- You can take steps to ensure that the person you've chosen has such a solid relationship with your children that the courts will uphold your choice if it is attacked by someone else.

## Testamentary guardian, a.k.a. fairy godparent

A *testamentary guardian* is a person appointed in a parent's will to look after the children. In almost every province, a parent can appoint a testamentary guardian — but making the appointment won't necessarily dissolve all parental worries. The effect of appointing a guardian depends on the province the family lives in and whether or not there is a surviving parent.

### If the other parent survives the testator

If the parents shared custody of the children and only one parent dies, the surviving parent will continue to be the guardian of the children. It doesn't matter that the parent who died named a different guardian by will — the deceased parent can't terminate the surviving parent's right to be guardian of the children. In some provinces, the appointment of the guardian has no effect at all in these circumstances, and in most other provinces the surviving parent can go to court to remove the guardian named by will. In a couple of provinces the guardian named by will can act as guardian, but has to act jointly with the surviving parent.

If the parent who died had sole custody of the children and the other parent survives, the surviving parent does not automatically become the guardian. But neither does the guardian appointed by will. Anyone who wants custody of the children will have to go to court to get it, and if there's more than one person asking for custody, they'll have to duke it out in front of a judge.

The surviving parent has the better chance of getting custody unless he or she is really an unfit parent. If the parent is unfit, then the guardian appointed by will may get the nod, so too if the children have been living safely and happily with the guardian. But because the judge has to decide what to do based on the best interests of the children (see the section called "If there's a custody battle" earlier in this chapter), not on the wishes of the people asking for custody, it's possible that the judge won't give custody to either the surviving parent or the guardian appointed by will.

### If one parent is already dead and then the second parent dies

Read another sappy story, this one called "Someday her prince will come," to give you the strength to go on with this orphan business.

## Someday her prince will come

Auguste was a wealthy widower with a young daughter named Danielle. Auguste married Rodmilla, a lady with two daughters of her own. Shortly after his remarriage, Auguste died of a heart attack. Rodmilla and her daughters treated Danielle cruelly, forcing her to do housework and not giving her any time during the daylight hours to read. As a result, she often passed the evening lying halfway into the cindery fireplace trying to get enough light from the fire to see her book. Danielle grew up knowing a great deal about domestic science (from working) and philosophy (from reading). She also had a deadly aim with an apple, and used it to bring down a handsome prince who rode through her father's property one day. He instantly fell in love with her, unburdened himself to her about his shoe fetish, punished her cruel stepfamily, and married her.

If you can put up with these stories, you can put up with anything. So let's keep moving.

If the second parent to die appointed a guardian by will, in almost all provinces the guardian will get custody of the children if the guardian agrees to the appointment — unless someone else applies to be guardian (and/or asks the court to remove the testamentary guardian). Then it's up to the courts to choose the guardian.

In some provinces, it's up the courts even if no one else wants custody or objects to the guardian: the appointment under the will lasts for only 90 days. During that time the guardian by will must apply to the court for a formal custody order. In the other provinces there is no legal requirement for the guardian under the will to get a court order granting custody. However, such an order may be necessary or at least desirable if the guardian wants to receive money left for the children's care, to register the children in school, or to consent to medical treatment for them. Financial institutions, schools, and doctors are apt to want proof of guardianship, and it's more reassuring to them to see a court order than a will.

If a guardian is appointed by will but other relatives and friends want custody in spite of the testator's choice, then everyone goes roaring off to court. In choosing among the various applicants, a judge doesn't have to decide that the guardian under the will is unfit before picking someone else to have custody. The judge will take the testator's wishes into account, but will make a choice based on the best interests of the children. (This takes us back to the section on custody battles again.)

Sounds like the guardian appointed by will may spend more time in court than with the kids. A testator who doesn't want the chosen guardian to feel oppressed (or bankrupt) from the very beginning should include a provision in the will that the estate will pay the guardian's legal costs.

## Preventing the fairy godparent from dissolving when splashed with water

You looked your family and friends over and chose as testamentary guardian the person you thought would best care for your children. But when you're gone, your choice won't necessarily be respected. People you rejected out of hand may show up yelling "Me, me!" and the judge (who's never met you, your kids, or any of the would-be guardians) may second-guess you and make his or her own choice. Is there any way you can get a little more control over the situation?

You may have noticed that "the best interests of the children" is a recurring theme when it comes to awarding custody of children. In order to make your choice of guardian stick, you can try to arrange things so that the court will be convinced that going with your choice will also be acting in the children's best interests.

How do you perform this trick? (No, flying monkeys are not the answer.) You have to start while you're still alive. When you choose someone to be guardian, if possible choose a person whose relationship with your children satisfies a good number of the "best interests of the children" factors. Look for a potential guardian who

- Is a relative (by blood or marriage).
- Has strong emotional ties with the children.
- Is living with the children (if not, then a person with whom the children would like to live . . . of course, your children may be at a stage when they'd like to live with anyone except you).
- Is able to look after the children.
- Can come up with good plans for the care and upbringing of the children.
- Lives in a stable family relationship.

And don't forget that the potential guardian should be someone who'll agree to be guardian. Make sure you ask before sticking a name in your will. "Sneak-up" or surprise guardianship doesn't work too well.

What if you don't know anyone who has a close relationship with your children — the kind of relationship the court will be looking for when deciding whether your choice of guardian is okay? Then it's time to get to work and create such a relationship. Keep in touch with whichever members of your family you consider fit to look after your kids, and encourage some bonding between them and the children. If your family looks hopeless, see whether any of your friends are suitable. And don't pin your hopes on just one individual — you may want to name an alternate guardian in your will in case your first choice gets cold feet. Faraway children look greener.

# The Duties of a Fairy Godparent

In fairy tales, the duties of a fairy godparent are pretty much restricted to showing up in the nick of time to rescue the child hero/heroine just when all seems lost. A guardian works harder and gets less time off. And doesn't get a magic wand that actually turns mice into pumpkins.

## Guardian of the person and guardian of the property

If a person is appointed the guardian of a child and nothing is said to limit the guardian's appointment, that person has the right and the responsibility to

- Care for the child and make decisions about how the child is raised (have custody of the child), and
- Look after the child's property.

It is possible, however, to appoint one person to care for the child (to be the child's *guardian of the person*) and another person to look after the child's property (to be the child's *guardian of the estate* or *guardian of the property*). In a will, it is usual to name a guardian of the person, and to make the executor the guardian of the property. The two guardians may be the same person or they can be different people. We'll talk more about choosing your guardians later in this chapter.

## Instructions for the guardian(s)

Instructions to the guardian of the property are usually left in the will. It's best to set up a testamentary trust for minor children, then the person looking after the property will be your trustee. We discuss this further in "The Little Bag of Gold" later in this chapter.

Instructions to the guardian of the person should be discussed face to face with the guardian. The better your chosen guardian knows you and your children, the more likely it is that he or she will know your values and have a sense of the way you would like your children to be raised. You might also want to leave a detailed letter for the guardian with your will, in which you set out your wishes about your children's general upbringing, their religious training and education, and the values you would like them have (fiscal conservative with a strong social conscience or bleeding heart liberal? Pepsi or Coke? Barney or Thomas the Tank Engine?). These instructions are not legally binding, but they will give the guardian some guidance and perhaps comfort. The letter will also be a useful tool in the guardian's hands when your children claim that if their parents were still alive they would have let them ____ (fill in the blank).

# The Little Bag of Gold

Next you've got to give some thought to the treasure that your children will live on until they're old enough to earn their own living.

In some fairy tales, good children are rewarded by having pearls and diamonds drop from their lips every time they speak. Don't count on this as a solution to the problem of supporting your kids after your death. (And don't forget that in the same tales, the brats are punished by having toads and spiders fall out of their mouths whenever *they* speak. Nothing irritates guardians more than having to mop up toads and spiders all over the house. In guardian circles, it's considered a lot worse than loud rock music.)

## Where will the money come from?

In most provinces, a person who is appointed guardian of a child is not required to spend his or her own money to support the child. That leaves it up to you.

So what's in your little bag of gold? It's the money and property you've left your children under your will, plus any insurance proceeds and pension benefits they are entitled to receive. If you're not sure whether you've arranged your affairs to provide properly for your children, go back to Chapters 2 and 3 on financial planning and Chapters 6 and 7 on life insurance. Do some calculating and then some planning.

## How will the money be managed?

If you leave money or property to children under the age of majority (18 or 19 depending on the province), you should set up a trust for the children in your will. (We talk about trusts for minors in Chapter 9, but thinking about your poor orphaned children may encourage you to read more carefully when we go over it again here.) If you leave property directly to a child under the age of majority, the provincial government will manage it according to rules set out by provincial law, until the child comes of age. The government will keep the child's money invested in very conservative investments and will give money to the person with custody only if it approves of the way that he or she plans to spend the money on the child. When the child comes of age, the government will turn all the money and property over to the child, pat the kid on the head, and tell him or her to enjoy. Setting up a trust and making your own rules sounds like a much better idea, doesn't it?

When you create a trust for minors, you instruct the trustee to invest the property you've left to the children. You can say what kinds of investments to make. (Just like the provincial government, you'll probably want safe investments, but you may want the trustee to be able to make some slightly riskier investments in order to increase the value of the trust property.) Then you can also add more detailed instructions about how the trust is to be managed. For example, you could tell the trustee to:

- Pay no income to the children. You may want all of the income to be reinvested so the capital amount of the property goes on growing until the trust ends.
- Pay part or all of the income earned by the trust property out to the children. You may want the children to use the trust income for clothes and books, or even sports and vacations. You can say exactly what the income can and can't be used for, or you can leave it up to the trustee to decide.
- Pay out some of the capital annually or as needed, if the income earned by the trust property isn't enough to pay for the children's necessities or activities.

Finally, you instruct the trustee to give the trust property to the children when they reach a specified age — 18 or 19 if you trust them to act wisely, or a more advanced age like 25 if you don't. Or you can hedge your bets and instruct the trustee to hand over the property in stages, say one-third at age 18 or 19, one-third at 21, and the last third at 25.

## Who will manage the money?

As we've already revealed to you, it is your trustee who will manage the money. But you have to choose the trustee. You'll want someone who is honest and who is knowledgeable about investments. Both qualities are necessary. A dishonest trustee will embezzle your children's money and an ignorant one will lose the money in bad investments. Either way, your kids will be left with no money. You'd also like your trustee to have good judgment if you're letting him or her make decisions about how much income or capital to pay out and when. And you want a trustee who won't play favourites if you have one trust but more than one child. And of course you want the trustee to have the time to take on the job, and the interest in doing it.

If you don't know anyone who meets all of the qualifications, you can name a trust company as your trustee. Trust companies have a track record in managing other people's money, and they don't die before the trust ends, or get sick of the job, or tired of your kids. As a compromise you can appoint more than one trustee, either two or more individuals or an individual (or individuals) and a trust company. If you name more than one trustee, they have to act unanimously unless you instructed otherwise.

If you think you know the perfect person to be your trustee, don't forget to choose (and name) an alternate trustee as well! If your perfect trustee dies and you didn't mention a second choice, your new trustee will be your old trustee's executor — whom you may not know from a hole in the ground.

We're just full of good advice at the moment. Here's some more. It may be wise to name different people to be the trustee and the guardian of the person. First, the skills needed to get teenagers to wipe their feet before they come into the house are not the same skills needed to manage investments. Secondly, having two people involved will help to provide a balance between your children's short-term and long-term needs. If you have only one person wearing both hats, he might want more money for the children's immediate care than there is income from the trust, and wouldn't hesitate to dig into the capital without giving thought to the future. Or she might think that it's more important to build the property than to provide a decent allowance for the children, and not be willing to give the kids enough money to enjoy their childhood.

If you name different people to be guardian and trustee, try to make sure that they get along reasonably well. You don't want your kids to become a battleground.

# The Hut at the Edge of the Forest

Here's one last thing to think about: Where will your children live? Will they move into the guardian's home, or will the guardian move into yours? This is a decision you should make together with the person you name as guardian.

If you decide that your home should be kept for the use of your children, you have to make special provisions in your will. You'll have to instruct your executor not to sell the house, or not to sell it until (for example) the children reach a certain age, or to deed it over to the children when they reach a responsible age. (But if you're wise you'll give your executor the power to sell your home if it's necessary.) Don't forget to mention what's to be done with the sale proceeds if and when the house is sold. You'll also have to set aside money in your estate to maintain the house.

If you don't go through this rigamarole about your home, it will be your executor's duty to sell it and divide the proceeds, along with the rest of your estate, among your beneficiaries.

# Happily Ever After

If this chapter does nothing else, it will encourage you to buckle up your seat belt, look both ways before crossing the street, and stop collecting brochures on bungee jumping, skydiving, river rafting, and alligator wrestling. And you will never again turn up your nose at broccoli, cauliflower, or flu shots. You want to stay alive until your children are grown up! It's easier to look after them yourself than to arrange for someone else to do it.

This chapter will also make you think twice before you let your kids sass their grandparents, aunts, and uncles (natural or honorary) or whack their cousins. From now on, you'll see your sane and decent relatives and friends as your pool of potential guardians and trustees. You won't want your kids to alienate a single one of them.

So . . . there's the happy ending we've engineered for you. From now on you'll live sensibly and safely and raise well-behaved, polite children. Then you won't have to worry about who'll mind the kids when you're gone.

# Chapter 12

# Giving Them the Business: What to Do with the Family Firm

### In This Chapter

- Deciding whether to sell your business or keep it in the family
- Considering when to sell or turn over control of your business
- Putting your plan into action
- Creating an emergency business plan

Nearly two million Canadians own their business or professional practice, either alone or with others. Are you one of them? And have you ever dreamed of your business being handed down from generation to generation . . . your portrait hanging on the boardroom wall . . . maybe even a bronze statue of you outside the head office . . . your descendants and their employees speaking of you in reverential tones as "our founder"?

Maybe that's not your fantasy at all. Maybe you'd just as soon your kids didn't follow you into the business you're in. But even so, you'd probably like to pass its value on to your family by selling the business and leaving them the money.

This much is sure: If you own your own business, deciding what to do with it is an important part of your estate planning. And deciding what to do isn't the end of it — you've got to take action, too. Whatever your decision about your business, it's much more likely to work out if you make plans than if you leave everything to chance.

## Take Stock of Your Situation

Your main choice lies between keeping your business in the family and selling it to someone outside your family.

We have to warn you right at the opening bell that it's not necessarily up to you to decide what to do with your business.

If you're a sole proprietor or the sole or majority owner of the shares of a corporation, the decision *is* pretty much yours. You own the business and you can do what you like with it. You'll have the power to hand it over to your family if that's what you want to do, or to sell it if you prefer.

If you are a partner in a business or a minority shareholder in a corporation, your choices are more limited. Your business associates very probably have a big say in what's going to happen.

## You may already be sold short

If you have partners or if you have fellow shareholders who together hold more shares in the corporation than you do, you don't have total control over your business. Whether you want to sell or you want to bring your family in, your partners or the other shareholders will want to stick their oar in. They may be able to prevent you from sharing ownership of the business with family members or passing ownership on to them. And they may be able to prevent you from selling your ownership interest to an outsider.

### If your business is a partnership

To be frank, it's rather unlikely that you will be able to transfer your interest in a partnership to a family member either during your lifetime or on your death.

You can transfer your partnership interest in an ongoing business to someone else (including a family member) only if your partners consent to the transfer. And they won't consent unless they think exchanging you for your family member is good for the business and for them as well. If there's a partnership agreement, it may require you to transfer your interest directly to your partners if you want out. And you can't add a new partner or partners without the consent of your existing partners.

If you die while still a partner in a business, you can't just leave your partnership interest to a family member and assume that he or she will take your place. If you have a partnership agreement it probably only requires your partners to pay your estate for your interest. It almost certainly doesn't say that the partnership has to take on someone you choose to replace you. If you don't have a partnership agreement, the partnership dissolves on your death. Then your family members simply inherit your share of any property belonging to the partnership. It would be up to your former partners and your family to decide whether they wanted to re-form the partnership together.

### If your business is a corporation

If your business is a corporation, you have to bring in new owners by transferring shares in the corporation to them. Anyone can buy shares in a public corporation on the stock market (although usually only the very rich can buy enough shares to get any kind of control over the business). But in a private corporation — which is the only kind of corporation you would be turning over to your family or selling to an outsider — the shareholders and/or the directors of the corporation have to give their consent before shares can be transferred. If you're not the only shareholder or not the majority shareholder of your corporation, it may be difficult or impossible to persuade all the necessary people to allow you to transfer your shares to a family member, or to anyone else for that matter. Just like partners, shareholders and directors don't want new owners wandering in off the street. (You'd also need consent to get the corporation itself to give or sell new shares to your family member.)

In addition, if you're thinking of selling, it's highly unlikely that an outsider would want to buy a minority share in a private corporation, even if the other shareholders agreed to the purchase. Actually, your family member might not thank you for a minority interest either. The only real market for minority shares in a private corporation is the other shareholders of the corporation.

## You may have options

If you're a sole proprietor or majority shareholder in a corporation, you're going to be able to decide for yourself whether to bring family members into the business — or whether to sell the business and pass its value on that way.

If you're bullish on keeping your business in the family, you might be interested to know that you're in the minority of Canadian business owners. A 1999 Deloitte & Touche survey of some 750 family-owned Canadian businesses with annual revenues of at least $1 million showed that only a third of owners thought it was important to keep the business in the family.

But if you're not afraid to buck a trend and you'd still like to hand down your business to your family, brace yourself for a bear market. Another survey, this one by the Family Firm Institute, an international organization that assists family businesses, showed that only about 30 percent of family-owned businesses survive into the second generation, 12 percent into the third generation, and 3 percent into the fourth generation and beyond. Of all family businesses in Canada, only 2 percent have passed through four generations or more. So even if nothing's stopping you from passing your business on to your children, your chances of creating a commercial dynasty are small.

So what's the plan here? You've got a choice. Should you try to keep the business in the family, or should you sell? In order to make your decision, you'll have to start thinking about the nature of your business, the abilities and interests of your children, and your own temperament.

### Look at your business

The characteristics of your business itself may determine whether or not it can be passed successfully on to the next generation. If it can't, the recommendation is: Sell. If you could use a little help pondering this matter, here are some points to consider:

- Must your business be operated by someone with special training or expertise? If you are a licensed professional or a skilled tradesperson, your business probably can't be carried on by a family member who isn't qualified in that trade or profession.
- Can your business get along without you or are *you* the business? Is your business based solely on your particular skills, talents and/or personality? If that's the case, it may be that *no one,* inside or outside your family, can take it over successfully. It only has value — income value — as long as you're running it, and there may be no value to pass on.
- How much is your business worth as a going concern? Is it worth enough to pass it on to all of your children who are interested in sharing in it? In other words, will they all be able to earn a decent living from it, either right away or after they've used their skills to expand it? Or will they starve? If the business won't support them, you would be doing them a favour to sell it and pass on the proceeds instead.
- How much has your business gone up in value since you started it? Selling your interest in your business or transferring it to a family member other than your spouse could trigger a capital gain or loss. (See Chapters 4 and 5.) If your business is a corporation, up to $500,000 of any capital gain may be tax free because of the capital gains deduction permitted under the *Income Tax Act* for qualifying small business corporations. If your business is a sole proprietorship or partnership, there's no deduction available. Will you have enough other money and property (or life insurance) to pay the tax on any capital gain that pops up when you give your business to your children? If you don't, selling your business may be the only way you'll get the money needed to pay the tax due.

### Look at your family (1): The advancers

Let's assume your business meets the requirements to be handed on to your children. Now let's look at the children. Every family has its advancing and declining issues, and the character and talents of your family members will determine whether it's wise or even possible to pass your business on to the next generation.

First of all, is there anyone in your family who is interested in taking over your business *and* who has the talent and ability to be successful? If your only child or all of your several children have the desire and the talent to carry on, you could be all set to start dynasty building.

Do none of your children have the talent to carry on (whether interested in doing so or not)? Again, you're all set — to sell to an outsider. There's no point in letting your children take over just to run the business into the ground. It will be best for them if you sell the business and give them the money to finance other enterprises they're better suited for.

But those two scenarios aren't the end of the possibilities. What if . . .

- You have several children, and they're all interested but only some are talented. Do you cause family strife by taking on some and rejecting the others? If you believe that taking on only some of your children will cause a lot of harm to your family, and you care more about your family than about your business, then you should consider a sale.
- You have several children with the interest and talent (whether they represent all of your children or only some of them). Do they get along well enough with each other that it's safe to bring them all in? Have their dispute resolution skills improved since they fought as children over the TV remote and whose turn it was to walk the dog? If they can't get along well as people, they'll have trouble getting along as partners, and an enforced partnership is almost certainly doomed.

## Something's rotten

Claudius, the highly competent CEO of Denmark Inc., was grooming his nephew to succeed him when he retired. He announced his succession plan at a shareholders' meeting to uniform delight. (One shareholder even described the nephew as "the expectancy and rose of the fair state," but she later had a water-related accident and cashed in her shares.) Unfortunately, after this Claudius found his nephew increasingly difficult to deal with. The nephew, not realizing that he could learn a lot from Claudius and thinking he could do a better job himself, began criticizing Claudius's leadership and even claimed that Claudius had arranged the sudden departure of his own brother, the previous CEO. Claudius tried to remedy the situation by having his nephew do more travelling on behalf of the corporation, but that turned out to be only a temporary solution. On his return from one business trip, the nephew organized a hostile takeover and forced Claudius to swallow a poison pill. The turmoil caused by the in-fighting soon led to the collapse of the corporation.

- You have talented, interested children who get along well with each other. But are they capable of working with and learning from *you*? Will they be willing to wait until you are ready to hand control over to them, or will they try to force you out of the business before you are ready? Have a look at "Something's rotten," on the previous page.

One last (somewhat gloomy) thought here. If it's a commercial empire you have in mind, even if your children get along well enough to cooperate as partners themselves, they may have trouble cooperating when it comes time to choose among their own children as their successors. That's the stage at which the McCain family business came unglued. There's a reason for that old expression, "Shirtsleeves to shirtsleeves in three generations"!

### Look at your family (2): The decliners

If you have more than one child and you decide (for various reasons, not restricted to those discussed above) to turn your business over to one or some of them rather than to all of them — what are you going to do about the children who've been left out of the business?

Your business has value. It may even be the most valuable thing you own. You may not care that you're not treating all your children equally in your estate plan by cutting some of them out of the business. But it's bound to cause trouble, and you may not want to increase your family's volatility (or turn your family into a hornet's nest). But then again, you may care very much about acting fairly towards everyone.

There are solutions to the problem of an unequal distribution of your estate, short of selling the business to an outsider, to save yourself a lot of grief. Here are some of them:

- You may have enough other money and property or enough life insurance that you'll be able to divide your estate equally among your children anyway.
- You may decide to make a gift of only part of the value of the business, and require your chosen successor to buy the rest of the business's value from you or your estate — so that you have enough money to leave equal shares to your other children. (Before you go for this solution, consider whether the business generates enough income for your child to be able to afford the purchase price you're asking. You don't want to sink your successor into debt.)
- You may decide to give ownership of the business to all of your children on the understanding that only one of your children will operate the business. In this case you have to consider whether the business is profitable enough to support several owners, and whether the silent partners are capable of actual silence.

### Look at yourself

Now, what about you? Can you do whatever is necessary to ensure a smooth transfer of control of your company to your children? Are you a floor trader at heart, working for yourself alone? Or are you the kind of person who can give up control of your business before you die, if that's what it will take to make the transition successful? Ask yourself:

- Can you bring yourself to choose a successor at all?
- Are you truly willing to involve your children in the ownership and/or control of your business before you retire?
- Are you capable of working *with* and perhaps *for* your children, rather than always being the boss?

If you answered "no" to any of these questions, you're probably not a good candidate for founder of a dynasty. Neither was a "very foolish fond old man."

## Market Timing

When's the best time to pass on your business or sell it? When you're hale and hearty, or when you're dead?

You may start thinking about this question in terms of when's the best time for *you* — when will *you* be ready to leave. Do you want to walk away from your business (and maybe out to the beach or golf course)? Hobble away? Or be carried out in a box?

### A very foolish fond old man

K. Lear of LearCorp (no relation to LearJet) had three daughters, only one of whom, Cordelia, had what it takes to run a complex corporation. Although he knew this in his heart, he couldn't bring himself to exclude his other two children, who loved him very dearly (or so they said whenever he talked about the net worth of the corporation). So he told his daughters that he was going to leave control of the corporation to the three of them jointly.

Cordelia was disgusted with this decision and left to join a competing corporation, RoiDeFrance Ltee. The other two daughters, although short on business smarts, were long on rivalry and eventually managed to force each other out of LearCorp.

When Lear died, driven mad by his daughters' antics, his corporation died with him. (His last words, in fact, were, "Now her price is fall'n.") LearCorp ended up with no value apart from its assets, which were purchased for a ridiculously small sum by Albany Takeovers Inc.

Your personal preferences loom large, but they have to be balanced against other factors.

## If you hold for the family

If you're going to hand over ownership of your business to your family, when should you do it? There are a number of things to take into account:

- When can you afford to retire from the business? If you don't have other income and investments to live on, and if your successors won't make enough from the business to pay you for it while they run it, you may have no choice but to hang on to the business yourself until you die.
- When can you afford the tax on the capital gain? If your business has gone up in value, you may have to pay capital gains tax when you transfer ownership of the business. If you don't have sufficient other money and property to be able to pay the tax without having to liquidate the business, you may have to hold on to the business until you die. At that point, life insurance you've bought for the purpose will help your estate cover the tax on the capital gain.
- Do you expect your business to continue to go up in value? If so, you may want to consider some form of estate freeze fairly soon that involves transfer of ownership (although not necessarily control) away from you. (See Chapter 5 for more on estate freezes.) If you do an estate freeze on your business, you may or may not have to pay capital gains tax on the current value of the business. But either way, future increases in value will belong to your children and will not be taxable in your hands. Your children will not have to pay any tax on increases in value until they dispose of the business.

Even if you decide that you can't afford to hand over ownership before you die, you should consider handing over control of your business — or at least partial control — while you're still alive. Bringing your family into the business while you're still around will increase their chances of successfully carrying on the business because

- They will have the opportunity to learn about the business from an expert — you.
- Your clients or customers will have an opportunity to get to know your children and transfer their trust and loyalty (now yours alone) to them.

### If you decide to sell

If you are planning to sell your business, you want to sell it for the highest possible amount. So you want to sell it when it's most valuable. Is that when it's a going concern? Or when you're finished with business life — well, with life in general — and your executor may be selling off just the business's property?

Most businesses are worth more as a going concern than as a collection of assets. And usually your business will be worth even more as a going concern if you're still around. A business that's in business has *goodwill*, which can be loosely defined as the likelihood that customers will keep coming back. If you stick around for a while after a new owner takes over, the customers are more likely to do that. For another thing, you can offer a buyer your expertise by agreeing to stay on while the buyer learns the ropes and gets to know your customers.

And there's yet another reason to sell while you're alive. You can arrange to have the sale price paid to you in installments spread out over several taxation years, and so reduce the tax payable on any capital gain. If you cling to your business until you die, you are deemed to have disposed of it at your death. Then your estate has to receive the full proceeds all at once and pay any taxes due in that same taxation year. This will come at a really bad time because you're deemed to have disposed of your non-business assets as well, and your estate will have to pay tax on any resulting capital gains. Just for fun, don't forget that everything in your RRSPs not left to your spouse will be considered income and be taxed as well.

## Place Your Orders

Once you've made the big decision — family succession or outside sale — you have to carry it out. Now let's look at what steps you need to take.

### If your business is a sole proprietorship

A sole proprietorship is fairly easy (from a legal point of view) either to transfer or sell. The business is essentially the assets (property) that the proprietor owns personally and uses to carry on the business. Once the sole proprietor has decided what to do, he or she can act right away.

### Keeping it in the family

If you want to hand over your business to a family member during your lifetime, you'll have to legally transfer ownership of all of the assets of the business. (You'll trigger a capital gain for yourself if your assets have gone up in value.)

If you want to hand over your business on your death, you will need a properly drafted will leaving the assets of the business to your chosen successor(s). (See Chapter 16 for more on wills.)

If you've decided on an estate freeze you'll need to make extra plans. An estate freeze is a lot more complicated than simply handing over your assets during your lifetime or leaving them in your will. (See the "Market Timing" section in this chapter and Chapter 5 for more on estate freezes.)

You'll probably want your successor to get not only the assets of the business but also all of the debts of the business. If you're giving your business away during your lifetime, you'll have to make some arrangements with your successor and your creditors for the payment of your business debts. If you're giving your business away in your will, your estate will be responsible for paying its debts. That could have the effect of reducing other family members' share of your estate — so take this into account when you're making your estate plan.

### Selling outside the family

Selling to an outsider is much the same as transferring to a family member — you transfer ownership of the assets used in your business to the purchaser and make arrangements for the payment of your business debts.

At the time of the sale, you'll want some tax advice about reducing the taxes payable on any capital gain you've triggered by the sale. For example, you may be able to arrange for the price to be paid to you in installments spread out over several taxation years.

## If your business is a partnership

If you're a partner in a business, your best plan probably is to have your partners buy your interest when you retire or die. That means you need a *partnership agreement* that deals specifically with retirement and death.

If you have no partnership agreement or you have one but it doesn't deal with retirement and death issues, your partnership will simply dissolve when you leave or die (the exception is a *declared partnership* in Quebec). If you have a two-person partnership, it will dissolve when you leave or die whether or not you have a partnership agreement. Once you reach the point of retirement or death, you (or your estate) will be at a disadvantage when it comes to negotiating a price for your interest in the partnership or your share of the partnership assets. That's because your partners aren't required to buy you out, and they may not have the money to buy you out anyway. And they have to agree before you can sell to an outsider — assuming you can find one who wants to join this partnership.

To prevent this financially unpleasant situation from coming to pass, you need a partnership agreement that deals with what happens when a partner wants to leave or retire or die. And you need it now, before you're actually ready to leave or retire or die.

You'll need to speak to a business lawyer about this, but your agreement should have:

- A buy-out clause *or* a buy-sell clause. If one partner wants out, either the rest of the partners buy that partner out or (usually only in small firms) that partner buys out all the other partners. (If no one is willing to buy, then the partnership is dissolved.)
- A retirement clause. The other partners buy out a partner who wants to retire. The clause will say how the price of the buy-out is to be calculated (the buy-out money will probably have to be borrowed).
- A clause that requires the other partners to buy the interest of a partner who has died from the dead partner's estate.
- A clause that requires the partners to have life and disability insurance on each other. The insurance proceeds can help fund a buy-out triggered by the death or disability of a partner.

It's possible, but uncommon, to have a partnership agreement that allows partners to sell their partnership interest to an outsider if the other partners approve of the new partner.

## If your business is a corporation

To transfer or sell your ownership interest in a corporation, you have to transfer or sell shares in the corporation. That sounds easy enough, but it isn't always that easy in practice.

### Keeping it in the family

If you are the only or the majority shareholder in your business corporation, you're free to transfer your shares to whomever you like. You don't need anyone's consent if you're the sole shareholder or the majority shareholder. So you'll simply sign the shares over to your family member while you're alive, or leave the shares in your will.

If you're just one of the shareholders and are not the majority shareholder, you'll need the consent of at least some of the other shareholders and/or the directors of the corporation to hand over your shares to anyone. If you want to be able to give or leave your shares to a family member, it would be best if you had a *shareholders' agreement* that says you can do that. You'll need to negotiate the agreement with your fellow shareholders before the time comes for you to make your dynasty-building move. The other shareholders may want their children to come into the business as well, so there could be interesting times ahead for the corporation.

### Selling to an outsider

If you are the only shareholder or the majority shareholder, again you can do whatever you like with the corporation. You're free to sell it to the buyer of your choice. (Unhappy minority shareholders might have a right to complain to the court about what you're doing, however.) You can sell a business corporation either by selling all of the corporation's assets or by selling its shares.

Whether you choose an asset sale or a share sale will depend largely on the tax consequences for you — consult your lawyer and accountant before you start negotiating a deal with a buyer.

If you are not the only shareholder or the majority shareholder, for all practical purposes your market is limited to your fellow shareholders or the corporation. But if you want to sell to either, you'll need to do some advance planning because without a shareholders' agreement in place,

- Neither the shareholders nor the corporation are automatically required to buy your shares.
- Neither the shareholders nor the corporation are required to offer a fair price for your shares.
- Even if the corporation and/or the shareholders want to buy your shares, they may not have enough money.

The upshot is, you want a shareholders' agreement that requires the other shareholders or the corporation to buy your shares from you or your estate and that says how the price is to be calculated. The agreement should also require the shareholders to be insured (life and disability insurance) so that there will be money to fund a share purchase on the death or disability of a shareholder. (If you just leave and don't die, the shareholders or corporation will probably have to borrow money to pay for your shares.) You might also want the agreement to give you or your estate the right to terminate the corporation's existence, so you can get your share of the corporation's property if the other shareholders or the corporation can't buy your shares.

# Don't Forget to Hedge

What if you were to die tomorrow?

Oops — sorry to be so abrupt. Are you okay? That was a nasty bump. Anyway, at least we're not asking you to think about dying today.

So far we've been talking about long-term planning for your business. But you must also think about what would happen to your business if you were to die or become incapacitated suddenly, before your long-term plan has played itself out. The odds are that plan would not be appropriate to deal with your unexpected death or illness.

What do we suggest? You need to line up an emergency replacement for yourself, have insurance in place, and put the right clauses in your will.

## Someone who can step in

Whatever your current situation and your long-term plans, you should make sure that there is someone who can step in and run your business, at least in the short term, if you were to die or become disabled suddenly.

### Who should that someone be?

If you plan to turn over your business to a family member and your successor is working in the business and is ready to take over, then your long-term plan will work in the short term as well. Your successor will simply get the nod before he or she expected it.

If you plan to turn over your business to your family but your children are either too young or too inexperienced to take over from you, the problem is harder to solve. You have to ask whether it's realistic to try to keep the business going until they are ready to take over. Does it make more sense to change direction and sell the business instead? But either way, you'll need someone to look after the business for the time being. That person could be your spouse or one of your senior employees, or a manager hired by you (or by your attorney under your power of attorney if you can no longer think straight), or your executor.

### What should that someone know?

Your emergency replacement should have some basic knowledge of the business — what the business does and how it operates. The more the person knows the better, but he or she should at least know:

- The names of your business's suppliers and customers or clients.
- Where to find your business records — corporate documents, major contracts, banking documents, insurance policies, accounts payable, accounts receivable, and so on.
- The name of the business's accountant. Your accountant will have information about the general financial health of the business, including details of major debts and sources of income.
- The name of the business's bookkeeper. The bookkeeper will have information about the day-to-day finances of the company, such as accounts receivable, accounts payable, and payroll information, and will probably know the names of the business's customers and suppliers and where most of the business records can be found.
- The name of the business's lawyer. Your lawyer has information about the structure of the business and perhaps also about its major contracts.
- The name and address of the business's bank, including the name of the bank manager. Your emergency replacement should have enough information to persuade a bank that has loaned the business money not to demand payment but to allow the business to continue to operate (either indefinitely or until a buyer is found).
- The names of senior employees who have knowledge about and can help with the day-to-day operation of the business.

## Insurance for your business

If you die or become disabled, your business is going to need money to help fend off the bears. It will need:

- Money to pay the debts of the business if the bank decides to demand payment on its loans.
- Money to pay for someone to run the business or to help your family run the business.
- Money to cover any reduction in the business's income as a result of your incapacity or death — to help cover ongoing expenses until the business is either back on its feet or sold.
- Money to pay the tax on any capital gain resulting from the deemed disposition of the business if you die. (See Chapter 5 for more on capital gains tax.)

The best way to make sure that your business will have the money it needs is to have the right kind of insurance in the right amount. So call your insurance agent. You may need to take out:

- **Overhead insurance:** A form of disability insurance that pays the fixed expenses of your business while you are temporarily out of commission.
- **Life insurance:** A policy on your life, payable to your estate, your spouse, or your children, that will provide money to pay the tax on the capital gain as a result of the *deemed disposition* of your business on your death (tax law assumes that you sell all your property just before you die) or other business debts for which your estate is responsible. Alternatively, the money can be plowed into the business.
- **Key person insurance:** Life insurance that your business takes out on your life because you're essential to the running of the business. The insurance proceeds provide the business with money to cover any expenses that must be paid to help the business survive — the cost of a replacement for you, consulting costs, debt payments, and so on.

## At the close

Since you can't know when you're going to die, you should draft the business-related parts of your will as if you're going to die tomorrow, in accordance with your short-term emergency plan. Your short-term plan may not necessarily be the same as your long-term plan, but you can and should revise your will as circumstances change.

- If you're grooming your children to take over from you and they're now ready to step in at a moment's notice, you can safely leave your business to them.
- If your children are not ready to take over immediately but should be ready in the near future, you could leave your business to them — but with instructions to your executor either to run the business personally or to hire someone to run the business until they are ready.
- If no one in your family is capable of taking over the business for the foreseeable future, you may be wiser to draft your will so that your business will be sold. If it was always your intention to sell your business, draft your will accordingly. But consider giving your executor the discretion and the powers to operate your business for a time. Your executor may be able to get a better price for the business if it's still in operation at the time of sale.

# Chapter 13

# You Gave at the Office, But . . . — Charitable Donations

### *In This Chapter*

- Thinking about making a donation to charity
- Deciding what to give, and how and when to give it
- Choosing a charity
- Getting tax benefits from a donation
- Asking others to donate in your memory

"I gave at the office" is a handy, if trite, way of politely telling canvassers to see whether the next-door neighbours are feeling more charitable. When you're making your will, though, there's no canvasser on your doorstep. There's no pressure on you, there's no request, there's not even a pleading look in someone's eye. The decision to leave something to charity is purely voluntary, and nobody needs to know about it except the lawyer drafting your will. The result of all this freedom, unfortunately, is that charity does not usually enter the mind of a person making a will unless the lawyer raises the subject.

Since the decision to give or not to give or how much to give is absolutely up to you, which way are you leaning?

If you've given to charities throughout your life, you might either be saying, "I've given enough" or "This will be my last chance to do something I think is important." If you've never given to charity before, you might either be saying, "It's a little late to start now" or else "This is a good time, since I won't miss what I give away."

In this chapter we'll help you to think about giving to charity as part of your estate plan and (should you decide that giving is a good idea) about the best way to do it.

# Thinking about Giving to Charity

The expression "last will" (as in Last Will and Testament) literally means your final wishes. A lot of your final wishes probably revolve around your family and looking after them, but shouldn't your final wishes reflect your entire life as you lived it? Family obligations are an important part of your life, but they're still only a part and not the whole.

Whatever your outside interests are, after your death is a good time to invest in them. Even if you never feel that you have enough extra money to give a significant amount to charity once the rent or mortgage is paid and food put on the table, you can probably afford to make a donation out of your estate. First of all, you're going to be dead and won't need that much cash where you're going. (Think of the afterlife as an "all-inclusive" kind of deal, like an otherworldly Club Med.) And secondly, the tax treatment of charitable donations on death can help reduce the tax your estate may have to pay.

## Why give to charity?

Some people secretly equate a charity with themselves. They might, for example, donate to organizations that are working to cure diseases that the donors are afraid of getting. So if you gave to the Cancer Society in the hope that they would find a cure for cancer before you got it, and then you got cancer anyway, it's perfectly understandable that you wouldn't see any point in giving them more money in your will.

But if you're one of the people who takes the longer view — that the planet, humans, and other animals and vegetables were here long before your entrance and will keep on going after your exit, and that they need as much help as they can get whether you personally are in or out of this world — then a donation in your will makes sense. You can get a lot of satisfaction from knowing that you've done one last thing for your community or for a cause that means a lot to you. And the cause or community may be even more grateful for your gift than your beloved relatives and friends. The charity may use the gift to ease suffering or create a lasting benefit, while your relatives might only use it to take a vacation, overindulge in rum punch, and whine about having waited for so long for so little.

## How much should you give?

If you have family members who are financially dependent on you, your first obligation, both morally and legally, is to them. (See Chapter 10.) It doesn't matter that the rainforest tree toads are endangered or that your favourite post mortem fantasy involves looking down from above and seeing your name inscribed on a plaque praising your generosity. You can't give more than a token amount to charity if you're not leaving enough in your estate to look after your dependent spouse or children.

But if your family is properly cared for, you can kick up your charitable heels.

- If you have no family at all, or none that you're speaking to, and no close friends, you may want to leave your entire estate to charity. This sounds horrifically depressing . . . maybe if you tell the charity in advance that you're leaving your whole estate to them they'll send someone over to befriend you.
- If you have family and friends but no one who actually needs your money as much as the endangered tree toads do, you may want to leave personal possessions with sentimental value and some of your money to the friends and relations, and leave the balance of your estate to charity.
- If you want or need to leave most of your estate to family or friends, you may want to calculate how much you can spare for charity.

## What are the tax advantages to leaving money to charity?

Isn't it amazing the way that we keep intertwining the highly entertaining topic of taxes with the mesmerizing topic of death? You're probably beginning to think that we keep talking about taxes just because we have a death-and-taxes fetish. That's not true. We do have fetishes, but they revolve around chocolate and shoes. Enough about us, though. Let's talk about those yummy taxes!

### Charity that begins at home

If you leave money or property to a registered Canadian charity in your will, your estate will be able to claim a tax credit in the return filed for the last year of your life, your *terminal return*. The tax credit reduces the tax that your estate pays on the income you earned before you died and on the taxable capital gains that your estate may have because of the *deemed disposition* of all of your property when you die (Canada Revenue assumes that you sell everything you own just before death) — not to mention the tax your estate will have to pay because your RRSPs are deemed to be cashed in when you die. (If none of this is ringing a bell with you, take our remedial tax course in Chapter 4.) If earned income and taxable capital gains have put your estate into the highest tax bracket, as is quite likely, your estate may save almost $50 in tax for every $100 in donations.

When you make charitable donations during your lifetime, the maximum that you can claim is 75 percent of the net income reported on your income tax return. But if charitable donations are made through your will or after your death, your estate can claim donations up to your total net income. And if the charitable donations in your will are greater than the net income in your final tax return, your executor can refile your tax return for the year before you died, and use the excess donation to get a tax credit to reduce that year's taxes. (Your estate will get a refund.)

There's quite a bit more to this tax stuff — including ways to get the biggest tax bang for your charitable buck — and we will inflict it on you in the section called "Ways to Give to Charity."

### Charity that begins abroad

If you want to give to a charity in another country, you don't necessarily have to forget about tax breaks here in Canada. A few foreign charities (in particular, U.S. educational institutions) have the same tax status in Canada as registered Canadian charities. Canada also has tax treaties with many other countries, and the provisions of the treaty with your charity's country may offer you some tax benefits. Before you make a donation to a foreign charity you should contact the charity itself and also Canada Revenue for advice. If you're thinking of making a significant donation, you should consult a Canadian tax lawyer.

Don't overlook the fact that many Canadian-registered charities work in foreign countries — the Red Cross, for example, many religious organizations, and organizations devoted to education, health, and the environment. So you may be able to do good abroad and do well tax-wise here at home too.

## Choosing the Right Charity

You may already have a favourite charity and you're planning to stick with it, dead or alive. But if you're not committed to a particular charity, how should you decide which one(s) to give to? There are several things you may want to take into account, not necessarily in the following order:

- The charity's purpose
- The charity's honesty and integrity
- The percentage of charitable donations that is used for charitable purposes (rather than for fundraising and other administrative costs)
- Whether the charity is registered with Canada Revenue
- Whether the charity is willing to accept your donation
- Whether the charity is willing to use your donation as you direct
- The kind of recognition that you will be given for your donation

## A charity that does the right kind of good

You may want to make a donation to a specific charity because it's active in an area that's important to you, or as a gesture of support and thanks. For example you may want to donate to:

- An organization that supports a cause that you believe in, such as literacy and education, animal rescue, protection of the environment, or protection of heritage buildings
- Your church, synagogue, mosque, or coven (for Wiccans)
- A charity that has helped you, a family member, or a friend during an illness
- An organization that carries on research about a disease that has affected you, a family member, or a friend
- A hospital in which you, a family member, or a friend were well cared for
- A school, college, or university that you or a family member attended
- A performing arts group whose productions you enjoyed

## A charity that's not good enough to be true

If you like a charity's objectives, you should check out some other matters too — especially if the charity is not well known.

Not every organization that requests money from the public for charitable purposes is what it appears to be. Money collected from donations may be going to the founders or administrators of the charity rather than to the stated goals of the charity. In other words, it's a scam.

Another point: Some charities are better than others at managing themselves efficiently. You would like to know how much of your donation will be spent on fundraising and administration and how much will be spent on a charitable purpose. In other words, will your donation go to the tree toads or to a receptionist?

A good way of answering questions about a charity's legitimacy and efficiency is to find out whether the charity is registered with Canada Revenue. Charities must meet strict criteria to become registered and to stay registered (see the next section). You can also question representatives of the charity directly, but they may not be in a hurry to tell you what you want to know.

## A charity that's on good terms with Canada Revenue

Well, look at that. We've managed to find a way to talk about Canada Revenue when we're supposed to be talking about how to choose a charity. We're pretty good at dragging taxes into every discussion, aren't we? But it's not that we have a thing for taxes. No, really.

When you make a charitable donation, you'll get a tax credit for it only if the charity is registered with Canada Revenue. To qualify for registration, an organization must

- Be set up and operated for *charitable purposes* and devote its resources to charitable activities. Canada Revenue recognizes four general categories of charitable purposes: relief of poverty, advancement of education, advancement of religion, and other purposes that benefit the community such as disaster relief; prevention and treatment of sickness and disability; care or protection of children, the elderly, people with special needs, and animals; and protection of the environment.
- Be resident in Canada.
- Provide a real benefit to the public (either the whole public or a significant part), and not use its income to benefit its members.
- Engage only in legal activities and, further, engage only in activities that won't get up the noses of government officials (the elegant way of saying this is that the activities must not be "contrary to public policy").

Some organizations may look like charities without *being* charities in the eyes of Canada Revenue. Service clubs and fraternal lodges, for example, are not considered charities because they provide social events for members even if they also provide services to the general community. (A separate organization for their charitable activities would qualify for registration as a charity.) Funds set up to accept donations for an individual (say a child awaiting surgery) or small group (say a family that lost their home in a fire) are not charities because the public as a whole does not benefit.

To stay registered, a charity has to spend at least 80 percent of most types of its annual donations directly on charitable activities. Charitable activities include paying the salaries of people who perform actual charitable work and buying equipment used in charitable activities (the doctor and her medical equipment), but do not include paying for administrative or fund-raising activities (the receptionist and his desk). A charity can pay only reasonable salaries to its members. It also has to keep proper records and make them available if Canada Revenue wants to inspect them, and it has to file an annual information return with Canada Revenue.

Canada Revenue maintains a searchable list of registered charities at its Web site (`www.ccra-adrc.gc.ca`). You can also get information by calling Canada Revenue's Charities Division at 1-800-267-2384.

There are about 78,000 charities registered with Canada Revenue. But you already knew that, didn't you? Because every last one of them has called you at dinner time.

## A charity that looks a gift horse in the mouth

Unless you're a well-known Colombian drug lord, no charity is going to turn down your gift of cash. A charity probably won't say no to publicly traded shares, either, because they can easily be turned into cash. (Things might be a little sticky if you try to give tobacco company shares to an emphysema society, or shares in an arms manufacturer to an organization promoting world peace.) But what if you don't want to give cash or cashable property? What if you want to donate your car to a service organization that delivers meals to the elderly? What if you want to leave a piece of art to a gallery or museum? What if you want to leave your baseball card collection to your church?

Making a *gift in kind* is not always easy. The meals-on-wheels organization may not want to own and insure its own vehicles, they may want only volunteers' vehicles to be used for deliveries. The art gallery or museum may consider your painting a third-rate work by a minor artist, or may be committed to building its collection around sixteenth century Flemish artists while your piece is seventeenth century. Your church may not want to be bothered having your baseball card collection appraised and finding a buyer so they can use the proceeds to fix the furnace.

Check with the charity before you make a firm decision to leave them something other than cash in your will.

## A charity that can't take a hint

It's not that you have a controlling personality . . . it's just that you feel you have a right tell the charity what it should do with *your* money. For example, you may have thought for years that your synagogue needed money to create a memorial wall; or you may be convinced that your farm property would be perfect for a summer camp for inner-city kids.

If you want your gift to be used for a specific purpose, check that purpose out with the charity first. The charity may not be willing or able to do what you want. Your synagogue may already be using all its walls (although they'd love to renovate their kitchen facilities), and the inner-city kids' organization can't afford to set up and run a camp (but it sure could use proceeds from the sale of your land to run its after-school program). If the charity cannot carry out your request, it may have to refuse your gift.

If the charity of your choice, when consulted, does not want to do what you want them to do, you have two choices. You can find another charity that will follow your orders. Or you can refocus on the charity's needs rather than your own wishes. If you choose this course, you can state in your will the purposes you would like your gift to be used for, but then give the charity discretion to decide how your gift will be used.

### A charity that will put your name up in lights

Some people prefer to be anonymous or at least unsung donors, while others like to be recognized and remembered (or have someone else honoured and remembered) for the contribution they've made. It won't be hard to find a charity that will agree not to mention your name. It will be harder to find a charity that will recognize your donation in the way you'd like. This is a matter you'll have to take up with the charity.

Depending on the size of your donation, the charity of your choice may be willing to publish your name in their donor list, put your name (or another's) on a plaque, or give a reception in your honour or memory. Charities that have buildings (churches, hospitals, universities, performing arts organizations) may be willing to name a room or a wing or even the entire building after you or someone of your choice . . . if your donation is big enough.

## Making Sure Your Donation Gets Where You Want It to Go

Once you've decided on a charity, there are two points to remember:

- Get the name right.
- Make alternate plans in case the charity dies before you do.

### Get the charity's name right

The most important thing is to name the charity correctly. Your will should refer to the charity by its full legal name and also give its address. This will reduce the chance that two charities with the same or similar names will end up fighting over your donation. If you leave a gift to the "animal welfare society," it's probably not your intention that the Humane Society and the Society for the Prevention of Cruelty to Animals should end up fighting over it like cats and dogs. The lady down the street who takes in strays might even join the free-for-all. There have been many lawsuits between competing charities over a donor's will — and it's not unheard-of for a court to rule that the cost of the fray should be financed by the gift in the donor's will.

Tracking down the right name and address of your charity is one of the things your lawyer will do when drafting your will. But if you're impatient, you can check Canada Revenue's searchable list of registered charities at its Web site (`www.ccra-adrc.gc.ca`), call Canada Revenue's Charities Division at 1-800-267-2384, or call the charity itself (if you think you know its name, that is).

### Guard against the charity's untimely end

A major charity is not likely to cease to exist between now and the time of your death — even if your death is decades away — but a small charity just might. It could fold when its present organizers lose heart about saving the tree toads, or it could join a larger organization and lose its objectives in the larger organization's objectives.

If you're concerned that your charity may get to heaven before you do, you can name another charity in your will as an alternate. Or in your will you can instruct your executor to choose a charity, keeping in mind your interests.

## Planned Giving

Many charities, especially the larger ones, have people whose job it is to encourage donations. They may be called Planned Giving Officers or Development Officers. Before you make a final decision about which charity and what donation, you can talk to charities' officers about matters such as:

- The correct name and address of the charity.
- The charity's willingness to accept your gift in kind.
- The charity's willingness to use your gift for a specific purpose.
- The charity's standard wording (if any) for use in your will.

If you are thinking about making a large donation to the charity, these officers will also be thrilled to speak to you about ways to structure your gift, including tax advice and advice on the different ways to give. Listen to them, drink their coffee and eat their cookies, even go out to lunch with them — but be sure to get your own legal and financial advice before you make any decision.

# Ways to Give to Charity

Now we're going to tell you about the different ways you can donate to the charity as a part of the estate planning process, and about what it all means from the point of view of taxes. The ways of donating include:

- Gifts of cash made by will
- Gifts of specific property made by will
- Gifts of life insurance
- Gifts of RRSP or RRIF proceeds
- Charitable gift annuities
- Charitable remainder trusts
- Memorial donations

## Gifts of cash made by will

You can leave cash to a charity in your will in one of two ways:

- You can make a gift of a specified amount of money to the charity. Just make sure that your estate will have enough cash or property that is easily converted to cash (such as GICs, RRSPs, or RRIFs) to cover the gift. If it doesn't, the amount of the gift does not necessarily get reduced. Instead, your estate may have to sell property to get the money for the gift. The property sold may be something that you would have preferred a family member or friend to receive, such as blue-chip stocks, a car, or a cottage.
- Or you can give the charity a share or percentage of the value of the *residue* of your estate — the residue is what's left in your estate after your executor pays your debts and taxes and hands out the gifts of cash and property that you made to named individuals.

These are the simplest and most common ways to make a donation to charity in a will. Your estate will be entitled to a tax credit of 17 percent of the first $200 in donations and 29 percent of donations over $200.

## Gifts of specific property made by will

Instead of leaving cash to a charity, you can leave specific property to the charity (a gift in kind) — for example, stocks or other securities, real estate, artwork, or a motor vehicle.

Your estate will have to pay capital gains tax on the property if it increased in value between the time you got it and the time you died. (This is true whether you donate the property or not.) But your estate will be entitled to a charitable donation tax credit for the property (17 percent of the first $200, and 29 percent of donations over $200), based on its fair market value at the time of your death. The tax credit can wipe out the capital gains tax payable on the donated property, as you can see in the example of "Frank arrives dead."

### Frank arrives dead

Frank, a successful real estate salesman, owned a solid silver trophy that he had received in recognition for his high sales volume. When he got the trophy, it was valued at $10,000. In his will he left the trophy to a favourite charity that promoted the benefits of atomic energy for all. During a vacation in San Francisco, he incautiously drank a "Glow in the Dark" martini whose active ingredient turned out to be radium. In the following 48 hours, he devoted his waning strength to discovering the recipe and the identity of the bartender, but finally landed dead on arrival at San Francisco General. His executor and the charity, although plunged into grief, worked out the tax aspects of the donation. The trophy was now worth $20,000.

**Capital gains tax:**

| | |
|---|---|
| Capital gain on the trophy ($20,000 – $10,000) | $10,000 |
| Taxable capital gain (50% of $10,000) | $5,000 |
| Tax payable at the top marginal tax rate (approx. 50%) | $2,500 |

**Charitable donation tax credit:**

| | |
|---|---|
| 17% tax credit on the first $200 of the donation | $34 |
| 29% tax credit on the balance over $200 ($19,800) | $5,742 |
| Total federal tax credit for the donation | $5,776 |
| Provincial tax credit (approx. — varies by province) | $2,888 |
| Total tax credits | $8,664 |

The charitable donation credit not only wipes out the capital gains tax payable of $2,500 but the remaining $6,164 can be used to reduce the total tax bill of the estate. This is an especially good deal considering that nobody, including the deceased's fiancée, Paula, could figure out what to do with the trophy anyway.

## Ebenezer's gift

Ebenezer, a famously jolly and generous gentleman, owned shares in the publicly traded Marley Clanking Chain Corporation. The shares were worth $10,000 when Ebenezer inherited them from the corporation's founder, and they were worth $20,000 when he later died laughing. In his will he left the shares to a charity in which he had been involved for many years, Christmas Present. Ebenezer's executor, Tim Cratchit, worked out the tax consequences of the gift as follows:

**Calculation of taxable capital gain in Ebenezer's estate:**

| | |
|---|---|
| Capital gain on the shares ($20,000 – $10,000) | $10,000 |
| Taxable capital gain (50% of $10,000) | $ 5,000 |
| Tax payable on normal taxable capital gain (at approx. 50%, since Ebenezer's estate easily reaches the top marginal tax bracket) | $2,500 |
| Capital gains tax payable on publicly traded shares donated to charity (approx. 50% of normal) | $1,250 |

Ebenezer's estate is still entitled to claim the full charitable donation tax credit on the shares' value of $20,000, which is approximately $8,664 (the exact amount depends on the province). This tax credit can be used to reduce the entire tax bill of the estate, not just the capital gains tax on the shares.

### *Special tax treatment for gifts of shares*

If your gift in kind to a charity is publicly traded shares, your estate gets a gift back! (At least until December 31, 2001.) The gift is from Canada Revenue and it's a reduction in any taxable capital gain on the shares. Only half of the normal taxable capital gain will be considered taxable in your estate. Have a look at the story of "Ebenezer's gift."

If you have both cash and publicly traded shares and you're thinking about making a donation to charity in your will, your estate's tax bill will be lower if you leave the shares to the charity and the cash to a relative or friend and you die before January 1, 2002. (But don't rush just to get the tax break!)

## *Gifts of life insurance*

If you think that there won't be enough money in your estate to fund the charitable donation you'd like to make, you can donate the proceeds of a life insurance policy on your own life to the charity you've chosen. There are two different ways to do this:

- You can donate the insurance policy to the charity while you are still alive. You can take out a new policy on your life naming the charity as the policy owner and beneficiary, or you can give ownership of an existing policy to the charity (the charity will name itself the beneficiary if you haven't already done so).

- You can hold on to your insurance policy and either name the charity as the beneficiary of the policy, or name your estate as the beneficiary and leave the charity an amount of money equal to the life insurance proceeds in your will.

As we show you in the next sections, the tax benefits to you and your estate are different depending on which option you choose.

### Donating the insurance policy

If you take out a new policy naming the charity as owner or if you assign ownership of an existing policy to the charity, the charity will become the beneficiary, and in all likelihood you'll pay the premiums. (The charity *could* pay the premiums, of course, but why would it want to? Their business is receiving donations, not making them.) When you die, the insurance proceeds will go directly to the charity. Charities like this option best because they own the policy, not you, and that means you won't be able to change the beneficiary if you should happen to have a difference of opinion with the charity or if you just decide you know someone who'll need the money more.

When you take out a policy naming the charity as owner, your estate will not be able to claim a donation tax credit for the proceeds paid to the charity when you die (because you didn't own the policy).

The only tax benefit you'll get is while you're still alive — any premiums that you pay for the policy are eligible for a donation tax credit in your annual tax return. If you donate an existing policy with a *cash surrender value* (that would be permanent insurance, as we explain in Chapter 7), you will be able to claim on your tax return, in the year you give away the policy, a donation credit based on the cash surrender value of the policy.

### Keeping the policy

If you keep ownership of the life insurance policy, you can name the charity as the beneficiary of the policy, or you can name your estate as the beneficiary and leave the same amount of money to the charity in your will. Either way, your estate will be able to claim a donation tax credit for the amount that is paid to the charity.

You will not be allowed to claim the insurance premiums you pay while you're alive as a charitable donation. But usually the tax credit your estate will get on the proceeds when you die will be far more than the credit you would be able to claim on the premiums while you're alive.

### How do you choose the beneficiary?

If you name the charity as beneficiary, when you die the insurance proceeds will be paid directly to the charity by the insurance company. Because the insurance proceeds go to the charity and not to your estate, your estate won't have to pay probate fees on the proceeds. (We discuss probate fees in

Chapter 5.) So you can reduce probate fees by naming the charity as beneficiary. On the other hand, if the proceeds don't go into your estate, they won't be available to pay your taxes and other debts. If there's not enough money in your estate to pay your taxes and debts, the charity will still get the full proceeds while gifts to your relatives and friends under your will may end up being reduced.

If you name your estate as beneficiary, the insurance proceeds will be subject to probate tax, but they will also be available to pay your taxes and other debts. If there's not enough money left over to give the full amount of planned gifts to relatives, friends, and charities, everyone's gift will be reduced.

## Gifts of RRSP or RRIF proceeds

You can donate the proceeds of your Registered Retirement Savings Plan or Registered Retirement Investment Fund to charity. If you do, you can either name the charity as the beneficiary of the RRSP or RRIF or you can name your estate as the beneficiary and leave the charity an amount of money equal to the proceeds of the plan or fund in your will.

The income tax implications are the same either way. When you die you are deemed by Canada Revenue to have cashed in all your RRSPs and RRIFs immediately before your death. The full amount of the RRSPs or RRIFs is added to your income in your terminal tax return, and your estate is responsible for paying the income tax. (We explain how all this works in Chapter 5.) Your estate will, however, be entitled to the usual donation tax credit (17 percent of the first $200 in donations, and 29 percent of donations over $200) based on the amount of the proceeds.

How should you decide, then, between naming the charity as beneficiary or in giving a gift in your will?

Think about the same things you think about if you are deciding how to donate an insurance policy. If you name the charity as the beneficiary, the RRSP or RRIF proceeds will not form part of your estate and will not be subject to probate tax, but then the proceeds won't be available to pay your taxes and other debts. If there's not enough money to go around, the charity will get the full proceeds while gifts to your relatives and friends under your will may end up being cut. If you name your estate as beneficiary, the RRSP or RRIF proceeds will be subject to probate tax, but they will also be available to pay your taxes and other debts. If there's not enough money to go around, everyone's gift will be reduced.

## Charitable gift annuities

You can make a donation to a charity while you're still alive in return for an *annuity.* But before we explain how a charitable gift annuity works, we'd better tell you how an ordinary annuity works.

### What's an annuity?

An annuity is an investment bought from a financial institution, usually an insurance company. You pay the financial institution a lump sum in return for its promise to pay you a fixed amount of money every year for either a set number of years (a *fixed term annuity*), until you die (a *life annuity*), or until both you and your spouse die (a *joint life annuity*).

If you buy a fixed term annuity, the fixed amount of the payments is calculated so as to repay you all the money you invested plus interest (at an agreed rate) over the number of years you choose. At the end of the term, you will have received all of your money back, plus interest. If you die before the term is up, what's left of the annuity will be paid to whomever you name as a beneficiary. You pay tax only on the interest portion of the payments, not on the repayment portion of the payments.

If you buy a life annuity, the fixed amount of the payments is calculated to repay you all of the money you invested plus interest for the number of years that you are expected to live. The insurance company decides how long you are likely to live, using the same kinds of mortality tables they use to calculate insurance premiums (see Chapter 7). If you live exactly as long as the insurance company expects you to, you will receive all of your money back, plus interest. If you live longer than the insurance company expects, it must keep on paying you the fixed amount until you die. If you die earlier than expected, the insurance company gets to keep your money — unless you buy a *guaranteed annuity,* which is more expensive. (If you buy a guaranteed annuity and die before a certain number of years have passed, the insurance company will make the rest of the payments to whomever you name as beneficiary.) As with a fixed term annuity, you pay tax only on the interest portion of the payments, and not on the repayment portion.

A joint life annuity works just like a life annuity. If you buy a joint life annuity, the fixed amount of the payments is calculated to repay you and your spouse all of the money you invested plus interest for the number of years that the two of you are expected to live (one of you will probably be expected to live longer than the other). If one of you survives the other and lives longer than expected, the insurance company has to keep on paying. If you both die before expected, the insurance company gets to keep the money.

### So what's a charitable gift annuity?

A charitable gift annuity is very nearly the same as a regular annuity. You take it out in the ordinary way, either as a fixed term annuity or a life annuity. The only special feature is that the charity gets any remaining value in the annuity after your death, instead of another beneficiary or the insurance company. Some charities issue their own annuities, others use insurance companies.

### Why buy a charitable gift annuity?

If you would like to make a donation to a charity while you're still alive but you need the income from the money to live on, an annuity can be useful. With other kinds of investments, the investor worries about preserving the capital so that it can go on producing income. With a life annuity, the *annuitant* (that's you, the investor) isn't concerned about the shrinkage in the capital because payments are guaranteed for life — no matter if the capital shrinks down to zero and below. The same is true of a term annuity if the term is longer than the annuitant truly believes he or she will live. Obviously there's a risk here, but if you outlive your term annuity, you may be so tickled to be alive that you won't care that you're poor.

The charity is agreeable to issuing you an annuity because it's gambling that you'll die while there's still capital left. Of course, no charity is going to go the annuity route with you if you look like you're going to outlive your capital. They prefer their annuitants to be kind of aged and doddery and pasty looking.

### Tax treatment of annuities

There are no plummy little tax surprises here. When you buy an annuity from a charity, you don't get a donation tax credit for any of the amount you can expect to receive back over the term of the annuity. (Those people at Canada Revenue are hardly ever caught napping!) You'll get a donation tax credit only if you pay more to the charity for the annuity than you can expect to get back. Then the credit will be based on the difference between what you paid for the annuity and what you're likely to get back.

When your annuity payments start, they will be made up of repayment of your investment plus interest earned on your investment. You will have to pay tax on the interest portion of the payments, but not on the repayment portion. So you won't be getting any special tax breaks, but you'll *feel* as though you are because you'll be paying tax only on part of your total annuity income. Okay, okay, we admit this is a pretty pathetic attempt to help you feel upbeat about paying taxes.

## Charitable remainder trusts

In Chapter 9 on trusts, we tell you about *charitable remainder trusts*. In a charitable remainder trust, you put income-producing property into a trust and get the income from the property for as long as you (or you and your spouse) are alive. The charity gets the trust property when you (or the second of you and your spouse) die.

Some charities promote charitable remainder trusts to donors, but it's not a particularly good idea from the donor's point of view. You do get a tax credit for the donation when the trust is set up, but you don't get a full credit because a real change in ownership won't happen until some time in the future. So the tax credit won't equal the total value of the property put into the trust. Over and above that, when you put capital property (anything other than cash) into the trust you are deemed to have disposed of it for income tax purposes. If the property has gone up in value since you acquired it, you will have to pay tax on the capital gain. The tax payable on the capital gain may very well be greater than the tax credit for the donation. (We tell you about taxes on capital gains in Chapter 4.)

## Memorial donations

If you want to donate to charity after your death, asking for memorial donations is a way of getting others to make the donation. It's not exactly cheating . . . you could think of it as "leveraging" your death. Or you could think of it as exercising power from beyond the grave (or urn) to encourage others to be charitable.

Mourners have traditionally sent flowers to funerals in order to show their respect, affection, or sympathy. A nice flower arrangement can cost tens or hundreds of dollars, and within a few days it's thrown into the garbage. It's pretty while it lasts but it's not much use to anyone. So more and more people are asking that mourners make a donation to charity rather than sending flowers. (It probably won't be long before someone establishes a charity for destitute flower sellers put out of business by the memorial donation trend.) You can ask that donations be made to the charity of your choice, or you can ask that donors give to a charity of their own choice.

If you would like memorial donations instead of flowers, let your family and executor know while you're still alive so it can be included in your obituary notice. Don't just leave instructions in your will, since it might not be read until after the funeral.

# Chapter 14

# Goodbye to All That: Plan Your Funeral and Organ Donation

### In This Chapter

- Planning a funeral
- Arranging to dispose of your body
- Paying for a funeral
- Donating organs and other body parts

As they say, you can't take it with you. But since you're leaving your body behind, you have to figure out what to do with it. This chapter will tell you what you need to know in order to pre-plan your funeral and the disposal of your body.

If you do any funeral planning, even if it's only choosing your favourite hymn or forbidding flowers you hate, don't just leave the instructions in your will! Wills often are not read until the funeral is over. Let your family and executor know about your wishes in some other way.

## The Last Word

Who gets to decide the details of your funeral and body disposal? Strangely, in law it's mostly none of your business what happens to your body after you're dead. If you've got an executor, it's the executor's responsibility to make funeral arrangements — and the executor doesn't have to pay any attention to what you wanted or to what your family and friends want. He or she only has to make arrangements suitable to your position in life. If you don't have an executor, your closest relative (starting with husband or wife but not in most provinces an unmarried partner, then in order a child, a parent, a brother or sister) gets to decide about funeral arrangements. Generally speaking, executors and families don't mind carrying out your wishes — but if yours are a bit unusual, it would be wise to run them by your executor and family just to make sure they're okay with them.

Even more strangely, although you're not allowed the final say about what happens to your entire body, you are supposed to get the last word about what happens to bits and pieces of it. Each province has a law that if an adult consents while alive to organ donation, the consent stays valid after death. The provinces passed this law to get around the earlier law (the same one that still applies to your funeral) that your consent to donate your organs ended as soon as you died and it was your executor's or family's decision to donate or not. Even now, however, a hospital usually won't accept your organs if you gave your consent but your family doesn't like the idea.

So be warned that you can spend a lot of time planning your funeral and signing donor consent forms, and your best-laid plans may not only go astray but may even shiver a timber or two on the rock of your executor and family.

# The High Cost of Death

Dying isn't expensive (it's prolonging life that costs so much) — but disposing of your body definitely is. You're easily looking at several thousand dollars. And you're not even going to be there to enjoy the festivities! One of the best reasons for pre-planning your funeral is to get an idea of exactly what all your hard-earned and hard-saved cash is buying.

If this were a wedding, you could elope and avoid the cost. But it's considerably more difficult to elope in order to avoid having to dispose of your body. Even if you decide to wander up to a remote mountain top in January and sit down and quietly freeze to death there, eventually someone will find your remains and your survivors will want to give whatever's left of you a send-off of some kind. So you might as well bite the bullet and make more traditional plans about your funeral and disposal of your body.

Funeral expenses are paid by your estate (including any life insurance proceeds), unless your executor and family are saps who don't realize that and pay out of their own pockets. Or unless you are eligible for money from the government or some private organization. These might include:

- A union, club, or fraternal organization of which you are a member
- Your employer, via your employment benefits package
- Provincial worker's compensation, if your death is caused by a work-related injury or disease
- The insurance company of a lousy driver who kills you, or your own insurer if you're in a no-fault-insurance province, or a provincial uninsured motorist accident claims fund if the lousy driver was also an uninsured driver

- If you're a veteran, the Last Post fund run by the Department of Veterans' Affairs
- The social assistance authorities, if you're on social assistance at the time of your death

This is a pretty pathetic-looking list, isn't it? The chances are very good that the cost of your funeral is going to be borne by you or your estate.

# It's Your Funeral

What kind of funeral arrangements do you want? If you want to go the whole nine yards — the visitation with casket open or closed, the flowers, the religious service in a funeral chapel or in your church, synagogue, or mosque, the graveside service — then you probably need the assistance of a *funeral home.*

If you just want to go straight from your place of death to a cemetery or crematorium (this is called "direct disposition" in the funeral industry — try to remember not to call it "direct deposit") you may prefer to deal with a *transfer service*. If there's no transfer service in your area, a funeral home can perform the same function. If you still want a religious service even though your body won't be present, you can have a memorial service rather than a funeral service.

## At the home sweet funeral home

What exactly is a funeral home going to do for you? Well, they could do all kinds of exciting things. They'll pick up your body, refrigerate it, embalm it if you ask them to (or, quite possibly, unless you specifically tell them not to), wash you, make up your face (love that orange foundation) or even do restorative surgery (this seems like a good place to draw the line and insist on a closed coffin), and dress you. Well, at least you're dead when all of this is going on.

They'll sell you the coffin, rent you a visitation room and the funeral chapel, provide a book for visitors to sign, make arrangements for a service in the chapel including clergy, flowers, music, and an order of service, get you some pallbearers and ushers, organize the details of burial or cremation, rent out a hearse and some limos, arrange for a police escort so your funeral procession can go through red lights and snarl up traffic for miles, and cater a reception for the mourners. And there's more. (These people are all-rounders.) They'll deal with the paperwork to get the death certificate and burial or cremation permit, put your survivors in touch with grief counsellors, and maybe even help your family apply for death benefits.

Since a funeral home is not a charity run for your benefit but a business run for its own benefit, it's going to charge to do all this. Now, you don't necessarily need every service they can perform, and you can tell the funeral home staff what you want if you're pre-arranging. However, the arrangements may come in a package and you may find that to get the things you want you may also have to take a few things you don't want. If you insist on picking and choosing only what you want, it may add up to more than the cost of a package. As we said, this is business.

Well, since it's business, treat it like business. Comparison shop before you buy.

## Shop 'til you drop

You're going to find shopping for a funeral home a rather . . . unusual . . . experience. Finding the right one for you isn't going to be on a par with finding hand-made Italian pumps that fit perfectly or the Swedish masseuse of your dreams. If you do happen to find funeral home shopping a sensual experience, you should stop immediately and seek professional help.

Here's the game plan for your shopping trip. First, discreetly ask around among family, friends, and associates who've gone through the shopping process recently, either for themselves or another. Get some recommendations. And it's just as important to know what funeral home gave them the creeps as it is to know what funeral home offered good service at an acceptable price.

Next, call three or four of the funeral homes that have been recommended to you and speak to the staff. Give them a general idea of what you'd like in the way of a funeral (for example, a visitation, no chapel service, and burial in the local area) and ask them to tell you roughly what it would cost. Ask about the price range of coffins they have on display and whether a brochure with a wider selection is available. Ask them to send you a current price list for their goods and services (many provinces require them to make a list available at no charge and with no obligation). Inquire if they belong to any funeral service associations. If you get the feeling that you're talking to beings who have just crawled out from under a damp rock, cross the funeral home off your list. If they seem to be decent people, considering the circumstances, make an appointment to visit.

When you pay your visit, look the establishment over generally (is this the kind of joint you'd be caught dead in?), view the coffins and any brochures, and inquire if they charge a fee if you buy your coffin elsewhere. Ask to see their standard pre-planning contract, and ask for an explanation of anything in it you don't understand. If there is no funereal activity there that day, you might even consider returning during a visitation to see whether they do a nice job.

If after making your phone calls and visits you're still undecided about which funeral home to choose, study the information you've collected from each one, comparing services and prices. If that doesn't help, maybe you should investigate more funeral homes. Or you can just say to hell with it and leave funeral arrangements up to your executor.

## Slip into something comfortable

A coffin is one of the more intensely interesting purchases you might make when you're shopping at the funeral home of your choice. Just think of the fun of going shopping for your own coffin! How about the classic Count Dracula model, with beautiful highly polished wood and red satin lining? It might cost quite a bit — a deluxe casket can cost several thousand dollars.

But you don't have to spend thousands on a casket. A basic casket costs about $500, and you should be able to find something that appeals to your taste and your wallet for somewhere between five hundred dollars and several thousand dollars. If you're looking at caskets in a funeral home, ask to see a brochure

### Hold the formaldehyde

We thought it was time to indulge your morbid curiosity about embalming. If you're a little bit squeamish, you can skip this sidebar.

Embalming involves draining out all your blood and replacing it with a preservative fluid such as formaldehyde. Yecch. Remember the smell of formaldehyde from high school biology classes? The embalming fluid will keep your buried body from decomposing for a certain length of time — not forever, but for anywhere from a few months to a few years. How long you'll look well preserved also depends on the local climate (cold and dry are good for your complexion, warm and damp are bad) and on the air-tightness of your casket. Your body is not going to decay significantly in the few hours or days between your death and burial or cremation if it's kept refrigerated . . . and to be frank, you will already have passed your "Best Before" date by the time you reach the funeral home.

So why is embalming fluid on tap at the funeral home? The funeral industry thinks people look better embalmed. But professional conservatism could be the answer. Embalming dates from the years before widespread refrigeration, specifically to the time of the U.S. Civil War in the 1860s, when a lot of bodies were being shipped home over long distances. It made sense then, but it doesn't make a lot of sense now — unless your body is in fact going to be shipped long distances. Some provinces, U.S. states, and foreign countries require bodies to be embalmed before they are shipped by public carrier (airline, railroad, ship, or truck).

Our advice? Just say no to embalming, unless there's a legal requirement for it. On the other hand . . . it will be your last kinky experience on this planet. Maybe you'd like to swing one final time.

showing their entire line. (Even if you fall in love with a particular model, you don't have to buy it on the spot. It's not as though you're going to take your purchase home with you.)

In some provinces you'll be able to find a discount coffin outlet. These outlets have a lower mark-up on coffins than funeral homes do. Maybe you'll be able to afford the Dracula model after all! There could be a bit of unpleasantness, however, if you're making your funeral arrangements through a funeral home and want to buy your coffin from a discount outlet. The funeral home's nose will be put out of joint to start with, and they may want to charge a handling fee of up to a couple of hundred dollars for using a coffin from outside (some provinces allow them to do this).

If your principles or your finances take exception to the spending of hundreds or thousands of dollars on a casket, there's still another way of getting yourself properly buried. Legally your body doesn't have to be put in a casket — all that's actually needed is an enclosed rigid container. Funeral homes and transfer services can provide a cardboard container for as little as $100, and fancier containers for a few hundred dollars. And if you want a flashier look for the funeral, you can rent a casket for the visitation or service (for about $1,000) and then be buried in a container.

## The funeral services contract

If you decide to pre-plan your funeral, you'll leave written instructions with the funeral home about your preferences. You can pre-plan without pre-paying. If you don't pre-pay, your executor will enter into a contract with the funeral home after your death and arrange with your bank to release funds from your estate to cover the costs.

If you do pre-pay, you can pay the entire amount up front, or you may be able to pay on the installment plan, or you can buy a life insurance policy to cover the amount. (Just because you're pre-paying doesn't mean that the price is guaranteed for the entire length of your life, though.) If you make a cash payment, some of the money (in some provinces, all of the money) has to be held in trust by the funeral home and not used until the services are actually performed.

If you're pre-paying, there should be a contract signed by both you and the funeral director, and each of you should keep a copy with original signatures (that is, don't accept a photocopy of the signed contract). It should set out

- What you want (casket model, details of visitation and service, and so on)
- The price

- Any amount you have already paid
- When and how any future amounts are to be paid
- What your rights to cancel the contract are (What if you move to another city? What if you're sick now but you miraculously recover? What if scientists unlock the secrets of immortality next year?)
- How much of your pre-paid money and accumulated interest will be refunded if you cancel

  A number of provinces have a "cooling-off" period of a few days to a few months, and if you cancel within this period you can get all your money back. If you want to cancel after the cooling-off period has ended, most provinces require a funeral home to refund the entire amount paid except for an administration fee (which can go as high as 12 percent in some provinces), but the rules about interest vary across the country.
- What will become of any money left over after the funeral (it should be returned to your estate and an itemized account of what was done and what money was spent should be given to your executor)

### A word from Canada Revenue

There may be tax advantages to pre-paying for your funeral. Now don't get all excited about this. We haven't.

The pre-planning that you do is considered an *eligible funeral arrangement* (an EFA to those in the know) if the funeral home has set things up in accordance with the requirements of the *Income Tax Act*. Money spent on an eligible funeral arrangement can't be deducted from income on your tax return like an RRSP contribution, but interest earned on the money salted away in the EFA isn't included in your reportable income. It doesn't even have to be included in your estate's income if it's used on funeral arrangements.

Now, before you start shouting "YEE-HA! Tax-free income!" keep in mind that (1) the income has to stay in an EFA until you die to remain tax-free, and (2) your money is not going to be invested by the funeral home in something that will make you rich — it will be invested as safely as possible. In the long run, income from an EFA will probably end up being used to offset inflation in the cost of the goods and services provided by the funeral home, if you live long enough after planning your funeral for interest and inflation to have a noticeable effect.

The really interesting thing about EFAs is how much you're allowed to put into them. You can contribute up to $15,000 for funeral services, up to $20,000 for cemetery services, and up to $35,000 for both. Here's what we think: if you've got $35,000, forget the funeral. Throw a great party while you're still around to enjoy it.

TIP

### For more words of wisdom

If you're keen on pre-arranging and pre-paying, you might want to contact your provincial board of funeral directors to find out more about funeral contracts in your province.

- Alberta: Alberta Funeral Service Regulatory Board (Edmonton)
- British Columbia: Ministry of the Attorney General, Cemeteries and Funeral Service Board (Victoria)
- New Brunswick: New Brunswick Board for Registration of Embalmers & Funeral Directors (Hampton)
- Nova Scotia: The Nova Scotia Board of Registration of Embalmers & Funeral Directors (Kentville)
- Prince Edward Island: Prince Edward Island Funeral Directors & Embalmers Association (Kensington)
- Manitoba: Manitoba Board of Administration Under the Embalmers & Funeral Directors Act (Winnipeg)
- Newfoundland: Newfoundland Board of Registration for Embalmers & Funeral Directors (St. John's)
- Ontario: Board of Funeral Services (Toronto)
- Quebec: Corporation des Thanatologues du Quebec (Sainte-Foy)
- Saskatchewan: Saskatchewan Funeral Service Association (Regina)

# At Your Disposal: Earth, Air, Fire, or Water?

Earth, air, fire, and water are the four elements that ancient philosophers believed everything was made of. So when it's time to return your body to the elements, which one will you choose? Do you want to be buried in the earth or at sea, do you want to be cremated, do you want to be returned to the air?

# Earth

If you choose burial in the ground, you'll be in the ground but not of the ground, so to speak. You don't get to cozy right up to the dirt, at least not for a while. You'll start off in the lovely casket — or possibly the cheap cardboard container — that you chose so carefully. Then you need a place to put it. So now you have to choose a cemetery.

## The cemetery

If your family doesn't already have a plot, or you haven't been casting a longing eye on a memorial garden on your route to work, you can contact your place of worship or a funeral home for suggestions about cemeteries. Or look in the Yellow Pages.

And before you ask, the answer is pretty much Yes: you have to be buried in a cemetery and not in the backyard or the woods. Even in the provinces that don't specifically say that dead human bodies belong only in cemeteries, if you leave instructions to be planted outside a cemetery your executor may run into trouble with the municipal zoning department, the public health authorities, the next-door neighbours, and the tabloid media.

Although the backyard is free, cemetery fees can be high. You have to buy a plot or a tomb (*interment rights*), the actual burial or entombment (*interment*), and some kind of monument so your friends and relations will know where to come and cry over you.

## Interment rights

It's no fun talking about "interment rights." It's not even any fun talking about "plots." Let's talk about graves instead. Graves come in different sizes. A "single" adult grave can hold two coffins, stacked. A *lot* contains more than one grave, so a two-grave lot could hold four coffins. Your family will be very touched if you go out grave shopping for yourself and come back with something for everyone.

If you prefer above-ground burial, in some cemeteries you can buy a *tomb* . . . also called a *crypt*. A tomb holds one or two coffins. If you're expecting company, go for a *mausoleum*. A family mausoleum can hold several coffins, a community mausoleum many more.

You can buy interment rights together with someone else, although this may seem like taking togetherness a little far. If you do, you and your significant interment other can be *joint tenants* (except in Quebec) or *tenants in common*. If you buy as joint tenants, when the first person dies complete ownership of the interment rights passes to the survivor. That means that the survivor has to sign a permission form to let the deceased be buried. If you buy as tenants in common, on the other hand, ownership of the deceased's interment rights pass on death to the deceased's estate, while the surviving tenant in common simply goes on having his or her interment rights. That means that the estate of the deceased *plus* the surviving tenant in common have to give permission to let the deceased be buried. If you buy interment rights all by yourself, only your estate has to give permission for you to be buried. Welcome to the wild and wacky world of interment!

Interment rights in a really nice cemetery can cost up to about $5,000. But you can find a Boot Hill for a lot less than that.

## Interment, or the yawning grave

Interment isn't that complicated if you've chosen a tomb, but if you've gone for a grave, interment involves locating the boundaries of the grave, digging the grave, placing the coffin in the grave, and filling in the grave. A cemetery might charge several hundred dollars to do all this.

## The monument

Now for the final touch, your monument. The cemetery may have by-laws about the size and shape of your monument, but the choice generally comes down to an upright stone (yes, you can even have weeping angels on top of it if that's what you want) or a marker, which is a granite or bronze plaque set flush with the ground. In some cemeteries you can have a memorial tree planted instead of having a monument.

You want your monument to look nice, because that's all anyone is going to see of you once you're in the ground. And you're going to have to pay for nice. You may spend several hundred dollars for a marker, and a thousand dollars and more for an upright granite stone. You may be able to (or even required to) arrange for a monument through the cemetery, or you may have to puddle off to the monument maker on your own.

## Extras

It's the little details that will make everyone remember your interment as a very special one. So you may want

- The excavated earth removed from the gravesite before the committal service starts.
- Artificial grass and coco matting placed at the gravesite during the service.
- A tent set up for the service.

You will almost certainly also want

- The gravesite levelled, tamped down, re-graded, and sodded after the burial.
- The gravesite levelled and resodded after the earth settles.

The cemetery will probably charge to do all of these things over and above the cost of the interment rights. They will probably also charge you extra for

- Interring the coffin at the deeper level so that a second coffin can be stacked above it later.
- Providing a concrete or steel outer container (a couple of hundred dollars) to prevent the earth from falling in as the casket decays (these are not required by provincial law but some cemeteries require them).
- Placing the container in the grave.
- Holding the funeral later in the day ("later" is usually after 3 or 4 p.m.) or on a weekend.
- Administering (determining ownership of the interment rights and getting permission for interment, filling out provincial documentation, maintaining the cemetery's files).

You've spent a bundle and it's just got you buried. What if you'd like your grave or tomb to look nice for a few years — at least until no one can be bothered visiting you? Probably the first thing to do is check the financial health of the organization that runs the cemetery. Cemeteries run commercially are required by law in most provinces to put aside money for continuing care (cutting the grass, re-grading the earth, removing the snow from a road through the grounds), but cemeteries run by religious organizations or municipalities usually are not. If your cemetery has money trouble, that means weeds and maybe worse in your earthly future.

That little problem aside, many cemeteries allow arrangements to be made for extra care of a grave, such as planting, caring for plants, and trimming the grass, either through an *endowment* (a lump sum of money given to the cemetery and earmarked for your grave) or through regular payments under a contract with the cemetery. An endowment for continuing care has the potential to be an eligible funeral arrangement (see "A word from Canada Revenue" earlier in this chapter).

### The contract

When you make cemetery arrangements, you'll want a contract in writing with the cemetery. It should

- Set out what you're buying.
- Set out the price and any amount you've already paid.
- Describe when and how any additional amounts are to be paid.
- Set out your right to cancel, or your right to have the cemetery buy back your interment rights. Although a grave is land, many provinces won't let you do a real estate flip — you won't be able to sell your plot to anyone else. Check that the contract or the cemetery by-laws require the cemetery

to buy your interment rights back (before you use them, of course) if you ask. There may be a fee for a buy-back.

- Have the by-laws of the cemetery attached to it. They govern things like the hours the cemetery is open, what can and can't be left at a gravesite, and whether pets are allowed to visit.

## Water

There used to be very practical reasons for burying people at sea — namely that they died at sea and in pre-refrigeration days nobody wanted them hanging around until landfall was reached. Nowadays, if you die at sea the authorities in the ship's next port of call will want to see your remains, so your body will be cooled somewhere instead of being chucked over the side.

If you're an old salt, or you're just crazy about the ocean, it's still possible to be buried at sea, whether you died at sea or on land. It's *possible* but it's far from easy. After you read the rules we're going to tell you about below, you'll probably give up the burial at sea idea just like everybody else who found out about the rules.

Burial at sea comes under the jurisdiction of the federal government (Environment Canada, Marine Conservation and Protection branch). And in a word, they would just as soon people were buried elsewhere. To encourage people to do exactly that, they require

- A permit for the funeral home or funeral association through which you're arranging the burial at sea. This permit costs about $2,500 . . . although it's good for an entire year and can be re-used by the home or association. Before the permit will be issued, a notice of intent to bury a body at sea must be published in a local newspaper and the deceased's doctor has to certify that the body is free from infection. It takes about eight weeks to process the application for the permit.
- No embalming. You're going to have to plan ahead very carefully to get around this rule. If no one applies for the permit until you're dead, it will be difficult to find a funeral home that will keep your body for several weeks in an unembalmed state. And if you keel over somewhere other than at the ocean's edge, keep in mind that a body usually has to be embalmed before a public carrier will transport it anywhere.
- A coffin for the body. It has to be designed not to release the body and weighted to keep it on the bottom.
- A site that isn't being trawled by fishing boats, or dredged, or washed by currents that will move the coffin elsewhere. This site, in addition, should be at least three nautical miles from land and in water at least 200 metres deep.

Now let's just suppose that you've said, "Yup, can do" to all four of these conditions. Then you have to go out and find a funeral home that's willing to arrange your burial at sea. That's hard to do because they'll worry about being sued by your family if your coffin gets fished up by a trawler some day, even though you think you found the perfect site.

So . . . Environment Canada has an alternative to suggest. Have the body cremated and scatter the ashes at sea. No permission required, no fee payable. By the way, you can also have your ashes scattered on a lake without permission, unless the lake is privately owned, or on a river.

# Fire

*Cremation* is becoming more popular than burial. Before a body is cremated, the provincial coroner's office has to be satisfied that there's nothing funny about the death — if questions about the death arise later on, there won't be any body to exhume and examine. So the coroner has to issue a certificate, and there's usually a required waiting period of 48 hours. If the coroner refuses to issue a certificate, there can't be a cremation.

Let's assume, however, that you will not die of strychnine poisoning at the hands of your family and that your cremation can go ahead. Read "Ready, aim . . . fire!" for a brief description of the cremation process. As with embalming, the squeamish may want to look away.

If you choose cremation, you may want to think twice about buying a fancy casket, because the casket is just going to go up in flames. You may prefer to opt for the cardboard container.

## Ready, aim . . . fire!

In cremation, the body, minus any medical devices such as a pacemaker or other implant or prosthesis that could explode, is put inside its casket or container into a small furnace (the cremation chamber). The temperature in the furnace is raised to about 1000°C. After about an hour and a half, the body's soft tissues (the flesh and organs) and the container or casket have been consumed by fire — all that's left is bone fragments. The fragments are pulverized to ash and put into a container. The container will weigh about two to four kilos. If you think that sounds heavy, remember we're talking about bone ashes, not wood ashes.

### How much will you get burned for?

The actual cremation costs a few hundred dollars, but then you start running into additional charges for administration, documentation, transfer of the body, witnessing of the cremation process (on request), a temporary urn, and shipping of the ashes. Once you add everything up, cremation is usually less expensive than burial, but it's still not exactly free.

### Ashes to dust

Your ashes, sometimes referred to as *cremains* but not by us or anyone we would invite to dinner, are now your family's to do with what they like. Better give them some hints about what *you'd* like. Not that you'll have any way of enforcing your wishes, of course, except perhaps through haunting. Your options include:

- Being kept in an urn (or a cookie jar or a tackle box or whatever pleases you) at home.
- Being buried in your urn (or whatever) in a casket burial plot or a cremation burial plot (less expensive than a casket burial plot but still up to several hundred dollars), with or without a monument.
- Being deposited in your urn in a cemetery's *columbarium*, which is a bunch of niches in a wall. A columbarium is usually more expensive than a cremation burial plot — it could cost a thousand dollars or more. You can usually have a marker for your niche.
- Being scattered in a cemetery, usually for a fee of a hundred dollars or more.
- Being scattered on private property with the owner's permission or on public property (Crown land) without permission. However, some municipalities have bylaws against scattering remains on private property.

## Air

Bet you're all agog to know what we've come up with here, since you probably can't think, off-hand, of a way of disposing of your body in air. Some cultures traditionally exposed the bodies of their dead to the air and allowed scavenger birds or animals to strip off the flesh . . . but that's not actually what we had in mind, and municipal by-laws in Canada tend to frown on that kind of thing anyway. Besides, while it's romantic to imagine eagles and falcons returning your body to the air, what you'd probably get in reality would be raccoons.

No, what we had in mind was — launching your ashes into space! True, space is a vacuum, so there's no air there, but there might be the odd molecule of oxygen whirling by. Anyway, here's the deal. A Texas company called Celestis (`www.celestis.com`) will, for a fee, launch seven grams of your ashes into space in its own little container on board a rocket. You can choose among earth-orbit, lunar orbit or impact, and a cruise through the solar system and out. If this sounds vaguely familiar to you, it's because you heard about the ashes of Gene Roddenberry and Timothy Leary being blasted into space on the first Celestis flight in 1997. This isn't a cheap option for disposing of your body — the least expensive, earth-orbit, costs several thousand dollars, and the other two cost twice as much. But it may be just perfect for you. To the moon, Alice!

# The Gift That Keeps on Giving: Organ and Body Donation

Body part donation is probably another subject that the squeamish would prefer to avoid. Unfortunately, most Canadians prefer to avoid it, with the result that Canada has one of the lowest organ-donation rates of all Western nations. Agreeing to donate your organs could save someone's life, and agreeing to donate tissue or bone could dramatically improve the quality of someone's life . . . so make yourself think about it. You can have a stiff drink first.

Donation of your entire body is a horse of another colour. Your body will probably be used by anatomy students for practice. If you're heavily into this donation thing, be warned that you have to make a choice between organ donation and body donation. Anatomy students don't want a body with important bits missing from it.

## Consenting to body part donation

As we mentioned at the beginning of this chapter, provincial law allows an adult to give lasting consent to donation of organs and other body parts. "Lasting" in the sense that it continues after death. You can give this consent by signing a donor card (in most provinces, the form comes with your licence) or by specifying it in a living will. We tell you more about living wills in Chapter 19.

You can agree to donate not only your organs (heart, liver, lungs, pancreas, kidneys) but other bits of you as well (heart valves, cornea, tissues, bones, skin, tendons and ligaments, bone marrow). You can be quite specific about which bits you want to donate and which bits you want to keep.

If you don't give your consent while you're alive to organ donation, your family can be asked after your death (by hospital personnel) for their consent. So if you don't really mind donating but you can't quite bring yourself to sign the donor card, you might mention to your family that they can give permission when you're dead. Generally speaking you'll stay intact unless you or your family consent to donation, but there are a couple of exceptions. In the odd province your corneas can be removed without consent. And in Quebec, neither your permission nor your family's is required for an organ donation if two doctors state in writing that there is serious hope of saving the life of the person who would receive the organ, that the operation is urgent for the recipient, and that it is impossible to get the family's consent in time.

If you're serious about organ donation, you should sign up with an organ transplant registry if there's one in your province. For example, there's the British Columbia Transplant Society, and the Multiple Organ Retrieval and Exchange Program of Ontario. If you want to donate bone marrow, you should register with Canadian Blood Services.

## This won't hurt a bit

Let's not beat around the bush. We're all agreed that we want to be completely dead, and not just enjoying a satisfyingly deep nap, before anyone starts removing pieces of us.

If you're donating something other than organs, you don't have to lose a moment's sleep over the question of complete deadness. But you might wonder a bit about being an organ donor, because someone who has undergone "total brain death" can be an organ donor. Then you start thinking about degrees of deadness and asking yourself whether totally brain-dead is as dead as you would like to be when donating a kidney. After all, some of us consider total brain death to be our normal state on weekdays from 9 to 5.

So here's the story on organ donation and total brain death. Organ donors are an elite group. They are people who have suffered brain damage in an accident or from a stroke or aneurysm and who are in a hospital on equipment that keeps oxygenated blood flowing to their organs. (Once blood stops circulating the organs suffer damage and are no longer usable — they can't be jump-started in a new body.) As you can see, only a very small number of people are eligible to donate organs, so chances are you'll never be called upon anyway.

But supposing you do suffer brain damage. When are you brain-dead even though your circulation system is still going? If you're permanently unconscious (either in a coma or a persistent vegetative state) you're not totally brain-dead. You've only undergone "cerebral brain death," because your brain stem is still alive even though your higher brain functions (thinking, seeing, hearing) have stopped. Your brain stem controls basic body functions like respiration and circulation. You're not totally brain-dead until the brain stem stops too. Then there is no independent respiration or circulation and you have to be put on equipment to keep your lungs working and your heart beating.

Now who gets to decide when you're brain-dead? This seems like an important question. The decider shouldn't be, for example, the guy who needs a new pancreas, or the mother of a kid who needs a heart transplant. Let us reassure you that nobody who stands to gain anything from your organ donation is allowed to be the one who says that you're gone, deceased, and defunct. By provincial law, the decision is made by two doctors who have no conflict of interest in declaring you brain-dead. Specifically, neither of the doctors can be closely associated with a person who will receive your organs. In addition, no doctor who plays a role in deciding whether you're totally brain-dead can participate in any way in transplanting your organs.

## No one thinks you're sexy anymore but someone may still want your body

Some people feel that the scariest thing about the afterlife is that Rod Stewart will be there too. But where will his body be? Let us now move on to the topic of body donation.

Medical schools and research institutions may accept donations of bodies for training students in anatomy and for research purposes. Contact the institution of your choice to see if they're accepting bodies. They may not be — they may already have all they want.

It is sad but true that certain people wish to donate their entire body to science not for love of humankind but in order to avoid paying for burial or cremation. The institution will bury or cremate your body at its own expense after its students or researchers are finished with you. On the other hand, the institution may ask that your estate or family pay the cost of transporting you to the institution in the first place.

# Part IV

# Putting Your Plan into Action

"You have to put some instructions in your will, Mr. Snead. You can't be sure that haunting your executor will work."

## *In this part . . .*

This part moves estate planning from theory to practice. We let you know why you need a will, show you a sample will and explain what the heck each section of it means, and tell you all the things that can go wrong with a will — especially one you write yourself! This part also tells you why you need documents (a *power of attorney* and a *living will*) that will allow someone of your choice to manage your finances and make decisions about your medical care if you become disabled before you die.

# Chapter 15

# If There's No Will There's No Way: Why You Need a Will

### In This Chapter

- Learning who gets your property if you die without a will
- Finding out who looks after your estate if you have no executor
- Learning about the problems that affect your estate if you have no will

The title of this chapter says it all — if you don't have a will, there's no way you can put your estate plan into action. In fact, if you don't have a will, your estate could be in a real mess.

A person who dies without a will is said to have died *intestate.* You can die intestate by never making a will at all, or by making a will that turns out to be invalid (because you are not legally capable of making a will or because your will is not properly signed and witnessed — see Chapter 16 for more details). If you die intestate, here are some of the consequences:

- Your property will be given away according to rules set by provincial law.
- There won't be an executor, carefully chosen by you, who will have the automatic right to look after your estate.
- Your estate may lose money while it is being administered.
- The property of your estate may not be given away in the form you'd like (even if it were going to the people you'd like).
- Your estate will probably end up paying more in taxes.
- If any of your beneficiaries are under the age of majority, any property that goes to them has to be managed by the provincial government.
- Your wishes about who will look after your children when you're gone may not be made known.

Now we'll tell you more about these nuisances and catastrophes, as we walk you through the rubble that will be your estate if you die with no will.

# Where Will Your Property Go without Your Directions in a Will?

If you don't have a will, your property doesn't just vanish when you die, and it doesn't get taken away from your family. Every province has a statute that sets out rules about how the property of an intestate person's estate will be given away. The rules are different in each province.

## If you are married

In every province, if you leave a spouse and no children or other relatives, your spouse will get your entire estate. If you leave a spouse and you leave surviving parents, brothers, and sisters, or nieces or nephews too, your spouse will still get everything (except in Quebec, where these relatives will also get a share of the estate).

In most provinces only a legally married spouse is entitled to receive a share of the estate of an intestate person. So if you think of yourself as being "married" to someone but are not legally married to that person, he or she may have no right to a share of your estate. Look at what happened to "Nicholas and Gregory."

### Nicholas and Gregory

Alexandra was married to Nicholas for several years, during which time they had five children. Nicholas and the children disappeared following an unpleasant incident involving armed revolutionaries, and Alexandra believed they were all dead.

In her grief she turned to Gregory, who became the love of her life and soon helped her forget her tragic past. They moved away from Alexandra's home town and lived together as husband and wife, supported by Alexandra's large inheritance from her grandmother, Victoria. But Gregory had enemies. One night they tried to dispose of him by variously poisoning, shooting, and drowning him — and although Gregory miraculously survived this attempt on his life, Alexandra was caught in the crossfire and died.

Alexandra's death made the national papers, and when Gregory (now permanently disabled) got out of the hospital, he was confronted by Nicholas, who, in another miraculous escape, had not died at the hands of the revolutionaries. Gregory was horrified to discover that Alexandra had not made a will and that Nicholas was entitled to take her entire estate. Gregory was certain that Alexandra would have left everything she owned to him, had she made a will — but as things turned out he was reduced to making a claim against Alexandra's estate to be supported as a dependant.

## If you are married with children

If you have both a spouse and children when you die intestate, your estate will be divided among your spouse and your children. (Again, in most provinces, a spouse means a legally married spouse.)

In some provinces the spouse gets a larger share than the children and in other provinces the children get the larger share. In some provinces the spouse gets a fixed amount (sometimes called a *preferential share*) and then whatever's left is divided among the spouse (again) and the children *per stirpes*.

Whoa! Where did that "per stirpes" thing come from? You were just going along, minding your own business, and WHAM.

"Per stirpes" is a Latin expression that means "through the descendants." It means if one of your children dies before you, your deceased child's children will get their parent's share, divided up among them. (The other way to distribute if one of your children has died is to have your other children take over the deceased child's share. It has a fancy Latin name too — *per capita*, meaning "by the heads.")

That's enough Latin class. Back to the spouse and the preferential share. In some provinces, the spouse may be entitled to receive the family home instead of, or as part of, the preferential share. In other provinces the spouse may be entitled to receive an interest in the family home in addition to the preferential share.

Some provinces also have family law statutes that may affect the size of your spouse's share of your estate. Your spouse may be able to choose to take the share offered under the family law statute instead of under the intestacy statute, if it will mean that he or she gets a larger share of your estate.

## If you are not married but you have children

Let's look at what happens if you leave children but no spouse when you die intestate. "Leave no spouse" means your spouse is either dead or divorced from you — or, in most provinces, alive and even living with you before your death but not legally married to you.

In this case, your estate will be divided equally among your children. If one of your children dies before you, his or her share will be divided among his or her children (that's per stirpes). In most provinces a partner who is not legally married to you will get nothing from your estate at all.

## All in the family

Rudolph was just on the point of marrying his cousin, Flavia, when he suffered a fatal hunting accident. He had not yet made his will, but if he had he would have given most of his property to Flavia, with a smaller gift to his other cousin (also named Rudolph). Rudolph had no living parents or children, but he did have a half-brother, Michael (known as Black Michael because of the profound depression he fell into when his many attempts to cause financial or physical harm to Rudolph were unsuccessful).

Rudolph's entire estate went to Michael — exactly the person Rudolph wouldn't have left a penny to if he had made a will! Flavia was incensed, and left the country to marry the other Rudolph, who was more dashing anyway.

## If you are not married and you have no children

If you have no (living, legally-still-married-to-you) spouse and no children when you die without a will, your estate will go to your other relatives. In the following order (in almost all provinces) it will go

- To your parents if they are alive, or to your surviving parent if one is dead.
- To your brothers and sisters if both your parents are dead. If any of your brothers and sisters are dead, their share will be divided among their children, your nieces and nephews (this is a per stirpes distribution to your brothers and sisters, if you were wondering).
- To other more distant relatives such as grandparents, aunts, uncles, and cousins, if you have no brothers or sisters or nieces and nephews.
- To the provincial government, if you have none of the relatives listed above. (The legal term for "goes to the government" is *escheats* . . . and it's not Latin, it's law French, as used in the courts in medieval England. You're getting an impressive language education in this chapter.)

Have a look at "All in the family," above, for an example of what can happen when there's no will.

## If you don't want this to happen to you . . .

Think about what will happen to your property if you die without a will. Is it headed where you want it to go? The odds are that provincial legislation won't accomplish the same distribution of your property that your own will would.

- Do you have a spouse and young children? Many people in that situation want their entire estate to go to their spouse, trusting him or her to know best how to handle family finances. Even if your children are grown up, you may prefer your estate to take care of your spouse first. But if you die without a will, your spouse may receive as little as one-third of your entire estate, depending on your province, and your children will receive the rest. (And if your children are minors, their share will be managed by the provincial government rather than by their surviving parent.)
- Do you have a partner to whom you're not legally married? In most provinces, as we have now said numerous times, if you are not legally married to your partner he or she will not automatically receive a share of your estate. He or she will get zip. Your partner may only be able to make a claim against your estate as a dependant (for more about the sad scenario of being a dependant, see Chapter 10).
- Are you separated but not yet divorced? If you are still legally married, in most provinces your estranged spouse will be entitled to a large share, perhaps all, of your estate. Ouch, that hurts!
- Do you have friends you'd like to leave something to? Friends aren't mentioned anywhere in the provincial statutes. Friends don't even get a whiff of your property to console them for your loss.
- Were you thinking of leaving something to charity? Charities don't figure in the provincial law either. If they don't get a gift in your will, they don't get a gift at all.

# Who Will Administer Your Estate?

If you die without a will, someone will have to be appointed by the court to act as administrator of your estate. Until then, no one has authority to start dealing with your estate until the formal appointment is made. That means no one can do necessary things like protecting the property of your estate, gathering it in, investing the cash, paying debts, and so on (see Chapter 10 for the full list of estate administration duties). However, your family will have the right to make your funeral arrangements. They don't have to leave you lying around until the administrator arrives.

The court will take an application from anyone who wants the job of administering your estate, and if it decides to appoint that person, it will issue a formal document naming the administrator. This document is called *letters of administration* in most provinces, although in Ontario they managed to come up with the light and charming name *certificate of appointment of estate trustee without a will*. The letters of administration are proof of the administrator's legal authority to administer your estate. They take the place of the letters probate that an executor has for proof of his or her authority.

## How will an administrator be found?

The provincial government first looks for volunteers if your estate needs an administrator. Any person who is entitled to receive a share of your estate may have the right to apply to be the administrator, although in many provinces the administrator has to be someone who resides within the province.

If more than one person wants the position, the provincial intestacy statute sets out who has the better right to be administrator. Usually, the closest relative who applies will be appointed, with your spouse (if you have one) having the best right. The court has the power to appoint two or more people to act as joint administrators.

If no one who's going to get something from your estate wants to volunteer, then the beneficiary or beneficiaries who will receive the biggest share of your property can agree to the appointment of a non-beneficiary as administrator.

Even if only one person applies to be administrator, the application may take several weeks to make its way through the court process. If more than one person applies and there's a contest between them, a court hearing will usually be required. That will make the process even longer. And your estate is still just sitting there, waiting. . . .

If you have no relatives and therefore no beneficiaries approved by the provincial statute, then a provincial government official will administer your estate. But that's okay, because your estate is escheating to the government anyway (so the government is getting all of your property). Your friends and favourite charities can wave goodbye as the administrator drags your estate away.

## The application for letters of administration

The application process for letters of administration is more difficult than for letters probate. Your administrator will probably be your spouse or a brother or sister or other close relative. You should know what you'd be putting them through if you die without a will.

The person who wants to be the administrator of your estate has to apply for letters of administration to the court, and notify all of your beneficiaries about his or her application. He or she has to provide various pieces of paper to the court, including a sworn statement that he or she is closely enough related to you to have the right to be your administrator. The applicant will also have to get all the other relatives with an equal or greater right to be administrator to consent in writing to his or her appointment. If the applicant can't get that consent, he or she can substitute a written statement from each of them that they do not wish to act as administrator. This is already sounding like a month's work, isn't it?

Once the court has appointed the administrator, he or she will probably have to *post security* with the court before being allowed to set to work. The purpose of making the administrator post security (hand over valuable property like money or a *bond* — an iron-clad promise to pay money — to the court) is to discourage the administrator from stealing from your estate or engaging in other questionable activities. The administrator will get the security back after the estate has been distributed — if he has kept his nose clean throughout the process. The administrator may not have to post security if all of the beneficiaries and all of the creditors of your estate agree in writing that it's not necessary.

# What Difficulties Will Arise in the Administration of Your Estate?

You've already caused a lot of trouble for everyone simply by not having an executor. But the problems associated with appointing an administrator are just the beginning. Even after you've got the administrator, the problems keep coming.

Here are the problems we're going to dwell on at greater length:

- Your administrator won't be given much flexibility in administering your estate.
- Your estate will miss out on ways of avoiding taxes.
- Your administrator may have to hunt down relatives no one has been in contact with for years (or ever) because they're now beneficiaries.
- The provincial government will be holding onto the piggy bank if any of your estate money goes to minor children.

Think this doesn't sound all *that* terrible? Then you'd better keep reading.

## A stranglehold on the administrator

Provincial law defines an administrator's powers and duties in managing your estate. An administrator, by law, does somewhat different things with your estate than an executor would do. This can have a really big effect on your estate.

### Converting property to cash

The general rule is that your administrator has to sell *all* of the non-cash property of your estate (rather than just enough to pay your debts) in order to turn your whole estate into cash, unless all of your beneficiaries agree otherwise. (In some provinces, real estate is treated differently. Unless it must be sold to pay the debts of your estate, a majority of the beneficiaries must agree before it can be sold.)

If your administrator has to sell property in your estate, he can't look over market conditions and decide when's the best time to sell in order to get the best price. He has to do it as soon as possible after becoming administrator.

### Investing the cash

Until the cash is distributed to the beneficiaries, your administrator must keep it in investments that are fixed by law in each province. These are investments that are generally considered to be very safe. (They're also very boring.) The permitted investments usually include:

- Government securities of Canada, a province of Canada, the United States of America, or the United Kingdom
- Canadian bank, trust company, or credit union deposits or guaranteed investment certificates
- First mortgages on land in Canada, as long as the mortgage is not for more than 75 percent of the value of the land or else the mortgage is insured by the Canadian Mortgage and Housing Corporation (CMHC)

Your provincial statute may allow your administrator to invest some of the estate's money (usually no more than about one-third) in slightly riskier investments such as certain types of corporate bonds and shares. Your administrator will not be able to invest your estate in anything not allowed by the statute, even if it's an investment that's reasonably safe and could earn your estate more money to give to the beneficiaries — even if it's an investment you owned when you died!

### Distributing your estate

Once debts and taxes are paid, your administrator must distribute your estate to the beneficiaries named in the provincial statute. Even if your beneficiaries agreed that your administrator didn't have to sell everything in your estate for cash, your administrator has no authority to give beneficiaries specific pieces of property unless (again) all of the beneficiaries agree. If your beneficiaries can't agree on which individual pieces of property can be given to which beneficiaries, your administrator will have to sell everything and just give the beneficiaries cash. So if there were items that you would have liked to give to particular people, those people — even if they're beneficiaries under the statute — may never get them.

## Increased taxes

Your estate will probably end up paying more in taxes if your property is distributed without a will. Without a will, it is hard to take full advantage of the tax planning strategies we tell you about in Chapter 5:

- The spousal rollover
- The principal residence exemption
- Naming your spouse, child, or grandchild as beneficiary of your RRSPs
- Charitable donations
- Making an RRSP contribution on behalf of your spouse

Below we'll explain why it's more difficult (and sometimes impossible) to make use of these strategies if you die without a will.

### The spousal rollover

In Chapter 5, we tell you that when you die you are deemed to dispose of all of your capital property at its fair market value. (Capital property is property with a long-term value, like real estate or shares in a corporation.) If your property has gone up in value since you got it, there will be a capital gain and your estate will have to pay tax on one-half of the capital gain.

As you'll also find in Chapter 5, there is an exception for property that you leave to your spouse. If you leave capital property to your spouse, there's a spousal rollover, and you are deemed to dispose of the property for the same cost at which you acquired it. As a result there will be no capital gain when you die. The capital gain is put off until your spouse disposes of the property. Then, your spouse's capital gain is calculated as if he or she got the property at the same cost you got it for.

So . . . if you have a valid will and you leave all your capital property to your spouse, your estate won't have to pay any capital gains tax.

But if you don't have a valid will? You do not lose the benefit of the spousal rollover entirely if you die without a will. There won't be any capital gains tax payable on the part of your estate that is paid to your spouse under the provincial intestacy laws. But if you have children (in Quebec if you have children *or* surviving parents, brother and sisters, and nieces and nephews), your entire estate will not be paid to your spouse. Your spouse may receive as little as one-third of your estate. And if capital property in your estate has increased in value, your estate will have to pay capital gains tax on the share of the estate that goes to anyone other than your spouse.

If you have a spouse and children and want them to share your estate — even if you like the provincial rules about how your estate is divided among them — it's best to make a will, for tax planning purposes. If you die without a will, you lose your chance to choose which property your spouse will receive and which property your children will receive. When you have the choice, you leave your spouse property that has larger capital gains and your children property that has smaller capital gains or no capital gain at all (such as your principal residence). Then your estate is able to take full advantage of the spousal rollover to pay the least tax possible.

### The principal residence exemption

If you dispose of your principal residence and make some money, that profit is normally not subject to capital gains tax. (That's true whether you're alive and just selling the place, or you "disposed" of it at the time of your death. See Chapter 5.) But tax law allows you to have only one principal residence. If you own more than one residence, when you dispose of one of them you have to choose which of your residences is your principal residence.

If you don't have a will, your administrator still gets to choose which residence is your principal residence at the time of your death (if you haven't made a designation while you were alive). But you lose the chance to take full advantage of the principal residence exemption by leaving one residence to your spouse (without capital gains tax because of the spousal rollover) and the other residence to someone other than your spouse (without capital gains tax because you designate it as your principal residence).

### RRSPs and RRIFs

When you die, all of your RRSPs and RRIFs are deemed to be cashed in. The full amount of the RRSPs and RRIFs will be added to your income and taxed along with your other income and capital gains in your terminal return.

There is an exception to this rule if you name your spouse as beneficiary of your RRSP or RRIF and the proceeds are paid into an RRSP or RRIF for your spouse. Then the proceeds are not considered your income, and neither your estate nor your spouse pays tax on the amount of the proceeds. (Your spouse must pay tax when he or she withdraws money from the RRSP or RRIF. See Chapter 5.)

There is another exception if your RRSP or RRIF proceeds are paid to your estate and you leave the proceeds in your will to your spouse or a dependent child or grandchild (or if you name the child as beneficiary of the RRSP or RRIF). Then, your executor and your beneficiary may file a joint form agreeing that the proceeds will be considered income of the beneficiary rather than of your estate. Your beneficiary can put off paying tax on the proceeds by transferring the money into his or her own RRSP or RRIF.

If you do not have a will, and you have not named your spouse as beneficiary of your RRSPs or RRIFs, your estate won't lose the benefit of this exception entirely. If the proceeds are used to pay your spouse's share of your estate or the share of a dependent child or grandchild, then your estate won't pay tax on the proceeds.

But your RRSP or RRIF proceeds may not go entirely to your spouse or dependent children or grandchildren. If you have children (in Quebec, if you have children or surviving parents, brothers and sisters, nieces and nephews) your entire estate will not be paid to your spouse. Your other relatives (who may not be dependent children or grandchildren) could get up to two-thirds of your estate. If the proceeds are used to pay the shares of these other relatives, your estate will pay tax on the proceeds.

Your administrator and your spouse (or other beneficiaries) will have to decide whether your RRSP or RRIF or your other property are being used to satisfy their share of your estate. Your administrator may not be able to take full advantage of both the RRSP/RRIF tax savings and the spousal rollover.

### Charitable donations

Your estate is entitled to a donation tax credit for any charitable donations you make in the year of your death or in your will.

If you do not have a will, your administrator will not have the power to make charitable donations on your behalf, even though that might have been your wish. So there's no chance your estate will be able to claim a charitable donation tax credit in your terminal return, either. To understand exactly what you're missing, see Chapter 13. A charitable donation in your will can reduce your tax bill significantly.

### RRSP contributions for your spouse

You may die without having used your RRSP contribution limit in the year of your death. If you die without a will, your administrator can't take your unused contribution and make a contribution to your spouse's RRSP and, by doing so, reduce the tax payable by your estate. If you leave a will, you *can* authorize your executor to make such a contribution to your spouse's RRSP.

## Government meddling

We mention in Chapters 9 and 11 that children under the age of majority cannot receive property from an estate themselves. It has to be put into trust for them until they come of age. When you make a will, one of the matters you take care of is creating a trust (with a trustee that you've chosen yourself) to hold property for children.

If you haven't left a will, the property of your estate still can't go directly to minor children. It still has to go into a trust. But if you die intestate, the trustee will be — depending on your province — a public official (often called, appropriately, the Public Trustee) or a person appointed by the court.

The trustee, whoever it is, will keep the child's money invested in very conservative investments, so it isn't likely to increase greatly in value while it's in the trust.

The trustee can pay money out of the trust to the person who has custody of the child. But the trustee isn't going to pay anything out unless he or she approves of the plan for spending the money on the child. The trustee is not going to feel kindly and indulgent towards the child and the child's guardian when they ask for money, because his or her actions are subject to review and even audit by other government officials and the court. The trustee is going to want to see a good, solid plan that doesn't sound like a frivolous waste of money.

The trustee will turn the property in trust over to the child as soon as the child comes of age (at 18 or 19, depending on the province). The kid doesn't even have to come up with a plan for the trustee in order to get the money. Maybe this newly wealthy teenager will invest the money in blue-chip stocks or complete boxed sets of Beethoven sonatas. But there's always the very remote chance that the kid will blow the money on a motorcycle or a recreational drug franchise.

### Mystery beneficiaries

The more remote beneficiaries named in the provincial intestate statute may turn out to be people you didn't keep in touch with. They may even turn out to be people you never met and didn't know existed. Your administrator will have to find them anyway, without benefit of your little black address book. The administrator may have to question your relatives and friends, advertise in the personal column of newspapers, or even hire a private investigator.

## What Happens to Your Estate If You Have a Will?

Are we allowed to have stage directions in a self-help book? We are? Okay.

> *In the background:* Radiant light slowly touches the horizon, builds to a brilliant glow. *Sound effects:* Voices of an unseen choir well up in beautiful four-part harmony. *Voice over* (deep and reassuring): "You have a will. All is well."

Did that seem a little overdone? Maybe we should have toned down the choir.

To be truthful, having a will isn't going to make everything perfect (for instance, you're still dead), but it's a lot better than *not* having a will.

Here's a summary of how things will be different if you have a will:

- Your property will be given away to the people and charities you've chosen. You will be the one who decides who gets specific items and who gets plain old cash.
- You can choose an executor — someone you trust to look after your estate and do the best job for your family and friends. Your executor will be able to start work right away after your death, and your estate won't be left in limbo for weeks.
- You can give your executor discretion to manage the property in your estate — to decide when to sell your property and how property in the estate can be invested. You don't have to tell your executor to convert all the property of the estate into cash, although you can if you wish. Your executor *has* to convert only enough to pay the debts and taxes of the estate and to pay gifts of cash to named beneficiaries. You can tell your executor how you want the estate's property invested, or you can leave it entirely up to the executor to decide what to do (your executor just has to handle the property the way a reasonably prudent business-person would handle his or her own property). And you'll be able to tell your executor whether to give your property to a beneficiary in its current form or make a cash payment. (See Chapter 10 for a rundown of an executor's job.)
- You can take advantage of tax planning strategies by carefully choosing how your property will be distributed among your beneficiaries, by making charitable donations in your will, and by directing your executor to make an RRSP contribution on behalf of your spouse to use up your unused RRSP contribution limit. (See Chapter 5.)
- You can use your will to set up a trust for beneficiaries who are under the age of majority. In your will you can give your trustee instructions on how to manage your children's money. (See Chapter 9 for more about trusts.)
- You can use your will to name a testamentary guardian for your minor children, so they'll be sure of your wishes for your children's care. (See Chapter 11 if you have a perverse need to know more about orphans.)

# Chapter 16

# The Will: An Alien Document Form

### In This Chapter

- Discovering that formal wills are not written in English
- Learning what a will says, in translation
- Learning the rules about how a will is signed and witnessed
- Finding out about do-it-yourself wills

If you've read this book straight through, you've slogged through fifteen chapters by now. We've led you across the treacherous swamps of financial planning, the rocky deserts of taxation, the dark chasms of life insurance. You've staggered past gifts and trusts and waded courageously into choosing beneficiaries and an executor. You've scaled the heights of dread over leaving behind your children and your business, and you've dashed over the quick-sands of funeral planning. Now, finally, we think you're strong enough to take a peek at a will. It will be an experience that you'll find . . . otherworldly.

## Get Ready, Get Set, Get Lost

Reading a standard will prepared by a lawyer is like turning on the hyperdrive and blasting out of the familiar solar system. It's very easy to get lost! But after all we've been through together, we wouldn't want to lose you. That's why we're going to take you away on a training jaunt. After you've completed it, you won't find yourself drifting helplessly and searching for a familiar landmark when you look for the first time (or the tenth time) at your own will.

A standard will can be very short or can go on for pages and pages. It is usually at least several pages long and contains a series of numbered paragraphs. Although every will is tailored to the needs of the individual, wills often follow a standard pattern. You can expect to find clauses that:

- Identify the *testator*, the person making the will (you).
- *Revoke* (cancel) all previous wills, to make it clear that this will replaces any earlier will you made.

- Name the *executor*, the person who will administer your estate.
- Leave all of your property to your executor *in trust*. (Please remain calm and do not unbuckle the restraints of your zero-gravity chair, as ignition is imminent. This isn't a scam dreamed up between your lawyer and your executor to grab your estate. The executor, as the trustee of your estate, is given a kind of ownership of the property in the estate after you die but has to hand the property out according to the instructions in your will.)
- Tell the executor to pay all valid debts, claims, and taxes of the estate.
- Tell the executor to give your *beneficiaries* (people and/or charities you've chosen to receive gifts) whatever is left in the estate after the debts, claims, and taxes have been paid.
- Give the executor certain legal and financial powers to manage your estate — power to keep or sell property in the estate, to invest cash, and to borrow money.
- Name someone to have custody of minor children, if you have any.

# . . . To Discover Strange New Words . . .

We have liftoff. The voyage is commencing.

To begin, we're going to show you what a complete standard will might look like. The first thing you'll notice is that it is not written in English. It's mostly written in Englatin, with some medieval French thrown in. You'll also notice that it follows the simple rule, "Why use one word when three will do?" As well, when it comes to sentence length, enough is never enough, and punctuation is almost totally banned (especially if it might put a sentence out of its misery). After we show you the will in all its glory, we'll take you through it paragraph by paragraph, translate it into English, and explain what's going on.

There is no one-size-fits-all will. Each person's will has to meet the needs and objectives of that particular person. So first we'll tell you something about our testator, John Robinson, and about his wishes.

John Robinson is married to Maureen Robinson. They have a grown-up daughter, Judy, and two younger children, Penny and Will. And who knows, they might have more children, depending on plot requirements and available alien technology.

John wants to leave his state-of-the-art atomic force microscope to his colleague, Dr. Zachary Smith; $10,000 to his daughter Judy; and $2,500 to the Alpha Prime Foundation to Save All Humanity Resident in Canada (a Canada Revenue–

registered charity). He wants to leave everything else to his wife if she is still alive when he dies. If his wife dies before he does, he wants to divide his estate among his children and wants each minor child's share of the estate to be held in trust until the child is 21 years old.

He wants his wife to be his executor if she is still alive when he dies. If his wife dies before he does, he wants his daughter Judy to be his executor. He wants his executor to have broad powers to deal with his estate and to be able to use her own judgment about what to do — because you never know when an intergalactic financial opportunity or disaster may occur.

Now that you've met John Robinson, have a look at Figure 16-1 to see what a sample will for him might look like. If you try reading it at all, we bet your eyes will get crossed around Paragraph III(a), and the rest of the will will go by in the kind of blur you normally associate with space travel at warp speed.

And bad as the will is, it could be worse! Because we leave out some things that a careful lawyer would have put in. For example:

- Because John and Maureen are the parents of young children, this will should include a paragraph naming someone to have custody of their children if both John and Maureen die. We have not included the clause because the wording varies from province to province. Not to mention from planet to planet.
- In some provinces, John might want to include language that would limit the right of a beneficiary's spouse to share in the property on a breakdown of the beneficiary's marriage. (We don't want to start any rumours, but what if Judy marries Dr. Zachary Smith instead of that nice Major West?)
- John might want to give his executor discretion to make an RRSP donation on his wife's behalf, to use up any unused RRSP contributions. (You shouldn't forget about possible tax deductions, even when the entire human race is threatened with extinction. If anyone survives, it will be the tax authorities.)
- John might want to direct his trustee to hold onto his home (or in this case, spaceship) for his children until they reach a certain age.
- If John has a business or complex investments, John's will might include clauses that give the trustee additional powers specifically designed to deal with them. (If John ever makes it to the uninhabited planet Alpha Prime, he could make a killing in the real estate market when the Rest of Humanity arrives.)
- John might want to include an insurance trust clause to deal with the proceeds of any insurance policies.

THIS IS THE LAST WILL AND TESTAMENT of me, JOHN ROBINSON, of the City of Jupiter 2, in the Province of an Unknown Part of the Galaxy.

I. I REVOKE all former wills and other testamentary dispositions made by me.

II. I NOMINATE, CONSTITUTE, AND APPOINT my wife, MAUREEN ROBINSON, to be the executor and trustee of this my will, provided that if my said wife shall have predeceased me or shall survive me but die before the trusts hereof shall have terminated or shall refuse or be unable to act or to continue to act as such executor and trustee, then I nominate, constitute, and appoint my daughter, JUDY ROBINSON, to be the executor and trustee of this my will in the place and stead of my said wife. I hereinafter refer to my executor and trustee for the time being as my "trustee."

III. I GIVE, DEVISE, AND BEQUEATH all of my property of every nature and kind and wheresoever situate, including property over which I may have a general power of appointment, to my trustee upon the following trusts, namely:

(a) To pay out of the capital of my general estate my just debts, funeral and testamentary expenses, and all estate, inheritance, succession duties, or taxes whether imposed by or pursuant to the law of this or any other jurisdiction whatsoever that may be payable in connection with any property passing (or deemed to pass by any governing law) on my death or in connection with any insurance on my life, or in connection with any gift or benefit given or provided by me either in my lifetime or by survivorship or by this my will or any codicil hereto, and whether such taxes and duties be payable in respect of estates or interests which fall into possession at my death or at any subsequent time; and I authorize my trustee to commute or prepay any such taxes or duties.
(b) To deliver to ZACHARY SMITH, if he survives me, my Atomic Force Microscope.
(c) To pay to my daughter, JUDY ROBINSON, if she survives me, the sum of TEN THOUSAND DOLLARS ($10,000).
(d) To give to the Alpha Prime Foundation to Save All Humanity Resident in Canada, located in Ottawa, Ontario, Canada, the sum of TWO THOUSAND FIVE HUNDRED DOLLARS ($2,500) for its general purposes. I declare that the receipt of the person who professes to be a treasurer or other proper officer for the time being of this charitable organization shall be a sufficient discharge to my trustee therefor.
(e) To pay, transfer, and assign the residue of my estate to my wife, MAUREEN ROBINSON, if she survives me for a period of thirty days, for her own use absolutely.
(f) If my said wife predeceases me or survives me but dies within a period of thirty days of the date of my death, to divide the residue of my estate into as many equal shares as there shall be children of mine then alive, and I declare that if any child of mine should then be dead and if any issue of such deceased child should then be living, such deceased child of mine shall be considered as alive for the purpose of such division.

My trustee shall set aside one of such equal shares as a separate trust for each child of mine who shall be living at the division date and shall keep such share invested and the income and capital or so much thereof as my trustee in her uncontrolled discretion considers advisable shall be paid to or applied to the benefit of such child until he or she attains the age of twenty-one years when the capital of such share or the amount thereof remaining shall be paid or transferred to him or her, any income not so paid or applied in any year to be added to the capital and dealt with as part thereof. If such child should die before attaining the age of twenty-one years, such share, or the amount thereof remaining, shall be held by my trustee in trust for the issue of such child who survive him or her in equal shares per stirpes. If such child should leave no issue him or her surviving, such share or the amount thereof remaining shall be held by my trustee in trust for my issue alive at the death of such child in equal shares per stirpes.

IV. I AUTHORIZE my trustee to use her discretion in the realization of my estate, with power to sell, call in, and convert into money any part of my estate not consisting of money at such time or times, in

(i)

**Figure 16-1:** A sample will for John Robinson.

such manner and upon such terms, and either for credit or for part cash and part credit as she may in her absolute discretion decide upon, or to postpone such conversion of my estate or any part or parts thereof for such length of time as she may think best. My trustee shall have a separate and substantive power to retain any of my investments or assets in the form existing at the date of my death at her absolute discretion without responsibility for loss to the intent that investments or assets so retained shall be deemed to be authorized investments for all purposes of this my will.

V. I DECLARE that my trustee when making investments for my estate shall not be limited to investments authorized by law for trustees but may make any investments which in her absolute discretion she considers advisable, and my trustee shall not be liable for any loss that may happen to my estate in connection with any such investment made by her in good faith.

VI. MY TRUSTEE may make any division of my estate or set aside or pay any share or interest therein, either wholly or in part, in the assets forming my estate at the time of my death or at the time of such division, setting aside or payment, and I expressly declare that my trustee shall in her absolute discretion fix the value of my estate or any part thereof for the purpose of making any such division, setting aside or payment, and her decision shall be final and binding upon all persons concerned.

VII. SUBJECT AS herein specifically provided, if any person other than a child of mine should become entitled to any share in my estate before attaining the age of majority, the share of such person shall be held and kept invested by my trustee and the income and capital, or so much thereof as my trustee in her absolute discretion considers advisable, shall be used for the benefit of such person until he or she attains the age of majority.

VIII. I AUTHORIZE my trustee to make any payments for any person under the age of majority to a parent or guardian of such person or to anyone to whom she in her discretion deems it advisable to make such payments, whose receipt shall be a sufficient discharge to my trustee.

IN WITNESS WHEREOF I have to this my last will and testament, written upon this and 1 preceding page, subscribed my name this 11th day of June, 20__.

SIGNED by the testator, JOHN ROBINSON, )<br>
as his last will, in the presence of us, )<br>
both present at the same time, who at )<br>
his request, in his presence and in the ) ______________________<br>
presence of each other have hereunto ) John Robinson<br>
subscribed our names as witnesses. )

WITNESS:

Signature: ______________________

Name: ______________________

Address: ______________________

Occupation: ______________________

Signature: ______________________

Name: ______________________

Address: ______________________

Occupation: ______________________

A formal will sure makes giant space spiders look cuddly, doesn't it? The dizziness and nausea you feel at this point could be associated with space sickness. Gravol might help. If not, some aliens swear by elastic bands around the tentacles.

# In Low Orbit around a Will

We weren't kidding when we said wills are not written in anything resembling English. They're written the way they are because this wording has stood up to legal challenges for years and years, and lawyers don't like to mess with success.

Now we are activating a translation device. We'll slowly move in for a closer look at the will, using full power to scan the document and make it comprehensible in a language spoken by humans.

## Identification

> THIS IS THE LAST WILL AND TESTAMENT of me, JOHN ROBINSON, of the City of Jupiter 2, in the Province of an Unknown Part of the Galaxy.

This part is easy. It identifies the document as a will and the testator as John Robinson. It also identifies his city and province of residence. Pat yourself on the back for understanding everything perfectly so far.

## Revocation of other wills

> I. I REVOKE all former wills and other testamentary dispositions made by me.

The making of a will generally cancels any previous wills. Clause I makes it clear that the testator does intend to cancel them. "Other testamentary dispositions" would include a *codicil*, an addition to an existing will that revises some part of the will. (Note: in the farthest western reaches of our galaxy, a codicil is a hallucinogenic fungus. It would be wise not to confuse the two.)

## Naming the executor

> II. I NOMINATE, CONSTITUTE, AND APPOINT my wife, MAUREEN ROBINSON, to be the executor and trustee of this my will, provided that if my said wife shall have predeceased me or shall survive me but die before the

> trusts hereof shall have terminated or shall refuse or be unable to act or to continue to act as such executor and trustee, then I nominate, constitute, and appoint my daughter, JUDY ROBINSON, to be the executor and trustee of this my will in the place and stead of my said wife. I hereinafter refer to my executor and trustee for the time being as my "trustee."

Clause II appoints John's wife, Maureen, to be his executor. If Maureen dies or is unwilling or unable to act as John's executor or to complete the executor's work, John appoints his daughter Judy to be executor. We tell you how to choose an executor and what an executor does in Chapter 10.

John named an alternate executor for Maureen (Judy), but has not named an alternate executor for Judy. (He was probably running out of trustworthy adults, and trust companies have not caught on much beyond the orbit of Pluto.) If Maureen dies and then Judy dies, Judy's executor will become John's executor.

After this clause you may lose track of the executor and wonder if she has fallen into a black hole. She hasn't, she's just changed her name. This clause names the executor as both executor and trustee, and the executor is referred to as "the trustee" for the rest of the will. (We tell you more than you want to hear about trustees in Chapter 9.) That's because the next clause sets up a trust for all of the property in John's estate and the executor is the trustee who deals with the property.

## Leaving property to the executor in trust

> III. I GIVE, DEVISE, AND BEQUEATH all of my property of every nature and kind and wheresoever situate, including property over which I may have a general power of appointment, to my trustee upon the following trusts, namely:

Clause III gives all of John Robinson's property to his executor, not for her own benefit but for the benefit of the people who will eventually receive the property under the will. These are the people to whom John's estate owes money, and the beneficiaries.

A "general power of appointment," in case you were wondering, is a very old-fashioned right over property that you rarely find in Canada any more.

John's instructions to his trustee about what to do with the property in trust are set out in the lettered sub-paragraphs that follow this clause.

## Payment of debts

> (a) To pay out of the capital of my general estate my just debts, funeral and testamentary expenses, and all estate, inheritance, succession duties, or taxes whether imposed by or pursuant to the law of this or any other jurisdiction whatsoever that may be payable in connection with any property passing (or deemed to pass by any governing law) on my death or in connection with any insurance on my life, or in connection with any gift or benefit given or provided by me either in my lifetime or by survivorship or by this my will or any codicil hereto, and whether such taxes and duties be payable in respect of estates or interests which fall into possession at my death or at any subsequent time; and I authorize my trustee to commute or prepay any such taxes or duties.

Paragraph (a) directs the executor (now of course known as the trustee) to pay all legitimate (valid) debts, claims, and taxes of John Robinson's estate, including the cost of his funeral. Most of the paragraph deals with the different ways that taxes might become payable. The executor is given the right (by John, not by Canada Revenue) to use her judgment about the timing of tax payments — she can put off paying (*commute*) or pay in advance (*prepay*).

Payment of debts and taxes is the executor's first responsibility. Nothing can be given to the beneficiaries until it is clear that there is enough money in the estate to pay the debts and taxes. If there is not enough money to cover them *and* the full amount of the gifts to the beneficiaries, the gifts to the beneficiaries will be reduced.

## Distributing the remaining property to the beneficiaries

After the executor pays the debts and taxes of John's estate, she must give the remaining property to the beneficiaries according to John's instructions. First she must give the specific gifts John made in his will. After the specific gifts are made, she must distribute the *residue*. The residue is what is left after debts, claims, taxes, and estate administration expenses have been paid and the specific gifts have been given out.

### Specific gifts

John's will contains three specific gifts, one of personal property and two of cash.

> (b) To deliver to ZACHARY SMITH, if he survives me, my Atomic Force Microscope.

This gift of property is worded in a typical way. There will be a gift only if Zachary Smith is alive when John dies. If Dr. Smith dies before John, Smith's heirs are not entitled to the gift. The microscope will become part of the residue of John's estate and go to other beneficiaries of John's.

Even though paragraph (b) doesn't say so, there will also be a gift only if John owns a microscope when he dies. If he doesn't own it at the time of his death, Dr. Smith will get nothing since the will does not provide for an alternate gift to him.

> (c) To pay to my daughter, JUDY ROBINSON, if she survives me, the sum of TEN THOUSAND DOLLARS ($10,000).

This is a typical gift of cash to an individual. There will be a gift only if Judy is alive when John dies. If Judy dies before John, her heirs will not be entitled to take the gift. The cash will become part of the residue of John's estate.

And there will be a gift only if there is $10,000 left in John's estate after his executor pays the estate's debts and gives Dr. Smith the microscope.

> (d) To give to the Alpha Prime Foundation to Save All Humanity Resident in Canada, located in Ottawa, Ontario, Canada, the sum of TWO THOUSAND FIVE HUNDRED DOLLARS ($2,500) for its general purposes. I declare that the receipt of the person who professes to be a treasurer or other proper officer for the time being of this charitable organization shall be a sufficient discharge to my trustee therefor.

This is a typical gift of cash to a charity. We go on at great length about charitable donations in Chapter 13, so you can go there to contemplate how to choose and name a charity, and what donation tax credits are available.

In the second sentence of paragraph (d), John is saying that the executor has done all that is expected of her if she gives the money to the charity and gets a receipt for it from someone who appears to be an officer of the charity. This paragraph is designed to protect the executor from liability if the person she pays the money to turns out to be the wrong person.

### Gift of the residue

> (e) To pay, transfer, and assign the residue of my estate to my wife, MAUREEN ROBINSON, if she survives me for a period of thirty days, for her own use absolutely.

John is leaving the residue of his estate (what's left after payment of his debts and taxes and the gifts to Dr. Smith, Judy, and the Alpha Prime Foundation) to his wife Maureen. "For her own use absolutely" means there are no strings attached — she can do whatever she likes with the property she receives.

(An alternative would be to give her the use of the property for her lifetime and then give it to the children.) But she only gets the residue if she lives for at least 30 days after his death. If she dies before John dies or less than 30 days after John dies, she will not inherit. Now what's that all about?

Suppose John and Maureen were in a cosmic radiation accident together. Without paragraph (e), Maureen would inherit from John even if she outlived him by only 15 minutes. The residue of John's estate would go to Maureen, and then would immediately become part of Maureen's estate and would be disposed of according to the provisions in *her* will. So John's property would be given to the people named by Maureen, not by John! Even if John and Maureen both name the same beneficiaries (as husbands and wives very often do), the property would have to pass through first John's estate and then Maureen's estate. That would result in extra work and expense.

Thirty days is the standard time period used in wills. There's no magic to the number 30 nowadays, but it was probably once considered a reasonable length of time to wait to see whether the second of two people who were injured or who sickened at the same time was going to live or die.

### Alternative gift of the residue

> (f) If my said wife predeceases me or survives me but dies within a period of thirty days of the date of my death, to divide the residue of my estate into as many equal shares as there shall be children of mine then alive, and I declare that if any child of mine should then be dead and if any issue of such deceased child should then be living, such deceased child of mine shall be considered as alive for the purpose of such division.

What happens if Maureen Robinson dies before John does? Who gets the residue of the estate then? Paragraph (f) gives the answer, and it's an eyeful. Let's scan it a bit at a time.

If Maureen dies before or within 30 days after John dies, John's estate is to be divided equally among his children. If Judy, Penny, and Will all survive John, and John has no other children by that point, then each of the three children will get one-third of the residue.

Then the next question is, What happens if a child also dies before John does? After all, some days there's an evil plasma creature lurking behind every rock.

When John was considering how to pass his estate on to his family, he had to think about whether the share of a child who died before him would simply go to his surviving children or whether it would go to any children that his deceased child had. This paragraph shows that John ended up deciding to divide a deceased child's share among that child's own children.

Here's an example of how this paragraph might work itself out, given the following situation:

> John dies, as the result of an unfortunate misunderstanding with a native of the planet Zifpox. At the time of his death, Maureen is already dead (unexpected meteorite shower, no shower cap) as is Judy (the espresso on the planet Tryffl is unbelievably strong). Penny and Will are both in their twenties. Will has a son, Robby. Judy is survived by her two daughters, Blawp and Spingo.

The residue of John's estate would be distributed like this:

- Penny will receive one-third of the residue.
- Will will receive one-third of the residue (and his son will receive nothing).
- Blawp and Spingo will receive Judy's one-third share and it will be split equally between them, so each of John's granddaughters will receive one-sixth of the residue.

In Figure 16-2 you'll find a chart as a navigational aid.

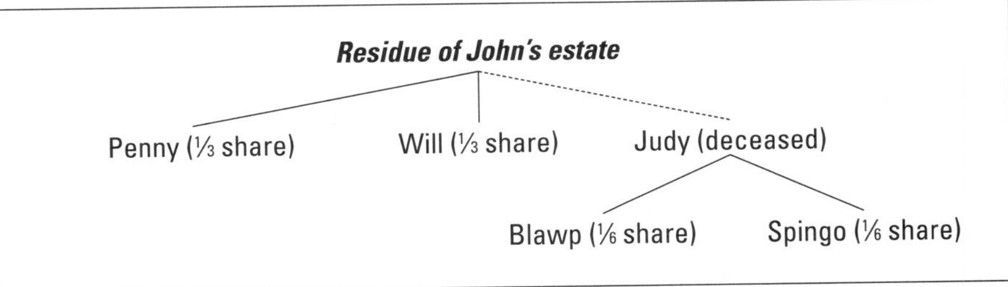


**Figure 16-2:** Here's how the residue of John's estate would be distributed.

## Trust for children under the age of 21

> (f) *continued* My trustee shall set aside one of such equal shares as a separate trust for each child of mine who shall be living at the division date and shall keep such share invested and the income and capital or so much thereof as my trustee in her uncontrolled discretion considers advisable shall be paid to or applied to the benefit of such child until he or she attains the age of twenty-one years when the capital of such share or the amount thereof remaining shall be paid or transferred to him or her, any income not so paid or applied in any year to be added to the capital and dealt with as part thereof. If such child should die before attaining the age of twenty-one years, such share, or the amount thereof remaining, shall be held by my trustee in trust for the issue of such child who survive him or her in equal shares per stirpes. If such child should leave no issue him or her surviving, such share or the amount thereof remaining shall be held by my trustee in trust for my issue alive at the death of such child in equal shares per stirpes.

The paragraphs are getting worse. It may be time to turn on the neutron shields for protection.

The rest of paragraph (f), which should not be approached without full anti-particle gear, tells John's executor what to do if any of John's children or grandchildren are under the age of majority (18 or 19, depending on the province or solar system) when John dies. Remember that a minor child cannot receive property directly. In Canada, if no trustee is named, then the provincial public trustee is supposed to look after a minor child's inheritance.

John instructs that the share of any minor child (or grandchild), including any interest earned on the share, is to be held in a trust set up specifically for the child, with John's executor as trustee. The share, plus interest, is to be turned over to the child when he or she turns 21. John could have instructed his executor to turn over the child's share as soon as the child reached the age of majority. However, he thought that any child would be better able to handle the inheritance at a slightly older age. And when you factor in light-speed travel, it could take John's executor the additional two or three years just to figure out how old everyone is anyway.

Until the child turns 21, John instructs his executor to use her own judgment about how much of the money to give to or spend on the child.

Finally, if a child dies before reaching the age of 21, that child's share will be divided among his or her children, if any. If the child has no children, then his or her share will be divided among John's other surviving children. If one of John's children has died (under 21) but has produced children, then the share that would have gone to John's child will be divided among those children. If you're wondering where we're getting all of this from . . . because frankly *you* don't see it there . . . part of what we've said is an expansion of the two little words "per stirpes" (see Chapter 15 for a discussion of this Latin phrase that means "through the descendants").

## Executor's powers

From this point on, the will mainly natters about giving the executor powers to deal with the estate. These include such things as the power to keep property of the estate in its current form instead of turning it into cash, the power to invest the estate's cash as the executor thinks best, the power to borrow money on behalf of the estate, and the power to buy property from the estate.

### Turning the estate's property into cash

> IV. I AUTHORIZE my trustee to use her discretion in the realization of my estate, with power to sell, call in, and convert into money any part of my estate not consisting of money at such time or times, in such manner and upon such terms, and either for credit or for part cash and part credit as she may in her absolute discretion decide upon, or to postpone such conversion of my estate or any part or parts thereof for such length of time as she may think best. My trustee shall have a separate and substantive power to retain any of my investments or assets in the form existing at the date of my death at her absolute discretion without responsibility for loss to the intent that investments or assets so retained shall be deemed to be authorized investments for all purposes of this my will.

Aren't these run-on sentences great? We hope you're not trying to read the clauses out loud, because you'll be dangerously short of oxygen by the time you come to a period. We wouldn't want you to faint when we're hardly halfway through our translation — you might miss something really exciting!

In clause IV, John gives his executor the power to keep any of the property of the estate in the form it's in when John dies, instead of selling it for cash. He also gives the power to delay turning property of the estate into cash. Under provincial law, an executor must turn all of the property of the estate into cash as quickly as possible — unless the will contains the powers given here.

### Investments

> V. I DECLARE that my trustee when making investments for my estate shall not be limited to investments authorized by law for trustees but may make any investments which in her absolute discretion she considers advisable, and my trustee shall not be liable for any loss that may happen to my estate in connection with any such investment made by her in good faith.

In clause V, John has given his executor very broad powers to decide how to invest any cash in the estate. Instead of restricting her to the very safe investments permitted under provincial trust legislation, John is allowing his executor to invest in any type of investment she thinks will be good. (This is wise, because provincial legislation has never seen the Intergalactic Stock Exchange during a trading session. It's true that you can easily lose your shirt and three of your five eyes, but on the other hand investors have been known to triple their pseudopod holdings in a single 20-second "trade blast.") John has also given his executor absolution: As long as she makes her investment decisions honestly, she will not be financially responsible to the beneficiaries if any of the investments lose money.

### Distribution in kind

> VI. MY TRUSTEE may make any division of my estate or set aside or pay any share or interest therein, either wholly or in part, in the assets forming my estate at the time of my death or at the time of such division, setting aside or payment, and I expressly declare that my trustee shall in her absolute discretion fix the value of my estate or any part thereof for the purpose of making any such division, setting aside or payment, and her decision shall be final and binding upon all persons concerned.

If it turns out that more than one beneficiary will share in the residue of the estate (which will happen if Maureen dies before or within 30 days of John's death), John's executor will have to divide the residue of the estate into the correct number of shares. Under this will, the shares have to be of equal value (we're getting this from paragraph III(f)).

John's estate may include some cash (in various currencies), some stocks, some rocks (picked up en route), his residence/vehicle, furniture, extraterrestrial art objects, and household goods. The only totally fair way to distribute the estate in equal shares would be to sell everything and split the cash. But, as with most estates, there are items that the beneficiaries would like to keep in the family. John, in clause VI, says that the executor can use her own judgment to decide to distribute some or all of the residue in its existing form. She'll be able to give each beneficiary a combination of cash and other property as long as the value of each beneficiary's share amounts to the correct percentage of the total value of the residue. If the beneficiaries can't agree on the value of individual pieces of property, the executor may have to get a professional valuation.

### Dealing with minors

John's will contains two more clauses to help his executor deal with beneficiaries who are minors.

> VII. SUBJECT AS herein specifically provided, if any person other than a child of mine should become entitled to any share in my estate before attaining the age of majority, the share of such person shall be held and kept invested by my trustee and the income and capital, or so much thereof as my trustee in her absolute discretion considers advisable, shall be used for the benefit of such person until he or she attains the age of majority.
>
> VIII. I AUTHORIZE my trustee to make any payments for any person under the age of majority to a parent or guardian of such person or to anyone to whom she in her discretion deems it advisable to make such payments, whose receipt shall be a sufficient discharge to my trustee.

Clause VII sets up a trust for anyone who may end up inheriting property under John's will while still a minor, but who is not already covered by the trust that looks after John's children and grandchildren. This is the ultimate "what-if?" clause because it addresses the possibility that when John dies his wife is dead and all of his children are dead without having left any grandchildren. John has not said where he wants his estate to go if that happens. As a result, his estate would be divided under provincial intestacy laws and might eventually reach a distant relative under the age of majority. If he has no relative, his estate will *escheat to the Crown* (become the property of the provincial government). If the estate escheats, this trust clause will be totally unnecessary — except on a small planet circling the star Tau Ceti, where the government is formed by citizens in the larval phase of development.

Clause VIII talks about the mechanics of making payments on behalf of beneficiaries who are minors. Since payments cannot be made directly to a minor, this clause gives the executor authority to make the payment to the minor's parent or guardian or to anyone else whom the executor considers suitable (for example, a school requiring payment of tuition fees, or Rigellian space pirates holding the minor hostage).

### Signing provisions

IN WITNESS WHEREOF I have to this my last will and testament, written upon this and 1 preceding page, subscribed my name this 11th day of June, 20__.

| | | |
|---|---|---|
| SIGNED by the testator, JOHN ROBINSON,<br>as his last will, in the presence of us,<br>both present at the same time, who at<br>his request, in his presence and in the<br>presence of each other have hereunto<br>subscribed our names as witnesses. | )<br>)<br>)<br>)<br>)<br>) | ______________________<br>John Robinson |

WITNESS:

Signature: ______________________

Name: ______________________

Address: ______________________

Occupation: ______________________

Signature: ______________________

Name: ______________________

Address: ______________________

Occupation: ______________________

This final clause says how many pages long the will is. That's so nobody will be able to slip an extra page in after John has signed (yes, there are people and life forms in this universe who would tamper with a will).

The clause also says the date on which John signed the will. It is important to include the date, since a new will revokes all wills that John made earlier. Without dates, it will be impossible to know which will came first if John has more than one signed will.

There's a strange blather beside the place for John's signature about how the will was signed with everyone in everyone else's presence. It almost sounds like the testator and witnesses are a troupe of contortionists. It's actually a description of the proper signing procedure for a will, and under the very next heading we'll untangle the whole business.

This completes our first orbit around the will itself. If little or nothing sank in on the first pass, you can set yourself on endless loop by returning now to the heading "In Low Orbit around a Will." Warning! If you do that, you will sooner or later run out of fuel. Then your orbit will decay and you will burn up in the atmosphere. Maybe it would be safer for you to read to the end of the chapter.

# Signing a Will

You may find it amusing to know that when lawyers talk about signing a will they use the term *execution*. Lawyers don't have their clients sign wills, they have their clients *execute* them. A very apt term, because at this point you'd probably just as soon take the will out back and zap it with a phaser as sign it.

There are two important matters that must be dealt with when a will is signed:

- Making sure that the testator is legally capable of making a will.
- Making sure that the legal formalities for signing a will are followed.

Signing a will is not something you do all by yourself in a darkened room. You have to have a cast of supporting characters — your witnesses and, if you're smart, your lawyer — all of whom have a role in these two matters. Your will, or parts of it, may be declared invalid after you die if it turns out that you were not legally capable of making a will and/or that you did not follow the legal formalities.

## The testator must be legally capable of making a will

A testator, to make a valid will, has to be over the age of majority (18 or 19, depending on the province). There are a couple of exceptions to this rule, but they're so minor that it's not worth taking up space to talk about them. In fact we've already talked about them too much now.

A testator must also be mentally competent to:

- Understand what a will is and what it does.
- Know and appreciate how much property he or she has.
- Appreciate who might have a claim to share in his or her estate.

And a testator must make the will freely, according to his or her own wishes, and not as a result of any violence or threats of violence, or pressure exerted by someone in a dominant relationship with the testator. (So tell everyone to stop shouting at you about what they want.)

If a testator doesn't meet these three conditions of age of majority, mental competence, and free will, the will can be set aside after death. Now how would a nasty thing like that happen? Someone who is not happy with his or her share under your will (and believes he or she would do better under provincial intestacy laws or the provisions of an earlier will) might challenge the validity of your will when your executor applies for letters probate. (This is in fact the normal course of events in the star system Lyra IV, but there they have special laws permitting the testator to be brought back to life to give any challenger a tongue-lashing, a procedure with a 122 percent success rate.) To meet the challenge here in Canada, your executor will have to prove that you were legally capable, based on the evidence of your witnesses and your lawyer, if you sensibly had one.

## Legal formalities for signing and witnessing a will

A will must be properly signed and witnessed in order to be valid.

### Signing

The testator has to sign the will in the presence of two witnesses, and the two witnesses must also sign the will, in the presence of the testator and in the presence of each other. Hmm, that still sounds like the contortion troupe. Let's try this again. What we mean is, the testator and the two witnesses must all be present and must all watch each other sign the will.

If any changes have been made to the will by hand after it was typed or printed (for example, if John Robinson came to his senses and at the last minute decided to leave his atomic force microscope to Major West instead of Dr. Smith, thus averting huge amounts of trouble), the testator and witnesses must all initial those changes. Otherwise it will be presumed that changes were made after the testator and witnesses signed the will, and they won't be valid.

If your will is longer than one page it is a good idea (although not legally necessary) for you and your witnesses to initial each page of the will other than the signature page. This makes it harder for someone to substitute different pages in your will after you sign it.

There should be only one original of the will for everyone to sign. If the testator wants to make the will available for other people to read or keep, photocopies of the original should be made after it has been signed.

### Witnessing

There are some people who just aren't cut out to be witnesses to a particular testator's will. In all provinces, a person who witnesses a will is not allowed to receive any gifts under the will. If the testator gives a gift to a person under the will and then allows that person to witness the will, the testator is giving with one hand and taking away with the other! The gift will fail and the person will never receive it. In most provinces, a gift to a beneficiary will also fail if the beneficiary's spouse witnessed the will. The purpose of these rules is to prevent a beneficiary from forcing a testator to make a will that favours the beneficiary. (In some provinces, a beneficiary who witnessed or whose spouse witnessed the will can apply to the court for an order allowing the beneficiary to receive the gift anyway.)

When your executor wants to apply for letters probate (see Chapter 10), at least one of your witnesses will be required to give evidence that he or she was a witness to your will and that the proper legal formalities were followed. This evidence usually takes the form of an *affidavit of execution* of the will — a document in which a witness swears under oath that the will was signed by the testator in the presence of both witnesses, and that both witnesses were present at the same time and signed the will in the testator's presence. Your lawyer will probably ask at least one witness to swear an affidavit of execution as soon as possible, because it may be difficult or impossible to find your witnesses after your death.

### Checking out the testator's legal capacity to make a will

If you use a lawyer to prepare your will, the lawyer owes a professional duty to you and your intended beneficiaries to make sure that you are legally capable of making a will at the time you sign it and that all legal formalities are followed. This duty requires your lawyer to be rather nosy. Your lawyer should:

- Meet with you personally, without any of your beneficiaries tagging along.
- Ask you about your family situation and property to make sure that you have not left out an obvious beneficiary and that you understand what's in your estate.
- Be satisfied of your reasons if you leave out an obvious beneficiary or treat unequally beneficiaries who might ordinarily be expected to be treated equally.
- Review any earlier will and ask why you are making any major changes.
- Arrange to have you medically examined, if your lawyer has any doubts about your mental capacity.
- Be present when you sign your will — unless your lawyer has given you complete written instructions on how to sign your will and is satisfied that you are mentally competent, and not acting under pressure or threats.

If someone challenges your will after you die, your lawyer will be able to give evidence that you were legally capable of making a will and that all of the legal formalities were followed. Your witnesses would probably be dragged in to give evidence too.

# After the Will Is Signed

After you sign your will, keep the original will in a safe place. If you don't have easy access to vault facilities of the Cerberus Corporation (franchises located in wealthier areas of the galaxy . . . Canada, alas, is in rather a downscale area), you could try

- Leaving the will with the lawyer who prepared it — most lawyers will provide storage in their wills vault, usually free of charge.
- Storing the will with the court (a service available in some provinces).
- Putting the will in a fireproof file cabinet in your home.

Do not store your will in your safety deposit box without giving your executor a copy to show to the bank, to prove his or her authority to open your safety deposit box.

Make sure you tell your executor where to find your original will.

If your lawyer is not holding your will for you, make sure that he or she gives you the affidavit of execution as well as the original will. Otherwise your executor will have to get the affidavit from your lawyer after you die — and some lawyers have been known to charge an administrative fee for locating the affidavit.

# Do-It-Yourself Wills

A will does not have to be prepared by a lawyer to be valid. It is possible, although not smart, to prepare your will all by yourself. Do-it-yourselfers could:

- Write out the entire will by hand (then it would be a *holograph will*, more about which below).
- Buy a pre-printed form from a stationery store and fill in the blanks.
- Prepare a will based on a sample lawyer-drafted will (like John Robinson's) or using computer software like the one on the CD, which we've included for information purposes.
- Buy a will "kit" and fill in a form using instructions in the kit.

But no matter how you go about it, you're asking for trouble when you prepare your own will. In Chapter 17, we tell you about all the things that can go wrong with a do-it-yourself will.

## Holograph wills

A *holograph will* is a will that is completely written out in the testator's own handwriting.

In Alberta, Manitoba, New Brunswick, Newfoundland, Ontario, Quebec, Saskatchewan, the Northwest Territories, and the Yukon, a holograph will is valid as long as it is dated and signed by the testator. It does not have to be signed in the presence of witnesses. In fact, in some of these provinces, a holograph will does not even have to be signed by the testator.

In British Columbia, Nova Scotia, and Prince Edward Island, a handwritten will must be signed and witnessed just like any other will in order to be valid (unless the testator is a member of the armed forces).

If the testator types out a will or fills in blanks on a pre-printed form, the document will probably not be considered to be a holograph will. That means it is not valid unless it has been signed and witnessed.

If you think that a holograph will is a three-dimensional image of you telling your survivors what you think of them and to whom you're leaving your money, then you're confusing it with a *hologram*. Hologram wills are not legal anywhere in this solar system. We're a bit behind the times. Actually, in the most advanced parts of this galaxy they've stopped using wills of any kind. Everyone lives until they've squandered their entire estate, and then they decompose.

# Chapter 17

# The Best Laid Plans: What Can Go Wrong with Your Will?

### *In This Chapter*

- Finding out how your will can go wrong through poor planning
- Finding out how your will can go wrong through poor wording
- Finding out how your will can go wrong through incorrect signing and witnessing
- Finding out how your will can go wrong through failure to keep it up to date
- Learning about the problems with using a "will kit"

Have you ever heard of Edward A. Murphy, Jr.? He was an engineer working with the United States Air Force in 1949 on rocket-sled experiments that were meant to test how much acceleration the human body could stand. Part of the experiment involved putting sixteen sensors on the test subject's body. There were two ways the sensors could be attached, a right way and a wrong way. Guess what? The person attaching the sensors managed to attach all sixteen the wrong way. That meant that the experiment, which wasn't so pleasant that any test subject in his right mind would want to repeat it, had been useless. Mr. Murphy, pondering this result, was moved to remark, "If there are two or more ways to do something, and one of those ways can result in a catastrophe, then someone will do it." You may be more familiar with another version of Murphy's law (that's right, this is the same Murphy), "Whatever can go wrong will go wrong."

Speaking of catastrophes — what if something goes wrong with your will? On one hand, it's not your problem. You're dead. It's your executor's problem. It's your beneficiaries' problem. On the other hand, you chose your executor carefully, and executors aren't a dime a dozen. You don't want to set your executor up for failure, or drive him or her to resign in a snit. As for your beneficiaries, they may be people you love dearly — but whether you love them or not, you went to quite a bit of trouble to make arrangements so they would be suitably looked after in your absence.

That means you might as well do your will right. The first time.

In this chapter we're going to tell you the kinds of things that can go wrong with your will, and how to avoid them.

# It's Unsinkable

Where can you go wrong in preparing your will? Almost anywhere. You can run into trouble at

- The planning stage — when you develop strategies for increasing the value of your estate and put together the overall scheme you want to follow in distributing your estate
- The drafting stage — when you choose the wording for your will
- The execution stage — when you sign your will
- The post-execution stage — when you should review your will regularly

But don't sink into a damp and icy gloom. Most problems can be avoided if you:

- Get professional estate planning advice,
- Have a lawyer prepare your will, and
- Keep your will up to date.

# Of Course It Will Hold!

When you plan your estate, there are many things to take into account, and there are quite a few problems that can arise if you don't plan properly. The mistakes you can make include failing to:

- Choose an executor who is capable of carrying out the required duties.
- Keep debts and taxes in mind.
- Take into account the claims that your spouse or dependants may have against your estate.
- Establish a trust for beneficiaries who are minors.
- Choose an appropriate person to have custody of your children.
- Make a plan to pass on your business.

We talk about these matters all through this book. That might be why they sound kind of familiar. Now we're going to take one more swing at them.

## What can happen if you choose the wrong executor?

Your executor is the linchpin of your estate plan. If you choose the wrong one, your plans can be seriously messed up. For example, an executor who is unwell or old and feeble when you die may drop out or die before his or her duties are completed. But that's not really such a big problem. One way or another, you'll still end up with an executor (your alternate executor, for example). But executors can do worse than get sick or bite the dust. An executor who performs the job incompetently or dishonestly can be bad news, big time.

### An incompetent executor

An incompetent executor may:

- Fail to file appropriate tax returns, leading to extra tax payments in the form of interest and penalties.
- Fail to take advantage of various tax-saving strategies such as making an RRSP donation for your spouse or taking advantage of unused capital losses, with the result that your estate loses money to the tax authorities unnecessarily.
- Pay debts that should be challenged (so your estate loses money) or fail to pay all of your legitimate debts (so your estate is sued).
- Make poor investment decisions, so that your estate doesn't increase in value as it could or even loses money.
- Distribute your estate before your debts and taxes are paid (with the result that the executor may have to pay some of them personally . . . ha ha, serves the twit right).
- Distribute your estate to the wrong beneficiaries or in incorrect shares or amounts.

### A dishonest executor

A dishonest executor may:

- Steal money from your estate, either by pocketing estate money outright or by overpaying himself or herself for services as the executor.
- Put his or her interests ahead of those of your estate, for example by buying property from the estate for a low price, or by directing paid estate-related work to himself or herself, friends, or family.
- Deliberately favour one beneficiary over another.

### Solution

We told you about what to look for in an executor in Chapter 10. Review that chapter and rethink your choice of executor if advisable. Make sure you've got an alternate executor — and, if necessary, a trust company as an *executor of last resort*.

## What can happen if you don't take debts and taxes into account?

Debts and taxes are paid off the top of your estate — your executor must pay the estate's debts and taxes before giving your beneficiaries a cent. There are special rules about where the money to pay them comes from, and if you don't give some forethought to paying debts and taxes, you might be surprised (if you were still alive) what your beneficiaries end up getting . . . or not getting . . . once those bills have been paid.

### How debts and taxes are paid

Without specific instructions in the will to proceed differently, your executor must use the *residue* of your estate to pay the debts and taxes on the estate. The residue is what's left of your estate once your executor has set aside

- Specific items of real and personal property that you have left to named beneficiaries, and
- Gifts of fixed amounts of cash that you have left to named beneficiaries.

First your executor will use the cash in the residue of your estate. If there's not enough cash, your executor will sell property in the residue to get cash. If there's not enough property in the residue to raise the cash needed to pay all of your debts and taxes, your executor will start using the cash that you left to named beneficiaries. When that runs out, your executor will sell for cash specific items of property that you left to a named beneficiary. Personal property is used first, and once it's used up real property is used.

### How things can go wrong

If you don't take your debts and taxes into account when planning your estate, or if you underestimate the amount of your estate's debts and taxes, you may get results you didn't expect. Here are some of the things that can happen.

- If there is tax payable on a specific piece of property given as a gift (such as capital gains tax on capital property or income tax on an RRSP), the tax will be paid first out of the cash in the residue of your estate, not out of the property. One beneficiary will get the property and another beneficiary (the one to whom you're leaving the residue) will get the tax bill.

- If your estate still has unpaid debts and taxes after your executor uses up the residue, the people to whom you have left specific gifts of cash may not receive their gifts — the cash that was supposed to go to them will have to be used to pay the debts and taxes.
- If your estate still has unpaid debts and taxes after your executor uses up the residue and the cash gifts left to named beneficiaries, the people to whom you have left specific gifts of personal property may not receive their gifts — that personal property will have to be sold and turned into cash.
- If your estate still has unpaid debts and taxes after your executor uses up the residue, the cash gifts left to named beneficiaries, and the personal property left to named beneficiaries, the people to whom you left specific gifts of real property may not receive their gifts — that real property will have to be sold and turned into cash.
- If there is not enough property in your estate to pay your estate's debts and taxes, your estate is said to be *insolvent*. Your executor will have to divide whatever money there is in your estate among the creditors of your estate, following rules set by provincial law. (The only good news here is that your executor and beneficiaries will not be made to dig into their own pockets to pay your debts.)

### Solutions

If you're pretty sure that you're going to die owing money — for example, if you have mortgage or big capital gains and don't have a lot of cash in your estate — take out life insurance in an amount that will cover what you expect to owe. See Chapter 6 for information about life insurance.

If it's taxes rather than debts in general that will cause trouble, plan your estate so that no tax is payable on particular property. For example, take advantage of the spousal rollover provisions to leave RRSPs or property subject to capital gains to your spouse. To avoid one beneficiary getting the property and another beneficiary getting the tax bill, you can also include instructions in your will that the tax on a particular gift is to be paid out of a specific fund (for example, out of the stocks you're giving the beneficiary). See Chapter 5, where we talk about estate tax solutions.

## What can happen if you neglect your spouse or dependants?

You have some relatives it doesn't pay to forget in your will. Because even though you forget them, they may not forget you. Then your careful estate plan can be shot to pieces, because these people have a first claim on your estate. They are:

- Your spouse, who under family law in some provinces may have a right to claim a minimum share of your estate, and
- Those who are financially dependent on you, who under succession law or dependants' relief law in all provinces may have a claim against your estate.

### Estate litigation

A spouse or dependant may start a legal action against your estate if you don't leave him or her enough money in your will. The time period to start an action is usually six months. The court often orders the costs of estate litigation to be paid out of the estate itself.

### Delayed distribution

Your executor cannot legally start giving your estate away to your chosen beneficiaries until the time limit for claims by a spouse or dependants has passed and no claim has been made. If someone does make a claim, your executor will not be allowed to give anything to your beneficiaries without first getting a court order, or else getting the consent in writing of everyone who has the right to make a claim against your estate. (If your executor gives any of your estate to your beneficiaries without getting that consent or a court order, the executor may personally have to pay the amount that a court later awards the dependant or spouse, if there's not enough money left in the estate.)

### Reduced shares

What happens to your other beneficiaries if you don't make adequate provision for your spouse and/or dependants? Their share of the estate will end up being reduced by the amount you should have left to your spouse and/or dependants in the first place, plus the legal and other costs involved in dealing with the claim. And they'll have to wait until any court proceeding started by your spouse and/or dependants is finished before they get what's left.

### Solution

In Chapter 10 we talk about the claims that your spouse or dependants might have against your estate. Make sure you make a proper provision for them from the outset, even if it means leaving less of your estate to people you really want to have it.

## What can happen if you don't set up a trust for beneficiaries who are minors?

If you leave property directly to a child under the age of majority, your executor can be required to pay the money or hand over the property to the provincial government. The provincial public trustee will manage it according to rules set out by provincial law, until the child's 18th or 19th birthday (depending on the province). The government will invest all of the child's money in very conservative investments, so there will probably be a low return on investment. Whoever has custody of the child will have to apply to the government any time money is needed for the child. The government will hand over money only if it approves of the plan to spend the money.

When the child reaches the age of majority, the government will turn all the money and property over to the child, whether or not the child is mature and responsible enough not to blow it all on tattoos and belly button rings.

### Solution

In Chapters 9 and 11 we talk about the importance of setting up a trust if you leave any money or property to a beneficiary who is under the age of majority. Then you, instead of the provincial government, have control over investment and spending decisions and can determine at what age the trust property is turned over to your child.

## What can happen if you don't name someone to look after your children?

If you don't name someone appropriate as your children's guardian, there is more likely to be a custody battle over your children, which the courts will have to decide without the benefit of knowing your views on the subject.

### Solution

We cover the guardianship question in Chapter 11. As you'll recall, an appropriate person would be someone the court will take to (for a long list of reasons we won't repeat here). Choose your potential guardian with our discussion in Chapter 11 in mind.

## What can happen if you don't make a plan to pass on your business?

A business that you own may be the most valuable thing in your estate. Don't waste a cent of it. If you don't plan properly,

- Your estate may end up paying more in taxes because you didn't do anything while you were alive to take advantage of tax-reduction or tax-avoidance strategies.
- Your estate may end up having to sell your business under poor market conditions, getting less than your business is really worth.

- Your estate may be unable to get the necessary consents to transfer your shares in a privately held corporation to your beneficiaries — then they'll neither be able to participate in the running of the corporation nor be able to sell out for cash.
- Your partners may be unable or unwilling to purchase your partnership interest from your estate, and then your estate may receive no money from your business.
- You may create arguments among family members who can't agree whether to try to run the business or sell it.

### Solution

We give you the goods on passing on your business, or at least the value of your business, in Chapter 12.

# Trust Me, I Know What I'm Doing

Are you thinking of writing your will yourself? We hope not. But just in case you are, in this section we'll tell you about some of the things that can go wrong with a will drafted by a non-lawyer.

Now don't get us wrong. Using a lawyer to prepare your will is not an absolute guarantee that there will be no problems. Even lawyers make mistakes. The difference between you and a lawyer, however, is that your beneficiaries can sue an incompetent lawyer and get money to correct the mistake. You're not insured against making mistakes when you draft a will — so your beneficiaries will just have to lump your mistakes.

If you take it into your head to write your own will, you can run into trouble in a lot of different ways, but here are some of the most common ones:

- You probably won't handle the residue of your estate properly.
- Your words may not make clear what you intend.
- You almost certainly won't consider all of the "what-ifs."
- You very likely won't give enough power to your executor.

## Residue

Two very common mistakes are to leave out the residue clause entirely, and to divide up the residue wrongly.

## To Russia with love

Mitchell, before undertaking a dangerous top-secret mission to steal a jet from a foreign power, wrote a will that gave his medals and uniforms to his friend, Pavel, his stocks and bonds to his sister, Natalia, his house and household goods and furniture to his brother, Pyotr, and his car and all his cash to his parents. Because he believed he'd given away everything he owned, he didn't include a clause giving away the residue of his estate. Mitchell forgot about his first edition of *Learn to Speak Russian Like a Russian*, which didn't fit into any of the categories he described, which he hadn't looked at since he was twelve years old, and which was very valuable by the time of his death.

Mitchell unfortunately crashes into the Ural Mountains. Who gets the valuable book? If the beneficiaries can't reach an agreement among themselves, then a court will have to decide.

### Leaving out a residue clause

The residue clause gives away whatever property you have left after you've given specific gifts. Think you can get around the residue clause by giving away everything you own in a specific gift? Mitchell did. Read "To Russia with love" to see what happened to his estate.

As you can see from reading Mitchell's story, there's a risk that you'll leave something out, and the court may have to decide what to do with your property. Going to court is expensive, and the legal fees will very likely come out of the estate. Further, your executor may not be able to distribute any of your estate until the matter has been settled — and the legal fees have been paid.

### Dividing the residue wrongly

If the residue of your estate is going to just one person, there's no problem here. But if you want to divide the residue among two or more people, you have to be careful how you say it's to be divided. If you make a mistake, the residue may end up being paid out as if you didn't have a will. Read "The wrong stuff" on the next page for an example.

## Unclear wording

Maybe *you* know what you mean, but will anyone else who reads your will? Your executor has to be able to understand your instructions in order to follow them.

Examples speak louder than explanation. You're the executor. What does the testator want you to do in the following situations?

### The wrong stuff

John wanted his estate to be divided equally among his four best friends, Alan, Wally, Gordo, and Gus. He wrote a will giving a couple of small specific gifts to distant family members and then directed his high-flying executor, Chuck, to divide the residue of his estate into four equal shares and to pay one share to each of his friends. Unfortunately, Gus died before John did, and John didn't change his will after that happened.

When John dies, where does the fourth share go?

It doesn't go to the other best friends. Under provincial law, it has to be paid out as though John had died without making a will. It ends up going to John's evil twin. To avoid this tragedy, John would have had to write in his will something like, "Divide the residue of my estate into as many equal shares as I have the following friends alive at the time of my death."

- The will says, "Divide my estate equally between my cousins." The testator has two first cousins, six second cousins, and ten third cousins. Does the testator want his estate divided *between* his two first cousins or *among* all of his cousins? Does it help any if we tell you that the testator rarely spoke to his first cousins but was on good terms with two of his second cousins?
- The will says, "I leave $10,000 to my brother and sister." Does the testator want you to pay $10,000 to the brother *and* $10,000 to the sister? Or to divide the $10,000 between them?
- The will says, "Divide my estate between my wife and my sisters." The testator has two sisters. Does the testator want you to give one-third of his estate each to his wife and his sisters or does he want you to give one-half of his estate to his wife and to divide the other half between his two sisters?

If your instructions are unclear, your executor may have to apply to the court for help in interpreting your will, or your beneficiaries may challenge your will in court. Your estate will probably end up paying the cost of court proceedings. And that gets paid before your beneficiaries get their gifts.

## Unconsidered "what-ifs?"

Your life only looks like a straight road when you look behind you. When you look ahead, you see forks in the road everywhere — what if you take a new job, what if you meet a new partner, what if a close relative dies unexpectedly? When you're writing a will, you can't assume that your life and your beneficiaries' lives are going to continue exactly as they are, right up to the time of your death. You have to explore the path at each fork, and consider the "what-ifs." If you don't, there will be results you didn't expect when your estate is distributed.

### What if you don't own then what you own now?

If your will gives a specific piece of property to a beneficiary but you no longer own that piece of property when you die, your gift will fail and your beneficiary will get nothing. For example, if your will says, "I leave my Humvee to my friend Riley," Riley will get nothing if you sell your Humvee and buy a stealth fighter jet before you die. Your stealth fighter jet will go to the person to whom you have left the residue of your estate. Riley will get the stealth fighter jet only if you leave a replacement gift in your will. Your will would have to say, "I leave my Humvee, or whatever other form of military transport I may own at my death, to my friend Riley."

If your will gives a cash gift to a named beneficiary and identifies a specific fund out of which the gift is to be paid, if the fund does not exist when you die the gift will fail and your beneficiary will get nothing. For example, if your will states, "I direct my executor to sell my collection of Polaroid photographs of MiG pilots engaging in aerial acrobatics and to pay to my friend Goose the sum of $5,000 out of the proceeds of the sale," Goose will get nothing if you sell your photograph collection before you die. If you want Goose to get $5,000 regardless, just leave him the money and don't specify the source. (Don't worry about your estate running out of cash — your aviator shades are easily worth five grand.)

### What if your beneficiary dies before you do?

If your will gives a specific gift of cash or property to a named beneficiary and the beneficiary dies before you, generally speaking the gift will fail. The cash or property will go to the person who's getting the residue of your estate. For example, if your will says, "I leave my fur-lined flying boots to my friend Ben," and Ben dies before you do, the boots will go to Keith, to whom you've given the residue of your estate. That may be okay with you. But what if you wanted Ben's daughter to get the boots? Or what if you wanted your assistant Harvey to get them? In some provinces there is a statutory provision that sends a gift that has failed on to the spouse and/or children of a beneficiary who predeceased you. The provision usually applies to beneficiaries who are close relatives of the testator — children, grandchildren, brothers, or sisters. That won't help here. And why count on the provincial government to solve problems that don't need to arise in the first place?

If you don't want the property to go back to the residue, make a gift of it to an alternative beneficiary if your first choice dies. If you want Ben's daughter to get the boots, your will should say, "I leave my fur-lined flying boots to my friend Ben, but if he predeceases me, I leave my fur-lined flying boots to Ben's daughter, L. Colony." If Ben's daughter dies before you do and you still don't want Keith to get the boots, then your will should say, "I leave my fur-lined flying boots to my friend Ben, but if he predeceases me, I leave my fur-lined flying boots to Ben's daughter, L. Colony. If Ben's daughter predeceases me, I leave my fur-lined flying boots to my assistant, Harvey."

## Vanishing point

Zack left the residue of his estate to his wife, Paula, if she survived him, to his children if she didn't, and to the children of any child who predeceased him. That's pretty standard stuff and it covers beneficiaries for three generations. Unfortunately, Zack and his entire family (his children were all under the age of 12) drowned while undergoing testing to see whether they'd be able to unbuckle their seat belts if they had to ditch a jet fighter in the ocean. Zack's estate went to his father, to whom he hadn't spoken in years. If Zack had thought about it, he would have preferred to give his estate to his personal trainer, "Drill Sergeant" Foley.

If you leave the residue of your estate to two or more people and one of them dies before you do, the residue will go to whoever is still alive. If you leave the residue to one person and that person dies before you do, the residue will be given away as if you had died without leaving a valid will. The same thing is true if you leave the residue to two or more people together, or to one or two people plus an alternate, and they all die before you. (We talk about intestate succession in Chapter 15.) How can that happen? Have a look at "Vanishing point" for an example.

If you want to control where the residue goes no matter what, name alternate beneficiaries until you run out of friends and relatives you actually want to give your property to. Then name a charity as *beneficiary of last resort.* If you don't, the provincial law of intestate succession decides who your beneficiary of last resort is — it will be the provincial government if you don't have any surviving relatives.

## Insufficient power to the executor

You may choose an excellent executor but then spoil everything by failing to give him or her broad enough powers to properly manage the assets in your estate. What can go wrong here?

- If you don't give your executor the right to decide when or whether to sell estate property, by provincial law your executor has to turn the property of the estate into cash immediately. You may not have wanted everything sold for cash, and your estate may not get that much cash if your executor isn't allowed to wait for good market conditions.
- If you don't give your executor the right to use your unused RRSP contribution to make an RRSP donation for your spouse, your executor won't be able to take advantage of this tax-saving strategy.

- If you don't give your executor the right to choose what kind of investments to make, or don't specify what kind of investments you want the executor to make, your executor will be restricted to making investments allowed by provincial law. These permitted investments are very conservative and will probably not bring your estate much of a return on investment.
- If you don't give your executor the right to decide whether to pay money out of trust to a minor beneficiary, and you don't specify in what circumstances a payment can be made, your executor may be unable to make any payment out to the minor — without applying to court — until the kid reaches the age when the trust ends.

### Now I really do know what I'm doing

Trust us, you don't. After reading this section, you may — or may not — be able to avoid the particular problems we've talked about. But there are lots of other problems to run into. If you insist on going ahead and drafting your own will, you'll be asking for trouble. And trouble has a way of obliging.

## What Happens If You Touch These Two Wires Together?

So your next bright idea is to execute your will without a lawyer's supervision, is it?

In Chapter 16 we tell you about the legal formalities that apply when you execute (sign) a will.

- The testator must have reached the age of majority.
- The testator must be mentally competent.
- The testator must be making the will freely.
- The will must be properly signed and witnessed.

These formalities apply even if you've got a do-it-yourself will. (And if you've got a holograph will, the only formality that doesn't apply concerns the signing and witnessing.) If you don't meet the legal formalities, all or part of your will may be invalid. Then either an earlier will you made will be the one that passes on your estate or, if you have no earlier valid will, the intestacy provisions of your province will govern what happens to your estate.

## Signed and witnessed

We're starting with the signing and witnessing, because that's the first thing everyone looks for when you're freshly dead and they light upon the will. It's easy to see whether a will has been signed and witnessed, but harder to see whether the testator was bonkers or being arm-twisted.

Your typed or printed or printed-and-handwritten will may not make it through the probate process if it's not properly signed and witnessed. Then it's not a valid will. Although some provinces have a law saying that a will that doesn't meet all the formal requirements may still be valid if it reflects the true intention of the testator, it's best not to count on a court fixing your mistakes.

### Geography

You and (in most provinces) two witnesses must all be present together in the same room and must all sign the will (you first) and must all watch each other sign the will.

Suppose you don't do it exactly right — suppose one of your witnesses wanders off to the kitchen in mid-signing, or you get your witnesses to sign on two different days — who's going to know?

In order to get your will probated (declared by the court to be your legitimate will), at least one of your witnesses will be required to swear under oath in an *affidavit of execution* that he or she was a witness to your will and that you and your witnesses were all present and all watched each other sign. Can you be sure that, after you're dead, one of your witnesses will lie under oath if you didn't do it right? Come to that, if you don't use a lawyer (a lawyer normally has the witnesses swear the affidavit immediately), can you be sure that your witnesses can be tracked down to swear an oath at all?

And what if you make a change by hand to your prepared will just before you and your witnesses sign it? Say you change "$10,000" to "$20,000," or "Alzheimer's Society" to "Parkinson's Foundation"? If you and your witnesses don't all initial any such changes, they won't be valid. The law will presume that the change was made *after* you and the witnesses signed the will.

Finally, suppose your will is two or more pages long. It's just a bunch of sheets of paper stapled or paper-clipped together. What's to stop some evildoer from rewriting one of the pages and slipping that substitute page into your will? Nothing much. That's why lawyers have the testator and witnesses initial each page of the will other than the signature page. Then a substitution is more difficult.

### Beneficiaries

It's not always that easy for a testator to find someone, and especially two someones, to witness a will. So you may just grab on to whoever's handy. The people who are handy are likely to be the people who are always hanging around — and *they're* likely to be the people you're leaving something to in your will.

A person who witnesses a will is not allowed to receive any gifts under the will. In most provinces a person whose spouse witnesses the will is also not allowed to receive any gifts under the will. So before you're even dead you've blown your will up. There may be hope, though. In some provinces, a beneficiary who was a witness to a will can apply to the court for an order allowing the gift to stand. Once again, you're hoping that a court will fix your mistakes.

## Mental competence and free will

If you're reading this book and you understand at least one word in three (one word in nine in the tax chapters), you're probably legally capable of making a will. However, that's not the legal test of mental competence. The legal test asks whether you've got your wits sufficiently about you to understand what a will is and what it does, know and appreciate how much property you have, and appreciate which people might have a claim to share in your estate. You also have to be acting freely, not under threats or violence, or under pressure from a person who has a dominant relationship with you.

### Proof

If your will is challenged after you die by someone who (hoping to get more from your estate under an earlier will or the provincial intestacy law) claims that you were mentally incompetent, or acted under pressure from someone dominant over you, your executor will have to defend your will in court by showing that you *were* mentally competent and acting of your own free will when you signed the will. If you didn't use a lawyer to prepare your will and supervise execution, you've taken away the executor's best evidence for the defence.

Remember, you'll be dead. You won't be able to jump up and say that you were perfectly right in the head when you made that will and nobody made you do it. The court hearing the case will have to rely on what people who are still alive observed about you.

If you use a lawyer to prepare your will, the lawyer will meet with you, ask questions about your family and property to make sure you know what's in your estate and haven't forgotten any obvious beneficiaries, ask about your reasons for leaving someone out or treating beneficiaries unequally, and want to know why you're making changes if you had an earlier will. If your lawyer has any doubts about your mind, he or she will arrange for you to have a medical examination. In other words, by the time a lawyer has finished preparing your will, he or she will have reached a firm conclusion about whether you were mentally competent and acting according to your own wishes. A lawyer would be able to give believable independent evidence about your state of mind.

### Holograph wills

A holograph will (one you write out entirely in your own hand — see Chapter 16) is easy to prepare. You sit down with a piece of paper and a pen. You don't need a lawyer, you don't need a witness (in most provinces), you just need you.

A holograph will is also dangerous, exactly because there is no lawyer and there are no witnesses. It can be challenged more easily by someone claiming that you were mentally incompetent or not acting of your own free will at the time you made it.

## Don't Worry, It's Not Loaded

You've probably heard "will kits" being advertised. The theory is that you'll save the money you would have spent on a lawyer and still get legal advice about how to write a will. Will kits claim to provide easy-to-use forms and step-by-step instructions on how to complete them.

We've looked at will kits and we're suspicious of them because

- The guides provide only limited advice about planning your will — they're very short (as opposed to this book, which is agonizingly long and still keeps telling you to see a lawyer).
- The easy-to-use forms tend to be blank in all of the difficult places and complete only in the places you could probably figure out on your own. (See "Drawing a blank" on the next page.)
- The guides give very little direction on the wording and language to use in completing the form — and as we've told you, wording and language can make or break your will.
- You're on your own when it comes to executing your will — the will kit people don't send over a lawyer to make sure that you're mentally competent, or provide witnesses to whom you're leaving nothing in your will.

A will kit may save you $150 to $250 in lawyer's fees. If your estate is worth more than a few hundred dollars, don't mess around on your own with a will kit. Get a lawyer to prepare your will!

### Drawing a blank

The will form in one leading will kit has pre-printed paragraphs revoking earlier wills, appointing an executor, stating that any gift to a minor is to be held in trust, and appointing someone to have custody of young children.

When it comes to gifts, all that's pre-printed are the words, "I make the following gifts:" followed by a blank space about ¾ of a page long, and then the words: "I give all of the residue of my estate to" followed by a blank space about ¼ of a page long.

The will form does not contain or leave space for (or directions to include) instructions to the executor to pay the debts and taxes of the estate or extra powers for the executor. We describe what can happen without such instructions in the "Of Course It Will Hold!" section earlier in this chapter.

# There's a Great View If You Just Lean Over Here

Even if you did everything right — you planned properly and you had a lawyer draft your will and oversee its execution — it can all go wrong with the passage of time and changing circumstances.

Unless your "what-ifs" were deadly accurate or totally comprehensive, you need to review your will on a regular basis, especially if there's a significant event in your life. Take your will out of storage, re-read it, and ask yourself if you need to revise it, if there's a change in

- Your personal life: If you marry, if your spouse or partner or any close relative dies, if you separate or divorce, if you meet someone new, if you have a new child, or if someone in your family develops special needs.
- Your business life: If your business becomes more (or less) successful, if you change the business you're in, or if you change the form of business you carry on (such as a change from a sole proprietorship to a corporation).
- Your executor's life: If your executor dies or becomes ill or suggests he or she would rather not take on the work involved in looking after your estate, or even if your executor moves away.
- The nature and value of your property: If you increase (or decrease) the value of your estate significantly, acquire new kinds of property (if you go from renting to home ownership or if you start building up an investment portfolio from scratch), acquire property in a different province or a foreign country, or find that you have growing debts.

- The law: If tax laws change (which they do almost daily), or if laws relating to the family or wills and estates change.
- Your place of residence: If you move to a different province or a foreign country.

Even one of these changes can mean that your will won't work the way you planned. So though it's a bit morbid, make a habit of reviewing your will regularly. In Chapter 23 we tell you more about the impact that your life can have on your will, and why your first will probably shouldn't be your last will.

# I Wish I Hadn't Done That . . .

By now you ought to be feeling thoroughly depressed and ashamed by the trouble your poor planning and execution have caused your survivors — and you haven't even gotten around to dying yet. But that's good! Because it means you've got a second chance to do things right the first time.

Get professional advice about how to plan your estate. Speak to a lawyer to find out how things like tax laws, family laws, and laws about making a will are going to affect you. For information about taxes and help with financial planning, you might also want to speak to an accountant or financial consultant. (More about accountants and financial consultants in Chapter 21.)

Have a lawyer prepare your will so it will reflect your true wishes *and* be written in language that will stand up to challenges in court (we can't claim that it will be written in language that you understand...). Have a lawyer involved in the execution of your will so that it will be signed and witnessed properly, and so that you'll leave behind at least one reliable witness who can say you were mentally competent and acting of your own free will when you signed.

Review your will regularly and keep it up to date. You want your will to provide the best solutions to current and future issues about caring for your family and friends with your estate.

# Chapter 18

# Affairs to Remember: Who'll Manage Your Money For You?

### *In This Chapter*

- Discovering what will happen to your income if you become disabled
- Understanding how your property will be managed if you become disabled
- Learning what a power of attorney is and what it does
- Learning how to create a power of attorney
- Finding out about alternatives if you become mentally disabled without having a power of attorney

We're getting tired of asking you, "What happens if you die?" So in this chapter we're going to change tactics and ask you, "What happens if your body fails or you lose your mind (and then you die)?"

You've got an estate (or else you're in the process of creating one), and that means you have all kinds of affairs to transact. You work to produce income, you make investments, you buy and sell property, you take out insurance, and you make a will. What would happen to you (and your estate) if you were no longer able to rush around attending to your affairs because you were physically or mentally disabled?

It's not uncommon for people to be disabled for a period of time — in some cases for years — before they die. It's not a scenario any of us likes to confront. For some people, disability is worse to face than dying.

While you're in the process of planning how to care for your family and friends after you die, you should also make plans to care for yourself and them if you become disabled.

# What Will Happen If Your Physical or Mental Health Fails?

You could just be walking along in apparently perfect health one day and keel over dead from a heart attack. Then you wouldn't have to worry about failing health, would you? And it certainly happens that some people are alive and in fine fettle in the morning and gone by the evening.

But that's not what happens to most people. A decline before death is much more common, whether it takes place overnight, or over a few weeks or a few years. That decline is likely to include a period of time when you're physically unable to get around (you might be in the hospital, or at home but too weak or tired to get out) or mentally unable to make sound decisions about your affairs. Read "Phenomenally powerless," below, to see what can happen.

## Looking after income

If you're still working when physical or mental disability strikes, you may have to stop working altogether or you may be able to find some other work — very likely at a reduced income. You may be eligible for worker's compensation benefits if the disability is work-related. If you became disabled as the result of an injury outside the workplace, you may be able to sue whoever caused the

### Phenomenally powerless

George was a successful businessman who ran a garage in a small town. He was an avid reader who learned foreign languages easily, an earthquake predictor, and an all-round good guy. He kept his affairs in order and had made a will.

One day George got zapped by a bolt of light out of the sky and was left with impaired mental abilities and a number of physical problems. He was no longer able to handle business at the garage or even work as a mechanic. He was mentally unable to make plans about how to support himself, his wife, Lace, and their children. Lace thought that he could sell some of his investments, or real estate that he owned, to get some money to tide them over — but George simply didn't have the physical or mental ability to look after this kind of business any more.

Lace asked George's broker if he would sell some of the investments without George's own instructions, and the broker said he couldn't do that. A real estate agent Lace contacted said that she couldn't deal with Lace because the property Lace wanted to sell was in George's name. Lace was at her wits' end about what to do for money. Her sole marketable skill was making chairs, and even at that the only customer she'd ever had was George.

injury for money to replace your lost income. If you have disability insurance (available before you become disabled through employment benefits and also through individual policies — see Chapter 3) you'll get payments, at least for a while, to cover some or all of your vanished paycheque. If you're retired when disability strikes, receipt of income probably won't be affected. Whether working or retired, you may be eligible for disability benefits from the Canada Pension Plan.

If your income falls after you become disabled and there's not enough income from another source to replace it, you'll probably have to sell some of your property (your stocks, your cottage, your house) to pay the bills. If you become completely impoverished you may be able to turn for help to social assistance. Wow, *that's* a thought to bolster your drooping spirits.

Your health may be poor enough that your provincial government will provide some home care services for you, or give you a place in a provincially subsidized long-term-care facility. For expenses over and above those the government will pay for, critical illness insurance and long-term-care insurance can help. (In Chapter 3 we also tell you about critical illness insurance and long-term-care insurance.) Once you're critically ill or in need of long-term care, it's too late to apply for such kinds of insurance.

This chapter is starting to make Chapter 14 on planning your own funeral seem really cheery, isn't it?

## Looking after business

How are you going to receive your income, pay your expenses, and take care of (or sell) your investments, real estate, and other property if you become disabled?

If you become physically disabled, you'll have trouble getting out and about. But with delivery from stores, credit card transactions, automatic bank deposit and withdrawal, Internet banking, telephone, e-mail and ordinary mail, and house calls when absolutely necessary from professionals such as lawyers and real estate agents, your life doesn't have to grind to a halt. Still, it would be convenient and might sometimes be essential to have someone else look after business for you.

If your mind weakens (whether or not your body remains willing) and you become mentally incapable, you won't be legally able to transact your legal and financial affairs whether you are physically able to or not. Perhaps worse, you might still be physically able to transact affairs that would do serious harm to yourself and your estate.

## You'd be surprised how often you need your mind

A person is considered to be mentally incapable of making legal and financial decisions when he or she is not able to understand information that is relevant to making a decision, or is not able to appreciate what is likely to happen as a result of making the decision.

If you become mentally incapable of looking after your own affairs, there are a surprising number of things you won't be legally able to do. You won't be able to enter into contracts — and that will cut off your personal ability, for example, to

- Buy or sell investments.
- Buy insurance.
- Buy or sell real estate.
- Buy or sell big-ticket items like a car.
- Open a bank account or rent a safety deposit box.
- Take out a mortgage.
- Rent an apartment or make arrangements to go into a seniors' residence or a nursing home.

They'll probably still take your cash down at the grocery store or pharmacy, and your bank may let you withdraw small amounts of money at reasonable intervals. But many merchants and almost all banks will get very nervous if you don't appear to be all there and you want to do something involving even a moderately large sum of money.

Other people you want to deal with may well go along with you too, if you don't look too glassy-eyed or talk too strangely (this is especially true if you transact business by mail or e-mail). However, there are two problems with this:

- You may, in your vacantness, want to enter into a contract that is harmful to you, or the other party to the contract may want to take advantage of your state of mind to defraud you.
- Even if the contract is perfectly fair, it can be challenged and set aside if someone realizes that you were not mentally competent when you entered into it.

### Looking for help!

Now that we've set up this grim vision of your future, you're likely hoping that we're going to tell you that there's a solution. And there is a solution! We have to leave it to medical science, unfortunately, to save you from suffering physical or mental disability. But we can tell you how to manage your affairs if you do become disabled.

## The Solution to Your Management Problems

If you are mentally incapable you will need someone else to conduct your legal and financial affairs for you all the time. If you are physically disabled you may need someone else to conduct your legal and financial affairs for you only some of the time. In order to give someone else the ability to look after your affairs, you need to prepare a *power of attorney*. A power of attorney is a document that gives another person authority to handle legal and/or financial affairs of the person who signs the document.

Before we go any further, we have to have a vocabulary section. That's because a power of attorney isn't known as a power of attorney in every province. We plan to call it a power of attorney throughout this chapter, but depending on the province it may be known as a *power of attorney for personal property*, a *power of attorney for financial decisions*, a *mandate*, or a *representation agreement*. Similarly, we're going to call the person who makes and signs the power of attorney the *principal*, although depending on the province this person might also be known as the *donor* or the *grantor*. Finally, we will refer to the person chosen by the principal to handle affairs as the *attorney*, although depending on the province this person might be known as the *attorney in fact*, the *agent*, the *donee*, the *mandatary,* or the *representative*.

Got it together now? The principal wants another person to look after the principal's legal and/or financial affairs, so the principal signs a power of attorney document appointing the person of his or her choice to be the attorney.

A power of attorney must be created when you are mentally capable. To be considered mentally capable of creating the power of attorney, you must be capable of knowing the value and kind of property you own and of understanding the powers that you are giving to another person.

# Powers of Attorney Come in Different Models

A power of attorney is quite flexible in its use. You don't have to be mentally or physically incapable to want one, you just have to want someone else to look after a legal or financial matter for you.

Examples, anyone? You can create a power of attorney that gives your accountant the power to handle all of your affairs for a short period while you're out of the country and out of reach, or one that gives your daughter the authority to sell your cottage, or one that gives your son the authority to instruct your lawyer what to do in a lawsuit you've started, or one that gives your nephew the authority to make deposits and withdrawals in your bank account. You can also create a power of attorney that gives a relative, friend, or professional adviser the power to look after all of your affairs for the rest of your life.

A power of attorney has no flexibility in one respect, though: It ends as soon as the principal dies. It cannot take the place of a will, and it cannot override the provisions of a will. And an attorney cannot make a will on behalf of the principal.

## Enduring or continuing power of attorney

An ordinary power of attorney is valid only as long as the principal is mentally competent. It automatically ends when the principal becomes mentally incompetent. For many people, of course, this is exactly the point at which they want the power of attorney to come into play.

This would be a much shorter chapter if there were no answer to this problem. Luckily, there is an answer, and unluckily, this chapter is quite long. The answer is the *enduring* or *continuing* power of attorney. It is intended to continue in effect even after the principal becomes mentally incompetent. What's needed to turn an ordinary power of attorney into an enduring power of attorney is a specific statement in the power of attorney document that the power of attorney is intended to continue after the principal becomes mentally incompetent.

## General or specific power of attorney

A power of attorney can be *general* or *specific*.

A general power of attorney gives the attorney power to make many or all financial and legal decisions on the principal's behalf. In most provinces, a general power of attorney gives the attorney authority to make any financial or legal decision that the principal could make, and to do any financial or legal act that the principal could do — except prepare or change the principal's will. The principal can impose limitations on the attorney's power when the document is prepared. But if the principal does not do so, the attorney has complete power to manage the principal's affairs. That includes, for example, receiving money and paying bills; opening and closing bank accounts; making bank deposits and withdrawals; making and cashing in investments; buying, mortgaging, and selling property; and hiring and firing workers (such as caregivers) for the principal.

A specific power of attorney gives the attorney power to carry out the transactions mentioned in the document. For example, it could allow the attorney to do personal banking, or to deal with stated sources of income such as investment income and dividends, or to carry out a particular activity such as selling a vacation property.

In Quebec, the situation is somewhat different. A power of attorney (called a mandate) only automatically gives the attorney (called the mandatary) the authority to make decisions and take actions that are necessary to preserve the principal's property, and it strictly limits the way in which the attorney can invest the principal's money. In addition, the attorney must get a court order to sell any of the principal's property. A Quebec power of attorney document must give the attorney "full administrative powers" in order to create a general power of attorney like that discussed above.

### Banking power of attorney

Banks have specific power of attorney documents for banking matters. You can usually get a form at your local branch, and if you only want to make a specific power of attorney for banking you don't need to go anywhere else to get a power of attorney. In fact, even if you have a general power of attorney prepared by your lawyer, your bank may insist that it needs a power of attorney for banking in its own form. You (or your attorney armed with a general power of attorney) may have an uphill climb to convince the bank employees that a general power of attorney includes a banking power of attorney.

If your bank refuses to accept the general power of attorney and insists on its own banking power of attorney, the bank's form should be checked over by a lawyer before you sign it, to make sure that it doesn't cancel the general power of attorney.

Since it may be too late for you to sign a banking power of attorney by the time your general power of attorney is needed, you should have a discussion with the manager of your bank branch at the time you're having a general power of attorney prepared. Ask whether the general power of attorney will be acceptable. If it looks like the bank is going to be stubborn, take the bank's form for the banking power of attorney to your lawyer for review.

# What's in a Power of Attorney?

The power of attorney document differs from province to province. In most provinces, though, a power of attorney document usually

- Names the attorney(s). If more than one attorney is being appointed, the document should say whether the attorneys may make decisions alone or whether they must agree on all decisions. Sometimes a power of attorney also names a substitute attorney who takes over if the original attorney is unable or unwilling to carry out the required duties.
- Cancels previously made powers of attorney. If there is an earlier power of attorney in effect and the principal wants it to continue in effect, the later document must make that clear. (It's this cancelling clause in the banking power of attorney that can lead to trouble if you've already got a general power of attorney.)
- Sets out the powers the attorney is to have. The attorney can be given all powers the principal has, or any part of the principal's powers — such as the power to carry out certain types of transactions (for example, banking) or the power to deal with certain types of property (for example, investments or real estate).
- Indicates whether or not the power of attorney remains in effect after the principal becomes mentally incompetent. If the document says nothing about this, then it ends when the principal becomes mentally incompetent. If it is meant to continue in effect, the document must say so in the words required by the law of the province in which the power of attorney is to be used.
- States when the power of attorney comes into effect. A power of attorney can come into effect immediately or at some time in the future. In some provinces it comes into effect as soon as it has been signed and witnessed. (To prevent the attorney from acting before the principal is ready to hand over the reins, the principal can have a third person — say the principal's lawyer — hold onto the document until the principal becomes mentally incapable.) In other provinces, the principal can decide when it will come into effect — on a specified date or on the happening of a specified event (usually the mental incapacity of the principal).

  If the power of attorney is to come into effect when the principal becomes mentally incapable, in some provinces the power of attorney document can say how it's to be decided that the principal has become incapable (for example, by the opinion of the principal's doctor or lawyer). If the document doesn't say anything about how to decide, then the provincial statute governing powers of attorney applies. In some provinces, the statute says that two doctors must agree that the principal is incapable. In other provinces, the statute says that a court must decide.

- Says whether the attorney is to be paid. In most provinces, the attorney is not entitled to be paid unless the power of attorney says so. If the attorney is to be paid, the document may set out the amount or the provincial government may set the rate.
- Makes conditions about how the attorney is to exercise his or her powers. The document can say that the attorney has to invest in certain types of investments, or consult with or report to the principal's family members or financial advisers, or keep financial records in a certain form.

# What's Involved in Preparing a Power of Attorney?

The main thing that's involved in preparing a power of attorney is a visit to your lawyer (or, in Quebec, a notary).

There's no legal requirement that a lawyer has to prepare the power of attorney document, however. It's perfectly legal for a person to write out his or her own version, or fill out a pre-printed form.

We strongly recommend that you *not* go the do-it-yourself route, though. A power of attorney is much like a will — there are special rules about who can be an attorney and who can be a witness, and it also takes some legal knowledge to know what to put in the document and what to leave out. Below we tell you about some of the things that can go wrong for do-it-yourselfers.

## The attorney

For the most part, choosing an attorney is not difficult. The attorney can be anyone who has reached the age of majority (18 or 19, depending on the province) and is mentally competent. Alternatively, the attorney can be a financial institution (usually a trust company).

Choose an attorney whom you trust and who you think would make the same kinds of decisions about your financial matters that you would make.

However, there can be some traps waiting for the principal who doesn't get legal advice and assistance:

- In some provinces, an attorney who is the spouse of the principal may run into trouble if he or she later tries to mortgage, sell, or otherwise transfer the family residence. Under the family law statutes in some provinces, *both* spouses must consent to such a transaction. One spouse won't be able to use a power of attorney to give the other spouse's consent to such a transaction. (That's to make sure that, for example, a devoted wife is not using the power of attorney to transfer or mortgage the family residence out from under her adored husband.) So it might turn out, in your province, that your spouse is not the best person to be your attorney if your family home may have to be sold or mortgaged.

- If the principal wants to name more than one attorney, the principal has to state in the document whether each attorney can act alone or whether the attorneys must act together. If you don't say anything, they must act together.
- The principal may forget to name a substitute attorney in case the first choice is unwilling or unable to take on or continue the job.

## The powers

A principal might well find it useful to have the help of a lawyer to give the attorney the proper powers. A do-it-yourself principal may make mistakes because:

- For the power of attorney to remain valid after the principal becomes mentally incompetent, there has to be specific wording in the document. If the required wording isn't used, the power of attorney may end just when it will be needed.
- If there is an earlier power of attorney that the principal wants to remain in effect (for example, a general power of attorney), a later power of attorney (for example, a banking power of attorney) must not contain a *revocation* clause that cancels the earlier one.
- If the principal wants to limit the attorney's powers in some way, or have the attorney show financial records to someone for review, that has to be dealt with specifically in the document.
- If the power of attorney is going to be used in connection with real estate, special wording may be required, as well as special signing procedures. In some provinces, the people witnessing the signing of the power of attorney may then have to swear an oath before a commissioner or notary public that they are the witnesses.
- If the principal has property in another province, one power of attorney may not be enough — a second power of attorney, valid in the other province, may have to be prepared.

## The process

It's just as important to get the details of creation of the power of attorney right as it is to get the right words in the document. A lawyer will make sure that all the legal requirements for properly giving a power of attorney are met.

### The principal must be in the right state

A lawyer will make sure that the principal has reached the age of majority (easy) and is mentally competent to give a power of attorney (harder). Your lawyer won't let you sign a power of attorney document if you're mentally incompetent — there wouldn't be much point, because it wouldn't be valid if you sign it while incompetent. If your lawyer has doubts about you, he or she may even refer you to a doctor for an examination before agreeing to assist you in creating a power of attorney. This is a safeguard to make sure that you know what you're doing when you give another person power over your financial affairs.

If someone later questions whether you were mentally competent when you signed the document, your lawyer will be able to give evidence that you were. Why would someone challenge your mental competence at the time you signed? Because that person doesn't like the attorney you chose or the decisions the attorney is making. If that person could prove to a court that you were not mentally competent when you made the power of attorney, the power of attorney would be declared invalid from the beginning. There is much less likely to be a challenge if you had a lawyer help you prepare and sign the document because a lawyer wouldn't ordinarily let you sign if you weren't right in the head.

### The document must be signed and witnessed

A power of attorney has to be properly signed and witnessed, just as a will does. In most provinces, two witnesses must be present when the principal signs the document and then the witnesses must also sign the document. The principal and the witnesses must all be present together to watch each other sign. (In some provinces, only one witness is required.) In some provinces, the witnesses may have to swear before a commissioner or a notary public that they are the witnesses.

The purpose of these rules is to make sure that no one is forging the principal's name on the power of attorney, or sneakily getting the principal to give a power of attorney without knowing it, or forcing the principal to give the power of attorney against his or her will.

### The witnesses must be eligible

Anyone who witnesses the signing of a power of attorney has to be eligible to be a witness. In almost all provinces, the witnesses must not be the attorney, the attorney's spouse, the principal's spouse, or the principal's child. Further, in some provinces only specified people such as judges, justices of the peace, lawyers, and doctors can act as witnesses.

The purpose of this rule is to make sure that the witnesses don't have their own stake in creating the power of attorney. Independent witnesses presumably won't help anyone to forge a power of attorney or force the principal to sign a document against his or her will.

### The attorney needs to know when it's time to take over

Finally, the attorney may need a lawyer's help to decide when the power of attorney can be used.

In provinces where the power of attorney comes into effect as soon as it is signed, the principal may want to instruct his or her lawyer to hold the power of attorney document and not give it to the attorney until the principal is mentally incapable. Then the attorney needs to know when to call up the lawyer and ask for the document. This is a matter you and your attorney should discuss with your lawyer.

In provinces where the power of attorney can come into effect when a particular event happens, the principal may state that the event is mental incapacity. Again, the attorney may need to talk to a lawyer to decide whether the event has happened. The principal may even have stipulated that his or her lawyer should decide when it has happened (the usual alternative is to have the principal's doctor decide).

If the power of attorney is intended to come into effect when the principal becomes mentally incompetent and the document says nothing about how it's to be determined that the principal is incompetent, the attorney may need a lawyer's assistance to find out what the provincial law says about determining incompetence. In some provinces two doctors are needed to give evidence, in others a court has to review the evidence and make a decision.

## Once the Power of Attorney Has Been Prepared

After preparing the power of attorney document, the principal should tell the attorney where the original document is being kept.

Don't keep your power of attorney in your safety deposit box! Your attorney may not be able to get into the box without having a power of attorney document to show the bank!

If the principal has confidence in the attorney's ability to decide when the principal is mentally incapable, the principal can even give the attorney the document to keep until it's needed. If the principal decides not to give the document to the attorney but to someone else to hold, the principal should give the holder instructions in writing that set out when the document should be given to the attorney. It's common for a principal to leave the document with his or her lawyer.

The principal can leave written instructions for the attorney along with the power of attorney document. In the instructions, the principal can tell the attorney how to exercise the powers given. For example, the principal who gives a general power of attorney could say that certain investments should not be cashed, or that a vacation property should be sold first if money is needed, or that the attorney should consult with family members before taking any action. These instructions (unlike restrictions written into the power of attorney document itself) do not have to be followed by the attorney, but the attorney may find it very useful to have some idea of the principal's wishes.

# What Happens When Your Attorney Takes Over?

When an attorney wants to exercise the powers given by the principal, he or she has to show the original power of attorney document. The attorney may also be asked to show identification to prove he or she is the person named in the power of attorney.

The attorney may be asked to hand over the power of attorney — a business may want to keep it on file for its own protection, nervous that it's not dealing with the principal in person. An attorney should never, ever give the original to someone else. The attorney can't act without it! A photocopy or a notarized copy (a copy certified identical to the original by a notary public) is good enough for giveaways.

## The duties of an attorney

Sure you trust your attorney — but you may be just a little bit relieved anyway to hear that your attorney can't run amok and do whatever he or she likes. By law, your attorney must always act honestly and in your best interests, must be reasonably careful in making and carrying out decisions, must avoid having any conflict of interest with you, must not make any secret profit from handling your affairs, and must keep records of all transactions.

In Ontario, your attorney, in addition, has to encourage you to participate in decisions (to the best of your ability), encourage regular contact between you and people who are supportive of you, and consult from time to time with these supportive people. Your attorney also has to put your financial needs above those of your dependants.

You can impose additional duties on your attorney by mentioning them in the power of attorney document itself.

# What Happens If There Is No Power of Attorney?

If you don't get around to making a power of attorney before your mind takes early retirement — or if you made one but someone goofed and it wasn't a continuing power of attorney, so it ended the moment you lost your mental competence *and* your legal ability to make a new power of attorney — your legal and financial affairs won't be completely screwed up . . . but close.

Others will be able to make certain kinds of arrangements to look after your affairs, but none of them will be as good as the arrangements you could have made yourself by creating a power of attorney. Your family or friends can create informal or formal mechanisms or, if everyone you know simply steps back a pace when the call goes out for volunteers, the provincial government can take care of your affairs.

It's tempting, but . . . about the worst thing your family or friends could do if you became mentally incompetent would be to get you to sign a power of attorney. (And they could be sorely tempted, like Alice in "Fool for love" on the next page.) Even if their intentions are good and they want to use the power of attorney only to make necessary arrangements that you would approve of, any action an attorney took could later be challenged in court and cancelled. The attorney (and any others who cooked up the idea) could also end up being sued by the people he or she dealt with using the power of attorney, and could perhaps even be charged criminally.

### Fool for love

Charly was a brilliant man, CEO of Algernon GenLabs, a $100 million company that was in the business of creating genetically enhanced mice with super intelligence. When Charly's own mental faculties began to slip, he managed to keep it a secret from everyone for a long time. Superstitiously, he refused to make a power of attorney — knowing, as he did, that he would need one in the near future.

When his family finally realized what was happening, Charly's wife, Alice, downloaded a power of attorney form off the Internet and filled in her own name to be appointed as his attorney. She explained to him what the document was for, but by this point he really wasn't capable of understanding. He signed it anyway because he loved and trusted Alice.

## Seat-of-the-pants arrangements

It's not possible to make informal arrangements to deal with complicated legal and financial affairs, but maybe something can be cobbled together to keep you from starving to death. For example, anyone can deposit cheques payable to you in your bank account. The trick will be getting any money *out* of your bank account — let's hope you had opened a joint account with someone even though you were too busy to make a power of attorney. If you didn't, the most likely informal arrangement is that a family member will pay your bills out of his or her own pocket, or that no one will pay your bills and the lights will go out and the heat will go off.

If some of your income is courtesy of the Canada Pension Plan, Guaranteed Income Supplement, Veterans' Affairs, or Old Age Security, a family member can apply to the Canadian government to be appointed as a trustee to receive the benefits. The person appointed as trustee will be able to cash your cheques. With any luck, he or she will use the money to pay your expenses. And why wouldn't the trustee? You can't party very hard on a federal government pension cheque, or flee very far.

## Formal arrangements

The only way a family member can look after your affairs (which now include looking after you) properly without a power of attorney is to get appointed by the court as your *property guardian* or *committee* (stress on the "ee" not the "mitt" — you can be this kind of committee without being a group). The name used depends on the province.

Getting appointed as a property guardian or committee is a big nuisance (think collecting a lot of information, finding doctors, notifying a whole bunch of people, getting consents, swearing affidavits, appearing at a court hearing, paying legal fees, and posting security with the court), and even if the court grants the appointment it may give very limited powers. For example, your property guardian would probably be allowed to invest your money only in specified safe investments. In some provinces your property guardian would have to pay into court any of your money not needed to meet your expenses and those of your dependants. (Then the money would stay there until the court gave permission for your property guardian to take some out.) Your property guardian probably would not be allowed to sell any of your investments or your real estate without getting court approval first. And the court probably wouldn't give its approval unless a sale was necessary to pay your expenses. Well, if you were too suspicious of your family and friends to give a power of attorney in the first place, maybe the court has the right attitude.

## Government arrangements

If no one wants to apply to be your property guardian, remember there's always someone to fall back on who will take care of your affairs — your provincial government. Doesn't that give you a warm glow of happiness? Particularly considering how often you've remarked to yourself and others that your provincial government does such a darned good job of running the province generally.

The *public trustee* or *public guardian and trustee* (depending on the province) can be called in to take over your affairs if you can't manage them. When someone notifies the public trustee about you and your property, the public trustee can make an application to court to be made your property guardian. (In most provinces, the public trustee can also be brought in without a court hearing if you have been certified mentally incapable by medical experts.) Even after the public trustee has been appointed, one of your relatives could still take pity on you and apply to have the trusteeship ended and to be made your property guardian.

Once in charge, the public trustee will take control of your property, receive your income, pay your expenses, and hold in trust money you don't need immediately (it will be invested — safely — to generate interest). The public trustee charges a fee for its work.

When you die, your estate doesn't just stay in the government's hands. It's distributed according to your will, if you have one, or the provincial law on intestacy (see Chapter 15), if you don't.

# Chapter 19

# While You're Up, Get Me a Ventilator: Who'll Care for You?

### *In This Chapter*

- Giving consent to medical treatment and health care
- Preparing a living will to allow another to give consent on your behalf
- Giving consent if you have no living will
- Having a guardian of the person appointed to look after you

In the last chapter we told you what to do so that your legal and financial affairs will be properly managed if you become unable to look after them yourself. Now we're going to deal with a matter that's just as important. If you can't look after your affairs, you probably can't look after yourself either. So who's going to look after *you*?

Although there's no such thing as universal legal and financial care in Canada, there is such a thing as universal health care. If you need to be looked after physically, you will be. If you need to be treated in a hospital, you'll be admitted to a hospital and treated — if there's a bed for you. If you need to live in a nursing home, a space will be found for you, once you get to the top of the waiting list. If you need home care, health care workers will come (although perhaps only eventually and occasionally).

So you don't really have to worry about making plans to get access to health care. (Or at any rate there's no point in worrying.) The thing you have to worry about is telling health care workers what you want. If you're sick or injured . . . or dying . . . you may not be physically or mentally capable of telling anyone your wishes. When that time comes it may turn out that you don't care what happens to you. But you probably care *now* — so this is when you should make your arrangements for a second-in-command who'll speak for you and tell everyone what you would say if you could.

# What Happens If You're Sick and Can't Speak for Yourself?

When you need health care, before you receive any care you have to give your consent. If you don't give your consent, a doctor or other health care worker can't treat you.

Giving consent isn't a big deal — you've probably given your consent to treatment dozens of times without noticing it. You're already interested in being treated when you show up at the doctor's office or the emergency room. So when the doctor says, "I'm going to give you an antibiotic shot," you roll up your sleeve. That's giving your *implied consent*. When the doctor says, "I'd like to listen to your chest," you take off your shirt. That's implied consent too. When the nurse says, "I want to take a blood sample," and you hold out your finger to be pricked, that's implied consent as well.

When you tell your doctor, "I'd like you to remove this wart," or "My throat is sore, would you look at it?" that's *oral consent* to treatment.

You may also have given *consent in writing* if you've ever had surgery in a hospital. You would have been asked to sign a consent form when you were admitted.

In order to give consent, you have to be conscious and you have to be in your right mind. Hmm, you're now wondering, not everyone who needs medical treatment is awake and rational — that could pose a bit of a problem. Consider the situation in "Red hot emergency."

In an emergency situation a doctor or other health care worker has the right, without getting the consent of the patient or anyone else, to give treatment that is urgently needed to save the person's life or maintain the person's health. If a family member is present, the doctor or other professional might consult with him or her, but it's not a legal requirement.

## Red hot emergency

Mike, Kelly, and Amy were taking the subway to work when a volcanic eruption (caused by the construction of a new subway line in a geologically unstable area) occurred. Molten lava began to engulf the subway train and all the passengers fled for their lives. Kelly was badly hurt and was unconscious by the time she was dragged to the surface by Mike and Amy. Paramedics on the disaster scene immediately began treating her for smoke inhalation and suspected internal injuries.

### Tremors

Lovely Denise and wealthy construction engineer Stuart were enjoying an affair. Suddenly the earth moved for them. Actually, the earth moved for everybody in town because an earthquake measuring 7.9 on the Richter scale occurred. Denise and Stuart were both injured. Although neither had life-threatening injuries, they both required reconstructive surgery. They signed consent forms and the operations proceeded. While Stuart was being operated on, his surgeon noticed a mole that could be pre-cancerous. He wanted to remove it and have it analyzed. He spoke to Stuart's wife, Remy, and asked for her permission.

In a non-emergency situation, a doctor or other health care worker has to get consent from you — or if you can't give consent, from someone acting on your behalf — before giving treatment or carrying out a procedure. Generally, the patient's closest relative, in a stated order (spouse first, then an adult child, then a parent, then a brother or sister), has the power to give consent if the patient has not made formal arrangements to appoint someone to give consent on his or her behalf. Read "Tremors," above, to see how this works.

# Why Is Your Consent Needed for Treatment?

When we say consent is needed for treatment, we don't mean that treatment physically cannot take place without consent. The doctor won't be vaporized if she touches you without your consent. A steel barrier won't descend between you and the nurse if you don't say, "Fine, go ahead."

The problem — not for the patient but for health care workers — is that it is a *tort*, a civil wrong, for any person to touch another person without the touchee's permission. The touchee can sue the toucher for the tort of *battery*, and get an award of money damages. So the reason a doctor (or nurse, etc.) can't provide health care without your consent is that the doctor doesn't want to get sued later. Doctors in Canada in fact *have* been sued and have lost and have had to pay compensation for giving necessary or even life-saving treatment to patients who did not want the treatment.

## Are There Special Rules about Giving Consent to Treatment?

In all provinces, a person over the age of majority (18 or 19, depending on the province) can legally consent to treatment or refuse treatment if he or she is able to understand information relevant to making a medical decision and is able to appreciate what is likely to happen as a result of making the decision. In most provinces, an older child who can appreciate the nature and consequences of medical treatment also has the right to consent to or refuse treatment. A parent of a younger child has the right to give consent or refuse treatment on behalf of the child.

In order to give true consent, known in the health biz as *informed consent,* the patient has to be given enough information about the proposed treatment to be able to make a reasonable decision. So the patient has to be told by the doctor (or other health care worker), without having to ask and certainly without having to beg and plead,

- What the nature of the proposed treatment is.
- What the significant risks of the treatment are.
- Whether there are any alternatives to the proposed treatment, and what they are.
- What is likely to happen if the patient does not receive the treatment.

The doctor must also answer any other questions that the patient has.

The legal ability to give or refuse consent to treatment can come and go. A person could be capable of giving consent during a meeting with his or her doctor to discuss surgery, but incapable of giving consent while unconscious during the surgery and semi-conscious following the surgery. During those times, a patient might need someone to give or refuse consent on his or her behalf.

You can refuse consent when you can't otherwise communicate by wearing a MedicAlert bracelet or keeping a written message with you. For example, for religious reasons some people carry a card in their wallet saying "No blood transfusion." Health care workers have to respect this refusal (even if not giving the treatment would lead to your death).

# What Kind of Treatment Are We Talking About?

There are all kinds of treatments that can't be given to you without your consent. You can't receive a flu shot or have a blood sample taken or have your appendix removed or be given a physical examination without consent. In fact, unless it's an emergency, you can't be treated — or even touched — at all without consent. So the kind of treatment we're talking about includes routine matters like a check-up, vaccination, *and* out-of-the-ordinary matters like surgery, radiation, or chemotherapy.

The kind of treatment we're talking about also includes treatment at the end of life — treatment that will keep you alive or at least hold death at bay, or that will make death easier.

A patient who is competent to give or refuse consent can refuse treatment that would save his or her life or prolong his or her life. The patient can also refuse to continue with treatment that has already been started. If a doctor disagrees with a competent patient's wishes, the patient wins.

## Treatment that prolongs life

Some of the treatments that a patient might receive to save or prolong his or her life, or stop death for some period of time, are surgery, blood transfusion, dialysis (machine cleaning of the blood if the kidneys fail), administration of drugs (for example, antibiotics to fight an infection such as pneumonia), and tube feeding (via a tube inserted into the stomach or abdomen). There's also CPR and use of a ventilator.

### Cardiopulmonary resuscitation (CPR)

CPR is used to try to restart heartbeat and breathing when they have stopped. When CPR is administered in hospitals, trained health care workers press on the chest and apply shocks to the heart to restart it; and they insert a tube down the throat into the windpipe and connect it to a *ventilator* to supply air to the lungs. Then drugs may be required to help the heart pump harder because blood pressure has fallen. You certainly won't feel great before you get CPR, but you won't feel so hot afterwards either.

If you ever happen to need CPR, it's not an optional kind of thing. If you need it and don't get it, you'll die. But if you get it, it won't necessarily save your life. In about 40 percent of cases it works well enough to get the patient as far as intensive care — but only about a third of those patients live to leave the hospital.

In many hospitals, CPR is given automatically to any patient whose heart and breathing stop. For some people, automatic CPR is a good thing. For others, it is a bad thing. If you're in the final stages of a terminal disease, or you've suffered very severe brain damage in an accident or as the result of a stroke, dying is probably the best course of action for you. You don't want to be CPR'd back to life so you can die again (and possibly be revived again) half an hour or half a day later, or so you can hang around in a permanent coma for a while.

In hospitals where CPR is automatic, a patient's doctor may ask the patient or the patient's family in advance to refuse it if it wouldn't benefit the patient. The doctor would ask for consent to putting an order *DNR* (Do Not Resuscitate) or a *no code* (same thing) or "No CPR" on the patient's chart.

### Ventilators

If a patient's lungs have been damaged by disease or injury, a ventilator can be used to help the patient breathe or to breathe for the patient. If the lung damage is bad enough, the patient will die if ever taken off the ventilator. A ventilator is uncomfortable, and patients are often sedated to be able to tolerate it.

A person being kept alive by a ventilator may have such a poor quality of life that he or she, or a family member acting on the person's behalf, may ask to have the ventilator disconnected. Or a doctor may recommend that it be disconnected because the use of the ventilator is only stretching out the dying process and not providing a real benefit. (This is where the expression "pulling the plug" comes from.)

## Treatment that eases death

Treatment that makes death easier includes withholding the various treatments mentioned above — because in some cases they don't prolong life, they just prolong dying — and *comfort care.*

Comfort care involves giving morphine in a high enough dose that the dying person does not suffer (from pain or from the sensation of suffocating if the respiratory system is failing) while dying. It's not always automatically given even when it's needed.

Patients sometimes need an advocate on hand not just to consent to comfort care but to demand it.

### What kind of treatment do you want?

Well, that's a stupid question, isn't it? How can you know until the time comes whether you want to be kept alive or gently shepherded out of this life? And when the time comes, you may not be able to communicate or even stay conscious.

## How Can You Make Your Wishes Known?

If you're conscious and mentally capable, you make your wishes about medical treatment known by telling your doctor and/or family what you want. If you can't speak you may have to write your wishes. If you can't speak or write you may have to talk with your eyes.

If you're not fully conscious or not mentally capable, the way to make your wishes known is by having prepared a *living will* while you were conscious and capable. A living will lets an earlier, mentally capable, version of yourself speak through another person when the later version of you can't.

A living will can do two things:

- It can appoint someone to make health care decisions for you.
- It can tell the appointed decision maker what decisions you would like made.

In some provinces, a living will is intended to deal with medical treatment only. In others, it can also deal with personal care decisions about things like housing, food, hygiene, clothing, or safety. You can find out more about living wills in your province from your lawyer, your provincial law society, or provincial government.

A living will comes into effect only when you're not mentally capable of giving consent to or refusing medical treatment. In most provinces, living wills are legally recognized and the instructions in a living will must be followed. They override the wishes of a patient's family, in the same way that the wishes of a mentally competent patient override the wishes of the patient's family. Even in provinces that haven't yet legally recognized living wills, the instructions will quite probably be followed too.

It would be too much to ask all the provinces to get together and use the same vocabulary about living wills. So there's a different name for a living will in almost every province. Depending on the province, the living will may be called a *personal directive,* a *representation agreement,* a *health care directive,* a *power of attorney for personal care,* a *mandate,* a *directive,* or an *authorization.*

Also depending on the province the appointed decision maker may be called an *attorney for personal care,* a *proxy,* an *agent,* a *representative,* a *substitute decision maker,* or a *mandatary.* In our discussion we'll refer to a living will and a substitute decision maker.

## What does a living will say?

The living will form is different in different provinces, but generally you'll find that the form covers several standard points.

### It names the person who will speak for you

Some people appoint just one substitute decision maker to make decisions on their behalf. Others appoint two or more decision makers, usually to make sure that someone will be available when needed rather than to create a safeguard against one person making the wrong decision. If you appoint more than one substitute decision maker but want one person to be able to act alone if a decision has to be made quickly, your living will should say that any substitute decision maker can make a decision individually. But if you want group decisions in case they're safer, the living will should say that the substitute decision makers must agree on all decisions.

Some people appoint a back-up substitute decision maker in case the original substitute decision maker can't or won't act. This is probably wise, because you can't know what the future holds for your substitute decision maker any more than you can know what it holds for you.

Later in the chapter we talk about who is eligible to act as your substitute decision maker.

### It may cancel a previous living will

When you make a living will and name a substitute decision maker and give instructions about your health care, you normally want to *revoke* or cancel any previous living will you made. After all, you're making a new one because you've changed your mind about what you want done or whom you want to decide on your behalf.

### It may list what health care decisions can be made

If provincial law allows a variety of decisions to be made by a substitute decision maker, a living will could give power to make all health care decisions, or (for example) power only to make decisions about medical treatment or power only to make decisions about food, safety, and hygiene.

### *It gives instructions about health care treatment*

If you live in a province that allows you to give a substitute decision maker the power to make decisions about different aspects of your health care, you could give a variety of instructions. You could say, for example, that if possible you would prefer to be cared for at home instead of in a hospital or nursing home. You could say that you'd like to be cared for in your daughter's home rather than your son's. You could say that you want to be bathed daily, and that you want to be dressed instead of being left in pyjamas. You could say that if you develop a tendency to wander and get lost you would prefer to have a caregiver with you at all times rather than being restrained in a locked area or a chair or bed with straps. You can give instructions about anything that concerns you or occurs to you. Whether it will be possible to carry out your instructions when the time comes is a question for another day.

The instructions you give about medical treatment are a different matter. They tend to be geared less towards everyday life and more towards the question of how long you want to live and in what state. Your substitute decision maker is not going to have a lot of trouble deciding to consent to routine maintenance for you. You don't need to sweat over giving instructions to have your blood pressure taken by the nurse in a nursing home.

Your instructions to the substitute decision maker about medical treatment could be very general — for example, you could instruct that you don't want any treatment that

- Will not cure you, *and*
- Will not improve your quality of life if it prolongs your life.

Or your instructions could be more specific — for example, that you do not want to be put on a ventilator or given CPR if you are in a permanent coma or vegetative state and suffer respiratory failure or heart failure. In fact, your instructions can be even more specific than that. You could run down a list of injuries and diseases and state in each case what treatment you would or would not consent to. That might be kind of a fun thing to do on a rainy afternoon.

If you're specific in your instructions, you'd better say how much discretion your substitute decision maker has to make a different decision. You might not want to miss out on a new medical treatment that could have you back on your feet in no time flat, or you might prefer not to be given experimental treatment that would be unpleasant but would provide little permanent benefit.

If you actually have a particular disease or condition when you make your living will, make sure that you and your substitute decision maker understand how the disease or condition is likely to progress, what the available treatment options are, what they involve, and whether they're likely to be successful.

You and your substitute decision maker should also familiarize yourselves with the standard life-prolonging measures we discussed earlier in the chapter under the heading "What Kind of Treatment Are We Talking About?" Talk to your doctor, or do research in a library or on the Internet.

### It may give instructions about organ and tissue donation

Your instructions to your substitute decision maker can also include your wishes for organ and tissue donation. You should know, however, that if you give advance consent to organ or tissue donation and members of your family are opposed when the time comes, the hospital will probably not accept your donation.

## How do you make a living will?

You can fill out a do-it-yourself form to make a living will. You don't have to have a lawyer (or, in Quebec, a notary). However, we think it's better to have a living will prepared by a lawyer. A lawyer will act as an objective person who can help you decide what instructions you want to leave and who can help you choose the best person to be the substitute decision maker. In addition, a lawyer won't forget to use any special language that the province wants in a living will.

A lawyer will also make sure that you are legally capable of making a living will, that your substitute decision maker is legally eligible to act, and that any special formalities in the making or signing of the document are observed.

### You have to be legally capable of making a living will

In some provinces you can make a living will if you are as young as 16, while in others you must have reached the age of majority (18 or 19, depending on the province).

To make a valid living will you must also be mentally capable. In some provinces this means that you must be able to "understand the nature and effect of the living will," and in others that you must be able to "make health care decisions by being able to understand and appreciate the consequences of treatment choices." That's the law . . . but if you're nutty as a fruitcake or comatose, a lawyer won't make a big inquiry into your understanding and appreciation.

### Not everyone is eligible to be a substitute decision maker

There are not a lot of qualifications required for a substitute decision maker. In some provinces a person as young as 16 can be named a substitute decision maker, while in others the person must have reached the age of majority (18 or 19, depending on the province).

The substitute decision maker, just like a patient who gives consent, must be mentally capable of understanding and appreciating the consequences of medical treatment choices and decisions. The substitute decision maker has to be mentally capable when called upon to act. That's one reason why it may be a good idea to name more than one substitute decision maker, or to name an alternate.

In Ontario, a person who is being paid to provide health care or residential, social, training, or support services for a person cannot be appointed as that person's substitute decision maker.

Whom should you choose as your substitute decision maker? First, go for someone you feel confident will carry out your wishes. Second, choose someone who isn't going to feel devastated and guilty if he or she has to make a non-life-affirming decision about you. Discuss your wishes in advance not only with your chosen substitute decision maker but also with your whole family so that your decision maker will be supported rather than attacked by your (other) relatives.

### Formalities involved in making a living will

You have to sign and date your living will. (If you're physically unable to sign, someone else may sign on your behalf.) Some provinces don't require that a living will be witnessed unless it was signed by someone on your behalf, while others require one witness or even two witnesses (depending on the province) to your signature. Again, ask your lawyer or check with your provincial law society or provincial government for more information.

In cases when a witness is (or witnesses are) required, the substitute decision maker cannot be a witness. Neither can the spouse of the person making the living will or the spouse of the substitute decision maker. The purpose of these rules is to prevent a person from being forced to make a living will or being forced to choose a particular substitute decision maker. The theory is that this sort of thing is less likely to happen if the living will is witnessed by people who have a little distance from the person making the living will and from the proposed substitute decision maker.

## After you've made a living will

There's no use making a living will if nobody knows what it says or can find it when it's needed. Your substitute decision maker could have a lot of trouble persuading your doctor or the hospital that he or she has the right to make decisions without the living will to show. Once you've made a living will, give the original to the substitute decision maker — or at the very least tell the substitute decision maker where to find the original.

Put the original of your living will in a safe place, but do not put it in your safety deposit box! Chances are that your substitute decision maker wouldn't be able to get into your box after you became either physically or mentally incapable.

Give a copy of your living will to your doctor(s) for the record. You may also want to give copies to other family members and/or your lawyer.

If you're suffering from a particular disease or condition, keep up to date on what medical treatment is available. You may want to revise your living will to give different instructions if there are significant advances in treatment. And don't forget to revise your living will if something happens to your substitute decision maker.

# What Happens When Your Living Will Comes into Effect?

Your living will comes into effect only when you become incapable of making a medical decision. It will probably be a health care worker — probably a doctor — who raises the red flag about your mental abilities and asks for someone else to come forward to give consent to treatment on your behalf.

When your substitute decision maker is brought in, in most provinces he or she has to follow the instructions in your living will rather than making a decision based on his or her own preferences. In some provinces, the substitute decision maker can consider your instructions but has the power to make his or her own decision.

What happens if there are no instructions? Consider Jo's dilemma in "Wild and whirling words."

## Wild and whirling words

Bill prepared a living will and named his ex-wife, Jo, as his substitute decision maker. In the living will he listed a number of medical conditions, such as cancer, stroke, heart attack, Lou Gehrig's disease, and sleeping sickness, and the treatment he wanted to receive in each case. Bill was subsequently caught in a level 5 tornado and injured by a flying cow. Jo was at a loss about what to do because Bill hadn't mentioned flying cows in his living will.

If your living will doesn't contain instructions that cover the situation the substitute decision maker is faced with, the substitute decision maker is supposed to follow any wishes you expressed before you became incapable, if they're known. If you didn't express any wishes, the substitute decision maker is supposed to think about what decision you would have made in the circumstances and base his or her decision on that. If the substitute decision maker really has no clue what you would have decided, he or she is supposed to base his or her decision on the nature of the medical treatment that's being proposed. Will the treatment improve or maintain your quality of life? And are the benefits of the proposed treatment greater than its risks?

# Arrangements If You Haven't Made a Living Will

If you don't have a living will, you don't have a substitute decision maker. You also don't have a substitute decision maker if the one you've named in your living will can't or won't act. In either event, the province will find one for you. One of your family members will be asked to give consent or refuse treatment on your behalf.

Generally, the first person to be asked will be your spouse. If you don't have one, your adult child will be asked. (If you have more than one child they may argue or they may agree as to what should be done. Hope they keep the argument short if it's preventing you from getting — or not getting — treatment.) If you have no adult children a parent will be asked, and if you've run out of parents an adult brother or sister can be asked. After that they'll turn to your closest adult next of kin. They won't go looking all over creation for next of kin, though.

If you need to be treated and you don't have any relatives who are interested enough in you to introduce themselves to the doctor, the doctor and/or hospital will contact the public trustee or public trustee and guardian of the province. The public trustee will make decisions on your behalf.

Even if you don't have a living will, anyone who gives or refuses consent on your behalf is supposed to follow your known wishes, not his or her own wishes. If the person doesn't remember you expressing any wishes about the matter, he or she is supposed to do what he or she believes you would do if you could express your wishes. If that approach fails, the family member giving consent on your behalf is supposed to consider whether the proposed treatment will improve or maintain your quality of life, and whether the benefits of the proposed treatment outweigh the risks.

If you've given no instructions about organ and tissue donation (in your living will, on the donor consent card available through the provincial driver's licensing department, or orally in front of two witnesses), your family members have the right to give or refuse consent at the time of your death. They'll be asked in the following order: your spouse, your adult child, your parent, your adult brother or sister, any other adult next of kin. If the highest person on the list says no, the doctor or hospital can't go further down the list looking for a different answer. If the highest person says yes but someone else who is also high on the list says no, the hospital probably won't accept the donation.

## Guardian of the person

If you don't have a living will, or if your living will covers only medical treatment and informal arrangements to look after you are breaking down, more action may be needed in order to take care of you properly. One of your relatives (or a friend) can apply to the court to be appointed your *guardian of the person*. If you have no concerned relatives or friends, the provincial public trustee or public trustee and guardian can apply to be appointed your guardian of the person.

### What can a guardian of the person do for you?

In some provinces, the guardian of the person will be given *custody* of you — that's right, just like you were a little kid. Then your guardian of the person has the same rights that a parent would have over a child.

In a few provinces, the powers of a guardian of the person are instead listed in detail. Then they include the power to decide

- Where you should live, and with whom.
- What health care you should have.
- What food you should eat.
- What social activities you should get involved in.

However the court order is worded, your guardian of the person will be responsible for your care. Your guardian will have to act in your best interests, make reasonable arrangements for your care, and be reasonably careful in making decisions about your care.

Doesn't this guardian of the person thing give you the creeps? Maybe dropping dead suddenly with a heart attack isn't such a bad thing after all.

### How do you acquire a guardian of the person?

A person who wants to be appointed your guardian of the person has to go through the same process as a person who wanted to be your property guardian or committee. (See Chapter 18.) He or she will have to get doctors to give evidence about your condition and will have to notify your relatives of the application to be made guardian, get consent (or proof of lack of interest) from the relatives, swear an affidavit, and possibly appear in court before a judge.

If the judge agrees that you're in need of care and protection because you're mentally incompetent to make health care decisions or incapable of caring for yourself, it will appoint a guardian of the person. If you've already got a property guardian, the court will probably prefer to appoint that person as your guardian of the person.

# Part V
# Do You Need Professional Help?

"No, I don't have a P.F.P. or S.F.C. from the I.C.B., but I do have an R.F.P. from the C.A.F.P."

## In this part . . .

This part helps you find help! Here we tell you how to find and work with a lawyer. We also show you what other assistants are out there — and how to use them to your advantage.

# Chapter 20

# The Best Defence: Your Lawyer as Your Estate Planning Coach

### *In This Chapter*

- Understanding why you need a lawyer
- Finding the right lawyer
- Learning about how lawyers charge for their work
- Dealing with an unsatisfactory lawyer
- Making the best use of your lawyer

The big game is coming up — and it's one of the most important you'll ever play. The name of the game? Looking after your family and friends . . . when you're no longer here to look after them.

The game isn't easy — there are a lot of traps and pitfalls waiting for you. But now you know some of the classic defensive moves — preparing a will and tax planning among them — and you're anxious to get into the game because it's dangerous to wait. So you're getting ready to head out onto the field. . . . Hold on — something's still missing! That something is an adviser who really knows the rules of the game and knows how to create a winning strategy. In other words, you need a coach.

All right, enough of this sports analogy stuff. It's making our heads feel like they've got footballs wedged inside.

In plain language, to plan your estate properly and carry out the plan by preparing a will and other legal documents, you need a lawyer. In this chapter we'll tell you the most important things you should know in order to find a good lawyer and to get your lawyer to do good work for you.

Then you'll be able to go out there and give 110 percent for your team.

# Why Do You Need a Lawyer?

As soon as anyone mentions the word "lawyer," the heckling from the bleachers starts. As in, Lawyers are expensive, right? It's going to cost a fortune to discuss estate planning with your lawyer and get your will prepared, right? So it's better to look for a cheaper alternative, right? Wrong! It can cost a lot *not* to have a lawyer prepare your will. On the next page, see what happened to Hart in "The estate chase."

This isn't to say that a little self-help isn't a good thing. Before you go to see a lawyer, there's nothing wrong with checking around and getting free or inexpensive legal information about wills and estates — from government Web sites (or general information Web sites, or even business promotion Web sites) or from books. In fact, you've shown remarkably good sense in buying this book. But just remember that the information you get from sources like these is not tailored to your specific circumstances. And neither are any documents you buy in a kit or download from the Internet. Lawyers like to say that a single fact can change an entire case.

Free legal advice and free legal documents are often worth exactly what you paid for them, and sometimes they turn out to be far more expensive than you dreamed.

## What about those guys who are sort of minor league lawyers?

In many provinces there are non-lawyers who offer legal services — and will drafting is quite often one of the services they offer. You might think it would be really clever to go to a *paralegal, legal consultant,* or *legal services provider* (they call themselves different things), because they're usually cheaper than lawyers and they must know what they're doing or they wouldn't be in this line of work.

Sorry to disappoint you, but they probably *don't* know what they're doing. In most provinces the paralegal industry doesn't have any standards. A paralegal can hang up her shingle without meeting any educational requirements and without having to get liability insurance to protect clients if she makes a mistake (lawyers are required to carry insurance). If a paralegal blows it, you'll probably have no one official to complain to. And there's often little point in suing someone who doesn't have insurance.

## The estate chase

Hart didn't think he had a big estate. He owned a house worth $200,000 and a cottage worth $75,000. He had a GIC worth $20,000, mutual funds worth $20,000, and a bank account with $5,000. And he owned the usual things like a car and some household furniture and appliances. So when he decided it was time to write his will, going to a lawyer sounded as though it would cost too much — especially when he could use a will kit that cost about $30. Anyway, he'd been sick of lawyers ever since spending a year at Harvard Law School. So he wrote his own will, leaving his house, his GIC, and money in his bank account to his wife, Susan, and his cottage and his mutual funds to his sister. Unfortunately he had spent his year at law school working on his contracts course and hadn't bothered to attend any wills and estates classes.

When Hart died, here's what happened: In the year of his death, he had income of $50,000. That meant that most of his estate was taxed at the top marginal rate of approximately 50 percent.

His house was capital property, but even though he'd bought it for $120,000 several years earlier there was no capital gains tax payable on the gain of $80,000 because of the principal residence exemption. So far so good.

He'd bought the cottage for $25,000, so there was a capital gain of $50,000 on it — one-half of $50,000 was added to his income in the terminal return. There was no principal residence exemption because you can only claim one principal residence. Too bad his will kit hadn't mentioned that there would have been no capital gains tax payable at all if he'd left the non-principal residence to his wife.

GICs (like money in the bank) don't attract capital gains tax because they're just cash — there's no capital gain. So it was kind of a waste for Hart to leave his GIC to his wife, since property left to a spouse doesn't attract capital gains tax anyway. His mutual funds, on the other hand, did attract capital gains tax, and they'd gone up in value by $10,000 since he bought them. If he'd left them instead of the GICs to his wife, there would have been no capital gains tax payable by his estate. Instead, one-half of $10,000 was added to income in his terminal return.

Finally, it was too bad that the will kit didn't mention that Hart had to give away *all* of his property in his will. Hart didn't think of putting in a "residue" clause that would give away the other things he owned apart from the specific gifts he mentioned. His wife and his sister both wanted his car and some of his other possessions as well. They had to get a couple of lawyers (Susan called in her dad, Kingsfield) to help them settle the dispute and write up an agreement. Both the lawyers charged for their services.

The final tally: Hart saved maybe two to four hundred dollars by not going to a lawyer, and his estate paid thousands of dollars in taxes that might have been avoided with a little professional legal help. Add in the aggravation, bad feelings, and legal fees caused by the lack of a residue clause in the will.

More to the point, in every province, paralegals are legally allowed to do only a limited number of things. They can represent clients before certain lower courts, such as small claims court, residential landlord and tenant court, and provincial offences court, and before some administrative boards and agencies, such as licensing commissions.

At the time of writing, they're not allowed to give legal advice or do legal work in other areas — and, in every province, that includes wills and estates. If you've seen an advertisement for a paralegal who does will preparation, it's because the law prohibiting them from doing wills is not being enforced.

Provincial governments have talked about the need to regulate paralegals for some time now. In the future, provinces may pass laws that set education and licensing requirements for paralegals, and they may pass laws that allow paralegals to do legal work in other areas, including wills and estates.

Should you use a paralegal then? After reading 19 chapters of this book, you should have a pretty healthy respect for what can go wrong in the planning of an estate and drafting of a will. The person who drafts your will should know what the potential problems are and how to avoid them. Check with your provincial government or provincial law society into the training standards set for paralegals in your province, before you let a paralegal muck around with your estate.

### Stick to the majors

Don't be afraid to go to a lawyer because you think it will bankrupt you. Lawyers deliberately keep the cost of preparing a will down — you can pretty easily find a lawyer who'll do your will for $300 or $400 or less. Lawyers look on wills as a kind of "loss leader." They don't expect to make money on the will — they hope to make their profit on other legal work you'll ask them to do once you get to know and love them, or on the administration of your estate after you die. Very often the executor of the estate asks the lawyer who prepared the will to help with probating the will and to advise on other matters that arise.

## When Do You Need a Lawyer?

If you're *still* not convinced that you need a lawyer, we'll recap for you some of the situations in which a lawyer would be really useful to you.

### When you're planning your estate and your will

While you're in the planning stages, your lawyer will be able to help you prepare a complete estate plan that answers all your needs by taking you through the foreseeable possibilities about your future and your family's future. Many

## What if . . .

**Scenario 1**

Client: "I want a very simple will. I just want to leave everything to my spouse."

Lawyer: "What if your spouse dies before you?"

Client: "In that case I want to leave everything to my kids."

Lawyer: "What if you die when your children are still young? Who should look after their money and for how long?"

Client: "I would like my brother to look after their money and manage it for them until they are 25."

Lawyer: "What if one of your kids dies before she is 25? Who should get her share — your other children, her children, or somebody else?"

**Scenario 2**

Client: "My neighbour has really helped me out since I've gotten sick. I'd like to leave him my car. It's about five years old."

Lawyer: "What if your neighbour dies before you do?"

Client: "Well, then I'd like his son to get the car."

Lawyer: "What if your car dies before you do and you get a new car? Do you still want your neighbour to have it?"

Client: "Oh, no. A gift of a new car would be too extravagant. If I have a new car, I'd like it to go to my son."

people who go through the estate planning process without professional assistance don't ask "What if . . ." enough times, and they end up with an incomplete plan that breaks down. Lawyers are great What-ifers. Look at "What if . . ." for some examples.

As well, your lawyer can

- Sort out the tax consequences of leaving certain kinds of gifts to certain kinds of beneficiaries.
- Help you decide whether to give gifts while you're still alive or wait to give your property away by will.
- Advise about the best way of making gifts in your lifetime.
- Tell you whether you have dependants you must provide for in your will.
- Tell you if you must leave at least a minimum gift to your spouse in your will.
- Tell you whether you must make a gift to someone as a result of an agreement or a promise you made.

## When you start to put your plan into action

When you're ready to go into action, your lawyer can

- Take the necessary legal steps to help you make a valid gift while you're alive, including such steps as putting property (real estate, for example) into joint ownership.
- Draft a will using language that will make sure your real intentions are carried out.
- Get the necessary information about a charity you want to benefit in your will.
- Draft a power of attorney that suits your needs.
- Draft a living will that reflects your wishes.
- Help you choose an attorney or a substitute decision maker who is legally eligible to fill the position.
- Explain all the legal concepts and technical language that you'll run into in a will, power of attorney, or (to a lesser extent) a living will.

## When it comes time to put pen to paper

When you're ready to sign all the important documents, your lawyer will

- Make a professional judgment about whether you are mentally capable of making a will, a power of attorney, or a living will. If your mental state is later called into question, your lawyer will be able to give evidence that you were legally capable of creating these documents.
- Make sure that you sign the documents properly.
- Choose as witnesses people who are legally eligible to witness you sign the documents.
- Make sure that special requirements about the witnessing of your signature are met.
- Have the witnesses sign the necessary additional documents that may be required to get your will probated.

## After you're gone

Once you're dead, you won't need a lawyer, will you? Well, let's hope not, anyway. It probably depends on where you end up and how you got there. But your estate and your executor will need a lawyer. At that point, a lawyer will be useful to

- Get your will probated.
- Provide help on request with preparing terminal tax returns and estate tax returns.
- Fight with Canada Revenue (sometimes Canada Revenue gets a bee in its bonnet about dead people's taxes, and then it's like a hornet at a picnic — almost impossible to get rid of).
- Set up long-term trusts.
- Transfer property from your name to the name of the estate and eventually into the names of the beneficiaries.

# What Lawyer Do You Want?

Now you're convinced. You need a lawyer. But which one? There are thousands of them out there. Well, don't worry — there are ways of picking the right one out of that mob. You'll be your own scout.

Lawyers don't all do the same kinds of work. There are lots of different specialties in law, like family law, real estate law, tax law, securities law, criminal law, and civil litigation. Those are only a few of the specialties. Many lawyers

### Not all lawyers stack up

Ed ran a law practice that consisted mainly of small real estate deals and lawsuits over car accidents. One day his keen-eyed law clerk noticed that a house deal appeared to involve contaminated land, so she hitched up her bra straps and set out to investigate. After organizing the clients in the house deal and all their neighbours into a class action lawsuit against the corporation that had contaminated the land, the law clerk managed to settle the matter for millions of dollars. Since most of the clients were now very ill from the contaminants, the law clerk was about to launch into giving them advice about wills and estate planning when Ed called a halt to the expansion of the law practice. He tactfully suggested to the clerk that they refer the clients to some other firm that had actually done estate planning and will preparation before.

### A tale of two lawyers

Frank has gorgeous blue eyes, but he also has a drinking problem that has led to losing all of his recent court cases. So he figures it's probably safer to settle any case that comes his way. Kaitlin, the sister of a young woman who's in a permanent coma because of a doctor's malpractice, brings him the case. She's a little uneasy about working with him since she noticed he has the shakes, but she decides to hope for the best. She's not very pleased when Frank strongly recommends settling this multi-million dollar case for $210,000. The client's verdict: Find another lawyer before it's too late.

Frank's partner, Daniel, is stone cold sober and has a charming smile but he seems to have better things to do than practise law. Play softball, to be precise. Joanne, his client in a matter involving an initiation hazing, has to keep after him to get him to do anything on the file. Eventually he brings the matter to a successful conclusion, but Joanne is left wondering why she had to nag Daniel as well as pay him to work for her. If she has legal problems in the future, she'll be looking for a few good lawyers.

specialize in one field, quite a few lawyers work in two or three fields, but no lawyer can be good at everything. It's much the same as with doctors — you wouldn't go to a dermatologist if you needed brain surgery, or to a cardiovascular surgeon if you were having mental problems, or to a GP if you were suffering from an exotic tropical disease.

Lawyers don't all act the same. They're people, just like their clients, and some of them are competent and some aren't. Some are easy to get along with and some aren't. You want a competent lawyer you can get along with. You'll be spending time with this person and paying his or her bills — might as well try to make the experience a good one.

## A lawyer who knows something about wills and estates

First of all, the lawyer you want is one who's already experienced in estate planning and drafting wills. You don't want to provide some lawyer with on-the-job training.

You may be able to find that experienced lawyer right around the corner. Sole practitioners (lawyers working alone) and lawyers in very small firms (two or three lawyers) often carry on a general practice, for example, a combination of real estate, some family law, and wills and estates. It's not uncommon for these lawyers to know quite a lot about wills and estates. They can usually be found in convenient locations — your neighbourhood rather than downtown in Lawyers' Alley. A sole practitioner or small firm is a good place to start when it's time to get personalized legal advice about estate planning and your will. If your estate is straightforward, you'll stick with the sole practitioner through the whole process. If you turn out to have complications — say if you need high-powered advice about taxes, trusts, or business succession plans — your lawyer can refer you to a specialist.

There are lawyers in medium-sized and big firms who do wills and estates work too. Wills and estates lawyers in the really big firms usually work with clients who are wealthy and require mega-help with their estate plans in order to keep taxes down. So these lawyers tend to be specialists in taxes, trusts, or estate freezes — areas that most people don't need extra-strength advice in. In a medium-sized firm you might find a specialist or you might find someone with a general practice just like a lawyer in a very small firm. It just depends on the lawyer and the firm.

The only real way to find out whether a lawyer knows enough or too much about wills and estates is to interview the lawyer. We'll talk about that later.

## A lawyer you like . . . or at least don't loathe

You could end up spending a fair amount of time with your lawyer . . . or it could feel like a fair amount of time when you're sitting around shooting the breeze about taxes and your upcoming death. It'll feel even longer if you don't think much of your lawyer — so don't hesitate to choose a lawyer at least partly on the basis of your feelings.

You want a lawyer who passes the competence test with you. You may not be able to judge whether a lawyer is working right up to the standard of other capable lawyers in this area of law, but you'll probably be able to tell if a lawyer is just bluffing and doesn't really know much more than you do.

You should also feel that you don't need to worry for a minute about your lawyer's honesty and integrity. If "honesty and integrity" aren't the words that come into your mind when you chat with a lawyer, but "slimeball" pops up, this isn't the lawyer for you. This is really a matter of instinct.

You want a lawyer to whom you feel you can talk freely. It's important to be able to say whatever's on your mind — it doesn't work to keep your lawyer in the dark about any aspect of your legal situation. You may feel more comfortable if you have a formal, business-like relationship with your lawyer. On the other hand you may prefer a more casual, less business-like relationship. It could be less intimidating.

Clients generally get more personal contact with a lawyer who's a sole practitioner or a member of a small firm. In a larger firm, you'll still get personal contact, but it may be with secretaries, clerks, and junior lawyers rather than mainly with your chosen lawyer. If it looks like you're going to be dealing with other people as much as with your lawyer, you can take your feelings about them into account too when you're deciding on a lawyer.

# Where Is the Lawyer You Long For?

Finding a good lawyer isn't (as they say) rocket surgery, but it may involve some leg work. We suggest that you proceed in the following way:

1. Get recommendations.
2. Do a little investigating.
3. Interview the finalists.
4. Make a decision.

## Recommendation

When you're looking for recommendations for a lawyer,

- Ask friends, relatives, or business associates for the names of lawyers who have done similar work for them (for example, who have drafted a will or power of attorney, or acted in estate matters). Don't just get the names — ask what they liked and disliked about the lawyers they used.
- Call a community legal clinic for suggestions.
- Contact your provincial law society for a list of lawyers in your area who specialize in wills and estates.

## Investigation

Unless you have absolute confidence in the judgment of the person who recommended a lawyer to you and your two hearts beat as one, don't just decide to go to the first lawyer mentioned to you. Narrow your list of possibilities by

- Finding out more about each lawyer's firm. If you think you're going to need an estate freeze, maybe you shouldn't be bothering with a sole practitioner who runs a general practice.

- Finding out the location of each lawyer's office. There's no point in choosing a lawyer who's inconveniently far away if you can find someone just as good who's easier to get to.
- Comparing the fee that each lawyer charges.

You can do all of this on the phone talking to a receptionist or secretary (and some lawyers even have their own Web sites with information about themselves and their practice). Don't be shy about asking about fees — just ask how much the lawyer charges for a simple or straightforward will. Also ask whether the lawyer offers the first half-hour of consultation free. (Many do.) You'll want to know this for your next step.

## Interview

If you end up with a short list of two or three lawyers who seem suitable, make an appointment to meet with each one. You're just going to have a chat to find out if this lawyer is the one for you. In the course of your chat, ask questions about

- How much experience the lawyer has in estate planning, drafting wills, and administering estates.
- What the lawyer's fees are.
- Whether your work will be handled by the lawyer personally or by others (other partners or associates, articling students, or law clerks).

In Chapter 24 we give you ten questions to ask a lawyer in the initial interview. You may find that you hardly have to ask anything — the lawyer may volunteer all the information you need. You'll probably also pick up some free legal advice about your own estate and will. Lawyers can't resist giving advice, even when they're not getting paid for it. But the lawyer will be perfectly aware that he or she is being interviewed for a job, and most lawyers will want to make a good impression on you.

By the end of your chat, you should also know whether you could work comfortably with this lawyer, or whether every meeting would feel like serving time in the penalty box.

## Decision

After you've looked over a lawyer or two or three and reviewed your notes about their experience, location, and fees, you should be able to settle on one. If you didn't think anyone you interviewed was suitable, you'll have to start over again at the recommendation stage.

# How Much Do Lawyers Charge?

"How much do lawyers charge?" is the wrong question to ask because the answer is probably "As much as it takes." And it takes different amounts to deal with different matters. The right question is "How do lawyers charge?"

## Yeah, okay, so how do they charge?

Lawyers have different ways of charging for their services, depending on the work they're doing. The usual ways are

- Billing at an hourly rate for the time they spend working for you.
- Charging a flat rate for a particular matter.
- Charging a *contingency fee*, which is a percentage of what the lawyer gets for the client if the lawyer is successful. Lawyers don't plan estates or draft wills for a contingency fee, though.

Besides their fees, lawyers also bill for *disbursements*, sums of money they have to lay out in order to do your work. Disbursements typically include long distance telephone calls, photocopies, document filing fees, and travel, among many possibilities. Sometimes they can really add up.

Lawyer's fees are subject to GST (or HST where applicable). Some disbursements are also subject to GST or HST.

## Billing at an hourly rate

For most matters, lawyers charge for the time they spend working for the client. That means charging for the time spent meeting with the client and holding telephone conversations with the client and with others on the client's behalf, drafting documents, and preparing letters to the client and others. Lawyers also charge for reading letters and documents received from the client or others, doing research, and *reviewing the file* (reading through the file folders that hold all the documents related to the client's case to remember what's there — before actually getting down to work). They even charge for making phone calls that aren't answered. Lawyers divide every hour into tenths, and start billing at 0.1 of an hour. A phone call that wasn't answered or that was answered by voice mail would be billed as 0.1 (one-tenth of the lawyer's hourly rate).

### What's the rate?

Lawyers' hourly rates vary considerably. A kind-hearted lawyer in a small firm might quote an hourly rate of $150 or less to a client who didn't have much money, while a super-duper lawyer in a big firm might charge a corporate client hundreds of dollars an hour.

If you need to see a specialist in a big firm, however, don't fixate on the high hourly rate. A specialist can often solve a problem much more quickly than a general practitioner — and may end up costing less than the general practitioner, who'll bill you for the time she spends educating herself about the law that applies to the matter (it may appear on your bill as "research").

If you're hiring a lawyer who's charging by the hour, be sure to ask what the hourly rate is. In fact, get it in writing. Sometimes the rate is negotiable — and sometimes you go with that rate or you go to the competition (and see if they'll do better). If your lawyer wants to raise the hourly rate after you've hired him, he has to tell you in advance and get your agreement.

Also ask, before any work is done, how long the lawyer estimates the work will take. If it turns out to take longer than estimated, your lawyer has to tell you (and get your agreement) before going past the estimate.

A lawyer who bills at an hourly rate should give you an account that shows not just the total number of hours but also a breakdown of how the time was spent. Ask for more detail if your bill doesn't contain enough.

### Retainers

A lawyer who bills at an hourly rate usually asks a client for a *retainer* before doing any work. A retainer is a deposit that is applied against the bill, usually enough to cover all of the estimated work or at least a substantial part of it. (Lawyers hate having to sue clients to get paid.) A retainer has to be held in a special trust account until the work is done and a bill has been prepared.

If the retainer is used up before the work is finished, the lawyer will ask for a further retainer. There's no legal limit to the number of times a lawyer can ask for a retainer. If a client won't give a retainer, the lawyer may very well not do the work the client wants done.

## Charging a flat rate

Lawyers don't always charge by the hour. For work that will take a fairly predictable amount of their time — such as acting on a house purchase or sale, or preparing a will or a power of attorney — they may be willing to quote a flat fee. Disbursements are usually charged over and above the flat fee, so be sure to ask how much they will cost.

Lawyers often ask for a retainer when charging a flat rate, just as when billing at an hourly rate.

### Charging a contingency fee

You probably don't need to know about contingency fees if all you want to do is plan your estate and have your will prepared, but for the sake of thoroughness we'll tell you about them anyway.

Contingency fees are mainly used when a client wants to sue someone (to collect a debt, for example, or to bring a lawsuit for personal injuries) but doesn't have enough money to pay legal fees up front or as the case proceeds. The lawyer's fee will be an agreed percentage (typically about one-third) of the amount of money collected from the other party to the lawsuit.

A lawyer will agree to a contingency fee arrangement only if the client has a good chance of winning the lawsuit and of collecting the money. If the client loses, the client doesn't have to pay. If the client wins but no money can be collected, the client doesn't have to pay. Win or lose, though, the client usually has to pay the lawyer's disbursements.

## What Should You Expect of Your Lawyer?

You probably expect a lot of your lawyer. You probably haven't broken down what you expect into categories, though. Provincial law societies have, however, in rules of professional conduct — and we're going to share that with you. Now you'll know at a glance what to expect when you hire a lawyer.

Lawyers' rules of professional conduct require them to

- Act with honesty.
- Provide legal services competently and promptly, and make sure that their assistants also act competently.
- Keep client information confidential.
- Act with the client's interests in mind only (rather than their own or anyone else's).
- Keep the client fully informed about what work is being done and what's happening in the matter.
- Act on the client's instructions only.

That's what law societies expect. But clients expect a little more than that. They expect their lawyer to treat them with respect and courtesy — for example,

- Not to keep them waiting for appointments.
- During appointments, not to deal with *other* clients and *their* problems (the lawyer's phone shouldn't even ring during an appointment).
- To explain legal matters in an understandable way, and not treat the client like a stupid person or a child.
- To return their phone calls within 24 hours.

# What Do You Do If Your Lawyer Annoys You . . . Or Worse?

We hope you'll be happy with your lawyer if you've chosen wisely. But what should you do if you're unhappy? Call the commissioner?

- If you have a one-time problem, such as a bill you can't figure out, a snippy secretary, or a phone call that wasn't returned, discuss it calmly with your lawyer. Remember that you're the lawyer's meal ticket — as a general rule, he wants to keep you on as a contented client.
- If you think that you've been overcharged by your lawyer, and are not satisfied with the lawyer's explanation of the bill, you can get help from the court. You can make an appointment to have the bill reviewed by a court officer in a procedure called an *assessment* or *taxation*. If the officer agrees that you have been overcharged, the bill will be reduced. (In some places it may take a while to get the appointment, and in the meantime your lawyer probably used your retainer to pay the bill.)
- If you don't feel that you're getting good quality legal work at a good price, or if you're not being treated well, you should look for another lawyer. But change lawyers the easy way. Don't get into a fight with your lawyer and stomp off to find someone new. Find the new lawyer first, and let her look after the details of telling the old lawyer he's fired and of getting your documents away from him.
- If you think your lawyer has screwed up the work he was doing for you, or if your lawyer has indulged in some form of professional misconduct such as refusing to answer your calls and letters, or making unwanted sexual advances to you, you should get in touch with the provincial law society. The law society will investigate your complaint. If it finds a complaint is valid, it has the power to discipline lawyers by reprimanding them, suspending them from practice, or even disbarring them. If a lawyer has carelessly done bad work for you, you may be able to recover any lost money through the lawyer's professional liability insurance.

- If your lawyer is really badly behaved and has done something like make off with your money to fund her gambling and cocaine habit, or has tossed you against the wall in a fit of rage, you can contact the law society *and* the police. Criminal charges can be laid against lawyers too. In addition, if your lawyer has deliberately harmed you (rather than carelessly harmed you by mismanaging your legal affairs), say by stealing your money, you can make a claim to the law society's compensation fund.

# How Do You Get the Most from Your Lawyer?

For the money you're paying, you want your lawyer to do the best possible job for you. *You* can help your lawyer to do the best job. Here's how:

- Do your homework. If you know something about the law concerning your particular matter, you'll be better able to explain your situation logically and tell your lawyer what you think you want. You'll also have an idea what documents you need to bring with you, and won't have to return later with essential pieces of paper. Bonus: The more you know about the law, the less time your lawyer will have to spend explaining it all to you. If you're being billed at an hourly rate you'd probably rather get the short version than the long version of the law school lecture.

- Collect all your information and documents. Only you know what you have — some of it may turn out not to be useful, but it's your lawyer's job to decide what's useful. It's your job to put together everything you've got. Appendix A, "Prepare to Meet Your Lawyer," at the end of the book (and also on the CD) will help you out here.
- Tell the truth. Your lawyer has to know the whole story in order to do a good job. Don't conceal information simply because it's embarrassing or puts you or your family in a bad light.
- Give clear instructions. Only you can tell your lawyer what to do. Your lawyer can set out your options for you and tell you what the consequences will be if you choose a certain course of action. Your lawyer can even recommend a particular course of action. But your lawyer can't just up and decide what to do and go off and do it. Your lawyer can't do anything until you've given your instructions. Make sure you tell your lawyer exactly what you want done.
- Don't wait too long. If you need legal help, it's best to get it sooner rather than later. If a problem arises, it can often be solved more quickly and cheaply if it's addressed early.

- Be available. Don't make it difficult for your lawyer to reach you — make sure there's a way to leave a message for you if you're not in (e-mail, voice mail, fax, someone to take a message). Return your lawyer's phone calls (leaving a detailed message if she's not in) and answer her letters promptly. If there are documents for you to sign, don't take off for the cottage or a conference without speaking to your lawyer first.
- Keep copies. If you've received letters or documents from your lawyer or sent documents to your lawyer, keep copies of them. Then you'll always know exactly what's been done or decided, and you'll reduce the chance of communication failures with your lawyer.

# Chapter 21

# Who's on First? The Rest of Your Estate Planning Team

### In This Chapter

- Knowing who (besides lawyers) offers estate planning advice
- Finding out how different estate planning advisers are paid
- Learning how to choose an estate planning adviser

When you jog out onto the estate planning field and see what you're facing, you may start to feel kind of lonely. As we tell you in other chapters, you need to do some financial planning, think about tax reduction strategies, consider taking out life insurance, choose an executor, think about creating a trust, and make up a business succession plan, among other things. So maybe you're thinking that a coach is all well and good for the legal stuff, but you wouldn't mind some teammates for support in other areas.

You know there are estate planning advisers out there apart from lawyers. You've seen ads for estate planning from people who claim to know what they're talking about. Maybe you've even been offered free estate planning advice! You'd like to find out more about these people . . . and we'd like to tell you more about them. We think you'll find that some are keepers and others should be sent to the showers — or even back to little league.

## The Coach, You've Met

Have you ever met the coach! We introduce you to lawyers at tedious length in Chapter 20. But (being lawyers ourselves) we can always find a little more to say on any topic. And this will warm us up for the rest of the chapter.

For now, lawyers are the only professional advisers who can legally prepare wills and supervise their execution, and are the most familiar with powers of attorney and living wills. It's a lawyer you want if you have questions that revolve around the law, and an awful lot of estate planning questions do revolve around the law. For many people, a lawyer can provide enough advice about all aspects of estate planning (taxes, trusts, gifts, business succession, and even whether insurance is needed) that they don't need to search out other advisers.

# Now Say Hello to the Boys on the Bench

You've decided you'd like to play the field a little before sitting down with a lawyer, so now we're going to introduce you to other potential team members. Here are most of the players who offer estate planning advice:

- Accountants
- Financial planners
- Bank, trust company, and credit union personnel
- Insurance agents or brokers

Some of these people are *professionals* (with accredited training), others are not. (Even the non-professionals often have professional-sounding designations — fancy strings of letters following their names. If you collect initials rather than baseball statistics, you'll have a great time in this chapter.) Some of them offer unbiased professional advice, others are just glorified salespeople.

How many, if any, of these advisers do you need? And if you need some of them, who's on first? What's on second? If you answered I don't know, you're already on third. Let's cut out this tomfoolery and look at the starting lineup.

# A Professional Accountant

You may think you'd like an accountant to help you prepare a financial plan, and you may see your estate plan as part of that overall financial plan. Or you may want to consult an accountant for tax advice about planning your estate. An accountant should be able to give you financial and tax advice about estate planning. Just don't forget that there's a lot more to estate planning than those two things.

In Canada, anyone can call himself or herself an accountant. So you don't just want "an accountant." That could be anyone who's taken a bookkeeping course, or can count to 10 (20 in bare feet). You want a professional accountant.

There are only three types of recognized professional accountants — *chartered accountants, certified general accountants,* and *certified management accountants.* These accountants have a professional designation and belong to government-recognized, self-regulating bodies, as lawyers do.

## Types of professional accountants

Of the three types of professional accountants, only two ordinarily offer tax and estate planning advice to individuals.

- Chartered accountants (CAs): CAs are regulated by provincial institutes of chartered accountants. They must have a Bachelor of Commerce or equivalent university degree, complete thirty months of supervised employment, take a series of professional courses, and pass a number of examinations, including a nationally administered Uniform Final Exam.
- Certified general accountants (CGAs): CGAs are regulated by provincial associations of general accountants. They must have a university degree, take a series of distance learning courses through the Certified General Accountants Association, complete between two and three years of supervised employment, and pass a series of examinations.

These are the really serious accountants, the ones who pay so much attention to detail that a whole industry of accountant jokes has been spawned.

> Doctor to patient: You have only six months to live.
>
> Patient: Oh no, what should I do?
>
> Doctor: Marry an accountant.
>
> Patient: I'll live longer if I marry an accountant?
>
> Doctor: No, but it will seem longer.

Both chartered accountants and certified general accountants are required to maintain third-party liability insurance, also known as *errors and omissions insurance,* which is designed to compensate a client financially if the accountant makes a mistake. (The client may have to start a court action to get any insurance money.) These accountants are also bound by professional standards and a code of ethics, and can be disciplined by the organization they belong to for doing poor work for a client or treating a client badly. If a client complains, the organization will investigate. So if a professional accountant does you wrong, something worse will happen to him or her than getting flicked with a wet towel in the locker room.

## How do accountants charge for their services?

Like lawyers, accountants usually bill at an hourly rate for the time they spend with you or working for you, or charge a flat fee for a particular matter.

Professional accountants are not allowed to receive a commission for selling the products of others or to receive payment from a third party in return for referring a client to that person for services. So you can expect a professional accountant to give you unbiased advice.

If you think you've been overcharged for the work an accountant has done for you, and speaking to the accountant or the accountant's manager in the accounting firm doesn't resolve it, you can take the matter up with the organization of which the accountant is a member. Some of them offer fee dispute resolution services.

## How do you find an accountant?

You want to find an accountant with experience in estate planning matters, with whom you'll feel comfortable working, and who will charge you a reasonable fee. How will you find a player like that?

- **Get recommendations.** Ask your lawyer, or friends, relatives, or business associates for the names of accountants who have done similar work for them. Contact your provincial institute of chartered accountants or certified general accountants' organization for the names of accountants in your area who specialize in estate planning.
- **Do a little investigating.** Call the accountant's office to find out a bit more about the areas in which the accountant has expertise. Ask about the accountant's standard hourly rate. Check the location of each accountant's office to see whether it's convenient for you.
- **Interview the lineup.** Once you've narrowed down the field to two or three accountants, make an appointment to meet with each one. You're looking for information about the accountant and for your personal reaction to the accountant, to see if you want to work with him or her. In the course of your chat, ask each accountant:
    - How much experience he or she has in estate planning.
    - What his or her fees would be for this work.
    - Whether your work will be handled by the accountant personally or by others.

# A Financial Planner

If you're interested in following investment strategies to increase the value of your estate, or you are planning your estate as part of an overall financial plan, you may start the estate planning process by looking for a financial planner. You'll find financial planners in financial planning firms, in banks and trust companies, and in investment firms.

There is very little regulation of the financial planning field. In every province except Quebec, anyone can call him or herself a financial planner. There is no minimum level of education and there is no professional training required before an individual can call himself or herself a financial planner.

## Are there any qualifications out there?

Outside of Quebec there are no laws that set qualifications for financial planners. Yet there are credentials galore in the financial planning field. They're granted by various organizations, usually following the completion of distance learning courses offered by the organization, and passing of examinations set by the organization.

Here's a sampling of financial planning organizations and the credentials they hand out:

- Registered Financial Planner (RFP). This designation is granted by the Canadian Association of Financial Planners (CAFP) and is recognized in Canada only. To qualify for this designation, a financial planner must have engaged in financial planning for at least two years and must complete 30 hours of continuing education in the year, pass examinations set by the CAFP, submit a sample financial plan that passes peer review, have a satisfactory record of business ethics, maintain errors and omissions insurance, and comply with the CAFP's code of professional ethics. A financial planner who receives the RFP designation must reapply for it every year and meet the same criteria.
- Certified Financial Planner (CFP). This designation, which is also recognized in Australia, Japan, New Zealand, the United States, and the United Kingdom, is granted in Canada by the Financial Planners Standards Council (FPSC). To qualify for this designation, a financial planner must have engaged in financial planning for at least two years and must complete a program of study approved by the FPSC, pass an examination set by the FPSC, complete 30 hours of continuing education each year, and comply with the FPSC code of ethics. The designation is renewed automatically as long as the CFP completes the required continuing education hours and complies with the code of ethics.

- Personal Financial Planner (PFP) and Specialist in Financial Counselling (SFC). These designations are offered by the Institute of Canadian Bankers (ICB) to financial services professionals after they have completed a series of distance learning courses (and exams) offered by the ICB, the ICB's "Designation Qualification Process" (no doubt referred to as the DQP), and six months of on-the-job training. The Personal Financial Planning Program teaches wealth-management skills. The Specialist in Financial Counselling Program teaches how to match (financial institutions') services and products to clients' financial goals.
- Financial Management Advisor (FMA). This designation is offered by the Canadian Securities Institute (CSI) following successful completion of self-study courses offered by the CSI in Canadian securities, financial planning, and wealth management.

## How are financial planners paid for their services?

Notice we didn't ask, "How do financial planners charge for their services?" That's because you may not be charged for the financial planner's services at all — at least not directly. But that doesn't mean that financial planners work for free.

Financial planners may be paid

- By charging the client a fee — either by billing at an hourly rate, or by charging a flat fee for a particular set of services.
- By charging a management fee that's a percentage of the value of a client's property under management.
- By earning commissions from insurance companies, financial institutions, and investment funds for selling their products to a client.
- By earning bonuses from companies, institutions, and funds for selling certain products or a minimum number of certain products.
- Through a combination of fees and commissions.

### What's the quality of the service you get?

You can be fairly sure of getting unbiased financial advice from a planner who only charges a fee for his or her service.

You can't be so sure of getting unbiased advice from a financial planner who is paid by commission or bonus, either wholly or in part. It is in the financial planner's interest to persuade you to buy what he or she has for sale, and even more so to persuade you to buy the product that gives the financial planner the highest commission or bonus.

As for financial planners who are salaried employees of companies such as investment brokerages, banks, trust companies, and insurance companies, even though they do not receive commissions they are still under pressure to sell the products their employer offers. They want to keep their jobs by meeting sales targets, and they probably wouldn't mind earning bonuses and salary increases as well.

### What kinds of products do financial planners sell?

Some financial planners who work on commission or for a brokerage or financial institution can offer you a wide range of products. Others only have a few. The kinds of products financial planners deal in include

- Mutual funds
- Guaranteed Investment Certificates (GICs)
- Segregated funds or guaranteed investment funds
- Registered Retirement Savings Plans (RRSPs)
- Registered Retirement Income Funds (RRIFs)
- Annuities
- Registered Education Savings Plans (RESPs)
- Life insurance
- Disability insurance
- Medical and travel insurance
- Tax-assisted investments and limited partnerships

### What's your game plan?

Keep in mind that someone working on commission or for a financial institution or brokerage may tend to advise you to build your estate plan around the product(s) that he or she sells. Your estate plan may end up heavy on insurance if the financial planner sells insurance, or on mutual funds if the financial planner sells mutual funds.

We don't mean to say that financial planners who are working on commission or for a brokerage or financial institution will always sell you products you don't need. The products may be just fine and perfect for your needs. But you have to take the advice you're given with a grain of salt.

Ask the financial planner about any commission or bonus he or she is getting on the recommended product(s), or what sales target he or she has for the product(s), and check out the product(s) independently, comparing them with similar products available elsewhere. You also need to think carefully, before you buy anything, about whether a product really fits in with your estate planning goals.

## How do you find a financial planner?

Since financial planners and their organizations are not subject to provincial legislation, as lawyers and professional accountants and their organizations are, we suggest that you choose a financial planner based on others' recommendations and your own investigation, rather than on the basis of credentials in the form of initials like the ones we discussed above — even if some of those initials look pretty spiffy, especially all strung together.

You want to find a financial planner with experience in estate planning matters, with whom you feel comfortable working, who does not get paid in commissions, and who will charge you a reasonable fee. In order to scout the talent,

- **Get recommendations.** Ask your lawyer or your accountant, or friends, relatives or business associates for the names of financial planners who have done estate planning work for them. If that doesn't produce any leads, contact your provincial chapter of the Canadian Association of Financial Planners (CAFP) for a list of Registered Financial Planners in your province, setting out their credentials, experience, and method of payment. The CAFP Web site (`www.cafp.org`) is helpful.
- **Do some investigating.** When you've got some names, call each financial planner's office to find out more about the areas in which he or she has expertise. Ask whether the financial planner receives commissions. Ask about the fee that the financial planner charges. Check the location of each financial planner's office for convenience.
- **Hold your own draft.** Once you've narrowed down the choices to two or three financial planners, make an appointment to meet with each one before you make your pick. Ask about:
  - His or her educational background — including university and courses taken for financial planning certification.
  - His or her experience in estate planning matters — how many years in the field and how many clients.
  - The availability of references from his or her clients.
  - The type of services he or she provides.
  - What products (if any) he or she receives commissions on.
  - What his or her fees are for the kind of work you want done.
  - Whether he or she carries errors and omissions insurance.
  - Whether your work will be handled by the planner personally or by others.

### What do you do if your financial planner drops the ball?

If you are not happy with the financial planner's work or the bill, discuss your concerns with the planner. If you're still unhappy and your planner works for a company, you can speak to the manager of the company. If that doesn't resolve the problem, you can take the matter up with whatever professional organization the planner belongs to. Some of the organizations offer dispute resolution services or can discipline members for breaching a code of conduct. If the financial planner makes a mistake that costs you a lot of money, you can sue him or her — but if you win your lawsuit you may not be able to collect your money unless the financial planner has errors and omissions insurance.

## Banks, Trust Companies, and Credit Unions

If you decide to go to a bank, trust company, or credit union for financial planning advice, you may be offered some advice about your estate as part of your financial plan. Your advisers will be employees of the bank, trust company, or credit union. They may or may not have some of the qualifications we talked about in the financial planners section (you can always ask), and their job description is more likely to be "sell products" than "give disinterested advice." You can give them some batting practice if you like by asking for their ideas about estate planning.

That's not game over, though. Trust companies in fact offer thorough estate planning advice (usually available only at certain branches). Most banks are now associated with trust companies and can refer a customer seeking estate planning advice to their trust company arm.

Many trust companies provide very informative free estate planning pamphlets. Anyone can get a copy of these pamphlets from the trust company, and many of them can be downloaded from trust company Internet sites.

Trust companies go further than pamphlets. They also employ estate planning advisers who help customers to develop an estate plan before a will is drafted or updated by a lawyer. These advisers are quite knowledgeable about estate planning issues, and the service is provided free of charge.

This sounds great! Free advice from knowledgeable people! Why didn't we tell you about this right up front at the beginning of the chapter? Well, because this service is offered *only* to customers who are going to name the trust company as sole executor or co-executor in their will. (Come on. You knew there had to be a catch, didn't you?)

If you go to a trust company for information about estate planning, expect a sales pitch for the appointment of the trust company as your executor. If you don't want to appoint the trust company, you won't get any estate planning advice.

Why do the trust companies provide an estate planning service for free? If you name a trust company as your executor, when you die your estate will be charged a fee for their estate administration services. (The fee will be based on the value of your estate and/or the work done.) So the service isn't so much "free" as "billed later."

If you do decide to appoint the trust company as your executor or co-executor, it's in the trust company's interest to make sure that your estate plan makes sense. That way it will be able to carry out the instructions in your will with a minimum amount of trouble.

# Life Insurance Agents or Brokers

If you need life insurance to build the value of your estate or to pay taxes or debts, you may edge into estate planning by speaking to an insurance agent or broker. An insurance agent or broker can give you advice about how much insurance you need, the kind of policy to buy, and how to get through the insurance application process. (You'll find tons of information about life insurance in Chapters 6 and 7.)

When we talk about an *insurance agent,* we mean a person who deals with only one insurance company and sells only that company's policies. When we talk about an *insurance broker,* we mean a person who deals with and sells the policies of several companies. A broker can get quotes on insurance policies from several companies, whereas an agent can get you an insurance policy from one company only.

Both agents and brokers are regulated and licensed by provincial governments.

## How are agents and brokers paid for their services?

Insurance agents and brokers are paid a commission by the insurance company for each policy they sell. Generally speaking, the more expensive the policy, the higher the commission. Commissions for permanent policies are higher than commissions for term policies. (Look at Chapter 7 to inform yourself about kinds of life insurance policies.) So insurance agents are like financial planners who work on commission — it's in the agent's or broker's interest to get you to buy an insurance policy, and to get you to buy a more expensive policy. If you're dealing with a broker, the more insurance a broker sells for a particular company, the higher the rate of the broker's commission. A broker can hardly be blamed for recommending one insurance company's products over another's if the broker will get a higher commission on it.

Because an agent's or broker's interests can be different from yours, it's important for you to choose carefully the agent or broker you go to for advice, compare insurance policies on your own before you buy, and think about whether any insurance that's suggested to you fits in with your estate plan as a whole.

Beware of insurance salespeople masquerading as estate planning specialists. Since insurance brokers and agents work on commission, you may end up with an estate plan built around insurance policies when another approach may be better for you. (We help you decide whether or not you need life insurance in Chapter 6.)

## How do you find an insurance agent or broker?

If you're in the market for a good insurance adviser, ask for recommendations from your family and friends, from your lawyer or accountant, or from the agent or broker you deal with for your car or home insurance. Then contact the recommended agents or brokers and ask each of them about:

- His or her qualifications to provide advice about insurance as part of an estate plan. Some agents and brokers hold various professional designations such as Chartered Life Underwriter (CLU), Chartered Financial Planner (CFP) and Chartered Financial Consultant (CHFC) — you might want to ask what courses and exams were required to get a designation. Ask particularly about qualifications related to estate planning rather than financial planning.
- His or her experience. How many years has he or she spent in the life insurance business, how long has he or she been giving advice about estate planning, and how many clients does he or she have? Or had? You should probably take a greater interest in the dead clients than the ones who are still alive. It's the dead ones who've tested the agent's or broker's expertise.
- Past performance. Can he or she give you references from clients? It's best not to be too fussy here — you can accept living clients as references.

- The amount of commission paid for the products he or she sells. (If it's a broker, also ask about different rates of commission from different insurance companies.)
- Errors and omissions insurance. Does he or she carry this liability insurance for clients' protection?

Decide whether you'll feel comfortable working with the people you interview. Then step up to the plate and make an appointment with one of them.

Insurance agents and brokers are sometimes willing to come to you, rather than making you come to them. You may prefer to meet in your chosen adviser's office instead of your living room, though. It's easier to leave an office, if you want to do some thinking before you make a decision, than it is to ask someone to leave your home.

## Forget about Stealing All the Way to Home Base

You might as well make up your mind from the beginning that if you want good estate planning advice, you're better off dealing with someone who will give you balanced and unbiased information and opinions. You're going to have trouble getting that from a person who has to sell you a product in order to earn a living.

There's no such thing as free estate planning advice. As you've seen, everyone who is in the business of helping you plan your estate gets paid one way or another.

## We're Back to the Coach Again

Your lawyer should be your main source of estate planning advice. (No, we're not getting paid a commission to say this.) An experienced wills and estates lawyer will have a fuller appreciation of the big estate planning picture than other estate planning advisers because so many estate planning issues are legal issues.

And you can count on a lawyer to be reasonably unbiased in referring you for additional help. A good lawyer will know when to call in the other players. Your lawyer might suggest that you

- Speak to an accountant if you need specialized tax advice in planning your estate or if you need financial planning assistance.
- Speak to a financial planner for help with financial planning or if you are looking for investment strategies to increase the value of your estate.
- Speak to representatives of a trust company if you are thinking of appointing an institutional executor.
- Speak to an insurance agent or broker if you need life insurance to pay taxes or debts or to increase the value of your estate.

# Part VI
# You're Not Done Yet

"I know I should tidy up, but I'm convinced that as long as I'm this disorganized I can't die."

## In this part . . .

This part sends you back to work. Now we tell you that it's not enough to make plans and create legal documents (a will, a power of attorney, a living will) to carry them out. You also have to organize your affairs so that your executor can carry out your plans. And we tell you that it's usually not enough to make plans once — we set out the changes in your life, others' lives, and the law that should be your cue to review your estate plan.

# Chapter 22

# Tidy Up Before You Go-Go — Putting Your Affairs in Order

### *In This Chapter:*

- Reducing the confusion that your illness and death will cause for your family
- Leaving documents and instructions that your family will need
- Leaving documents and instructions that your executor will need
- Understanding why the documents will be needed
- Choosing the best place to leave your documents and instructions

This is not an exciting chapter. It's mainly about document organization, the kind of drudge work you're dying to get away from. Worse, there's not much benefit to you personally in this work. You'll be gone before most of the documents are needed. At least when you do ordinary drudge work like vacuuming the dog hair out of the car you get something out of it for yourself.

You're doing all this estate planning for the sake of your family or other people who are close to you. Don't let the last act of your life or the first act of your death be to drive them nuts! If there's information they're going to need, make sure it will be available to them.

If you already keep your important documents in neat file folders in your neat home office, this chapter won't be too bad for you. You'll probably still have some work to do . . . not too much. But if you are in the habit of stuffing bills, mortgages, and passports into the handiest drawer (which explains how the instructions for the fax machine ended up in the bathroom medicine chest) or an old shoe box, you'll have a lot of work to do.

# How Can You Prevent Your Death from Causing Confusion in Your Family?

There will probably be a period of time just before and just after your death when your financial and medical affairs are pretty much up in the air. You need to prepare for that as well as for your death.

## Before you kick the bucket

If you're incapable of looking after your finances in the days (or weeks, or months) before your exit, you'll need a power of attorney to cover the situation. So do it now — while you're still fully capable of looking after yourself and your business — and then don't forget to tell your family that you've got a power of attorney. You can check out powers of attorney in Chapter 18.

If you're incapable of making decisions about your medical care, either because you're unconscious or you're gaga, you'll need a living will to allow your family to make decisions about the care you receive. Have it prepared at the same time as your power of attorney. Make sure your family knows about it as well as your power of attorney. For more on living wills, go to Chapter 19.

## After you kick the bucket

Your power of attorney will become invalid the moment you die. At the same time, your bank accounts will be frozen for most purposes and your safety deposit box will be inaccessible until your executor gets organized and, in some cases, gets letters probate. (We explain this and other parts of your executor's job in Chapter 10.)

You should make a point of telling your dependent family members — yes, we mean while you're still in the land of the living — about the arrangements you've made to take care of them after your death (life insurance policies and benefits plans naming them as beneficiaries, as well as provisions in your will). Then they or your executor will be able to contact the insurance company or benefits plan administrator to get the money as soon as possible. If they don't know that you've arranged to look after them, they may despair and sell your beer stein collection for food even before the will has been opened.

Your family will find your insurance very helpful at this time — the proceeds of your insurance policy will reach them much faster than the funds in your estate. But it will still take a little while for the insurance company to satisfy itself that you're dead and pay the policy proceeds to a family member you've named as the beneficiary.

If your family is financially dependent on you, you want to make sure they don't go hungry in the midst of plenty. (Let's assume you arranged things so that your estate will be able to support them plentifully.) You want them to be able to get at some cash for immediate expenses like food and mortgage or rent payments. You can do this by having a joint account with a family member and always keeping enough there for emergency expenses. The joint account holder should be able to go on making withdrawals after your withdrawal from the scene.

# What Documents and Instructions Will Your Family Need?

Your family will run into trouble helping either you (while you're alive) or themselves (whether you're alive and incapable or dead) if they don't have the necessary documents and marching orders from you.

## If you don't just drop dead but become incapacitated before you die

If you depart this world in stages, the first person who needs important documents from you will probably not be your executor but family members who have to look after you and your affairs. So you'll want them to have easy access to

- Your living will. Your substitute decision maker should have a copy of your living will and should know where the original is. Your doctor should have a copy of the document too.
- Your power of attorney. Give your named attorney a photocopy and tell him or her where the original is. With your lawyer is okay. In your sock drawer is okay. In your safety deposit box is *not* okay unless your attorney has signing rights to get into your box and knows where the key is.
- Information your family may need to help them deal with the government or your employer — things like your social insurance number, old age security number, marriage certificate, armed services record (if any), employment contract, and employee number.
- Information your family may need to help them deal with your mortgage lender or landlord — things like your mortgage payment schedule or your residential lease.

### When you die

Once you're gone, your executor has to take over the job of looking after the details. Your executor may be a close family member who's already familiar with your affairs, a more distant relative, a friend, a business associate, or even a trust company.

If your executor is not a close family member, make sure that your family knows who your executor is! They'll want to go bug the executor to get started on the work associated with administering your estate.

## What Documents Will Your Executor Need?

Your executor will arrive on the scene and immediately need lots and lots of pieces of paper. Not making sure that your executor will have what he needs will really make him regret your death. He will daily wish you were alive again — even just for a minute — so he could punch you in the nose.

### The duties of an executor

In order to understand why you need to organize your documents for your executor, you have to understand what your executor is going to do. You can review the duties of an executor in Chapter 10, where we go on about them at great length. As we tell you there (and this time we'll be briefer), your executor has a duty to

- Make your funeral arrangements.
- Collect information about your estate.
- Apply for letters probate.
- Protect the property of your estate.
- Gather in the property of your estate.
- Make an inventory of the property of your estate, and value the property.
- Pay your legitimate debts and your estate's taxes.
- Distribute the estate to your beneficiaries, according to the instructions set out in your will.

Your executor also has to

- Keep your property invested in proper investments until it is needed to pay your debts and taxes and to distribute to your beneficiaries, and
- Account to your beneficiaries — give them a statement setting out what was received into your estate and what was paid out or distributed.

However, these two duties don't require any document organization on your part, so you can forget about them.

### Making your funeral arrangements

If you've already made your own funeral arrangements, your executor needs the pre-arrangement documents so she'll know which funeral home to send you to. If you've also pre-paid, your executor will need the contract and receipt for your payment. If you have interment rights in a cemetery, your executor will need to know whether you own them alone (in which case only your estate — via your executor — has to give permission to get you buried there) or with someone else (in which case the surviving owner and possibly the estate as well will have to give permission). (We explain all these funeral and burial options in Chapter 14.)

If you haven't done any pre-arranging, your executor may need information for your death certificate and a statement of your preferences for your funeral and disposal of your remains.

Whether or not you've pre-arranged, you can use the "Instructions for Your Executor" form that you'll find at the end of this book as Appendix B and also on the CD-ROM that comes with this book.

The information required for your death certificate form, which will be filled out by the funeral home, includes

- Your name
- Your usual residence address
- The place and date of your birth (your birth certificate would be handy)
- Your marital status (your marriage certificate might also be handy, as well as any divorce decrees or spousal death certificates)
- Your occupation
- The names of your mother and father (birth certificate again)

The information required also includes the place and date of your death . . . but let someone else worry about that.

When you leave directions about your preferences for your funeral, think about the following matters (go to Chapter 14 if you need inspiration):

- The funeral home you would like to use, perhaps one your family has traditionally used and that has information about past funerals in your family.
- Whether you want to be embalmed — well, *want* is probably too strong a word — or whether you absolutely don't want anyone coming near you with formaldehyde.
- Whether you want an open casket and whether you want cosmetics applied.
- What clothes you'd like to be buried in, if you have a favourite outfit.
- Whether you'd like to have some particular item buried with you, such as a piece of jewellery, a book, or a photograph.
- Your obituary — you can write one for yourself or ask someone else to write it.
- Whether you want a visitation.
- Whether you want a funeral service (you're present, in body if not in spirit) or a memorial service (after your body has been buried or cremated).
- Whether there are people you are sure will want to attend your funeral, and whether your funeral should be delayed a few days to accommodate them if necessary.
- Details of your funeral or memorial service:
  - The person you would like to officiate at the service.
  - Where the service should be held (funeral home, place of worship, or elsewhere).
  - What form of service you would like used.
  - What passages (from a religious text, poem, or book) you would like read.
  - What music you would like played, and by whom (if you have, for example, a family member or friend who plays the organ or violin — or, not to be narrow-minded, the electric guitar or the bassoon).
  - What hymns you would like sung. Note: "My Way" is not a hymn, and please think twice before you ask your mourners to sing it.
  - What special prayer(s) you would like said.
  - Whether you would like a eulogy and, if so, whom you would like to deliver it. (If you hate eulogies, you'd better say so plainly.)

  - The people you want to act as pallbearers (the funeral home can supply muscle pallbearers if your pallbearers are more the honorary sort) or ushers.
  - Whether you would like a reception following the service and where it should be held.
  - Whether you would like memorial donations instead of or in addition to flowers.
- Details of your preferred disposal arrangements:
  - Whether you want to be buried or cremated, or even whether you want to be buried at sea.
  - If you choose to be cremated, what you would like done with your ashes — whether they should be buried or put into a columbarium in the urn, or whether they should be scattered in a particular place.
  - Your preferred cemetery.
  - The kind of monument you would like (upright stone or marker), and the inscription you would like.
  - Whether you would like a memorial of some kind placed somewhere other than your grave — for example, a tree or a bench in your favourite municipal park.
- How you would like your funeral arrangements paid for — out of a specific bank account or insurance policy, or through an employment benefits plan.

### *Collecting information about your estate*

You should leave an inventory of your property among your documents. It's unlikely you'll be able to keep your inventory right up to date to the time of your death, but it should contain at least general information about what you own and where further information about your property can be found. If you prepared an inventory of your possessions for Chapter 2 you could use that. But it would be better if you filled out the more detailed "Inventory for Your Executor," which you'll find at the end of this book as Appendix C and also on the CD-ROM.

Your property includes:

- Real estate. What's the address of each piece of land?
- Bank accounts. What's the name of the bank or trust company, and the account number?
- Investments. Who's your broker? (Your monthly statements will be really useful.) If you have no broker, what are your investments (GICs, Canada Savings Bonds, mutual funds, shares, and so on)?

- RRSPs and RRIFs. What's the name of the institution that manages the plan or fund? State whether the beneficiary is a named individual or your estate.
- Valuable capital property, such as artwork, jewellery, antiques, and collections. Describe each item.
- Insurance policies. What's the name of the insurance company, the face amount of the policy, and the name of the beneficiary (an individual or your estate)?
- Pension plans. What's the name of the institution that runs the plan? It's also useful to mention whether any of your surviving family members are entitled to benefits after your death.
- Debts owed to you. What's the name of your debtor and the reason for the debt?

In addition to the information suggested above, for each asset also state:

- The approximate value of the property. Don't get carried away here. Be realistic or conservative. Your executor will use your inventory to apply for letters probate, and in almost all provinces probate fees are calculated on the value of your property. In the case of especially valuable items (such as a house, for example), your executor may need to get an expert appraisal of the property.
- Whether you own the property together with another person (and if so, what that person's name is). If you own property jointly with a right of survivorship, the property passes directly to the joint owner on your death and does not form part of your estate.
- Where the property is located, especially if it is not in your house or one of your usual haunts like the cottage or your office.
- Where the documents relating to the property are located. These documents could include ownership documents, valuation of the property, insurance on the property, loans made to buy the property or made against the property, lease on a building or locker where the property is stored, and so on.

Your executor is responsible for paying your debts, so don't forget to leave information about:

- Mortgages. What's the address of the property and the name of your mortgage lender?
- Loans (such as a car loan). What's the loan for and what's the name of the lender?
- Back taxes and utility payments. Who's your creditor?

- Credit cards. What institution issued the card, and what's your account number?
- Business debts, if you are a sole proprietor or partner in a business, or if you have guaranteed a debt for a corporation. Who's the creditor? What's the security for the debt?

In addition to the information above, also include information about

- The approximate balance of the debt.
- Where the documents relating to the debt can be found.
- Whether anyone else has responsibility to pay the debt too, either as a co-borrower or as a guarantor.

### Applying for letters probate

In order to apply for letters probate (which are discussed in Chapter 10), your executor will need:

- Your will — the signed original, not a photocopy.
- The name and address of the lawyer who prepared the will. Even if your lawyer doesn't have the original will, he or she probably has the Affidavit of Execution (signed by the witnesses to your will), which the probate court will want to see before it grants probate. (We tell you all about this requirement in Chapter 16.)
- The inventory of your estate, with approximate values of your property.

Once armed with letters probate, your executor will be able to get physical and legal access to your property.

### Protecting the property of your estate

To protect the property of your estate, your executor will need

- Your inventory, including approximate values, so he or she knows what property you have in the first place.
- Any insurance documents you already have for any of your property.
- Any appraisals you have for individual items.
- Information about any existing security measures, such as an alarm system (your executor will want the code).
- Information about partners, employees, and business advisers, if your business forms part of your estate (if you are a sole proprietor or partner). Your executor will either have to keep your business running or begin shutting it down.

Your executor may find it necessary to insure property you don't currently have insured, or to put some of your property into a safety deposit box or secure storage.

### Gathering in the property of your estate

Your executor must gather in your estate. As we tell you in Chapter 10, that means that she must find and take possession of all the property that is part of your estate. To do so, your executor will need:

- Your inventory (beginning to feel some pressure to prepare one?) — and the inventory should include the location of any piece of property that's not in your house, cottage, or office. If you've hidden any of your valuable property, your executor will need to know the hiding place. (Reflect on the problems executor Ippolit encountered in "Please have a seat.")
- Any documents showing your ownership of property (such as a land deed, car ownership, and share certificates).
- Anything required to reach your property, such as keys, safe combinations, codes, or passwords.

If all the property in your house, cottage, safety deposit box, storage locker, and so on doesn't belong to you, make a note of that on your inventory list too, and give the name and address of the real owner.

Part of the gathering-in process may involve helping your survivors to get life insurance proceeds and survivors' pension benefits. If your survivors are entitled to receive anything directly from an insurance company, a pension plan, or a government plan, make sure that information is available too — make it part of your inventory.

## Please have a seat

Ippolit was named executor of his wealthy mother-in-law's estate. At least he thought she was wealthy . . . but when he gathered in the estate there didn't seem to be much in it. He began selling off her property such as cars and household furniture to pay debts and taxes. Then he found out that his mother-in-law (fearful of civil unrest and revolution among the oppressed classes) had converted most of her several million dollars in wealth into diamonds and had sewn them into one of her twelve dining room chairs. Unfortunately the dining room suite had just been auctioned off and the chairs had been sold singly or in pairs to several different people. Looking on the bright side, the dining room suite brought in $2,500.

### Making an inventory and valuing the property of your estate

When your executor makes an inventory of your estate, the inventory you prepared will, once again, be invaluable!

One of the main purposes of this step in estate administration is to figure out whether items of your property have increased in value since you got them. (This is for the purpose of calculating capital gains tax on your terminal return; see Chapters 4 and 5.) That means your executor will need to know what the value of any piece of capital property was when you got it and the value as of the day of your death.

Any documents you have showing the value of capital property when you acquired it will be very useful. A bill of sale would be good, or an appraisal for insurance purposes. If you don't have such documents, your executor will have to find someone to give an appraisal as of the date you got the property. (Or as of the beginning of 1972 — whichever is later. As we explain on the following page, capital gains tax was first imposed in Canada in 1972, so capital gains are only calculated from then.)

In addition, it would be helpful for you to provide your executor with the names of appraisers you've dealt with in the past — real estate agents, jewellers, your stockbroker, antique or collectible dealers, your accountant. They can be asked to value your property.

### Paying debts and taxes

Your executor has really been through the mill by now, identifying what you own, figuring out where you put it, and placing a value on it. And he or she still hasn't got to the really icky part yet — paying your debts and preparing your terminal return and paying the taxes due. Oh well. Better your executor than you. Your executor isn't going to feel quite the same stab of anguish as you would if you had to do this yourself.

Your executor probably won't be besieged by people falsely claiming that you owed them a hundred (or a hundred thousand) bucks, but he or she still has to take care to pay only legitimate debts. A legitimate debt is one you really owe and in that exact amount. You provided all the essential information about your legitimate debts as part of your inventory.

Or maybe you didn't. If you don't leave enough clues about your debts, then your executor has to advertise for your creditors (in local newspapers). Your executor may also have to argue (and maybe even get into a lawsuit) with a creditor about whether there's a debt and how much it is. Don't waste your executor's time and your estate's money by forgetting to mention your debts.

Now, as for your taxes. . . . You can put off hearing about your chores relating to taxes by reading Chapter 5 about taxes and your estate. But if that sounds like a fate worse than death, back to the chores. Your executor will need

- Your previous tax returns — so say where they can be found (at your accountant's, or third shelf up in the back linen closet).
- The name and address of your accountant, if you had an accountant prepare your returns in the past.
- Your inventory, particularly the part that shows your capital property such as a cottage or other piece of real estate that is not a principal residence, your investments, valuable art, antiques or collectibles, and so on.
- Your will, which says whether any of your capital property is being rolled over to your spouse (or any other eligible person) and which your executor therefore doesn't have to include in the capital gains calculation in your terminal return.
- Any documents showing your cost of acquiring capital property. These documents could include bills of sale from the time of purchase, appraisals dating to the time of purchase, and trade slips for investments that show the cost of buying and the broker's commission. If you bought or received capital property before December 31, 1971, your executor needs to know the value of the property as of February 1972. (February 14, 1972, was the official "Valuation Day" for capital property acquired before capital gains tax came into effect in 1972. Trust Canada Revenue — or Revenue Canada as it was then known — to make such a romantic gesture to the taxpayers of Canada!)
- Any documents showing your income for the taxation year, and documents relating to your RRSPs or RRIFs (which will be taxed as income in your terminal return).

### Distributing your estate

By the time your executor has been mucking around with your estate for months or a year, he or she will be glad to get rid of it by giving it away to the people named in your will. Your executor will probably be able to find your spouse and your children without too much trouble, but your second cousin Fred (who gets your favourite fly-fishing lure) or your dear school friend Laurinda (who gets your Royal Albert teacup with the gold rim and purple butterfly) may be harder to locate. Look on the next page at what executor Earl had to go through in "The searcher"!

### The searcher

Earl Dorincourt quarrelled with his son, who then left the country and never saw his father again. But when he died a few years later he left a will naming his father executor of his estate. In the will he left his property to "my son" — but neglected to mention where his son might be found. Earl spent a fortune hunting for his grandson, and eventually located the boy, named Cedric, in Brooklyn, N.Y. Then, just as Earl was about to celebrate the end of his quest, a boy named Tom turned up and claimed to be Earl's only grandson. Thank God for DNA testing! Tom was identified as an impostor and Cedric scooped the estate.

If you remember in your will people whom your executor or close family don't know or haven't kept up with, leave a note of their current addresses among the documents you're accumulating for your executor.

## Where Are Your Documents Now?

Are your documents scattered around your kitchen? Hidden under your mattress? Filed under "Personal" at your office? Locked up in your safety deposit box? Squirrelled away at your lawyer's office? Buried in the back yard? If your documents are currently in several places, consider reducing your document repository sites. Try to keep your important documents in one place.

And think twice about putting your documents away too securely. True, they contain information you don't normally share with a lot of people — maybe you don't even share it with your spouse or children. But if you hide them they may not be found when they're needed, or not in time to be useful. If you put them in your safety deposit box, no one without signing authority will be able to get in (even if you leave the key and box number lying around) — and in the event of your death the bank or trust company may not let your executor remove anything from the box (except possibly your will) until he or she has letters probate.

Easter egg hunts and car rallies can be fun, but there's a time and a place for everything. And your death isn't the time and your residence, office, and surrounding area are not the place for a treasure search that can last for months.

# Chapter 23

# It's Even Better the Second Time Around: Updating Your Estate Plan

### *In This Chapter*

- Facing up to the fact that you have to plan your estate more than once
- Knowing when you need to revise your estate plan
- Finding out about the events that cancel all or part of your existing will
- Learning how to update your will, power of attorney, and living will

In Chapter 1 we tell you that estate planning is not a one-time exercise but a continuing process. If you've made it through twenty-one more chapters, you probably hope that we were just joking when we said that. We weren't. In this chapter we're going to explain to you why you need to review and revise your estate plan, and when and how you revise it.

## What's Involved in Reviewing Your Estate Plan?

You were ready for some kind words and good wishes from us at this point, as we prepare to send you off to lead the rest of your life. The last thing you wanted to hear from us is that you have more work to do. Unfortunately, that's *exactly* what you are going to hear from us. We're going to tell you to review your estate plan on a regular basis. The only way you can escape this never-ending chore is to die.

Reviewing your estate plan means taking another look at:

- Your plans for giving a share of your estate to family and friends
- Your financial arrangements, such as investment strategies, tax reduction or avoidance strategies, gifts to family members during your lifetime, and life insurance

- Guardianship arrangements for your children
- Succession arrangements for a business that you own
- Your will
- Your beneficiary designations on your life insurance policies, RRSPs, RRIFs, and pensions
- Your power of attorney
- Your living will

# Why Do You Need to Review and Revise Your Estate Plan?

Why do you need to revise your estate plan? Well, why did you need an estate plan in the first place? Because you wanted to make sure that, when you die,

- You have done everything in your power to see that your family will have enough money to manage without you and your income.
- Your property will go to the people you want to have it.
- A person you chose will look after your estate.
- You have a say in who will look after your minor children.
- Your debts can be paid with the least damage to your estate.
- The taxes and probate fees your estate has to pay will be as low as possible.
- The future of any business you own has been looked after.

Think about it. The amount of money your family needs will change as your family grows, shrinks, or reconfigures itself. Your debts may increase or decrease significantly, which means rethinking your debt-payment plans. The value or nature of your property will probably change, so you'll need to reconsider tax strategies in order to keep taxes as low as possible.

Your relationships will probably change as well. You may revise your opinion about who needs help after you're gone, and how much — or you may get into a feud with someone you had chosen as a beneficiary and swear that that person won't get a cent from you, even over your dead body. Your executor may die or become ill, or you may part ways with that person too. You may want to reconsider your choice of guardian as your children and the guardian you have chosen grow older, or as you end old relationships and enter into new ones.

A business you own may be a wild success, or it may dwindle away to nothing. As your children grow up you may find (contrary to your expectations) that they want to join you in business, or that they wouldn't touch it with a ten-foot pole. You may have intended to run your business your whole life, and then receive an offer to purchase that you can't refuse — or discover that health problems will force you to sell out or shut down.

Any of these changes in circumstances can mean that your present estate plan is no longer constructed to meet your objective to provide properly for your family and friends after your death.

# When Should You Revise Your Estate Plan?

You should think about revising your estate plan as changes occur in your personal life, for example:

- If you marry, if your spouse or partner dies, if you separate or divorce, or if you meet a new partner.
- If you have children, as your children grow up, and as your children become independent.
- If you develop serious health problems.
- If a member of your family develops special needs.
- If you move and change your province or country of residence.
- If your executor of first choice will not be able to act (we stuck this in under your personal life because most people choose a close relative or friend as executor).

You should also think about revising your estate plan if there are changes in your financial and economic life, for example, changes in

- The nature and value of your property
- A business you own

Finally, you need to revise your estate plan and will if there are changes in the law, particularly tax law, family law, and succession law.

You think your life is the same old grind and nothing much ever happens? Don't count on it, at least as far as your estate plan is concerned. Change has a way of creeping up on people, so even if you think your life is in a rut, it's a good idea to run a review every few years. You may be surprised how out of date your earlier plans and arrangements have become. And if you're right that absolutely nothing in your life has changed, reviewing your estate plan will be an exciting project to light up your humdrum existence.

# Changes in Your Personal Life

Whether pleasant or unpleasant, major changes in your personal life (even short of your own death) can have a great impact on your estate plan.

## If you get married

Getting married is a big event, and it calls for a reassessment not just of your toothpaste arrangements but of your entire financial strategy. So you'll want to go over your estate plan carefully. In particular you'll want to go over your will.

When you marry, any will that you signed before your marriage is automatically cancelled as a result of your marriage. If you die before you sign a new will, you will die without a will, and provincial intestacy law will govern what happens to your estate (it will go to your spouse and surviving relatives in a fixed order: see Chapter 15). Learn from what happened to Leo's estate in "Julia couldn't wait."

Obviously the purpose of this rule is not to annoy you but to protect your new husband or wife if you didn't have the forethought to do it yourself. That's why the only exception to this rule proves the rule. If you sign a will before you get married and the will clearly states that it's being made *in contemplation* of your marriage, that will continues to be valid after you get married (and die).

Even if you don't want to make any changes in your existing will, you still must sign a new will just to keep your old arrangements valid. However, keeping your old arrangements may not be a realistic option once you are married — you'll at least have to take into account your spouse's potential claim as a dependant and his or her claim to a minimum share of your estate under provincial family law legislation. (See Chapter 10.)

### Julia couldn't wait

Billionaire Leo Farnsworth, a former football player, was engaged to marry society-lady-about-town Julia. Shortly before his wedding, he met social activist Betty and fell in love with her. He bankrolled her cause of saving the environment and made a will leaving her his entire estate. He felt obliged, however, to go ahead with his marriage to Julia. Shortly after the wedding he drowned in the bathtub. His last thoughts were of Betty and how she would make much better use of his money than Julia. Julia, after scooping Leo's estate, graciously gave Betty a musical instrument that Leo had been fond of. Betty started dating a football player named Tom and forgot Leo.

## If your spouse dies

If your spouse dies, your will in general continues to be valid. However every gift to your spouse will fail. If you die without changing your will, any gift of specific property you made to your spouse will go to an alternate beneficiary you named or (if you didn't name an alternate) fall back into the residue of the estate. If you left the residue of your estate to your spouse, it will go to an alternate beneficiary of the residue you named. If you didn't name an alternate (or the alternate has also died), the residue will be distributed as if you had died without a will. Provincial intestacy legislation will govern what happens to it. (See Chapter 15.)

The upshot of all this is, if your spouse dies you have to review your will to see whether you need to name a new person to receive whatever property you originally left to your spouse. If you named your spouse as your executor and didn't name an alternate executor, you will have to come up with a new executor as well.

You'll also have to rethink your tax planning strategies, since you will not only have lost your spouse but also the ability to use the primary tax-saving strategy — the spousal rollover (see Chapter 5). It may well be that your taxes will be higher than before, in which case you will have to come up with a plan for your estate to pay the additional tax. Or you can quickly remarry and regain your access to the spousal rollover. Are we coming across as a little heartless here? Or just tasteless? Don't worry about sparing our feelings when you answer . . . clearly we have none.

## If your marriage breaks down

When you run headlong into marital problems, rethinking your estate plan may take a backseat to fighting, trying to get custody of the kids, worrying about finances, and wondering if you'll ever be able to get a date. Even if your lawyer doesn't drag your estate plan into the fray, you shouldn't wait too long to go over it.

### If you and your spouse separate

Your will continues in effect if you and your spouse separate and do not divorce. If you die before divorcing and before changing your will, your spouse will be entitled to receive any gifts you made him or her in your will, and to act as your executor if named as executor. Look what happened to Nina's estate in "Rats!"

## Rats!

Truly, Nina and Jamie loved each other madly. They married and made mutual wills leaving all of their property to each other. After a time, Jamie began to drive Nina crazy because he insisted on keeping the house too hot and having extra comforters on the bed, and always came in slightly behind the beat when they played piano-and-cello duets. She kicked him out, but found she missed him terribly. She was ecstatic when he returned to her . . . but it wasn't long before he was driving her crazy again — besides doing the things that had annoyed her before, he now spoke Spanish with a terrible accent and constantly had friends over to watch videos.

So Nina left and took up with Mark and decided to devote her life to him and advocacy for the mentally disabled. Unfortunately, she never changed her will, and when she died of a rat bite a few years later her entire estate went to Jamie rather than to Mark. Mark would have used the money from her estate to build a drop-in centre for adults with Down syndrome, but Jamie spent it on an industrial furnace, gas fireplaces in every room, and a video library.

### If you and your spouse divorce

If you and your spouse divorce, in most provinces any gift you made in your will to your former spouse will be cancelled when the divorce decree comes through. If you die without changing your will, any gift of specific property you made to your spouse will go to an alternate beneficiary you named or (if you didn't name an alternate) fall back into the residue of the estate. If you left the residue of your estate to your spouse, it will go to an alternate beneficiary of the residue you named. If you didn't name an alternate (or the alternate has died), the residue will be distributed as if you had died without a will. If you named your spouse as your executor, the appointment will be cancelled. If you haven't named an alternate executor, you will have to come up with a new executor. If you don't name a new executor, when you die someone will have to apply to the court to be made *administrator* of your estate.

This sounds familiar — where have you read it before? A couple of headings back, actually. If you and your spouse divorce, your estate will be distributed just as if your former spouse had died before you. It may give you a nasty little thrill, to think that succession law looks upon your former spouse as a dead duck.

Just as with the death of a spouse, you'll have to think about who your beneficiaries should now be and reconsider your tax-planning strategies. (You may have gained your freedom, but you've lost that spousal rollover.)

### If you have new financial responsibilities as a result of marriage breakdown

There's one big difference between death and a divorce. When you revise your estate plan following separation or divorce, remember to take into account any responsibilities you have under a court order or separation agreement — to pay support, for example, or to keep your life insured in favour of your spouse or ex-spouse.

## If you have children

If you made your present estate plan before you had children, you'll definitely want to revisit it after your first child arrives . . . and probably after each additional child arrives — just to make sure that your arrangements will cover them properly.

As your children grow, you'll find that each has his or her own particular needs and you may want to reconsider your affairs to take that into account. One child may need family funding through a long university program such as medicine, another may have his or her own children when quite young (and quite poor) and need extra financial help to look after them. If one of your children has major financial requirements, you may want to do what you can to balance your arrangements so that your other children are treated fairly.

As your children become independent, they may need less from you — a share of your estate will be a pleasant windfall, no more. Or they may in fact need more, as they struggle to hold down a job and raise and educate their own children in a world of rising prices. You'll want to take any grandchildren you have into account in your plan as well. They're probably not your responsibility but they may require more financial help than their parents can give them.

## If you develop serious health problems

If your health starts to fail, your income may be affected, as may your financial planning priorities. Family relationships may change, for better or worse. Your plans for a business that you own may change. You may have to sell your home to cover health care expenses, or mortgage it to be able to afford necessary renovations. That means that health problems are another cue for you to look at your estate plan again.

## If a family member develops special needs

If one of your children is born with disabilities, or a family member is badly injured in an accident, or your aging spouse requires extra care, you have to look your estate plan over to see whether it's adequate to deal with the situation. You may need more life insurance because the cost of looking after your family has gone up. You may never have thought of setting up a testamentary trust or a living trust until now, but it may turn out to be a good idea. You may even need to change the testamentary guardian you appointed in your will, to ensure that someone who is both willing and strong enough will look after a child with mental or physical disabilities.

## Changes in your residence

A move from anywhere to anywhere else can have an effect on your finances and estate. You may find that your income goes much further in your new home town — or that you can hardly make ends meet on what was formerly a comfortable salary. Your new house may cost a lot more and form a bigger chunk of your estate than before, or it may cost a lot less and free up income for investment. So take out your estate plan for another look . . . if you can find it among the boxes and furniture that are strewn all over the place.

If you leave your executor behind when you move, it may be wise to choose a new executor who will be on the scene, geographically speaking, when you make your final exit.

A move to another province or another country can involve changes in the law as well as changes in your finances. You should get some professional advice about how your move affects your estate from this point of view. More about this under the next headings.

### If you move to another province

Many provincial laws affect estate planning. If you move to another province, there may be different laws on such matters as:

- The age at which a person can make a will
- The right of your spouse to claim a minimum share of your estate, and what that minimum is
- The right of your dependants to claim support from your estate
- How your business will be affected by your death
- How a will, power of attorney, and living will are prepared and signed
- The amount chargeable for probate fees

After you unpack, arrange a visit with a local lawyer to go over your will and estate plan to see if you need to make changes.

### If you move to another country

The laws governing estates are not the same in the United States and other countries as they are in Canada. You may find yourself in a country with big death taxes, income and capital gain tax rules you've never even imagined, completely different rules about your spouse's rights over your estate, and even special succession laws for property owners who are not citizens.

If you move to another country you will definitely need professional advice about things like

- Whether you need a new will to cover property in the new country
- What automatic rights your family members (including an unmarried spouse) have to share in your estate
- Whether beneficiaries living outside the country will receive the full amount of any gift you leave them (or whether the local government will take something off the top — or even refuse to allow property or cash to be sent to another country)
- What estate tax avoidance or reduction strategies are available
- What effect your change of residence will have on any Canadian pension rights you have factored into your estate plan

You even need to review and revise your estate plan if you buy property in another country and live there for only a part of the year.

It's possible to have more than one will, if you have property in more than one country (even if you have property in more than one province, in fact). You may decide, after getting professional advice, that you need two wills to carry out your estate plan properly.

You can get into all kinds of trouble when you try to have more than one will, so don't even *think* about doing this without the help of a lawyer. You have to be careful that your later will in one country or province does not revoke your earlier will in the other country or province. And then you must be careful not to give away the same property twice.

Finally, the laws relating to preparing and signing a will can differ from country to country.

### Changes in your executor's life

Your plan is that your executor will outlive you . . . but being named an executor is no guarantee of immortality or even of a long and healthy life. You will need to name a new executor if the person you originally named in your will dies and you haven't named an alternate. You'll also need to name a new executor if the one you have is no longer willing or able to take on the duties of an executor.

If your executor is already dead when you die and you haven't named an alternate, your executor's executor will become your executor. The funny buzzing noise created in your head by the preceding sentence may be nothing compared to the funny things the unknown executor will do to your estate.

If the executor you named is still alive but doesn't want to take on the job when you die, someone among your surviving friends and relations will have to apply to court to be made *administrator* of your estate (see Chapter 15) if you don't name a new executor. If an administrator has to be appointed, that will delay administration and distribution of your estate.

## Changes in Your Financial and Economic Life

It's exhausting even to contemplate all the things that can happen in your personal life that may affect your estate plan! Let's hope you don't actually have to go through them all. And there's no relief in sight. Financial and economic changes can have just as much impact on your estate plan.

### Changes in the nature and value of your property

Over the course of your life — or over the course of a wild week on the real estate or stock market — the value of the property you own may go way up or down in value. You could become an Internet millionaire or you could be the victim of a natural or man-made disaster that reduces the value of your home or business to approximately zip.

The kind of property you own may change, like Scottie's (next page) in "Rich and strange." You buy a house and then the next thing you know you're retiring and giving up homeownership in favour of renting a place in Canada and one in Florida. Or you may move from investing in GICs that earn income to buying stocks that shoot up in value and leave you with a big capital gain.

### Rich and strange

Scottie quit his job as a cop to go into the make-over business. Following his huge success in making over his girlfriend, Judy, to look like his ex-girlfriend, Madeleine, he became much sought-after and made a lot of money. But something was missing from his life. Finally he realized what it was — he wanted to become a BASE (Building Antenna Span Earth) jumper! He used much of his cash and mortgaged his home to buy the necessary climbing apparatus, parachutes, and plane tickets to foreign countries with tall buildings, broadcasting towers, bridges, and cliffs for him to jump off. Now Scottie's estate (which he is leaving to Judy and Madeleine in equal shares), formerly free of debt, has little cash and a big debt.

Whatever financial and economic changes happen, you'll want to rethink your estate plan. You may need to deal with the change in the tax bill your estate will have to pay or with the payment of debts. For example, you may need to take out more life insurance so that debts and taxes don't wipe out your estate, or you may need to look for different tax-avoidance strategies. You may also want to re-think how you've divided up your property in your will if you're trying to treat everyone in your family equally.

And you may want to change your executor — if you decide that you need someone with more sophisticated business or investment skills, or if you sadly realize that the high-powered team of professionals you appointed will no longer be necessary.

## Changes in your business

A business you own, alone or with others, could be a valuable part of your estate. (See Chapter 12 for an in-depth discussion of estate planning if you own your own business.) You need to keep your estate plan in mind whenever your business undergoes a change. For example:

- When you start up a business or change the form of your business (say from a partnership to a corporation), you should consider estate planning when you and your associates negotiate a partnership or shareholder agreement. If you want your family to be able either to run the business or sell out profitably after your death, those matters need to be addressed in the agreement.
- If the value of your business changes, you need to think about whether your arrangements to pass on its value will be fair to everyone in your surviving family. Maybe at one time it was fair to leave your house to one child and the proceeds of sale of your business to another — but is that true now?

- If your business enters into the next generation because your children are coming on board, you need to think about whether your succession arrangements will work properly to achieve your and their goals. For example, will the business need a shot of cash, best provided by insurance on your life, to steady it financially when you die? You also need, once again, to think about whether your plans to distribute your estate are fair. In your will, should you give everyone a share of the business, so they can all taste the profits? Should you require your successor to buy all or part of the business from the estate so that the successor doesn't get a windfall at the expense of other family members?

In Chapter 12, we advise you to draft the business-related parts of your will as if you were going to die tomorrow. The reason for this is to make sure that your arrangements are appropriate for the business as it is now, not as it might be if you live for many more years. This approach means you need to revise your will as your business circumstances change.

# Changes in the Law

Most of the changes that affect your estate plan will be quite noticeable to you. You'll clue in pretty quickly that you're getting married, having children, divorcing, feuding with relatives, burying your executor, or becoming fabulously rich through your business.

Changes in the law are much less noticeable. You might read about a new law in the paper — if it's a slow news day for lack of stories about mass slaughter or movie stars' sexual shenanigans. But it's just as likely that you'll never hear about the creation or cancellation of laws that could be important to your estate plan. Even lawyers have to work quite hard to find out what lawmakers have been up to lately.

The areas of law that are most likely to have an impact on your estate plan and will are tax law, family law, and wills and succession law.

It's a good idea to check in with your lawyer every few years and have him or her go over your estate plan with an eye to changing laws. When a very significant change in law occurs, sometimes lawyers notify their clients and ask them to come in for a chat.

## Tax law

The federal *Income Tax Act* is huge and is constantly being rewritten as the government creates schemes to keep itself and the tax-paying (and voting) public happy. Among the many changes that occur on a regular basis:

- Income tax rates change, either up or down.
- Capital gains tax rates change.
- Tax reduction opportunities are given and taken away — RRSPs, RRIFs, and RESPs are examples of tax reduction opportunities.
- Tax breaks are given to businesses or taken away.

Each province also has an income tax act, containing provisions that can affect your estate plan.

## Family law

In provincial family law, probably the most likely thing to change is the rights of one spouse over the property of the other spouse. This could mean that your estate will turn out to be smaller or larger than you expected (depending on which spouse you are), or that your spouse has a larger (or smaller) claim against your estate.

## Succession law

The thing to watch for in provincial succession law in the next while is a change in the definition of a spouse. At the moment, in order to get a share in the estate of a partner who dies without a will, in every province a spouse has to be legally married to the partner. Over the past few years, the definition of a spouse in numerous areas of the law has gone from "legally married" to simply living together like a married couple for a fixed period of time. In certain legal areas, the definition has even gone from "partners of the opposite sex" to partners of the opposite *or* same sex. There's a good chance that some or all of these changes will eventually find their way into succession law.

## Other areas of law

Provincial laws concerning living wills and powers of attorney experience turbulence from time to time. For example, living wills are not yet legally recognized yet in every single province, but it's probably only a matter of time until they are. The forms required and the legal formalities for completing living wills and powers of attorney also undergo change every now and then in some provinces. (See Chapter 18 for more about powers of attorney and Chapter 19 for more about living wills.)

Provincial laws about probate fees can also change. And that doesn't always mean that the fees go up. In Quebec, for example, the fee was changed to a low flat rate. (See Chapter 5 for more about probate fees.)

# How Do You Change Your Will?

If you decide that you need to make changes in your will to update your estate plan, you can either amend your will by making a *codicil* or you can revoke your will and replace it with a new will.

Do not try to change your will by writing changes on the original will. The changes will be easy to attack after your death. You must be legally capable of making a will even if you're just making handwritten changes to your will, and any changes must be properly signed and witnessed — just like a will. If you don't meet these requirements (which we describe in Chapter 16), any changes you make have no effect on your will.

## Making a codicil

A codicil is a written document that makes a change or changes to an existing will. It can add provisions to the will, it can cancel certain provisions of the will, or it can cancel certain provisions and substitute new ones. In fact, one codicil could do all of those things, in different parts of the will. It's possible to have more than one codicil to a will. A new codicil can also change existing codicils.

When you sign a codicil you must satisfy the same requirements as for the signing of a will (see Chapter 16). For the codicil to be valid:

- You must be legally capable of making a will. That means, generally, that you have to be able to understand what a will is and what it does, what property you have, and who might have a claim to share in your estate.
- You must be acting freely, not under threats or violence, or under pressure from a person who has a dominant relationship with you.
- The codicil must be properly signed and witnessed, just like a will. You and two witnesses must all be present together in the same room and must all sign the codicil and must all watch each other sign the codicil. If your lawyer isn't supervising the signing of the codicil, be careful whom you choose as a witness. A person who witnesses a codicil is not allowed to receive any gifts under the codicil. In most provinces, a person whose spouse witnesses the codicil is also not allowed to receive any gifts under the codicil.

Once a valid codicil is made, the will and codicil are read together. The changes set out in the codicil become part of and change the original will.

Be sure to let your executor know that you have made a codicil, and store your will and codicil together.

A codicil can be challenged in court just as a will can. If a court finds that you were not mentally competent when you signed the codicil, or you were pressured into making it, or the codicil was not properly signed and witnessed, then it won't be valid and won't have any effect. Your will won't be changed by the codicil.

### Revoking and replacing your will

You can *revoke* (cancel) your will by physically destroying it. If you destroy your will and you don't make a new will before you die, you will die intestate, and provincial intestacy law controls what happens to your estate (see Chapter 15).

The better way to cancel your will is to sign a new will that states that it revokes any earlier wills. The new will then takes effect and your old will is revoked. Most lawyers recommend that you destroy your old will after making a new one, to make sure that no one tries to probate the old will, either mistakenly or intentionally.

### A codicil or a new will?

People often make a codicil instead of a new will because they believe that a lawyer will charge less for preparing a codicil than for the preparing a new will. In fact, there may be no difference in cost, or only a very small one — especially since almost all lawyers keep their clients' wills in computerized form.

It's fine to use a codicil if your instructions will be clearly understood by someone reading your will and the codicil. But you should have a new will prepared if you are making a lot of changes to your will, if you already have several codicils, or if using a codicil will make your instructions confusing.

## Don't Forget Your Pensions and Insurance Policies

Your estate plan almost certainly has more documents hanging around it than just a will. When you change your estate plan and will, don't forget about your life insurance policies, pensions, RRSPs, or RRIFs. You may want to change the beneficiary or beneficiaries you named earlier.

## Life insurance policies

You have the right to change the beneficiary of any life insurance policy unless you designated the beneficiary *irrevocably*, in which case you cannot change your beneficiary without the beneficiary's consent. (See Chapter 6 for more about naming a beneficiary of your life insurance policy.)

If you are divorced or separated, make sure that you are not prevented from changing your beneficiary by the terms of your separation agreement or a court order.

To change the beneficiary on a life insurance policy, you must sign a written document revoking your earlier designation and naming a new beneficiary. You can do this by writing and signing a note yourself, or you can contact your insurance company to find out if there is a form your company would like you to use. Or you may change the beneficiary by including a direction to that effect in your will.

Be sure to notify your insurance company in writing of the change in beneficiary. Otherwise the insurance company may pay out the proceeds to the wrong person.

## Pension plans

You will probably not be able to change the beneficiary under your pension plan if you have a spouse and/or dependent children.

If you are a member of a pension plan, when you die your spouse (including an unmarried partner of the opposite sex in many plans, and even the same sex, in some plans) will be entitled to receive a pension or a refund of your contributions plus interest. If you have dependent children, they may be entitled to receive a pension either immediately or on the death of your spouse.

As long as you have a spouse (and in some plans, dependent children), you cannot direct your pension plan to pay a pension or refund to anyone else. If you do not have a spouse (or in some plans, dependent children), under some plans you may name a beneficiary to receive a pension or a lump sum payment. Under other plans, this payment will be made to your estate. If you are permitted to name a beneficiary for your pension plan, you are also permitted to change the beneficiary. Contact the administrator of your pension plan to find out what forms you must complete to name or change a beneficiary.

If you and your spouse separate or divorce, the value of your pension may be the subject of negotiations when you and your spouse divide up your property. You and your spouse may decide to trade the value of your pension rights against the value of other property you own, or you may decide to split the pension benefits themselves. Most provincial and federal pension benefits laws allow pension rights to be divided between the spouses according to the provisions of a separation agreement or court order. Contact the administrator of your pension plan to find out what your plan permits you to do and how you go about doing it.

### RRSPs and RRIFs

You have the right to change the beneficiary on your RRSP or RRIF. Contact the bank, trust company, or other plan administrator to find out what forms you must complete to change your beneficiary.

## And Don't Forget Your Power of Attorney and Living Will Either

With all this upheaval in your life, your power of attorney and living will may require some attention too.

### Power of attorney

When you revisit your power of attorney, ask yourself whether you still want the same attorney, and whether he or she is still willing and able to take on an attorney's duties (see Chapter 18).

Generally, powers of attorney can be revoked by tearing up the original. In some provinces you must revoke your power of attorney by a written document that is formally signed and witnessed.

If you revoke a power of attorney, you should notify your attorney in writing and also ask for the return of the original power of attorney document (if your attorney has it). If your attorney has been dealing with anyone on your behalf such as your bank or your stockbroker, be sure to write to those people telling them that the power of attorney has been revoked.

After you've revoked your power of attorney, remember to make a new one!

## Living will

The changes in your life that prompted you to review your estate plan may affect your thinking about your choice of substitute decision maker and the instructions you put in your living will. (See Chapter 19.)

If you made your living will while you were healthy and you're now suffering from a particular disease or condition, you'll want to find out what medical treatment is available. You may want to rewrite your living will to give instructions relating specifically to treatment for that disease or condition.

Don't forget to revise your living will if something happens to your substitute decision maker. If you've got a living will but no substitute decision maker, one of your relatives, in an order set out by the province (spouse first, then adult child, then a parent, and so on), will be called on to act as your substitute decision maker.

If you make a change to your living will, be sure to retrieve any copies of the older version from your substitute decision maker, doctor, lawyer, family members, or any others. Remember to give your up-to-date living will to your substitute decision maker and to your doctor.

# Part VII
# The Part of Tens

"According to this financial calculator, we won't have an estate to leave until 2018."

## In this part . . .

This part is the famous Part of Tens! It's an encore inspired by the thunderous applause you gave us for Chapters 1 to 23. We offer you 10 questions to ask when you interview lawyers before making your final choice, and 10 ways to use your computer when you're planning your estate.

# Chapter 24

# Ten Questions to Ask before You Hire a Lawyer

### In This Chapter

- Knowing the questions to ask a lawyer
- Knowing what to ask yourself

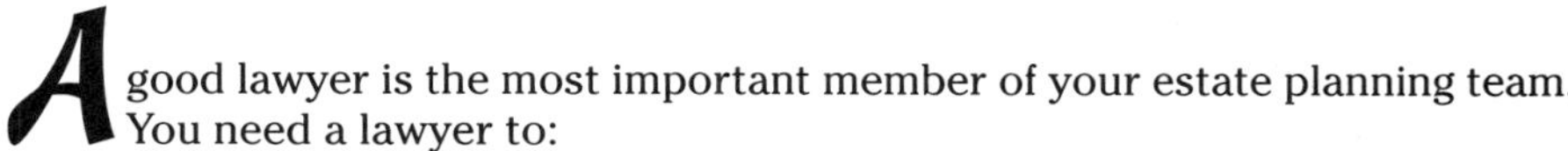

A good lawyer is the most important member of your estate planning team. You need a lawyer to:

- Help you plan your estate.
- Prepare your will, power of attorney, and living will documents.
- Make sure that your will, power of attorney, and living will are properly signed and witnessed.

After you're gone, you won't need a lawyer but your executor will, to:

- Get your will probated
- Help administer your estate

It's very important to choose the right lawyer, because you'll be relying on the lawyer's advice, not to mention paying for it! How do you go about finding the lawyer of your dreams?

- Get recommendations from friends, relatives, or business associates.
- Make some telephone calls or see if the law firm has a Web site to find out more about the lawyer's firm, location, and fees.
- Interview the finalists to see which one is the lawyer for you.

The following ten questions address the most important matters in choosing a lawyer. The first nine questions are for the lawyer. The last one is for you.

# Ask the Lawyer

### How much experience do you have in estate planning and estate administration?

You want a lawyer who's already experienced in the kind of work you need done. You don't want to be a lawyer's work-study project.

Does the lawyer have experience in preparing wills, powers of attorney, and living wills? How long has the lawyer been doing this kind of work? How many wills has the lawyer prepared? Does the lawyer have experience in planning estates of the same value and with the same types of property as yours? Is the lawyer willing to seek the help of outside specialists such as tax accountants if necessary?

Your executor will probably ask the lawyer who prepared your will for help in administering the estate, so you'd also like some information on behalf of your executor. Does the lawyer have experience in working with executors in administering estates? How many estates has the lawyer administered?

### How will you charge me for the work you do, and how much will you charge me?

A lawyer may bill you at an hourly rate for the time spent working for you, or charge a flat rate for preparing your will, power of attorney, and living will.

If the lawyer is going to charge you by the hour, find out what the hourly rate is and how long the lawyer estimates the work will take. Once you hire the lawyer, he or she has to get your agreement to raise the hourly rate, and has to tell you (and get your agreement) before going past the estimate.

If the lawyer is going to charge you a flat fee, find out how much time the lawyer is willing to spend with you for that fee. Ask what the lawyer will do if he or she needs to spend more time with you.

Ask if the lawyer will want you to pay a *retainer* (a deposit paid before the work is done that is applied against the bill), and if so, how much.

### Will you be doing the work on my estate plan personally, or will the work be done by others?

Unless the lawyer is a sole practitioner with no employees, someone else will be doing at least some of the work, even if it's just the typing and photocopying. If the lawyer works in a firm, other lawyers, articling students, or law clerks may be involved. There's not necessarily anything wrong with that, but you should know up front whom you're hiring. You may want to know more about and perhaps even meet these other players, depending on how involved they're likely to be.

### How long will it take before my documents are ready for me to sign?

Perhaps you have reasons for wanting your estate plan put into place very soon: you may be getting married, going on a trip, or undergoing surgery; or you may have been recently diagnosed with a life-threatening illness. Even without specific reasons, now that you've finally gotten up the gumption to tackle your estate plan, you probably want everything wrapped up sooner rather than later.

Some lawyers are better at taking on work than at actually getting it done. Tell the lawyer when you would like the work completed, and ask if he or she can have it done by then.

### Will you explain the documents to me in detail before I sign them?

If you've read Chapter 16, you know how difficult it can be to understand what a will says. You want a lawyer who's willing to take the time to translate your will into English and answer any questions you might have.

### Will I have to come back to your office?

Some lawyers make house calls for estate planning clients who are older or unwell and find it hard to get out to a lawyer's office.

If you have to come back, how many times will you have to come back? Just once to sign the documents? Or for another one or more meetings to give the lawyer information and/or to discuss your estate plan before the lawyer prepares the documents?

### Will you hold my will, power of attorney, and living will for safekeeping?

Most lawyers have a vault in which they keep their clients' estate planning documents. Some lawyers provide safe storage of documents for free, others charge a fee.

Whether or not the lawyer charges a fee for holding your documents, find out whether there will be an administrative fee charged to your executor or family members for locating your documents and releasing them.

### Will you keep me up-to-date on changes in the law that might affect my estate plan?

Some law firms send out regular newsletters to their clients to keep them advised of developments in the law on any number of topics. Even if the lawyer's firm does not do so, the lawyer you hire should notify you of any changes in the law that might cause you to rethink and revise your estate plan.

### How often should I review my estate plan with you, and what will it cost?

Ask the lawyer what changes in your circumstances should cause you to talk to him or her about possible changes to your estate plan. The lawyer should also suggest that you have a look at your estate plan every few years, and then contact him or her if you think changes are necessary.

The lawyer will probably tell you that the cost of reviewing your estate plan will depend on how much time it takes to do the review, and then how much, if anything, needs changing. He or she should be able to give you some kind of idea of how much it would cost to:

- Simply review your estate plan
- Prepare a codicil to your will
- Replace your will, power of attorney, and/or living will

## Then Ask Yourself

Ask the questions we've set out before you choose a lawyer. Listen to the answers carefully — not just to what the lawyer says, but to how the lawyer says it. And then you need to ask yourself a question.

### Do I want to work with this lawyer?

Listen to your instincts — do you feel comfortable with this lawyer? Do you like this lawyer? Does this lawyer treat you with courtesy and respect?

Were you kept waiting for your appointment or were you ushered into the lawyer's office right on time? Did the lawyer act as though he or she were doing you a favour by meeting with you or were you made to feel welcome? Did the lawyer allow himself or herself to be interrupted by telephone calls and visits from staff during your meeting or was your meeting quiet and uninterrupted? Did the lawyer make a point of explaining things to you in an understandable way or did he or she treat you like a child or a moron because you don't know a lot about law?

If you like the answers to all of the questions you asked the lawyer and yourself, then you're ready to say, "You're hired!"

# Chapter 25

# Ten Tips for Using Your Computer for Estate Planning

### *In This Chapter*

- Getting financial planning help
- Finding income tax information
- Looking for insurance help
- Locating legal information
- Getting government information
- Looking into organ donation
- Investigating charities
- Researching your living will
- Getting organized

Estate planning involves a lot of work, and it's drudge work at that. We wouldn't blame you for trying to palm off at least some of it onto someone — anyone — else. But if you do, don't be surprised if your targeted helpers all run screaming at the very thought. Even the family dog may start to back away from you when you enter the room. Is there anywhere to turn for help? In fact there is. Sitting there quietly on a desk is something with a brain and no legs to run away — your computer!

## Get Financial Planning Help

Use the CD versions of the tables in Chapter 2 to help you figure out your net worth and your monthly expenses.

Use the Scotiabank financial planning software on the CD to help you in your net worth and your cash-flow calculations.

Research financial planning topics on the Internet with information portal sites like Yahoo! Canada (www.yahoo.ca) or Canoe (www.canoe.com). Some sites have net worth and budget calculators.

## Find Income Tax Info

Get tax guides, publications, and forms from Canada Revenue's Web site at www.ccra-adrc.gc.ca.

Find tax information from the Canadian Tax Foundation at www.ctf.ca or from the Web sites of various accounting firms (you can find their sites through Yahoo! Canada).

## Look for Insurance Help

Visit the Web sites for Canadian Life and Health Insurance Association (www.clhia.ca) and Insurance Canada (www.insurance-canada.ca) for general information about insurance.

Find life insurance needs calculators at insurance company Web sites (you can find their Web sites through Yahoo! Canada) or at Free Insurance Quotes.com (www.free-insurance-quotes.com).

## Locate Legal Information

Visit the Access to Justice Network (www.acjnet.org) or the University of Toronto's Bora Laskin Law Library (www.law-lib.utoronto.ca) for general legal information and links to other legal sites such as governments, provincial law societies, and public legal education organizations.

Check out Web sites for law firms in your province (you can find them through Yahoo! Canada). They often post articles about legal topics of general interest.

## Get Government Information

Find statutes and other government information on your provincial government's Web site:

| | |
|---|---|
| Alberta | www.gov.ab.ca |
| British Columbia | www.gov.bc.ca |
| Manitoba | www.gov.mb.ca |

| | |
|---|---|
| New Brunswick | www.gov.nb.ca |
| Newfoundland | www.gov.nf.ca |
| Nova Scotia | www.gov.ns.ca |
| Ontario | www.gov.on.ca |
| Prince Edward Island | www.gov.pe.ca |
| Quebec | www.gouv.qc.ca |
| Saskatchewan | www.gov.sk.ca |

## Find Help with Funeral Planning

Find links to provincial funeral services associations and lists of member funeral homes listed by province at the Funeral Service Association of Canada Web site (www.fsac.ca).

Search the Web for funeral homes, cemeteries, and funeral planning services using Yahoo! Canada.

## Look into Organ Donation

Visit the Canadian Association of Transplantation Web site (www.transplant.ca) for information about organ donation and links to other Web sites including organ donor registries.

## Investigate Charities

Check Canada Revenue's searchable list of registered charities at www.ccrc-adrc.gc.ca to check whether the charity of your choice is there.

Visit the Web sites of individual charities for information about the charity. The Web sites for some of the larger charities contain information about planned giving.

## Research Your Living Will

Visit the Web site for the University of Toronto's Joint Centre for Bioethics (www.utoronto.ca/jcb) for information about living wills and kinds of medical treatment you may wish to agree to in advance or refuse in advance.

Use the Internet to research a disease or condition and treatment options.

## Get Organized

Use the CD version of Appendix A, “Prepare to Meet Your Lawyer,” to help you get the most from your lawyer. Use the CD version of Appendix B, “Instructions for Your Executor,” and Appendix C, “Inventory for Your Executor,” to make your life easier now and your executor’s life easier later.

# Appendix A

# Prepare to Meet Your Lawyer

To plan your estate properly and carry out the plan, you need a lawyer. While you're in the planning stages, your lawyer will be able to help you prepare a complete estate plan that answers all your needs by taking you through the foreseeable possibilities about your future and your family's future. When you're ready to put your plan into action, your lawyer can draft your will and other legal documents, such as a power of attorney and a living will, that reflect your wishes. We tell you the most important things you should know in order to find a good lawyer and to get your lawyer to do good work for you in Chapter 20.

Use the form in this appendix (also on the CD) to make sure your lawyer has all the information necessary to do the best job possible for you.

# Prepare to Meet Your Lawyer

## INFORMATION ABOUT YOU

Have you ever made a

- ☐ Will?
- ☐ Power of attorney?
- ☐ Living will?

If so, you should bring the documents to your meeting with your lawyer.

## INFORMATION ABOUT YOUR FAMILY

**Marital Status**

Are you currently

- ☐ Single. If you are living with someone, bring any cohabitation agreement you have signed.
- ☐ Planning to marry. If so, bring any marriage contract you have signed or are thinking of signing.
- ☐ Married. If so, bring any marriage contract you have signed.
- ☐ Separated. If so, bring any separation agreement you have signed or are thinking of signing, and any court orders that have been made.
- ☐ Divorced. If so, bring your divorce decree and any separation agreement and court orders.
- ☐ Widowed. If so, bring a copy of your spouse's will.

**Your Children**

| | Child #1 | Child #2 | Child #3 | Child #4 |
|---|---|---|---|---|
| Name | ________ | ________ | ________ | ________ |
| Date of birth | ________ | ________ | ________ | ________ |
| In your custody or another's | ________ | ________ | ________ | ________ |
| Disabilities or special needs | ________ | ________ | ________ | ________ |

Bring any documents, such as a separation agreement or court order, that affect your relationship with your children.

Who would you like to look after your underage children if both parents are dead?

________________________________________

**Your Grandchildren**

| | Grandchild #1 | Grandchild #2 | Grandchild #3 | Grandchild #4 |
|---|---|---|---|---|
| Name | ________ | ________ | ________ | ________ |
| Date of birth | ________ | ________ | ________ | ________ |
| Disabilities or special needs | ________ | ________ | ________ | ________ |

**Other Family Members or Friends** whom you have a moral obligation to support financially

| | Person #1 | Person #2 | Person #3 |
|---|---|---|---|
| Name | | | |
| Date of birth | | | |
| Disabilities or special needs | | | |

**Pets to Be Cared For**

| | Pet #1 | Pet #2 | Pet #3 | Pet #4 |
|---|---|---|---|---|
| Name | | | | |
| Date of birth | | | | |
| Special needs | | | | |

## INFORMATION ABOUT YOUR PROPERTY

**Real Estate**

| | Property #1 | Property #2 | Property #3 |
|---|---|---|---|
| Address | | | |
| How is it owned (by you alone, by you and another)? | | | |
| Approximate value | | | |

**Vehicles**

| | Vehicle #1 | Vehicle #2 | Vehicle #3 |
|---|---|---|---|
| Description | | | |
| How is it owned (by you alone, by you and another)? | | | |
| Approximate value | | | |

**Bank accounts**

| | Account #1 | Account #2 | Account #3 |
|---|---|---|---|
| Location | | | |
| How is it owned (by you alone, by you and another)? | | | |
| Approximate balance | | | |

**RRSPs and RRIFs**

| | Plan/Fund #1 | Plan/Fund #2 | Plan/Fund #3 |
|---|---|---|---|
| Location | | | |
| Beneficiary named | | | |
| Approximate value | | | |

**Pension Plans**

| | Plan #1 | Plan #2 | Plan #3 |
|---|---|---|---|
| Employer | | | |
| Beneficiary named | | | |
| Approximate value | | | |

**Investments** (bonds, GICs, shares, mutual funds, etc.)

| | Investment #1 | Investment #2 | Investment #3 |
|---|---|---|---|
| Description | | | |
| How is it owned (by you alone, by you and another)? | | | |
| Approximate value | | | |

**Life Insurance**

| | Policy #1 | Policy #2 | Policy #3 |
|---|---|---|---|
| Insurance company | | | |
| Beneficiary named | | | |
| Face amount of policy | | | |

**Valuable Personal Possessions** (electronic equipment, art, antiques and heirlooms, jewellery, silverware, furs)

| | Possession #1 | Possession #2 | Possession #3 | Possession #4 |
|---|---|---|---|---|
| Description | | | | |
| How is it owned (by you alone, by you and another)? | | | | |
| Approximate value | | | | |

**Furniture and Household Contents**

How are they owned (by you alone, by you and another)? ____________________

Approximate value ____________

**Money Owed to You**

| | Amount #1 | Amount #2 | Amount #3 |
|---|---|---|---|
| Owed by | ________ | ________ | ________ |
| Owed because of | ________ | ________ | ________ |
| Due on | ________ | ________ | ________ |
| Approximate amount | ________ | ________ | ________ |
| Supporting documents (mortgage, contract, court order, etc.) | ________ | ________ | ________ |

**Your Business**

Description ______________________________

Address(es) ______________________________

______________________________

______________________________

How is it owned (sole proprietorship, partnership, corporation) and what is your share?

______________________________

Approximate value (of assets less liabilities if sole proprietorship or partnership, of shares if corporation)

______________________________

## INFORMATION ABOUT YOUR DEBTS

**Mortgages**

| | Mortgage #1 | Mortgage #2 | Mortgage #3 |
|---|---|---|---|
| Address of property | ________ | ________ | ________ |
| Name and address of mortgagee | ________ | ________ | ________ |
| Approximate outstanding balance | ________ | ________ | ________ |

**Loans**

| | Loan #1 | Loan #2 | Loan #3 |
|---|---|---|---|
| Description (car, line of credit, etc.) | ________ | ________ | ________ |
| Name and address of lender | ________ | ________ | ________ |
| Approximate outstanding balance | ________ | ________ | ________ |

**Outstanding Taxes and Penalties**

Canada Revenue ________

Property taxes ________

Other ________

**Family Law Support Orders**

| | Family member #1 | Family member #2 | Family member #3 |
|---|---|---|---|
| Amount of payment | ________ | ________ | ________ |
| Frequency of payment | ________ | ________ | ________ |
| Probable end date | ________ | ________ | ________ |

**Court Judgments against You**

Amount of judgment ________

Date of judgment ________

**Have you ever declared bankruptcy?** ______
If so, bring those documents to your lawyer.

## OTHER ADVISERS

**Lawyer**

Name ________ Address ________

Kind of work done for you ________

**Accountant**

Name________ Address ________

Kind of work done for you ________

**Bank Manager**

Name________________________ Address of bank branch________________

Kind of work done for you ____________________________________________

**Broker**

Name________________________ Brokerage ________________________

Address ________________________________________________________

Kind of work done for you ____________________________________________

**Financial adviser**

Name________________________ Address ________________________

Kind of work done for you ____________________________________________

**Other**

Name________________________ Address ________________________

Kind of work done ________________________________________________

## LIFE INSURANCE AND PENSIONS

***Life insurance***

| | Policy #1 | Policy #2 | Policy #3 |
|---|---|---|---|
| Description | ____________ | ____________ | ____________ |
| Beneficiary | ____________ | ____________ | ____________ |

***Pension Plans***

| | Plan #1 | Plan #2 | Plan #3 |
|---|---|---|---|
| Description | ____________ | ____________ | ____________ |
| Beneficiary | ____________ | ____________ | ____________ |

## YOUR WISHES FOR YOUR WILL

Your first choice(s) for executor(s) ________________________________

Alternate choice(s) for executor(s) ________________________________

## *Specific Gifts*

***Personal effects***

| | Item #1 | Item #2 | Item #3 | Item #4 |
|---|---|---|---|---|
| Description | | | | |
| Beneficiary | | | | |

***Real estate***

| | Property #1 | Property #2 | Property #3 | Property #4 |
|---|---|---|---|---|
| Description | | | | |
| Beneficiary | | | | |

***Vehicles***

| | Vehicle #1 | Vehicle #2 | Vehicle #3 |
|---|---|---|---|
| Description | | | |
| Beneficiary | | | |

***RRSPs and RRIFs***

| | Plan/Fund #1 | Plan/Fund #2 | Plan/Fund #3 | Plan/Fund #4 |
|---|---|---|---|---|
| Description | | | | |
| Beneficiary | | | | |

***Investments***

| | Investment #1 | Investment #2 | Investment #3 | Investment #4 |
|---|---|---|---|---|
| Description | | | | |
| Beneficiary | | | | |

***Cash***

| | Amount #1 | Amount #2 | Amount #3 | Amount #4 |
|---|---|---|---|---|
| Amount | | | | |
| Beneficiary | | | | |

***Pets***

| | Pet #1 | Pet #2 | Pet #3 | Pet #4 |
|---|---|---|---|---|
| Name of pet | | | | |
| Beneficiary | | | | |

***Family business***

Description ______________________________

Beneficiary______________________________

***Other***

Description ______________________________

Beneficiary______________________________

***Residue***

**(What's left over after you have made all your specific gifts)**

**If you have a spouse:** Would you like all the residue to go to your spouse, would you like none of the residue to go to your spouse, or would you like some of the residue to go to your spouse and some to others? ______________________________

______________________________

**If you have children:**

How would you like to divide your estate among them? ______________________________

______________________________

What should happen to one child's share if that child dies before you? ______________________________

______________________________

If your children are young, until what age should their shares be held in trust? ______________________________

How should a child's trust fund be used? (For example, not used until child comes of age, used for child's education, paid out to child as a regular allowance, etc.)

______________________________

**If you have grandchildren:**

How do you want them to share in your estate? ______________________________

What should happen to one child's share if that child dies before you? ______________________________

______________________________

If your grandchildren are young, until what age should their shares be held in trust? ______________________________

How should the grandchildren's trust fund be used? (Not used until child comes of age, used for child's education, paid out to child as a regular allowance, etc.)

______________________________

**If you have no immediate family:**

Would you like to give friends or other relatives a share of your estate? _______

Names of friends or relatives ____________________

____________________

What should happen to someone's share if he or she dies before you? ____________________

____________________

Would you like to give something to charity? _______

Name of charity or charities ____________________

Approximate amount you would like to give ____________________

Is there anyone you wish to exclude from your will who might expect to be mentioned in your will?

____________________

## YOUR WISHES FOR YOUR POWER OF ATTORNEY

Your first choice(s) for your attorney(s) ____________________

Your alternate choice(s) for your attorney(s) ____________________

When would you like the power of attorney to come into effect — immediately, when you become physically disabled, suffer from minor mental disability, or suffer from major mental disability?

____________________

Do you want the power of attorney to give your attorney(s) all the powers that you have to deal with your affairs, or would you like to limit the attorney(s)' powers?

____________________

## YOUR WISHES FOR YOUR LIVING WILL

Your first choice(s) for your substitute decision maker(s): ____________________

Your alternate choice(s) for your substitute decision maker(s): ____________________

What are your wishes about prolonging your life or hastening your death? ____________________

____________________

____________________

# Appendix B

# Instructions for Your Executor

Your executor has a lot to do when you kick the bucket, including collecting your important documents, making your funeral arrangements, and generally making sure your wishes for your estate are followed. We go on about the duties of an executor at great length in Chapter 10. In Chapter 22, you'll find more information about how to leave things in good shape.

Use the form in this appendix (also on the CD) to make sure your executor can get a running start on the job.

## INSTRUCTIONS TO MY EXECUTOR

**My will:**

You will find the original of my will in the following place: ____________________

____________________

**The following are my wishes for organ and tissue donation:**

☐ I wish to donate the following: ____________________

____________________

☐ My consent to donation documents can be found in: ____________________

☐ I have notified the following registry that I would like to donate: ____________________

☐ I wish to donate my body:

☐ I have contacted the following institution to pre-arrange body donation:

____________________

☐ I have not contacted any institution but would like to donate my body to:

____________________

☐ I do not wish to any of my organs or tissues to be donated.
☐ I do not wish to donate my body.

**The following are my wishes for my funeral:**

**If Pre-Arrangements Have Been Made**

I have pre-arranged my funeral at the following funeral home: ____________________

☐ I have prepaid my funeral.
☐ I have not prepaid my funeral.

My funeral has been pre-arranged but not pre-paid and I would like it to be paid out of the following bank account(s) or insurance policy or benefit plan:

____________________

____________________

My documents relating to pre-arrangement or pre-payment can be found in:

____________________

____________________

I own a plot at the following cemetery: ____________________

☐ I own the plot alone.
☐ I own the plot with the following person:

My documents relating to the plot can be found in: ____________________

____________________

**Funeral Arrangements** If No Pre-arrangements Have Been Made:

☐ I would like to use the following funeral home: ____________________
☐ I leave it to you to choose a funeral home.

I would like my body to be treated in the following way:

☐ Embalmed ☐ Not embalmed
☐ Made up ☐ Not made up

I would like to be buried in the following clothes: ____________________

____________________

If possible, I would like to have the following item(s) buried with me: ____________________

____________________

I would like my obituary to appear in the following papers: ____________________

____________________

☐ I have written my obituary. You will find it in: ____________________

____________________

☐ I would like the following person or people to write my obituary: ____________________

____________________

☐ I do not want a visitation.
☐ I would like a visitation.
☐ For the visitation, I would like my coffin to be open.
☐ I do not want an open coffin.
☐ I would like a funeral service. OR ☐ I would like a memorial service.

If necessary, I would like my funeral service delayed a reasonable length of time to permit the following people to attend:

____________________

____________________

I would like the following person to officiate at my service: ____________________

If he or she is not available, then my second choice is: ____________________

I would like the funeral service to be held at: ____________________

____________________

I would like the following kind of service: ____________________

I would like the following passage(s) to be read at the service: ____________________

____________________

____________________

____________________

I would like the following music played at the service: ____________________

____________________

I would like the following person or group to play the music at the service: ____________________

____________________________________________________________

I would like the following hymns sung at the service: ____________________

____________________________________________________________

____________________________________________________________

I would like the following prayer(s) to be said at the service: ____________________

____________________________________________________________

____________________________________________________________

☐ I don't want anyone to deliver a eulogy.
☐ I would like the following person or people to deliver a eulogy: ____________________

____________________________________________________________

I would like the following people to be pallbearers at a funeral service: ____________________

____________________________________________________________

____________________________________________________________

I would like the following people to be ushers at a funeral or memorial service: ____________________

____________________________________________________________

____________________________________________________________

I would like a reception following the funeral, to be held at: ____________________

____________________________________________________________

☐ I would like memorial donations instead of flowers.
☐ I would like mourners to be given the choice between memorial donations and flowers.

**Disposal Arrangements** If No Pre-arrangements Have Been Made

☐ I would like to be buried.

☐ I would like to be buried in the following cemetery: ____________________

____________________________________________________________

☐ I leave it to you to choose a cemetery.

☐ I would like a monument:

☐ An upright stone
☐ A marker

Description of the stone or marker I would like: ____________________

____________________________________________________________

I would like the following engraved on my monument: ____________________

____________________________________________________________

____________________________________________________________

☐ I would like to be cremated:

☐ I would like my ashes to be scattered at: ______________________________

______________________________

☐ I would like my ashes to be buried at: ______________________________

______________________________

☐ I would like my ashes to be put in a columbarium at: ______________________________

______________________________

If my ashes are buried or put in a columbarium, I would like the following engraved on my monument:

______________________________

______________________________

☐ I realize it is difficult to do, but I would like to be buried at sea if possible:

My preferred location is: ______________________________

______________________________

☐ Other instructions for disposal of my remains: ______________________________

______________________________

______________________________

☐ I would like a memorial tree planted for me at: ______________________________

______________________________

☐ If possible, I would like a memorial plaque put up for me at: ______________________________

______________________________

I would like the following engraved on the memorial plaque: ______________________________

______________________________

______________________________

Other instructions for a memorial: ______________________________

______________________________

______________________________

**Payment**

I would like the cost of my funeral and disposal to be paid out of the following bank account(s), insurance policy, or benefit plan:

______________________________

______________________________

______________________________

______________________________

## Appendix C

# Inventory for Your Executor

When you die, your executor will arrive on the scene and immediately need lots and lots of pieces of paper. Not making sure that your executor will have what she needs will really make her regret your death. Look at Chapter 22 for more about tidying up your documents and collecting the information your executor will need.

Use the form in this appendix (and on the CD) to prepare an inventory of your important documents and where your executor can find them.

## INVENTORY FOR MY EXECUTOR

Inventory made as of: ____ / ____ / ____
DAY/MONTH/YEAR

The original of my will is located in: ______________________________

______________________________

The name and address of my lawyer: ______________________________

______________________________

The name and address of my financial adviser or accountant: ______________________________

______________________________

The name and address of my insurance agent: ______________________________

______________________________

I have a safety deposit box at the following bank or trust company:

| Name and address of bank | Location of key |
|---|---|
| | |
| | |
| | |

My important documents (e.g., investment certificates, bonds, share certificates, ownership documents, loan documents, valuations of property, etc.) include the following:

| Document | Location |
|---|---|
| | |
| | |
| | |
| | |
| | |

I have money in the following bank accounts:

| Address of bank | Account number | If joint account, joint owner is |
|---|---|---|
| | | |
| | | |
| | | |

I own the following RRSPs or RRIFs:

| Name of institution | Description |
|---|---|
| | |
| | |

I am a member of an employee pension plan at the following institutions:

| Institution name and address | Plan name or number |
|---|---|
| | |
| | |

I own the following life insurance policies:

| Name of insurance company | Face amount of policy | Named beneficiary |
|---|---|---|
| | | |
| | | |

I have a stock portfolio with the following broker: ______________________

For stocks owned jointly, the joint owner is: ______________________

I own or rent the following real estate:

| Address | If jointly owned, joint owner is | If mortgaged, mortgagee is |
|---|---|---|
| | | |
| | | |

I own or lease the following vehicles:

| Description of vehicle | Location | If jointly owned, joint owner is |
|---|---|---|
| | | |
| | | |

I own personal property that is kept outside my residence(s):

| Description | Location |
|---|---|
| | |
| | |

The following property is being held by me but belongs to someone else:

| Description of property | Name and address of owner |
|---|---|
| | |
| | |

I am owed money by the following people or organizations:

| Name of debtor | Description of debt | Amount owed |
|---|---|---|
| | | |
| | | |

I owe money to the following:

| Name of creditor | Description of debt | Amount owed |
|---|---|---|
| | | |
| | | |

WARNING! I have concealed valuable property in the following places (so be careful about throwing anything out!):

| |
|---|
| |
| |
| |

# Appendix D

# About the CD

This appendix gives you the scoop on the CD-ROM. It tells you what you'll find on the CD, what system requirements your computer needs to use the CD, and how to install the software included.

Here's some of what you can find on the *Wills and Estates For Canadians For Dummies* Planning Kit CD-ROM:

- AOL Canada: Software to sign you up for an Internet account with AOL Canada, a commercial Internet service provider (ISP) available locally for many Canadian cities, as well as a large set of Internet software.
- Financial software from Scotia McLeod. Use these interactive calculators to help with your estate planning.
- A sample will form.
- Interactive versions of forms and tables from the text.

In this appendix, we tell you how to install and get more information about the programs on *Wills and Estates For Canadians For Dummies* Planning Kit CD-ROM.

## System Requirements

Make sure that your computer meets the minimum system requirements listed below. If your computer doesn't match up to most of these requirements, you may have problems using the contents of the CD.

- A PC with a Pentium or faster processor, or a Mac OS computer with a 68040 or faster processor.
- Microsoft Windows 95 or later, or Mac OS system software 7.8 or later.
- At least 32MB of total RAM installed on your computer; for best performance, we recommend at least 64MB.
- A CD-ROM drive.
- A monitor capable of displaying at least 256 colors or grayscale.

- A modem with a speed of at least 14,400 bps.
- A sound card for PCs. (Mac OS computers have built-in sound support.)

If you need more information on the basics, check out these books published by Wiley Publishing, Inc.: *PCs For Dummies,* by Dan Gookin; *Macs For Dummies,* by David Pogue; *iMacs For Dummies* by David Pogue; *Windows 95 For Dummies, Windows 98 For Dummies, Windows 2000 Professional For Dummies, Microsoft Windows ME Millennium Edition For Dummies,* all by Andy Rathbone.

# Installing the Programs from Microsoft Windows

To install the items from the CD to your hard drive, follow these steps:

1. **Insert the CD into your computer's CD-ROM drive.**
2. **Click Start→Run.**
3. **In the dialog box that appears, type** D:\Start.EXE.

   Replace D with the proper drive letter if your CD-ROM drive uses a different letter. (If you don't know the letter, see how your CD-ROM drive is listed under My Computer.)
4. **Click OK.**

   A license agreement window appears.
5. **Read through the license agreement, nod your head, and then click the Accept button if you want to use the CD — after you click Accept, you'll never be bothered by the License Agreement window again.**

   The CD interface Welcome screen appears. The interface is a little program that shows you what's on the CD and coordinates installing the programs and running the demos. The interface basically enables you to click a button or two to make things happen.
6. **Click anywhere on the Welcome screen to enter the interface.**

   Now you are getting to the action. This next screen lists categories for the software on the CD.
7. **To view the items within a category, just click the category's name.**

   A list of programs in the category appears.
8. **For more information about a program, click the program's name.**

   Be sure to read the information that appears. Sometimes a program has it's own system requirements or requires you to do a few tricks on your computer before you can install or run the program, and this screen tells you what you might need to do, if necessary.

9. **If you don't want to install the program, click the Back button to return to the previous screen.**

   You can always return to the previous screen by clicking the Back button. This feature allows you to browse the different categories and products and decide what you want to install.

10. **To install a program, click the appropriate Install button.**

    The CD interface drops to the background while the CD installs the program you chose.

11. **To install other items, repeat Steps 7–10.**

12. **When you've finished installing programs, click the Quit button to close the interface.**

    You can eject the CD now. Carefully place it back in the plastic jacket of the book for safekeeping.

## Installing the Programs from a Macintosh

To install the items from the CD to your Mac hard drive, follow these steps:

1. **Insert the CD into your computer's CD-ROM drive.**

   In a moment, an icon representing the CD you just inserted appears on your Mac desktop. Chances are, the icon looks like a CD-ROM.

2. **Double-click the CD icon to show the CD's contents.**

3. **Double-click the License Agreement icon.**

   This is the license that you are agreeing to by using the CD. You can close this window once you've looked over the agreement.

4. **Double-click the Read Me First icon.**

   The Read Me First text file contains information about the CD's programs and any last-minute instructions you may need in order to correctly install them.

5. **To install most programs, open the program folder and double-click the icon called "Install" or "Installer."**

   Sometimes the installers are actually self-extracting archives, which just means that the program files have been bundled up into an archive, and this self extractor unbundles the files and places them on your hard drive. This kind of program is often called an .sea. Double click anything with .sea in the title, and it will run just like an installer.

6. **Some programs don't come with installers. For those, just drag the program's folder from the CD window and drop it on your hard drive icon.**

# What You'll Find on the CD

Here is information about the goodies that are on the CD and how to use them.

*Shareware programs* are fully functional, free, trial versions of copyrighted programs. If you like particular programs, register with their authors for a nominal fee and receive licenses, enhanced versions, and technical support. *Freeware programs* are free, copyrighted games, applications, and utilities. You can copy them to as many PCs as you like — for free — but they offer no technical support. *GNU software* is governed by its own license, which is included inside the folder of the GNU software. There are no restrictions on distribution of GNU software. See the GNU license at the root of the CD for more details. *Trial, demo,* or *evaluation* versions of software are usually limited either by time or functionality (such as not letting you save a project after you create it).

## Windows programs

### Acrobat Reader

Evaluation version. Acrobat Reader, from Adobe Systems, is an evaluation version that lets you view and print Portable Document Format, or PDF, files. The PDF format is used by many programs you find on the Internet for storing documentation, because it supports the use of such stylish elements as assorted fonts and colorful graphics (as opposed to plain text, or ASCII, which doesn't allow for any special effects in a document).

For example, a document on the CD-ROM is the manual for Eudora Light. That document, a PDF file, requires you to use the Acrobat Reader program to view or print it.

To install Acrobat Reader, follow Steps 1 through 6 in the section "Installing the Programs from Microsoft Windows," near the beginning of this appendix. When you see the main menu, click the Working Offline category, click the Acrobat Reader option, click the Install button appropriate for your version of Windows, and follow the prompts that appear on-screen to complete the installation.

You can now run Acrobat Reader at any time by clicking the Start button, choose Programs and then Adobe Acrobat, and then click the Acrobat Reader icon.

To find out more about using Acrobat Reader, choose Reader Online Guide from the Help menu. You can also get more information by visiting the Adobe Systems Web site at `www.adobe.com`.

### AOL Canada

Commercial product. AOL Canada is a commercial online service provider that has local telephone access from most areas of Canada. The software provided by AOL Canada on the CD-ROM includes an easy-to-use interface to the Internet programs you will want to use, as well as a large selection of the Internet client programs.

Before you sign up for an account with AOL Canada, check whether it's accessible from your location as a local telephone call. If you have access to the Web, you can check the AOL Canada Web site, at `www.aol.ca` or call 1-888-AOL-HELP to speak to a customer service representative. While you're on the phone with AOL Canada ask about local phone numbers, and check to see whether its pricing has changed.

Some of the programs on the CD-ROM can also be found in the AOL software. In most cases, the ones on the CD-ROM are more recent versions, so you may want to install them rather than the versions from AOL Canada.

To install the AOL Canada programs, follow Steps 1 through 6 in the section "Installing the Programs from Microsoft Windows" near the beginning of this appendix. On the main menu, choose the Connecting category and then the AOL option, click the Install button appropriate for your version of Windows, and follow the prompts that appear on-screen to complete the installation.

The installation program asks whether you want to make a New or Custom installation. A New installation installs all the programs in the preceding list; a Custom installation enables you to pick the ones you want. The installation program prompts you for all the information necessary to open an account with AOL Canada, including a credit card number. The program checks your modem, dials a toll-free or local number to register you, and returns with your password and other groovy information.

The AOL Canada installation reboots your computer. Make sure that you're not running any other applications while you're installing it.

To run the AOL Canada program in Windows 95 or Windows 98, press the Start button, and then choose Programs and then AOL Canada.

### WinZip

Shareware version. WinZip, from Nico Mak Computing, is a shareware version of an invaluable file compression and decompression Windows shareware utility. Many files you find on the Internet are *compressed,* or shrunken in size via special programming tricks, both to save storage space and to cut down on the amount of time they require to be downloaded. You may also occasionally receive compressed files (ZIP files) as e-mail attachments. After you have a compressed file on your hard disk, you can use WinZip to decompress it and make it useable again.

To install WinZip, follow Steps 1 through 6 in the section "Installing the Programs from Microsoft Windows" near the beginning of this appendix. When you see the main menu, choose the Working Offline category and then the WinZip option, click the Install button appropriate for your version of Windows, and follow the prompts that appear on-screen to complete the installation.

To run WinZip, click the Start button, choose Programs and then WinZip, and click the WinZip 7 32-bit icon.

The first time you launch WinZip, it displays a bunch of messages and configuration questions. When you're asked whether you want the program to operate in WinZip Wizard or WinZip Classic mode, we recommend that you choose WinZip Classic, which we consider easier to use. After you've answered all the questions, WinZip is ready to go.

For information about using WinZip, choose the Contents option from the program's Help menu or double-click the program's Online Manual icon in its folder. To find out even more about WinZip, visit the program's Web site at `www.winzip.com`.

## Macintosh programs

### Acrobat Reader

Evaluation version. Acrobat Reader 4.0, from Adobe Systems, is an evaluation version that lets you view and print Portable Document Format, or PDF, files. The PDF format is used by many programs you find on the Internet for storing documentation, because it supports the use of such stylish elements as assorted fonts and colorful graphics (as opposed to plain text, or ASCII, which doesn't allow for any special effects in a document). For example, the manual for Eudora Light on the CD-ROM is a PDF file that requires you to use the Acrobat Reader program to view or print it.

To install Acrobat Reader, follow the steps in the section "Installing the Programs from a Macintosh," near the beginning of this appendix. When you see the main window, choose the Working Offline folder and then the Acrobat Reader folder. Open the Reader folder first and then double-click the Reader Installer icon. Follow the prompts that appear on-screen to complete the installation. If you would like to add the capability to search for specific words or phrases in PDF documents to your version of Acrobat Reader, open the Search folder and double-click the Search Installer icon.

You can now run Acrobat Reader at any time by double-clicking the Acrobat Reader icon. If you want to view the manual for Eudora Light, for example, after you have installed the program, open the Eudora folder and double-click the file with the Acrobat Reader icon.

To find out more about using Acrobat Reader, view the Acrobat.pdf file that was installed in the same folder as the program. You can also get more information by visiting the Adobe Systems Web site at `www.adobe.com`.

### AOL Canada

Commercial product. AOL Canada is a commercial online service provider that has local telephone access from most areas of Canada. The software provided by AOL Canada on the CD-ROM includes an easy-to-use interface to the Internet programs you will want to use, as well as a large selection of the Internet client programs.

Before you sign up for an account with AOL Canada, check whether it's accessible from your location as a local telephone call. If you have access to the Web, you can check the AOL Canada Web site at `www.aol.ca` or call 1-888-AOL-HELP to speak to a customer service representative. While you're on the phone with AOL Canada ask about local phone numbers, and check to see whether its pricing has changed.

Some of the programs on the CD-ROM can also be found in the AOL software. In most cases, the ones on the CD-ROM are more recent versions, so you may want to install them rather than the versions from AOL Canada.

To install the AOL Canada components, follow the steps in the section "Installing the Programs from a Macintosh," near the beginning of this appendix. When you see the main window, open the Connecting folder and then the AOL folder. Double-click the AOL Install.1 icon and follow the prompts that appear on-screen to complete the installation.

The installation program asks whether you want to make a New or Custom installation. A New installation installs all the programs in the preceding list; a Custom installation enables you to pick the ones you want. The installation program prompts you for all the information necessary to open an account with AOL Canada, including a credit card number. The program checks your modem, dials a toll-free or local number to register you, and returns with your password and other groovy information.

The AOL Canada installation reboots your computer. Make sure that you're not running any other applications while you're installing it.

### StuffIt Expander and DropStuff with Expander Enhancer

Stuffit Expander (Commercial product) and DropStuff with Expander Enhancer (Shareware version). StuffIt Expander, from Aladdin Systems, Inc., is an invaluable file decompression utility for the Macintosh. Many files you find on the Internet are *compressed,* or shrunken in size via special programming tricks, both to save storage space and to cut down on the amount of time they require to be downloaded. You may also occasionally receive compressed files as e-mail attachments. After you have a compressed file on your hard disk, you should use StuffIt Expander to decompress it and make it useable again.

DropStuff with Expander Enhancer is a complementary product that enables StuffIt Expander to handle a wider variety of compression formats and to decompress files more quickly on Power Macintosh computers.

To install these programs, follow the steps in the section "Installing the Programs from a Macintosh," near the beginning of this appendix. When you see the main window, open the Working Offline folder and double-click the StuffIt Expander Installer icon. Follow the prompts that appear on-screen to complete the installation. After you have installed StuffIt Expander, go back to the Working Offline folder and double-click the Install DropStuff w/EE 4.5 icon, and once again, follow the prompts to complete the installation.

You typically run StuffIt Expander indirectly because it activates automatically when you download a compressed file or double-click a compressed file. When StuffIt has finished its work, you can toss the compressed file in the trash can and use the normal files that have been generated.

For more information about StuffIt Expander and DropStuff with Expander Enhancer, visit the Web site of these two programs at `www.aladdinsys.com`.

## Forms and other documents

*Author files* is where you'll find forms and documents from the text. The forms on the CD-ROM come in a couple of flavours:

- **Rich Text Format files.** Use this version if you use a version of Microsoft Word prior to Word or if you use another word processing program such as WordPerfect, WordPro, or WordPad. After you install these forms, they appear in the following folder: C:\Wills&Estates.
- **Adobe Acrobat (PDF) files.** Some files (such as the sample will) can only be seen if you install the Adobe Acrobat Reader. You cannot modify these forms, but you can print them out. The forms in Adobe Acrobat format that come with *Wills and Estates For Canadians For Dummies* Planning Kit are installed along with the Word forms or the RTF forms. Look for them along with your other forms.

| Forms at a glance | | |
|---|---|---|
| ***Number*** | ***Title*** | ***Description*** |
| Table 2-1 | What You Owe | In order to take stock of what you've got, you'll need to get an accurate idea of what you own and what you owe. Make a list of everything you own and its value. |
| Table 2-2 | What You Own | Make a list of everyone you owe money to and the current balance that you owe in each case |
| Table 2-3 | Your Net Worth | Your net worth is what you would be worth financially after paying off all of your debts. To calculate your net worth, subtract the total of your debts from the total value of what you own. |
| Table 2-4<br>spend. | Your Monthly Expenses | Start your financial planning by calculating, on a monthly basis, what you earn and what you |
| Table 5-1 | Estimate Your Capital Gains | Make a list of everything that you are *not* leaving to your spouse. Don't worry about property that will not be subject to capital gains, such as cash, GICs, treasury bills, or your principal residence. Estimate your capital gain for each remaining piece of property by doing the calculation shown in Table 5-1. |
| Table 5-2 | Add Deemed Income from Gifts of RRSPs and RRIFs | The full value of your RRSPs and RRIFs will be taxed as income received by your estate. The combined total of the balances in all of your RRSPs and RRIFs plus your taxable capital gains total is the amount on which your estate will be taxed as a result of the gifts you are making in your will. |
| Table 5-3 | Calculate the Actual Amount of Tax Payable in Your Terminal Return | Use this table to calculate your taxes. |
| Appendix A | Prepare to Meet Your Lawyer | Use this as a way to collect information and documents to bring to your lawyer. For more information, see Chapter 20. |
| Appendix B | Instructions for Your Executor | Using this form will take some of the guesswork out of your executor's job. See Chapter 22 for more. |

| Number | Title | Description |
|---|---|---|
| Appendix C | Inventory for Your Executor | Use this form to prepare an inventory of your property and where further information about your property can be found. Leave it somewhere that your executor can find! See Chapter 22 for more information. |

### Financial calculators

In addition to the tables mentioned above, the CD includes several interactive financial calculators from Scotia McLeod. Use this financial software to calculate your net work and your cash flow and to plan for your retirement.

## Troubleshooting

We tried our best to compile programs that work on most computers with the minimum system requirements. Alas, your computer may differ, and some programs may not work properly for some reason.

The two likeliest problems are that you don't have enough memory (RAM) for the programs you want to use, or you have other programs running that are affecting installation or running of a program. If you get an error message such as `Not enough memory` or `Setup cannot continue`, try one or more of the following suggestions and then try using the software again:

- **Turn off any antivirus software running on your computer.** Installation programs sometimes mimic virus activity and may make your computer incorrectly believe that a virus is infecting it.
- **Close all running programs.** The more programs you have running, the less memory is available to other programs. Installation programs typically update files and programs; so if you keep other programs running, installation may not work properly.
- **Have your local computer store add more RAM to your computer.** This is, admittedly, a drastic and somewhat expensive step. However, if you have a Windows 95 PC or a Mac OS computer with a PowerPC chip, adding more memory can really help the speed of your computer and allow more programs to run at the same time. This may include closing the CD interface and running a product's installation program from Windows Explorer.

If you still have trouble with the CD, please call the Customer Care phone number: (800) 762-2974. Outside the United States, call 1 (317) 572-3994. You can also contact Customer Service by e-mail at `techsupdum@wiley.com`. Wiley Publishing, Inc. will provide technical support only for installation and other general quality control items; for technical support on the applications themselves, consult the program's vendor or author.

# Index

## A

Access to Justice Network, 390
accidental death insurance, 101–102
accountants
  certified general, 338
  chartered, 337
  errors and omissions insurance, 337
  fees, 338
  finding, 338
  professional, 336–337
Acrobat Reader, 417, 419
actuaries, 89
adjusted cost base, 51
adjusted sale price, 51
administrator
  charitable donations, 241
  conversion of property to cash, 238
  distribution of estate, 238
  duties, 237–238
  finding an, 236
  investments, 238
  letters of administration, 235, 236–237
  powers, 237–238
airplane crashes, 95
annuities
  charitable gift, 207–208
  contingent, 90
  definition of, 207
  fixed term, 207
  guaranteed, 207
  joint life, 207
  life, 207
  reversionary, 90
  tax treatment, 208
AOL Canada, 417–418, 420
artwork and antiques, 23
assets, 10, 22–25
attorney, 287, 291–292, 295–296
attribution, 120, 124, 134, 141
authorization. *See* living wills
automobiles, 23, 41

## B

bank accounts, 22
banks, 343–344
beneficiaries, 160
  changing, 379–381
  charities as. *See* charitable donations
  choosing, 148–155
  dependents, 152–153, 269–270
  direct or indirect gift, 150–151
  disinheritance, 154–155
  distribution to, 246, 252–256
  estate as, 92–93
  individual as, 92
  insurance trust, 91, 93
  on intestacy. *See* intestacy
  joint ownership, 149
  life insurance, 86, 91–93, 149, 379, 380
  minors, 150–151
  non-survival of, 275–276
  obligations, 152–155
  pension plans, 149, 379, 380–381
  promises, 154
  reason for giving, 149
  and removal of trustee, 137
  RRSPs and RRIFs, 65–66, 149, 379, 381
  separation agreements, 154
  spouse as, 59, 62–66, 153–154
  taxes, 142, 143
  testamentary freedom, right of, 151–152
  timing of gift, 150
  tool for making gift, 149
  trusts, 125, 126
  as witnesses, 279
body donation, 227
body parts, donation of. *See* organ donations
Bora Laskin Law Library (University of Toronto), 390
burial
  cemetery, 219
  contract, 221–222

crypt, 219
extras, 220–221
graves, 220
interment rights, 219–220
joint tenants, 219
mausoleum, 219
monument, 220
at sea, 222–223
tenants-in-common, 219
tomb, 219
business
as asset, 23
changes in, 375–376
characteristics, 180
corporation, 179, 187–188
emergency planning, 191
emergency replacement, 189–191
family succession, 180–182, 186, 187–188, 189
goodwill, 185
as inheritance, 179–183
insurance, 190–191
key person insurance, 191
life insurance for, 191
market timing, 183–185
overhead expense insurance, 46, 191
partnership, 178, 186–187
sale of, 185
selling or keeping, 177–183
sole proprietorship, 185–186
succession plan, lack of, 271–272
successor, 179–183
survival of, 179–183
unequal distribution of estate, 182
unexpected death or illness, 189–191


## • C •


Canada Customs and Revenue Agency. *See* Canada Revenue
Canada Pension Plan, 88, 297
Canada Revenue, 49
Charities Division, 201
Web site, 199, 201, 390, 391
Canada Trust, 159
Canadian Association of Financial Planners, 339
Canadian Association of Transplantation, 391
Canadian Life and Health Insurance Association, 390
Canadian Mortgage and Housing Corporation, 238
Canadian Securities Institute, 340
Canoe, 390
capital cost allowance, 52
capital gains
adjusted cost base, 51
adjusted sale price, 51
attribution, 120
calculation of, 51–52
capital cost allowance, 52
capital property, 53, 62–64
deemed disposition, 53, 62
gifts, 70, 119–120
shares, gifts of, 204
and spouses, 53–54
taxable, 51–52
capital losses, 54–56, 76–77
capital property, 62–64
car insurance, 40
cardiopulmonary resuscitation (CPR), 303–304
cash surrender value. *See* life insurance
caskets, 215–216
CD-ROM software
Acrobat Reader, 417, 419
AOL Canada, 417–418, 420
DropStuff with Expander Enhancer, 420–421
forms, 421–423
installation (Macintosh environment), 416
installation (Windows environment), 415–416
PDF files, 422
problems, 423–424
Rich Text Format files, 421
shareware note, 421
StuffIt Expander, 420–421
system requirements, 413
WinZip, 418–419
Celestis, 225
cemetery, 219–222
certificate of appointment of estate trustee with a will. *See* letters probate
certificate of appointment of estate trustee without a will. *See* letters of administration

Certified Financial Planner (CFP), 339
Certified General Accountants Association, 337
certified general accountants (CGAs), 337
changes in life
- business, 375–376
- children, birth of, 371
- divorce, 370–371
- executor's life, 374
- health problems, 371
- marriage, 368
- marriage breakdown, 369–371
- moving to another country, 373
- moving to another province, 372–373
- property, nature and value of, 374–375
- separation, 369
- special needs of family member, 372
- spouse, death of, 369

charitable donations, 60, 75
- accurate name, 201
- alternate charities, 201
- amount of, 194–195
- annuities, 207–208
- anonymity, 200
- cash made by will, gifts of, 202
- charitable purposes, 198
- charitable remainder trusts, 209
- choosing the right charity, 196–200
- to foreign charities, 196
- gifts in kind, 199, 203–204
- information, 391
- intestacy, 241
- legitimacy of charity, 197
- life insurance, gifts of, 204–206
- living trusts, 135–136
- memorial donations, 209
- objectives of the charity, 197
- planned giving officers, 201–202
- publication of your name, 200
- purpose of, 194
- registered with Canada Revenue, 198–199
- RRSPs and RRIFs, 206
- scams, 197
- shares, gifts of, 204
- specific charity, 197
- for specific purpose, 199–200
- tax advantages, 195–196

charitable gift annuities, 207–208
charitable remainder trusts, 209
chartered accountants (CAs), 337
Chartered Financial Consultant (CHFC), 104, 345
Chartered Financial Planner (CFP), 104, 345
Chartered Life Underwriter (CLU), 104, 345
child welfare legislation, 165–166
children
- *see also* minors
- best interests, 170
- custody, 162–166
- custody battle, 164–165
- foster homes, 166
- guardians of, 162
- in need of protection, 165–166
- orphaned, 167–168
- residence, 175
- review of estate plan, 371
- testamentary guardian. *See* testamentary guardian
- trusts, 173–174

Civil Code, 138
co-executors, 159
co-ownership, 122–123
codicil, 378–379
coffins, 215–216
committee, 297–298
consent for treatment
- emergency situations, 300
- implied, 300
- informed, 302
- lack of living will, 311–313
- legal requirements, 300, 302
- necessity of, 301
- oral, 300
- refusal of, 302
- treatments, types of. *See* treatments
- in writing, 300

consideration, 117
contingent annuity, 90
corporate bonds, 22
corporation
- business as, 179
- as estate freeze, 74–75
- shareholders' agreement, 188
- shares, gifts of, 204
- transfer of ownership interest, 187–188

court award or settlement, 95

credit cards, 40, 42
credit unions, 343–344
cremation, 223–225
critical illness insurance, 48
custody, 162–166
custody battle, 164–165

• D •

damages, 95
deemed disposition, 53, 62, 142, 191, 195
Deloitte & Touche, 179
dependents, 152–153
directive. *See* living wills
disability, income after, 284–285
disability insurance, 45–46
  amount of, 46
  entitlement to benefits, 46, 285
  necessity of, 45
  where to get, 45–46
discretionary trusts, 129
disinheritance, 154–155
divorce, 12, 370–371
do-it-yourself wills, 264
  execution of, 277–280
  holograph will, 264, 280
  mistakes. *See* mistakes in will preparation
  residue, 272–274
  will kits, 280–281
document storage, 363
double indemnity rider, 101–102
DropStuff with Expander Enhancer, 420–421
duress, 116

• E •

eating out, 41
eligible funeral arrangement, 217
emergency fund, 36, 44
emergency planning
  emergency fund, 36, 44
  insurance, 44–48
employment benefits, 41
employment pension plans. *See* pension plans
entertainment expenses, 41
Environment Canada, 222, 223
estate
  definition of, 9–11
  income earned by, 89
  information about, 357–359
  as legal being, 11
  taxes. *See* tax planning
  terminal return, 195
estate freeze, 60, 71–75
  corporation, 74–75
  gifts, 72
  promissory note, 72
  sale to child or grandchild, 72
  trusts, 73–74, 134
  types of, 72–75
estate planning
  basics, 11–12
  best time for, 15–16
  computer, using your, 389–392
  lawyers, 320–321
  necessity of, 12–14
  ongoing process, 12, 16
  professional help, 18–19
  review of estate plan, 365–367
    *see also* changes in life; legal changes
  tools of, 14–15
estate trustee with a will. *See* executor
execution of will
  beneficiary as witness, 279
  changes, 262, 278
  do-it-yourself wills, 277–280
  free will, 279–280
  initials, 278
  legal capability of testator, 261, 262–263
  legal formalities, 261–263
  mental competence, 279–280
  witnesses, 261–262, 278
executor
  alternate, 159, 268
  changes in executor's life, 374
  choosing, 158–159, 160
  co-executors, 159
  conversion into cash, 257
  debts and taxes, payment of, 361–362
  dishonest, 267
  distribution in kind, 258
  distribution of estate, 362–363
  duties of, 354–363
  estate, information about, 357–359
  funeral arrangements, 355–357
  gather in estate, 360
  incompetent, 267
  instructions for, 403–407

insufficient power, 276–277
inventory, 361, 409–413
investments, 257
of last resort, 268
legal responsibilities, 157–158
letters probate, 359
minors, dealing with, 258–259
naming in will, 250–251
powers, 256–260
protection of estate property, 359–360
refusal to act, 159
role of, 156–157
in trust, 246, 251
trust company as, 159
unused capital losses, 77
valuation of property, 361
expenses
assessment of, 28–33
life insurance amounts, 87–88
reduction of, 39–41

## • F •

Family Firm Institute, 179
financial information, 353
Financial Management Advisor (FMA), 340
financial planners
fees, 340–341
finding, 342
problems with, 343
products, 341
qualifications, 339–340
Financial Planners Standards Council (FPSC), 339
financial planning
assets, 22–25
expenses, 28–33
goals, 21, 35–37
income, 27–28
information, 389–390
liabilities, 25–26
net worth, 26–27
first-to-die policy, 101
flight insurance, 102
Free Insurance Quotes.com, 390
funeral arrangements
burial, 218–222
coffins, 215–216
cooling-off period, 217
costs of, 212–213
cremains, 224
cremation, 223–225
direct disposition, 213
eligible, 217
embalming, 215, 222
executor, information for, 355–357
funeral home, 213–215
funeral services contract, 216–218
information, 391
pre-payment, 216–218
provincial boards of funeral directors, 218
in space, 225
transfer service, 213
your say in, or lack thereof, 211
funeral home, 213–215
Funeral Service Association of Canada, 391
furniture, 23

## • G •

gifts
*see also* beneficiaries
affordability, 118–119
alternatives to, 120–124
capital gains tax, reduction of, 70, 119–120
to charity. *See* charitable donations
confidential, 135
current taxes, 71, 120
direct or indirect, 150–151
as estate freeze, 72
as estate planning tool, 14
expensive, purchasing, 41
failed, 275
in kind, 199, 203–204
legal definition, 114–115
promises, 117–118
purpose of, 114
reasons, 69–70
regret, 118–120
as tax planning strategy, 60
taxes on, 119–120
unintentional, 116–117
valid, 115–116
goals, 21, 35–37
choices, 37
costs of, 36
emergency planning, 36

long-term, 36
medium-term, 36
short-term, 36
goodwill, 185
government
benefits, 11
information, 390–391
savings bonds, 22
group insurance, 105, 107, 112
Guaranteed Income Supplement, 297
guaranteed investment certificates, 22
guardian of the person, 312–313
guardianship, 162

• H •

health care directive. *See* living wills
health issues
consent for treatment. *See* consent for treatment
guardian of the person, 312–313
health care, access to, 299
living wills. *See* living wills
long-term-care insurance, 48
out-of-country medical insurance, 47
holograph will, 264, 280
home insurance, 40
household contents, 23

• I •

income
assessing your, 27–28
family, after death, 88–89
family members, 39
increasing your, 37–39
new job, 38
overtime, 38
raises, 37
renting out space, 39
tax on, 50
taxable, 56–57
work more, 37–38
income replacement, 87–90
income splitting, 120, 142
income taxes
*see also* tax planning
annuities, 208
avoidance, 58
capital gains, 51–54
capital losses, 54–56
changes in law, 376–377
eligible funeral arrangement, 217
estate taxes, 49–50
estimating, 79–80
evasion, 58
as expense, 39
foreign, 81
income, 50
income splitting, 120
information, 390
and intestacy, 239–241
tax brackets, 56–57
tax planning goals. *See* tax planning
taxable income, 56–57
trusts, 140–143
incompetence. *See* mental incompetence; physical incompetence
individual insurance, 102–105, 106–107, 111–112
informed consent, 302
Institute of Canadian Bankers, 340
insurance
business, 190–191
companies, 103
critical illness insurance, 48
disability insurance, 45–46
for emergency planning, 44
errors and omissions, 337
group, 105, 107, 112
individual, 102–105, 106–107, 111–112
information, 390
key person insurance, 191
liability insurance, 47
life. *See* life insurance
long-term-care insurance, 48
out-of-country medical insurance, 47
overhead expense insurance, 46, 191
permanent insurance, 99–100
trust, 91, 93
Insurance Canada, 390
inter vivos trust. *See* living trusts
interment rights, 219–220
Internet information, 390–392
intestacy
administration of estate. *See* administrator
changes in law, 377
charitable donations, 241

consequences, 231
legal marriage, requirement of, 232
married with children, 233
minor children, 241–242
not married and no children, 234
not married but have children, 233
per stirpes, 233
preferential share, 233
principal residence, 240
remote beneficiaries, 242
RRSPs and RRIFs, 240–241
spousal rollover, 239–240
spouse, 232, 233
succession, 58, 155, 232–235
taxes, 239–241
Investing For Canadians For Dummies (Tyson and Martin), 43
investment strategy, 43–44, 121

## • J •

jewellery, 23
joint
account, 353
custody, 162
ownership, 15, 149
policies, 101
tenants, 123, 219
Joint Centre for Bioethics (University of Toronto), 391

## • K •

key person insurance, 191

## • L •

law society, 331–332
lawyers
after death, 323
assessment, 331
communication with, 325–326
competence, 324
contingency fee, 330
disbursements, 328
estate planning, 320–321
execution of documents, 322
fees, 318, 320, 328–330
finding, 326–327
flat fees, 329–330
GST, 328
helping your, 332–333
honesty and integrity, 325
hourly rate, 328–329
interviewing, 327
main source of estate planning advice, 346
necessity of, 336
preparations for meeting your lawyer, 394–402
problem with your, 331–332
professional conduct, rules of, 330–331
putting your plan into action, 322
recommendations, 326
retainers, 329
specialists, 324–325
taxation, 331
ten questions to ask before hiring, 385–388
what-if scenarios, 321
wills, 272, 320–321
legal changes
family law, 377
living wills, 377
powers of attorney, 377
probate fees, 377
succession law, 377
tax law, 376–377
legal information, 390
letters of administration, 235, 236–237
letters probate, 156, 359
liabilities, 25–26
liability insurance, 47
life insurance, 10, 15, 45
accidental death insurance, 101–102
agents and brokers, 103–105, 110–111, 344–346
amount of, 87–91, 108
applying for, 105–107
as asset, 22
beneficiaries, 86, 91–93, 149, 379, 380
for business, 191
cash surrender value, 98, 205
as charitable donations, 204–206
comparison shop, 110–111
contents of policy, 111–112
contingent annuity, 90
contracting party, 112
cost of, 108–111
debt payment, 91

definition of, 85–86
direct purchase from, 104
double indemnity rider, 101–102
face amount of policy, 85, 97
federal government, insured by, 103
first-to-die policy, 101
flight insurance, 102
group insurance, 105, 107, 112
guaranteed life, 98
income replacement, 87–90
individual insurance, 102–105, 106–107, 111–112
as inheritance, 91
joint policies, 101
lapse, 112
life insured, 86
major expenses, payment of, 91
mortality tables, 109
mortgage insurance, 101
necessity of, 86–87
permanent insurance, 98
premiums, 85
proceeds, 352
purchasing, 102–105
rating factors, 108–110
reversionary annuity, 90
second-to-die policy, 101
term insurance, 97–98, 99
universal life, 98
whole life, 98
liquidator. *See* executor
living trusts, 123–124
attribution, 134, 141
charity, donations to, 135–136
confidential gifts, 135
definition, 128
discretionary, 129
estate freeze, 134
income-producing property in, 134
probate fees, avoidance of, 136
special needs trust, 135
tax rate, 142
transfer of property into, 141
trust agreement, 93, 128
living wills, 17–18
backup substitute decision maker, 306
cancellation of previous, 306
coming into effect of, 310–311
contents, 306–308
do-it-yourself, 308
formalities, 309
health care decisions, type of, 306
information, 391
instructions as to treatment, 307–308
lack of, 311–313
legal capacity, 308
legal changes, 377
organ donations, 308
preparation of, 308–309
purpose of, 305
revisions to, 382
storage of, 309–310, 353
substitute decision maker, 306, 308–309
when to prepare, 352
loans, 72, 121
long-term-care insurance, 48

## • M •

mandate. *See* living wills; power of attorney
Marine Conservation and Protection, 222
marriage, 368
marriage breakdown, 369–371
Medical Information Bureau, 107
MedicAlert bracelet, 302
memorial donations, 209
mental incompetence, 17–18, 279–280
definition of, 286
disability, income after, 284–285
living will, 17–18
power of attorney. *See* power of attorney
minors
*see also* children
direct or indirect gift to, 150–151
intestacy, effect of, 241–242
public trustee, 150–151
testamentary guardian. *See* testamentary guardian
testamentary trusts, 130–131, 255–256, 270–271
mistakes in will preparation
debts and taxes, lack of specific instructions, 268–269
delayed distribution, 270
dependents, neglect of, 269–270
estate litigation, 270
executor, bad choice of, 267–268
insufficient power to executor, 276–277

minors, trust for, 270–271
non-survival of beneficiaries, 275–276
property not owned on death, 275
reduced beneficiary shares, 270
residue, 272–274
spouse, neglect of, 269–270
succession plan, lack of, 271–272
testamentary guardian, 271
money owing to you, 23
mortality tables, 109
mortgage insurance, 101
mortgage renegotiation, 39–40
Murphy, Edward A. Jr., 265
mutual funds, 22

• N •

needs, 16–17
negligence, 91–95
net worth, 26–27
non-lawyers, 318–320

• O •

Old Age Security, 88, 297
organ donations, 212, 225–227
body donation, 227
cerebral brain death, 226–227
consent, 225–226
corneas, 226
information, 391
living wills, 308
Quebec, 226
total brain death, 226
out-of-country medical insurance, 47
overhead expense insurance, 46, 191

• P •

paralegals, 318–320
partnership, 178, 186–187
pension plans, 11, 22
beneficiaries, 149, 379, 380–381
death benefits, 94
as income, 88
per stirpes, 233
permanent insurance, 98, 99–100, 108
personal directive. *See* living wills
Personal Financial Planner (PFP), 340
personal information, 353
physical incompetence
disability, income after, 284–285
living will, 17–18
power of attorney. *See* power of attorney
planned giving officers, 201–202
power of attorney, 17
attorney, 287, 295–296
banking, 289
coming into effect of, 294
contents of, 290–291
continuing, 288
on death, 288, 352
definition of, 287
do-it-yourself, admonishment against, 291
donor, 287
eligible witnesses, 294
enduring, 288
general, 288–289
grantor, 287
lack of, 296–298
legal changes, 377
legal requirements, 293–294
notarized copy, 295
for personal care. *See* living wills
powers in, 292
preparation of, 291–294
principal, 287, 293
revisions to, 381
signed and witnessed, 293
specific, 288–289
storage of, 294–295, 353
when to prepare, 352
principal residence, 60, 67–68
definition of, 67
exemption, 67–69
intestacy, 240
multiple residences, 68
single residence, 68
probate fees, 82
avoidance through living trust, 136
changes in law, 377
insurance as charitable donation, 205–206
professional advisors, 18–19
accountants, 336–338
banks, 343–344
credit unions, 343–344
financial planners, 339–343
free advice, 346
free legal information, 318

lawyers. *See* lawyers
life insurance agents and brokers, 344–346
non-lawyers, 318–320
paralegals, 318–320
trust company, 343–344
promises, 117–118, 154
promissory note, 72, 121
property guardian, 297–298
property taxes, 40
public guardian and trustee, 298
public trustee, 150–151, 298

## • Q •

Quebec
declared partnership, 186
liquidator. *See* executor
organ donations, 226
power of attorney (mandate), 289
property ownership in, 123

## • R •

real estate, 23
refund of premium form, 65
Registered Education Savings Plan (RESP), 122
Registered Financial Planner (RFP), 339
Registered Retirement Investment Fund. *See* RRSPs and RRIFs
Registered Retirement Savings Plan. *See* RRSPs and RRIFs
rental, 121
representation agreement. *See* living wills; power of attorney
residue, 81
alternate gift of, 254–255
common mistakes in do-it-yourself wills, 272–274
gift of, 253–254
leaving out residue clause, 273
non-survival of beneficiaries, 275–276
unclear wording, 273–274
wrongful division of, 273
RESPs, 122
reversionary annuity, 90
review of estate plan, 365–367
*see also* changes in life; legal changes
revisions
changes in life. *See* changes in life
legal changes. *See* legal changes
life insurance policies, 380
living wills, 382
pension plans, 380–381
power of attorney, 381
RRSPs and RRIFs, 381
wills, 378–379
Royal Trust, 159
RRSPs and RRIFs, 22
after death tax-planning, 76
beneficiaries, 65–66, 149, 379, 381
charitable donations, 206
contribution limit, 241
on death, 64–65
intestacy, 240–241
refund of premium form, 65
spouse as beneficiary, 65–66

## • S •

sale, 72, 122, 185
savings, 37–42
credit card debt, 42
expenses, cutting your, 39–41
income, increasing your, 37–39
investment strategy, 43–44
setting aside, 42–43
Scotiabank financial planning software, 389
second-to-die policy, 101
separation agreements, 154, 380
settlor, 125
shareholders' agreement, 188
shares, gifts of, 204
special needs trust, 132, 135
spendthrift trusts, 131–132
spousal rollover, 54, 55, 63, 76–77, 141, 239–240
spousal trust, 129–130
spouse
as beneficiary, 59, 62–66, 153–154
capital gains and. *See* spousal rollover
capital property left to, 62–64
death of, 369
entire estate, inheritance of, 59, 62–66
income, 88–89